Creating Value with Social Media Analytics

Managing, Aligning, and Mining Social Media Text, Networks, Actions, Location, Apps, Hyperlinks, Multimedia, & Search Engines Data

Gohar F. Khan

Printed in the United States of America.
Published by CreateSpace, Seattle, WA 98108-0683, U.S.A.
ISBN: 1977543979
ISBN-13: 978-1977543974

"Gohar F. Khan has a flair for simplifying the complexity of social media analytics. *Creating Value with Social Media Analytics* is a beautifully delineated roadmap to creating and capturing business value through social media. It provides the theories, tools, and creates a roadmap to leveraging social media data for business intelligence purposes. Real world analytics cases and tutorials combined with a comprehensive companion site make this an excellent textbook for both graduate and undergraduate students."

—Robin Saunders, Director of the Communications and Information Management Graduate Programs, Bay Path University.

"*Creating Value with Social Media Analytics* offers a comprehensive framework to define, align, capture, and sustain business value through social media data. The book is theoretically grounded and practical, making it an excellent resource for social media analytics courses."

—Haya Ajjan, Director & Associate Professor, Elon Center for Organizational Analytics, Elon University.

"Gohar Khan is a pioneer in the emerging domain of social media analytics. This latest text is a must-read for business leaders, managers, and academics, as it provides a clear and concise understanding of business value creation through social media data from a social lens."

—Laeeq Khan, Director, Social Media Analytics Research Team, Ohio University.

"Whether you are coming from a business, research, science or art background, *Creating Value with Social Media Analytics* is a brilliant induction resource for those entering the social media analytics industry. The insightful case studies and carefully crafted tutorials are the perfect supplements to help digest the key concepts introduced in each chapter."

—Jared Wong, Social Media Data Analyst, Digivizer

"*Creating Value with Social Media Analytics* is one of the most comprehensive books on social media analytics that I have come across recently."

—Bobby Swar, Assistant Professor, Concordia University of Edmonton, Canada.

The book comes with a companion site (www.analytics-book.com) which hosts important resources, including the following:

- Up-to-Date Tutorials
- Lecture Slides
- Case Studies
- Test Bank
- Sample Data
- Sample Syllabus
- Research Articles

INTENDED AUDIENCE

This non-technical book offers theories, tools, and practical skills for creating value with social media data while developing critical thinking of analytics-business alignment, strategy, security, ethics, and privacy issues. It is suitable for:

- Academics, researchers, and students who study and research social media and analytics.
- Business executives, managers, and owners who are engaging with customers through social media and are keen to employ data-driven decision-making.
- Individual consultants and consulting firms who undertake social media related assignments for clients.
- People with no prior technical skills and knowledge of social media analytics, and
- Even those in government who formulate social media related policies that influence a firm's performance in the face of the Internet.

CONTENTS

Contents

Contents

Contents

Contents

Contents

FIGURES

Figures

TABLES

PREFACE

Often termed as the 'new gold,' the vast amount of social media data can be employed to identify which customer behaviors and actions create more value. Nevertheless, many brands find it extremely hard to define what the value of social media is and how to capture and create value with social media data.

In *Creating Value with Social Media Analytics*, we draw on developments in social media analytics theories and tools to develop a comprehensive social media value creation framework that allows readers to define, align, capture, and sustain value through social media data. This book offers concepts, strategies, tools, tutorials, and case studies that brands need to align, extract, and analyze a variety of social media data, including text, actions, networks, multimedia, apps, hyperlinks, search engines, and location data. By the end of this book, the readers will have mastered the theories, concepts, strategies, techniques, and tools necessary to extract business value from big social media data that helps increase brand loyalty, generate leads, drive traffic, and ultimately make sound business decisions. Here is how the book is organized.

PART 1: UNDERSTANDING THE VALUE

Chapter 1: Creating Value with Social Media Analytics

This chapter lays down the foundation of the book by introducing a generic *social media value creation model* (VCM), which we explore in the rest of the book in detail. The social media VCM is inspired by the well-known Michael Porter's Value Chain (Porter, 1985). The model explains the process of value creation through a set of activities that firms need to undertake to create value with analytics. Throughout the chapter, we define and equally explore several tangible and intangible social media analytics values to firms and customers. We also provide a detailed discussion on social media return on investment (ROI) and construct a variety of social media value metrics to measure it. A real-world *case study* is also part of the chapter, which shows how *Jack in the Box* used social media analytics to create value.

Chapter 2: Understanding Social Media

Social media is a big part of our lives today; it is almost impossible to imagine our lives without it. This chapter introduces *social media* and its underlying technologies including the Internet, Web 1.0, Web 2.0, Web 3.0, and Web 4.0. A discussion on the use of social media for business purposes is also part of the chapter. The chapter also identifies common *social media issues*.

Chapter 3: Understanding Social Media Analytics

Chapter 3 introduces the *eight layers of social media analytics framework*, which we examine in the subsequent chapters in detail. The chapter explores social media analytics concepts, tools, history, and industry. A detailed discussion is included on uses of social media analytics for business intelligence purposes. The chapter also draws a distinction between *social media analytics* and *business analytics* with examples. We also discuss four types of social media analytics: descriptive analytics, diagnostic analytics, predictive analytics, and prescriptive analytics and everyday social media analytics limitations and issues.

PART 2: ALIGNING THE VALUE

Chapter 4: Analytics-Business Alignment

Configuring and understanding social media tools alone is not enough. To get the most out of social media analytics, it should be *strategically aligned* with business strategy. Chapter 4 discusses strategies and techniques to align social media analytics with business goals. We also provide a detailed discussion on *social media strategy* formulation and its components, such as social media ownership plan, content strategy, account strategy, platform strategy, and implementation plan. The chapter also provides an analytics maturity model that organizations use to assess their current state of analytics maturity and provide a structured path towards improving data analytics competence for enterprise-wide business decision-making.

PART 3: CAPTURING THE VALUE

Chapter 5: Capturing Value with Network Analytics

Networks are the building blocks of social media and are formed as social media users make friends, follow brands, like and share content, review and rate products, and forge professional ties. Chapter 5 deals with *network analytics* which is the science and art of identifying influential nodes (such as people and organizations) and their position in the network. We also discuss *network-level properties* (such as clustering coefficient, diameter, and density) and *node level properties* (such as degree, betweenness, and eigenvector centralities) in detail. We also explain network structure driven strategies and different types of social media networks, such as friendship networks, professional networks, and content networks. The chapter also includes a *case study* and a systematic tutorial on NodeXL for analyzing social media networks.

Chapter 6: Capturing Value with Text Analytics

Chapter 6 is dedicated to *text analytics*, the second layer of social media analytics. In this chapter, we explore a variety of textual elements of social media along with the steps needed to carry out text analytics, its purpose, and the tools of text analytics. The chapter also includes a case study on the use of text for business intelligence purposes and a systematic guide on analyzing social media text (e.g., tweets and comments) using *Semantria for Excel* and *IBM Watson Analytics for Social Media.*

Chapter 7: Capturing Value with Actions Analytics

Chapter 7 deconstructs the third layer of social media analytics, that is, the *actions analytics*. The chapter explains extracting, analyzing, and interpreting the actions performed by social media users, such as likes, dislikes, shares, mentions, and endorsement. The chapter also includes a *case study* on action analytics and a systematic tutorial on *Hootsuite's analytical* tool.

Chapter 8: Capturing Value with Search Engine Analytics

Search engine data are gateways into the minds of customers. Search engines analytics focus on analyzing historical search data to gain valuable insight into trends analysis, keyword monitoring, and advertisement spending statistics. This chapter explains search engines analytics and search engine optimization (SEO) techniques and strategies. A detailed discussion on search engine types, black and white SEO techniques, and offsite and onsite SEO techniques is also part of the chapter. We also provide systematic guidelines for using *Google Trends* and *Google Correlate* to analyze search engine data.

Chapter 9: Capturing Value with Location Analytics

Location matters. Chapter 9 deals with *location analytics*, which is also known as spatial analysis or geospatial analytics. The chapter outlines tools and techniques to mine and map the location of social media users, contents, and data. A real-world *case study* on mining mobile phone data and a systematic guide on geo-mapping tabular business data using *Google Fusion Table* and *ArcGIS Online* are also provided.

Chapter 10: Capturing Value with Hyperlinks Analytics

Social media traffic is carried out through the hyperlinks embedded within it; thus hyperlink (e.g., in-links and out-links) analysis can reveal, for example, Internet traffic patterns and sources of the incoming or outgoing traffic to and from a source. *Hyperlink analytics* is discussed in this chapter. A real-world *case study* and systematic guidelines on hyperlink analytics using *VOSON* are also included.

Chapter 11: Capturing Value with Mobile Analytics

Mobile apps are the next frontier in the social business landscape. Chapter 11 deals with *mobile analytics.* A useful *tutorial* on analyzing and understanding in-app purchases, customer engagement, and demographics is included in the chapter. A real-world *case study* is also included in the chapter.

Chapter 12: Capturing Value with Multimedia Analytics

The last but not the least layer of social media analytics *is multimedia analytics.* Social media multimedia analytics is the art and science of harnessing business value from video, images, audio, and animations, and interactive contents posted over social media. Chapter 12 also introduces multimedia analytics tools, techniques, and strategies.

PART 4: SUSTAINING THE VALUE

Chapter 13: Social Media Analytics Capabilities

Having sound *social media analytics capabilities* can place a firm in a superior business position, which can generate greater value for a company and its shareholders. To harness value from the social media data, organizations need sophisticated social media analytics capabilities, particularly predictive and prescriptive analytics abilities. This chapter discusses the analytics capabilities that firms need to leverage social media for *competitive advantage.*

Chapter 14: Social Media Security, Privacy, & Ethics

Engaging through social media introduces new challenges related to privacy, security, data management, accessibility, governance, and other legal and information security issues such as hacking and cyber-warfare. Chapter 14 discuss these issues in detail alongside a *framework for social media risk management.* A case study on *social media risks assessment* is also part of the chapter.

ACKNOWLEDGMENTS

I would like to thank the following individuals without whose help this book would never have been completed.

Jared Wong, Social Media Data Analyst, Digivize.
Marc Smith, Director, Social Media Research Foundation.
Rob Ackland, CEO, Uberlink.
Laeeq Khan, Director, Social Media Analytics Research Team (SMART) Lab, Ohio University.
Haya Ajjan, Director & Associate Professor, Elon Center for Organizational Analytics, Martha and Spencer Love School of Business, Elon University.
Bobby Swar, Assistant Professor, Concordia University of Edmonton, Canada.
Gabrielle Iglesias, Asian Disaster Preparedness Center.
Görkem Çetin, Countly.
Hannah Tregear, Customer Marketing Manager, BrandWatch.
Jacob Wood, Assistant Professor, Chungnam National University.
Lora Wan, Enterprise Development Representative, Hootsuite.
Manho Lee, the Seoul Metropolitan Government, South Korea.
Ryan Seams, Support Team, Mixpanel.
Seth Redmore, VP Marketing, Lexalytics, Inc.
Zorica Nedovic-Budic, Professor Chair of Spatial PlanningArchitecture, Planning & Environmental Policy, University College Dublin.

Part 1: Understanding Social Media Value

Chapter 1

Creating Value with Social Media Analytics

"For every $20 you spend on web analytics tools, you should spend $80 on the brains to make sense of the data."—**Jeff Sauer**

Learning Outcomes

After completing this chapter, the reader should be able to:

- Have an in-depth understanding of social media value creation concepts.
- Comprehend a generic social media value creation model.
- Understand different types of social media values to customers and firms.
- Have an in-depth understanding of social media ROI
- Formulate social media metrics for measuring return on investment.
- Comprehend analytics investment stages.
- Understand different components of analytics infrastructure.

INTRODUCTION

Social media data is considered the '*new gold*' and valuable source of hidden business insights. Organizations can leverage the vast amount of social media data to start identifying which customer behaviors and actions create more *value*. A study conducted by MIT Sloan Management Review found that 67% of the total 2,500 survey respondents reported that by employing analytics their companies gained a *competitive advantage* as well as helping them to innovate (Kiron et al., 2013). The case study included at the end of the chapter shows how '*Jack in the Box*' used social media analytics to identify influencers and measure the success of content amongst its audience.

Nevertheless, many businesses struggle to generate value from social media data (Kiron et al., 2014). In fact, many businesses find it extremely hard to define what the value of social media is and how to create value with social media data. A study conducted by the Altimeter Group found that 56% of marketers still list the "*inability to tie social media to business outcomes*" as the most significant challenge of measuring social media return on investment (ROI) followed by the lack of analytics experience and resources.

SOCIAL MEDIA ANALYTICS VALUE CREATION MODEL

Creating value with social media analytics entails harnessing cost-effective and commercially worthy insights from social media semi-structured and unstructured data that can ideally lead to competitive advantage. Figure 1.1 shows a generic *social media value creation model* (VCM). The social media VCM was inspired by the well-known Michael Porter's Value Chain (Porter, 1985). The model explains the process of value creation through a set of activities that firms need to undertake to generate value with social media data. These activities include, 1) defining what the value is, 2) aligning the value creation with business objectives, 3) capturing the value using analytics, and finally, 4) sustaining the value for a long period. The model also provides analytics infrastructure that can be understood as the support activities of the value creation journey. For the value creation to happen, firms should possess social media analytics capabilities, routines, information technology (IT) and financial assets, and conduct procurement activities. We explore elements of the model, in detail, in this and the subsequent chapters. Figure 1.1 also maps each chapter to the value creation model.

VALUE OF SOCIAL MEDIA

From a business perspective, *value* includes all sets of *tangible* and *intangible* assets that determine the overall success of a firm in the long run. Firms engaging through social media expect to get more sales and cost savings (financial value), brand awareness, and relationship building (non-financial value), to name a few benefits. Similarly, customers have their expectation from engaging with firms through social media, such as, getting discounts and lowering their transaction cost (financial value), and being part of the brand community (non-financial value).

Consequently, the social media value creation process should start with succinctly defining and understanding the nature of the value that firms wish to deliver and harness from social media. The value derived from social media can be categorized into two (see Table 1.1):

1) Value to Firms
2) Value to Customers

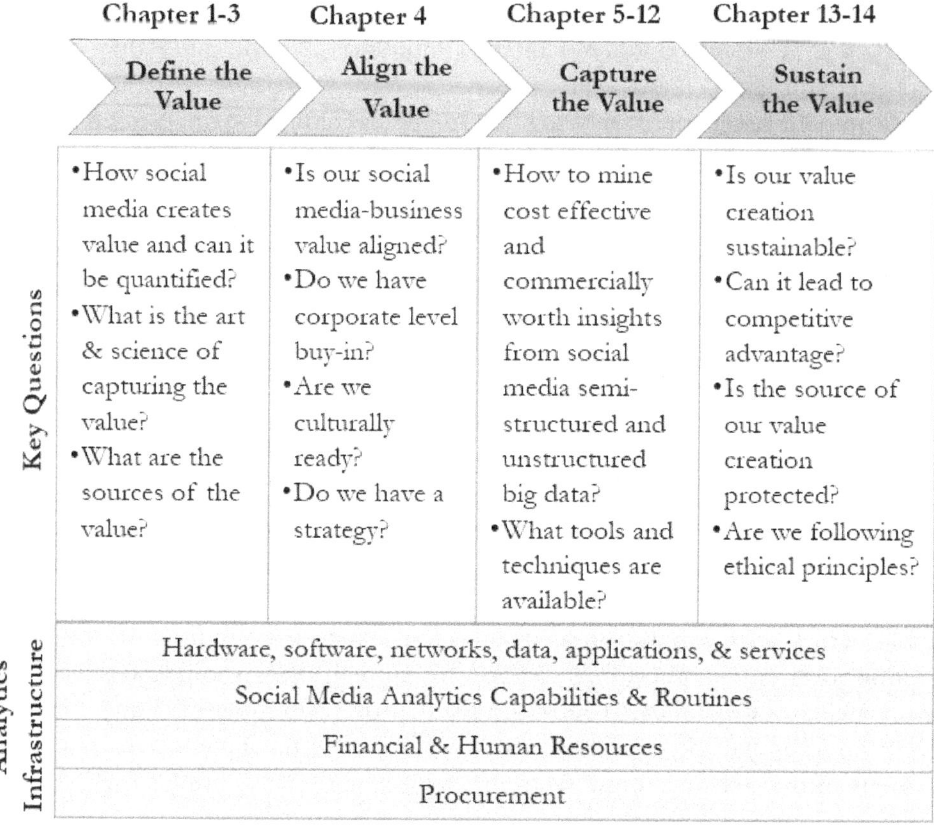

Figure 1.1. Social media analytics value creation model

Value to Firms

Social media *value to firms* (V2F) includes all forms of tangible and intangible assets that firms derive (or wish to derive) from social media investment and engagement. Consequently, we can further divide social media V2F into two categories.

1) Tangible Social Media V2F
2) Intangible Social Media V2F

Social Media Tangible V2F

Tangible or *financial* V2F from social media can come in a variety of forms including more sales, leads, market growth, and cost reduction. Research, for example, suggests that positive comments over social media can lead to significant financial value. A study showed that an eBay seller could earn an additional $45.76 (that is 10% more than the mean selling price) with the help of more than 675 positive opinions expressed online (Livingston, 2005). Another study showed that emotional words in social media text (such as hope, worry, and fear) have a significant impact on share market indices (Antweiler & Frank, 2004). Table 1.2 (created based on Wamba et al. (2016)) provides several examples of business value generated with analytics.

Table 1.1. Classification of tangible and intangible V2F and V2C

	Value to Firms	Value to Customers
Non-Tangible Value ☺☺☺	• Brand awareness • Brand name • Brand loyalty • Customer engagement • Mass collaboration • Crowdsourcing • Idea generation • Connectivity • Customer satisfaction • Product/service promotion • Website traffic	• Product awareness • Brand association • Brand connectivity • Brand involvement • Service quality • Information quality • Product quality • Net promoter score • Information attainment • Brand consideration • Customer effort score
Tangible Value $$$	• Brand sales • Repeat sales • Market share • Market growth • Repeat volume • Cost savings • Customer acquisition cost • Customer retention cost • Customer lifetime value • Path to purchase	• Discounts • Competitive price • Group buying • Social buying • Volume discount • Promotions • Low transaction cost • Savings • Easy buying • Fun buying

An important point to note is that financial V2F from engaging through social media is not always immediately apparent. Traditionally, firms believe that when a customer views or clicks on their Facebook ads they should then make a purchase. A customer viewing a product through a Facebook feed or clicking on a social advertisement may not immediately make a purchase or be impressed by a brands well-crafted social media content. However, eventually, comments, views, likes, and clicks may create brand awareness and bring more traffic to a website; which in turn may lead to more sales. In simple terms, getting value from social media is not as black and white as firms think. The value creation from social media is complicated and sometimes may take longer to realize.

Table 1.2. Social media analytics & business value

Business Value	Type	Explanation	Firm (s)
Customer Engagement	Intangible	Running customer engagement program to promote brand and CSR activities to donate money to charity (Baird & Parasnis, 2011).	American Express
In-store sales	Tangible	Using the eGift program on Facebook in 1,500 locations in 16 countries to drive a measurable impact on sales (Baird & Parasnis, 2011).	Cold Stone Creamery
Service Improvement	Intangible	Use customer recommendation to improve the existing product, service, and packages (Chui, 2013).	Danske Bank
Brand Presence	Intangible	Using Facebook to engage users with polls on their favorite foods and sports.	Citi Bank
Rich Customer Experience	Intangible	Using gamification techniques in their social media community to reward points based on the usage of credit cards (Virgili & Káganer, 2012).	Barclays
New Idea and engagement	Intangible	Using Connect+, a social media platform that allows external companies and individuals to share their ideas on specific problems (Huston & Sakkab, 2006).	Procter & Gamble
Crisis Management	Tangible	Tweets for each monitored movie IMBD.com reported approximately 25% total sales during opening weekends (Purcell, 2011).	Bank of America
New Business Development	Intangible	Using opinion and recommendation on a social media platform to identify new business segment (Kite, 2011).	KIA Motors and The Royal Bank of Canada
Increase in Gross Sales	Tangible	Approximately 25% total sales increase due to tweets about movies during opening weekends (Simonoff & Sparrow, 2000).	Box office (IMBD.com)
Stock Indices	Tangible	Emotional keywords in social media such as hope, worry, fear, and timing had a significant impact on share market indices (Antweiler & Frank, 2004).	Stock Exchanges (NYSE)

Intangible Value V2F

In addition to financial gains, engaging through social media creates *intangible values* for brands. Research studies suggest that social media engagement has a significant positive impact on a brand's reputation, trust, and loyalty (Kim and Ko, 2012). According to a study by DEI Worldwide (2008), 70% of consumers they surveyed have visited social media platforms to obtain information about products and services. Using the information found on social media platforms, 49% of these consumers made a purchase decision. 60% indicated that they use social media sites to pass along information to friends; and 45% who use social media engaged in electronic word-of-mouth (DEI Worldwide, 2008).

Intangible V2F that comes from social media includes (Kim & Ko, 2012):

- Gaining insights into customer's values and behaviors.
- Tracking the impact and effectiveness of social media campaigns, and
- Understanding brand reputation and engagement purposes, and customers' value, relationship, and brand equities.

A study by Kim and Ko (2012) showed that social media activities by luxury brands, such as entertainment, interaction, trendiness, customization, and word of mouth significantly and positively affect a customer's perception of value equity, relationship equity, and brand equity. Value equity is a customer's objective assessment of the value of a brand (Vogel, Evanschitzky, & Ramaseshan, 2008). Relationship equity "expresses the tendency of customers to stay in a relationship with a brand' and brand equity is a 'customer's subjective and intangible assessment of the brand over and above its value" (Kim and Ko, 2012, p. 1481).

Getting intangible value from social media is usually immediate. For example, for Bank of America, the intangible value came from using sentiment analysis to recognize and control critical issues by gathering 41,000 comments from social media platforms (Purcell, 2011). Twitter-based sentiment analysis creates intangible value by accurately predicting a future event, such as an election result (Tumasjan, Sprenger, Sandner, & Welpe, 2010). Facebook paid ads can produce instant intangible value in the form of brand awareness (through likes, shares, and views) and website traffic. However, the magnitude of the brand awareness will depend on the quality of the ad content and the dollar amount spent on it.

Association Between Tangible and Intangible

Most value derived from social media is intangible. However, tangible and intangible values are closely associated. Eventually, the intangible value of social media may lead to tangible value and vice versa. For example, brand awareness and website traffic generated due to Facebook ads campaign (which is intangible value) may contribute to product sales (which is a tangible value). Alternatively, a social media led brand awareness campaign may convert prospective customers into actual customers. Using a social media ads experiment, Khan et al., (2017) showed that the *Social Facebook ads* (the ads that invite customers to like a brand) are instrumental in customer engagement and conversation; which ultimately has a positive effect on product sales. Mainly because after 'Liking' an ad, the customer becomes part of a likers' community where they are exposed to product-related updates and discussions.

However, the association between tangible and intangible gains from the social media is usually hard to establish. Because there are many external variables involved that are difficult to isolate or control. Furthermore, negative opinions posted on social media may affect tangible gains adversely. A research study, for instance, showed that adverse opinion could reduce the price as much as 11%, about $19 from a mean price of $173 (Lucking-Reiley, Bryan, Prasad, & Reeves, 2007).

Value to Customers (V2C)

Like brands, by engaging through social media, customers also expect to gain specific values/benefits from it. Social media *value to customers* (V2C) includes all forms of tangible and intangible benefits that social media users wish to derive from engaging with brands. Therefore, we can further divide social media V2C into two categories:

1) Tangible V2C
2) Intangible V2C

Tangible V2C

The tangible value that customers expect to gain from social media is financial. For example, in a focus group interviews in 2017 at The University of Waikato, we asked a group of 56 respondents to list all possible tangible benefits they expect to gain from engaging through social media with brands. Ninety percent (90%) of the respondents reported that through social media they expect to get discounts, better deals, promotions, and competitive prices.

Intangible V2C

The intangible value that customers expect to gain from social media is non-financial. During the same focus group, we also asked the respondents to list the intangible value that they expect to gain from social media engagement. The intangible value reported were brand awareness, being part of the community, getting the latest information and news, faster response to customer complaints and questions, and ease of comparing product/service quality and features with that of competitors.

SOCIAL MEDIA RETURN ON INVESTMENT

In pure business terms, *return on investment* (ROI) are the gains from an investment less the cost of an investment (Cronin, 2014). Figure 1.2 conceptualizes the process of deriving returns from social media investment. Firms make financial and/or non-financial investments in social media. Examples of *financial investments* include paid social media ads, search engine optimization (SEO), and paid media. *Non-financial investments* include organic SEO and organic ads. Such investments usually lead to brand reach, engagement, likes, comments, clicks, Google ranking, and user-generated content. These returns are collectively known as *social media returns*. The social media returns, in turn, lead to financial (such as lead generation and sales) and/or non-financial returns (such as brand and relationship equities). The social media returns also affect corporate website traffic, which may lead to further financial and non-financial returns.

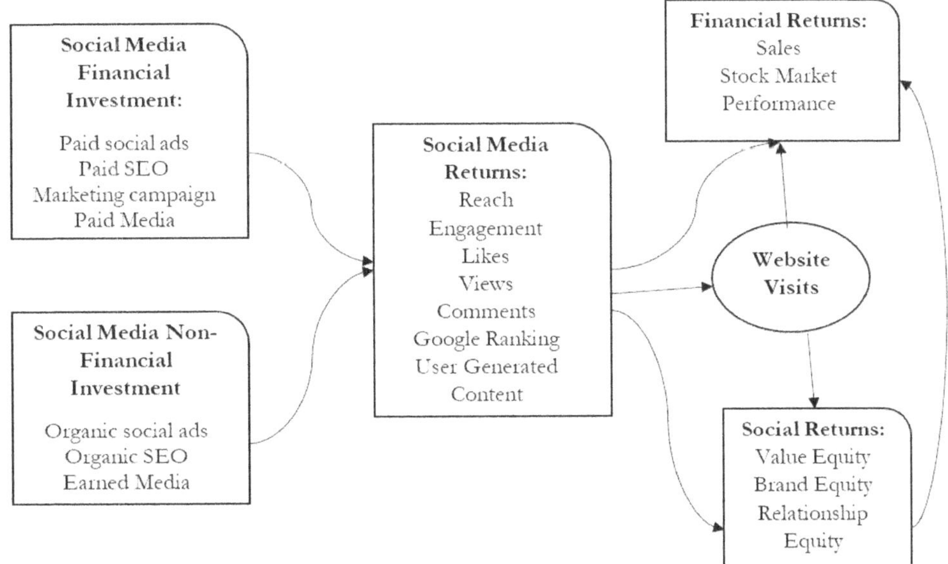

Figure 1.2. The process of getting returns from social media investment

ANALYTICS INVESTMENT STAGES

Business investment is about allocating resources (e.g., time and money) in the expectation of some returns in the near future.

Due to the massive amount of social media data generated, brands are increasingly recognizing the importance of investing in analytics capabilities: to understand their customers better; to identify growth opportunities, and to stay ahead of the competition. For instance, a report by Economist Intelligence Unit (EIU) and ZS (a global sales and marketing firm) found that 70% of 448 business executives and professionals they interviewed considered sales and marketing analytics as a "very" or "extremely important" investment (The Economist, 2015).

Like any other business investment, analytics investment is a difficult choice to make and goes through three stages (Verhoef, Kooge, & Walk, 2016):

Analytics Enthusiasm (Investment Phase)

This stage is marked by the top executives' firm belief about analytics, its potential business value, and the need for data-driven discussion. Hoping to create value with big data, firms make a significant investment in analytics technologies and capabilities. The firm belief is mostly driven by successful examples of analytics implementation by competitors or by the extensive sales and marketing efforts of the analytics vendors or stories in the business press.

Analytics Disappointment (Frustration and Disinvestment Phase)

The enthusiasm soon fades away when years of analytics investment produces disappointing results and several failed projects. At this stage, firms start to redesign their investment strategies, and in some cases, leading to divestment of analytical technologies and capabilities.

Analytics Realism Phase (Reinvestment Phase)

Based on the knowledge gained from past failures, firms refine their analytics expectations and formulate realistic analytics investment strategies. The reinvestment is led by realistic expectation, business value creation potential of analytics, and its return on investment.

SOCIAL MEDIA ROI CONTROVERSY

Most business ROI is measured in purely financial terms. However, when it comes to *social media ROI*, a vast majority of business managers find it hard to measure such returns quantitatively. Whereas the top management always demands concrete measures on their return on social media investment (Weinberg & Pehlivan, 2011). The question of measuring social media ROI is a very controversial issue. Due to the nature of social media, the returns gained from it should not always be measured in purely monetary instruments. Instead, business managers should use platform-specific social media metrics (such as likes, shares, comments, views, posts, and dislikes) to gauge the effectiveness of social media engagement efforts (Hoffman and Fodor, 2010).

Furthermore, Khan et al., (2017) argue that the current practice of measuring social media metrics are challenging, because they are understood as discrete or isolated social actions. To be more exact, let us consider an example of a Facebook's brand fan page and the 'Like' button. When a user likes a brand's fan page many things happen, including the following:

- The person who likes the page becomes a part of the liker's community where he/she can engage with the other customers who also liked the page, contribute comments, and post contents.
- friends of the liker are informed through their news feeds, and
- New updates/posts from the brand's page start appearing on the liker's news feed.

To the brand in question, this means a multiplied exposure of the product/service/content which is proportional to the size of the liker's network (Khan et al., 2017). In other words, the 'Like' button carries a *network externality effect* for the brand. The network externalities and *Metcalfe's law* are two prominent concepts in economics and networks studies. In a purely economic sense, a positive or negative network effect is present when the value of a network product or service increases or decreases as more people use it. If measured from the network externality point of view, one can argue that social media ROI is derived not only from the actions (likes, shares, and views) per se but also from the additional exposure that results from the network externality, which is proportional to the number of friends that a liker has.

Consequently, seeing social media metrics as discrete actions misalign with the fundamental philosophy of social media, which is inherently a network media where people from different types of networks create and share content, interests, and expertise (Khan et al., 2017). Table 1.3 shows some prominent social media metrics (or actions). In line with Khan et al., (2017)'s argument, they are reclassified as networked actions (which carry a network externality) and discrete actions (which do not carry a direct network externality and visibility). A detailed discussion on how to measure network returns is beyond the scope of this book; however, it is available in Khan et al., (2017)'s article. Unfortunately, despite its potential, current analytics platforms do not provide network externality based metrics.

SOCIAL MEDIA VALUE METRICS

One way to gauge social media value or returns on social media investment is through value metrics or *key performance indicators* (KPIs). KPIs are quantifiable measures used to gauge a company's success at reaching targets.

Table 1.3 Summary of the prominent social media networked and discrete metrics

Platform	Examples	Network Metrics	Discrete Metrics
Personal Social Networks	Facebook; Google+.	Likes; Shares; Comments; Views; Posts; Dislikes; Engagement.	Clicks; Reach; Personal Messages.
Professional Social Networks	LinkedIn	Profile Views; Connections; Endorsements; Likes; Comments; Following.	Direct Messages.
Academic Social Networks	Research Gate	Endorsements; Citations; Profile Views; Reads; Scientific Reputation Score; Followers; Followings; Downloads.	Direct Messages; Full-text Requests.
Content Communities	YouTube; Flicker.	Likes; Dislikes; Views; Shares; Comments; Subscribers; Favorite.	Time Watched; Embeds; Hyperlinks; Downloads.
Blogs	WordPress	Comments; Posts; Search Ranking; Likes.	Referrals; Clicks; Visitors; Unique Visitors; Views; Search Terms; Bookmarked; RSS Feed Subscribers; Bounce Rate; Sessions; Average Session Duration; Return Visits.
Microblogs	Twitter	Tweets; Mentions; Following; Followers; Favorites; Replies; Lists.	Direct Message
Search Engines	Google Bing	Search Engine Ranking	Clicks; Search Terms; Search Trends.

The value of having KPIs is that they help a business stay focused on achieving their goals and objectives. Brands can mainly develop two types of KPI:

1) V2F Metrics
2) V2C Metrics

V2F Metrics

Once brands identify key business goals, they can then develop *V2F metrics* or KPIs to measure how efficiently a company is achieving these goals. After the KPIs are developed and employed, brands can then use social media analytics to extract and analyze the data for measuring the KPIs.

The *eight layers of social media concept* introduced in chapter 3 can be used to develop business-specific KPIs. We provide a detailed discussion on KPIs in the subsequent chapters. Table 1.4 provides a list of example business goals and potential social media KPIs for measuring these goals. Essential social media V2F metrics include the following.

Social Media Engagement (SME)

It is the overall responsiveness and interaction of a brand with its customers through social media. In essence, it is the communication connections between brands and its stakeholders through various social media channels. The essential idea of SME is to encourage customers to interact and share their experiences while brands stay responsive to such communications.

When it comes to *active* social media engagement, the number of followers is not essential, what is crucial is how many of these followers are actively interacting with the content and are regularly in conversation with a brand. In other words, what matters is the brand's active number of followers.

Since social media platforms vary significantly regarding scope, engagement, and use, SME metrics must be platform specific (see Table 1.4). For example, if a brand's objectives were to measure social media engagement through Twitter, KPIs for this would be:

- *Re-tweet %:* percentage of *re-tweets* in the total tweets of a brand in a particular time frame. Re-tweets here are the tweets of the followers re-transmitted by brands.
- *Replies %*: percentage of *replies* in the total tweets of a brand in a particular time frame.
- *User Mentions*: the average number of people (followers/fans)

mentioned per tweet by a brand.

In the case of Facebook, SME metrics include:

- No. of times content generated by brands.
- No. of times content generated by fans.
- No. of times content shared.
- No. of comments posted by fans.
- No. of replies posted by brands.

Social Media Influence (SMI)

Social media influence (SMI) is the capacity or ability of brands to have a positive effect on social media users, fans, and followers. The positive effect can result in brand loyalty, persuasion of prospects, buying decisions, and positive behaviors. We can use the following KPIs to measure SMI over Twitter:

- *Tweets favorited*: the proportion of a brand's tweets favorited by other Twitter users.
- *Re-tweets*: the proportion of a brand's tweets re-tweeted (or transmitted) by Twitter users.
- *Brand mentions*: it is the average number of times a brand is mentioned per tweet by Twitter users. Higher is better.

Even though we used two similar metrics (i.e., re-tweets and mentions) to measure SME and SMI, if observed closely, the perspective is different. In the case of SME, the V2F (engagement) is measured from a brand perspective while in the SMI case it (influence) is quantified from a customer's perspective.

Social Media Popularity (AMP)

In the management literature, *brand popularity* is defined as the extent to which a brand is widely purchased by the general public (Kim & Chung, 1997). Over social media, it is the overall fame or social media share of a brand. Ultimately, popularity over social media may lead to financial and social returns for a brand. On Twitter, for example, we can measure a brand's popularity as follows:

- *Followers*: it is the number of fans/supporters of a brand. Higher is better.
- *Follower/following ratio*: it is the ratio of followers per person followed. A ratio of more than 1 means a brand is more popular than its competitors.
- *Listed*: it is the number of people who added a brand to their public list.

Table 1.4. Examples of social media KPIs

Business Value	Potential KPI		
	Twitter	**Facebook**	**Search Engines**
Engagement	• *Retweet %:* Percentage of re-tweets in the total tweets of a brand in a particular time frame. • *Replies %:* Percentage of replies in the total tweets of a brand in a particular time frame. • *User Mentions:* the average number of people mentioned per tweet by a brand.	• No. of times content generated by brands. • No. of times content generated by fans. • No. of times contents shared. • No. of comments posted by fans. • The average number of comments on posts in which a brand was tagged. • The total number of Facebook posts. • No of replies posted by brands. • The average time between two Facebook posts of a brand. • The standard deviation of the time between two Facebook posts of a brand. • The number of posts in which a brand was tagged.	• No. of people searching for a brand. • No. of new topics/idea researched related to a brand. • The ratio between organic vs paid search results.
Influence	• *Tweets Favorited:* the proportion of a brand's tweets favorited by other Twitter users. • *Re-tweets:* the proportion of a brand's tweets re-tweeted (or transmitted) by Twitter users. • *Mentions:* number of times a brand is mentioned by name.	• No. of likes a page has received. • No. of times content is viewed. • No. of times content is clicked. • The total number of likes on posts of a brand. • The total number of	• No. of quality in-links to your website. • Company website ranking on a search engine result page. • Trustworthiness of the in-links to

Business Value	Potential KPI		
	Twitter	Facebook	Search Engines
	Higher is better.	shares on posts of a brand. • The average number of likes on posts in which a brand was tagged. • The average time between two Facebook posts in which a brand was tagged.	your website.
Popularity	*Followers:* the number of fans/supporters of a brand. Higher is better. *Follower/Following Ratio:* it is the ratio of followers per person followed. A ratio of more than 1 means a brand is more popular. *Listed:* the number of people who added a brand to their public list.	*Followers*: the number of fans/supporters of a brand. Higher is better. *Reach*: the total number of people who are exposed to an advertisement or social media content. The total number of people talking about a brand.	• No. of referrals. • The volume of a search engine's traffic.

Business Value	Potential KPI		
	Twitter	**Facebook**	**Search Engines**
Lead Generation	• *Click-Through Rate:* the ratio of users who clicked on a link in a tweet to the total number of users who viewed a tweet. • *Conversion Rate:* the ratio of users who took desired actions (e.g., purchasing, sign-in) to the total number of users who visited a company website. • No. of users' intentions (e.g., buy, recommend) expressed in Tweets.	• *Click-Through Rate*: the ratio of users who clicked on a specific link to the total number of users who viewed Facebook ads. • *Conversion Rate*: the ratio of users who took desired actions (e.g., purchasing, sign-in) to the total number of users who visited a company website. • No. of users' intention (e.g., buy, recommend) expressed in comments; • The sum of all people indicating their presence at a brand; • The number of check-ins the page has received.	• *Click-Through Rate*: the ratio of users who clicked on a specific link to the total number of users who viewed a search engine's ads. • *Conversion Rate:* the ratio of users who took desired actions (e.g., purchasing, sign-in) to the total number of users who visited a company website.

MEASURE WHAT MATTERS

When it comes to KPIs, one of the critical questions that surface is, "*how many should a brand have?*" A simple answer would be to measure what matters most. There are several KPIs that brands could potentially measure; however, not everything that is measurable should be measured. In fact, a business should not drown itself in such a large volume of KPIs that they start to lose focus. Consequently, managers should only focus on KPIs that generates more value for its stakeholders.

ANALYTICS INFRASTRUCTURE

Analytics infrastructure (AI) is the overall social media analytics capabilities (skills), routines (practices), information technology (IT), and human & financial assets that can be employed to create value with social media analytics.

SMA Capabilities and Routines

SMA capabilities and routines are the interlocking systems of competencies and practices that enable organizations to create value through social media data (Bekmamedova & Shanks, 2014). These include technological, organizational, people, environmental, and cultural capabilities and routines that an organization needs to define, align, capture, consume, and sustain SMA value creation and support effective organizational decision-making (Karim et al., 2016). For instance, to capture value from unstructured social media data (such as tweets), a manager needs to allocate appropriate technological assets and people with relevant analytics competencies. To interpret and consume the insights gained, organizations need to embed it into daily business practices. We discuss several SMA capabilities in chapter 13.

IT Assets

IT assets include hardware, software, networks, data, applications, and systems that are essential for creating value with social media data. IT assets provide a solid base for exploiting value through statistical modeling, estimation, validation, and scoring (Grossman, 2009). It enables organizations to employ existing tools and develop a new application for efficiently harnessing insights from social media data. Unlike traditional business analytics, social media analytics require new sets of IT assets. For example, to access and harness structured and semi-structured externally hosted social media data, the organization requires complex tools (such as APIs) and databases (e.g., Hadoop) capable of storing and analyzing this big data.

Financial and Human Resources

Acquiring and deploying human and financial resources is crucial for building and attaining social media analytics capabilities. *Skilled analytic professionals*, for example, are in high demand and hard to acquire and retain. A study by MIT Sloan Management Review reported that 40 percent of the companies they interviewed struggle to hire and retain skilled analytics professionals (Ransbotham, Kiron, & Prentice, 2015). In addition to the people who can extract and analyze data, finding people with the abilities to interpret and consume big data is even harder to acquire. To meet the future analytics demand from industry, the universities from around the world are now offering analytics related majors and qualifications. Nevertheless, they are far from producing enough skilled people to fill the gap[1]. Here are some common strategies companies can leverage to find analytics talent (Ransbotham et al., 2015):

- Develop existing talent by launching internal social media analytics training and educational programs. Having such programs will, 1) deepen existing analytics abilities, 2) provide data scientists with a chance to improve their skills and brighten their career prospects, 3) build and strengthen community among analytics workers, and 4) signal a commitment to analytics that can attract new analytics talent.
- Work collaboratively with academia to nurture analytics talent and actively recruit on campuses that offer data analytics programs and qualifications.
- Develop analytics oriented internships and student projects as a recruiting tool as well as to nurture future analytics business leaders.
- Establish clear and rewarding career paths with IT assets in place, which are most likely to attract analytics talent.
- Build analytical teams by bringing people with complementary skills, as data scientist may excel at different aspects of analytics. Some may be better at statistics, and other excel at programming and algorithms.

Analytics Procurement

Analytics procurement is the process of finding, acquiring, and retaining IT assets: hardware, software, networks, data, applications, and systems that are essential for creating value with social media data.

---

1 *Deloitte analytics trends, 2016, http://deloi.tt/2bY9VTF.*

ANALYTICS CHALLENGES

The organizations that are seeking to become more analytics-driven face many challenges. Research points to several analytics-related managerial, organizational, technological, and process challenges, such as a need for a precise data and analytics strategy, the right human resources to establish a data-driven cultural change, and the issues surrounding data and information ethics when using data for decision making (Vidgen, Shaw, & Grant, 2017). Analytics-driven value creation also demands the alteration of existing organization structures creating room for business analytics units to comprise business analysts, data scientists, and IT personnel. Furthermore, the organizational need to align business analytics capability with their business strategy (analytics-business alignment) is discussed in chapter 4.

Using a Delphi study with practitioners and interviews with business analytics managers in three case organizations, Vidgen, et al. (2017) reported the following top 10 challenges faced by analytics-driven organizations.

Managing Data Quality—assuring data quality aspects, such as accuracy, data definition, consistency, segmentation, and timeliness.

Analytics Driven Decision Making—linking the analytics produced from big data with crucial decision-making in business.

Analytics Strategy—having a clear big data and analytics strategy that is aligned with organizational strategy.

Data Availability—the availability of proper and reliable data to support analytics-driven decision-making.

Analytics Skills Building—building analytical skills in an organization and the training/education needed to upskill employees in general to utilize big data and analytical tools.

Migration Issues—existing IT tools and application/architecture are hard to migrate to and manage big data and analytics.

Measure Customer Value/Impact—hard to qualify the real impact of big data on customers. How to measure the real value that big data can bring to organizations?

Analytics Skills Shortage—challenging to acquire skilled data scientists who can handle big data analytics.

Establishing a Business Case—hard to demonstrate the tangible benefits and return on investment of analytics to top management.

Getting Access to Data—considering that big data is scattered around the applications and the Internet, it is hard to get access to it. Likewise, most social media data is privately held by individuals and social media organizations (such as Facebook and Google).

CASE STUDY 1.1

JACK IN THE BOX: IDENTIFYING INFLUENCERS IN A COMPETITIVE MARKET

Introduction

Jack in the Box Inc., based in San Diego, is the restaurant company that operates and franchises Jack in the Box® restaurants, one of the largest hamburger chains in the USA. It boasts of more than 2,200 Jack in the Box restaurants across 21 states and Guam. Additionally, through a wholly owned subsidiary, the company operates and franchises Qdoba Mexican Eats®, a leader in fast-casual dining with more than 690 restaurants in 47 states, and the District of Columbia and Canada.

The Problem

Innovation and a pioneering attitude have always been at the heart of Jack in the Box. The restaurant chain has been responsible for many industry "firsts" since it opened for business in 1951. Jack in the Box was the first major hamburger chain to develop and expand the concept of drive-thru dining. It launched the first ever breakfast sandwich in 1969, and it was the first quick-serve restaurant chain to integrate video graphics in order-confirmation displays in 1997. The quick-serve restaurant (QSR) market is competitive. Jack in the Box competes with some of the most influential brands in the world, such as McDonald's, Taco Bell, and Burger King. To gain a competitive edge on these large organizations, Jack in the Box made use of social analytics to help maximize the work the brand was already undertaking with influencer marketing. Influencer marketing is much more than a popular phrase. By identifying and building relationships with influencers, companies can harness their reach to broadcast far more meaningful messaging, with much more significant impact than they might be able to generate through their channels. Jack in the Box had already identified, and was engaging with some important influencers but knew social analytics could help reveal others and present new opportunities for the business.

What is influencer marketing, and how does it work? Influencer marketing is a straightforward notion: a brand using the influence of an individual to increase awareness, reach new audiences, scale its message, or increase sales of its products. Speaking broadly, this may include celebrity endorsements or sports sponsorship; campaigns that take place offline, via traditional media. Social analytics is a useful component in finding those influencers that are not necessarily established as celebrities but carry much sway with others in online spaces. With the growth of content marketing, subtler, less direct tactics may be employed where the influencer is promoting a piece of content from a brand, rather than explicitly giving an endorsement for a particular product or service. The specific goal may be referred traffic, backlinks, lead generation, direct sales, or merely mass awareness. How precisely the influencers are sourced and engaged with will depend on the objective, and any measurement framework will need to match the campaign's goals. Jack in the Box's aim was to identify new influencers who were not currently engaging with the brand. The business also wanted to understand the extended interests of fast food fans, to get a richer understanding of the audience. It was also interested in campaign measurement, understanding what activities and actions around its campaigns were resonating and performing best with its audience.

What did they do?

When starting to think about influencers, one of the best ways to start the search is to use keyword Queries. In other words, determining which words or phrases are commonly used among those customers a brand is trying to target. For Jack in the Box, this meant its brand as well as its prime competitors. In many cases, a Query will focus on the brand's actual products, but it can also be valuable to search more broadly across a particular category or topic. Enterprise-level social media analytics from Brandwatch allowed Jack in the Box to craft incisive Queries like this, meaning the brand was able to find high-influence individuals not just talking about the brand name, but also about specific menu items or fast food in general. Dashboards within Brandwatch Analytics then provided categorization and visualization tools to help the team manage and display the relevant data.

Hashtag Analysis

Figure 1.3 represents the leading hashtags used during February in Jack in the Box conversation.

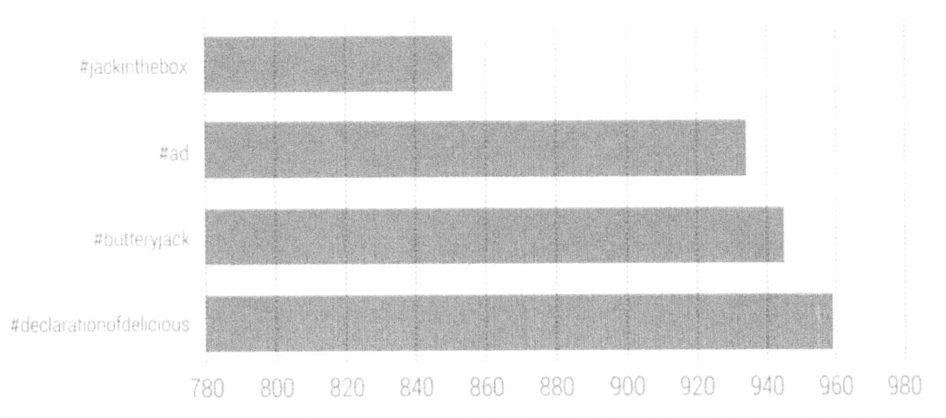

Figure 1.3. Leading hashtags in Jack in the Box conversation

These preliminary results showed that #DeclarationOfDelicious was the most popular choice of hashtag among its audience, helped by a Super Bowl-timed push by the brand. Engagement with the hashtag was mostly passive, with much of the conversation emanating from authors sharing Jack in the Box's promotion announcement. Approximately 90% of mentions featuring #declarationofdelicious were retweets. Several organic mentions (non-retweets) came from local media personalities, particularly in local radio (see Figure 1.4).

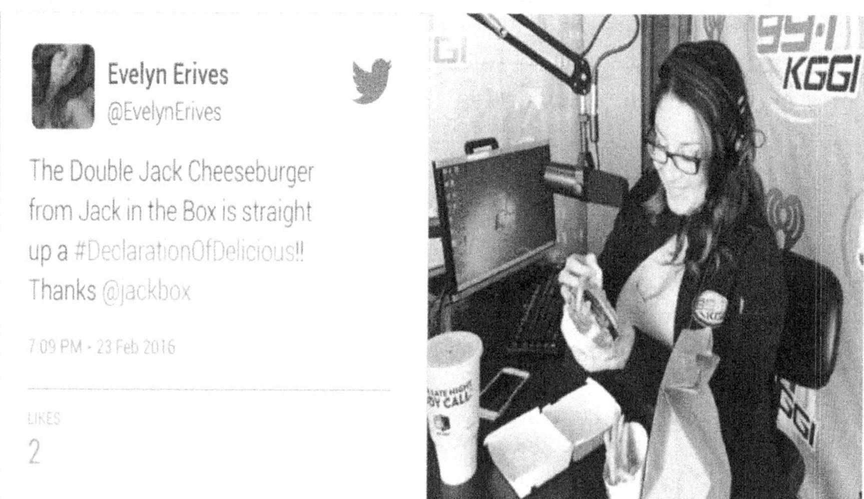

Figure 1.4. Organic mentions from local media personalities

The hashtags #butteryjack and #ad were used in the same highly retweeted post from YouTuber @MirandaSings, which also drove a peak on February 13th (Figure 1.5).

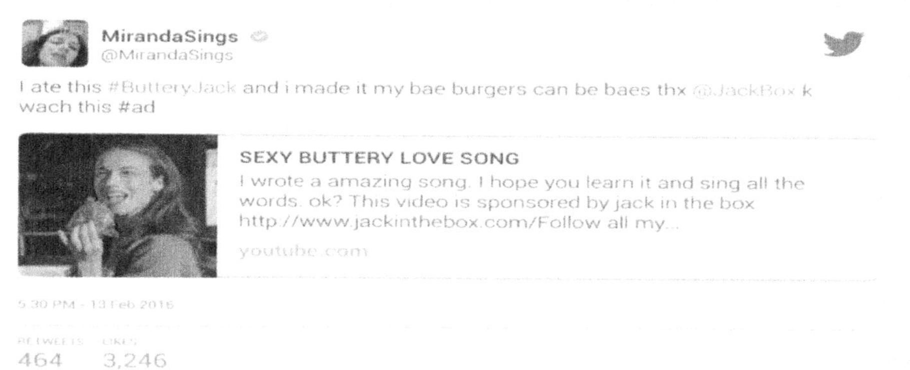

Figure 1.5. YouTuber @MirandaSings

The video posted by the YouTube sensation was then responded to by another YouTuber, and Miranda's husband Joshua David Evans, driving further passive engagement (Figure 1.6).

So... @MirandaSings has been romancing the #ButteryJack at @JackBox lately. Why can't she look at me that way? #ad

SEXY BUTTERY LOVE SONG
I wrote a amazing song. I hope you learn it and sing all the words. ok? This video is sponsored by jack in the box http://www.jackinthebox.com/Follow all my...

7:12 AM - 14 FEB 2016
RETWEETS LIKES

Figure 1.6. YouTuber Joshua David Evans

The hashtag #ad, used by online personalities like Miranda Sings, helped drive a retweet-led conversation for Jack in the Box. Continued endorsement of these personalities could help drive future brand awareness for Jack in the Box.

Author Analysis

It is probably the most repeatedly referenced vanity metric for any mainstream discussion about online influencers: number of Twitter followers. The public nature of the platform means, theoretically, that anybody can attract followers from anywhere. However, those followers need to be first earned and then rewarded for them to stay engaged and help the profile spread further. Therefore, a substantial base of Twitter followers is a valuable asset to any individual and is the first essential way of judging influence on the platform. Figure 1.7 represents the leading authors within Jack in the Box conversation in February. The authors have been sorted by total mentions; taking into account both tweets and retweets. Each of the below authors retained a high retweet: tweet ratio, suggesting a great deal of passive engagement with conversation around Jack in the Box.

MOST MENTIONED TWEETERS WITHIN JACK IN THE BOX CONVERSATION

Tweeter	Followers	Tweets	Retweets	All Tweets	Tweeter Bio
@jackbox	75,000	2728	6970	9698	"Ruler of the fast food world"
@alimaadelat	140,000	44	4389	4433	"Forbes-Listed marketer of the year"
@mirandasings	2,250,000	57	923	980	"Really famous actor/singer/dancer/model/ magician on youtube"
@joshuadtown	327,000	14	159	173	"Husband, YouTuber, Host of What's Up Internet... Be nice to people"
@uclambb	27,000	36	74	110	Official Twitter account of the UCLA Men's Basketball Team

Figure 1.7. Top authors in the conversation

"*With influencer marketing, it is important to identify the difference between influencers and advocates; while advocates may engage with a brand a lot it does not make them influential. I like to see the linkages a person has within different communities, to find the influencer who connects a number of communities together*" DR. JILLIAN NEY, CEO, DISRUPTIVE INSIGHT.

Sentiment Analysis

Sentiment analysis is the process used to determine the attitude, opinion, and emotion expressed by a person about a particular topic in an online mention. Sentiment analysis aims to categorize these mentions into positive, negative, or neutral mentions to help a brand measure the overall customer sentiment behind their brand. Jack in the Box used sentiment analysis within the Brandwatch Analytics dashboards to understand the reaction to its brand over February and March 2016. The leading brand Twitter handle, @jackbox, attracted engagement in both months. February saw a higher volume of positive mentions, primarily due to Super Bowl-associated promotions that drove uplift in the conversation for Jack in the Box that lasted through the end of February. YouTube generated consistent positive brand interactions in both February and March. Looking further into the data, an organic influencer was identified. @sheaserrano was an influencer who generated positive brand interactions for Jack in the Box.

Demographic Insights

Demographic Insights from Brandwatch Analytics lets brands find out more about the people behind the online conversation. It provides demographic data about the Twitter audience and the individuals talking about a brand, as well as a host of dashboards and tools for analyzing that data. With this new feature, brands are able to analyze the tweeters within their Query (search) results, both as a group and individually, including its:

- Account type (whether they are an organization or an individual)
- Gender
- Interests
- Profession
- Location

Using Demographic Insights, Jack in the Box saw that 'sports' was the dominant interest among the Jack in the Box audience in both February and March. Some, but not all, of this was due to sports-related influencers, such as the official Lakers basketball team's Twitter handle @Lakers tweeting about Jack in the Box in March. These tweets resonated with sports fans and helped drive an increase in mentions for the organization. Due to the online reaction to the Super Bowl campaign, consumers who are also football fans in February drove the brand conversation. The official Jack in the Box hashtag associated with the Super Bowl commercial #declarationofdelicious was included in these footballs fans' Tweets.

Results

The research has helped the marketing communications team within Jack in the Box to identify new influencers and emphasize interests that resonate with their audience. The analysis has provided the organization with insight into how its campaigns affect people and the reaction people have. This analysis also reinforced that compared to principal competitors in the QSR market, they have a much smaller presence, and therefore, Jack in the Box will look to learn how to grow in this area. Jack in the Box has an overall online objective to create compelling, relevant conversation to drive brand advocacy. With insights and analysis gathered with Brandwatch Analytics, the organization has vital information available to them, which will help the business to achieve its goals and bold ambitions for the future.

Source: https://www.brandwatch.com/case-studies

REVIEW QUESTIONS

1. Explain different types of tangible and intangible social media values to customers and firms.
2. Explain the social media analytics value creation model with examples.
3. Explain the concept of social media return on investment.
4. Explain the network externality argument in the context of social media ROI.
5. Define social media engagement, interactivity, and popularity metrics.
6. Explain three stages of analytics investment.
7. Explain the overall social media analytics capabilities needed to create value with social media analytics.

CHAPTER 1 REFERENCES

Antweiler, W., & Frank, M. Z. (2004). Is all that talk just noise? The information content of internet stock message boards. *The Journal of Finance, 59*(3), 1259-1294.

Baird, C. H., & Parasnis, G. (2011). From social media to social customer relationship management. *Strategy & Leadership, 39*(5), 30-37.

Bekmamedova, N., & Shanks, G. (2014, 6-9 Jan. 2014). *Social Media Analytics and Business Value: A Theoretical Framework and Case Study.* Paper presented at the 2014 47th Hawaii International Conference on System Sciences.

Chui, M. (2013). *The social economy: Unlocking value and productivity through social technologies*: McKinsey.

Cronin, J. J. (2014). Teaching ROI Analysis in an Era of Social Media. *Journal of Advertising Education, 18*(2), 28-35.

DEI Worldwide. (2008). the impact of social media on purchasing behavior. Engaging Consumers Online, available at www.deiworldwide.com/files/DEIStudy-Engaging%20ConsumersOnline-Summary.pdf

Grossman, R. L. (2009). What is analytic infrastructure and why should you care? *SIGKDD Explor. Newsl., 11*(1), 5-9. doi:10.1145/1656274.1656277

Huston, L., & Sakkab, N. (2006). Connect and develop. *Harvard business review, 84*(3), 58-66.

Karim, A., Khan, N., & Khan, G. F. (2016). *A SOCIAL MEDIA ANALYTICS CAPABILITY FRAMEWORK FOR FIRM'S COMPETITIVE ADVANTAGE.* Paper presented at the PACIS 2016 Proceedings, Taiwan.

Khan, G. F., Mohaisen, M., & Trier, M. (2017). The network ROI. *working paper.*

Kim, A. J., & Ko, E. (2012). Do social media marketing activities enhance customer equity? An empirical study of a luxury fashion brand. *Journal of Business Research, 65*(10), 1480-1486. doi:http://dx.doi.org/10.1016/j.jbusres.2011.10.014

Kim, C. K., & Chung, J. Y. (1997). Brand popularity, country image and market share: An empirical study. *Journal of International Business Studies, 28*, 361-386.

Kiron, D., Ferguson, R. B., & Prentice, P. K. (2013). From Value to Vision: Reimagining the Possible with Data Analytics. *MIT Sloan Management Review: Spring Research Report*, 1-19.

Kiron, D., Prentice, P. K., & Ferguson, R. B. (2014). The analytics mandate. *MIT Sloan Management Review, 55*(4), 1-25.

Kite, S. (2011). Social CRM's a Tough, Worthy Goal. *Bank Technology News, 24*(6), 30-31.

Livingston, J. A. (2005). How valuable is a good reputation? A sample selection model of internet auctions. *Review of Economics and Statistics, 87*(3), 453-465.

Lucking-Reiley, D., Bryan, D., Prasad, N., & Reeves, D. (2007). Pennies from eBay: The determinants of price in online auctions*. *The journal of industrial economics, 55*(2), 223-233.

Porter, M. E. (1985). *Competitive Advantage: Creating and Sustaining Superior Performance.* New York: Simon and Schuster.

Purcell, B. (2011). Bank of America insights make a case for social media data analytics Retrieved from http://beyondthearc.com/blog/2011/customer-experience/bank-of-america-insights-make-a-case-for-social-media-data-analytics

Ransbotham, S., Kiron, D., & Prentice, P. K. (2015). The Talent Dividend: Analytics talent is driving competitive advantage at data-oriented companies. *MIT Sloan Management Review.*

Simonoff, J. S., & Sparrow, I. R. (2000). Predicting movie grosses: Winners and losers, blockbusters and sleepers. *Chance, 13*(3), 15-24.

The Economist. (2015). *Broken Links: Why analytics investments have yet to pay off, available at: https://www.zs.com/-/media/files/publications/public/broken-links-why-analytics-investments-have-yet-to-pay-off.pdf?la=en*. Retrieved from

Tumasjan, A., Sprenger, T. O., Sandner, P. G., & Welpe, I. M. (2010). Election forecasts with Twitter: How 140 characters reflect the political landscape. *Social Science Computer Review*, 0894439310386557.

Verhoef, P. C., Kooge, E., & Walk, N. (2016). *Creating Value with Big Data Analytics: Making Smarter Marketing Decisions*: Routledge.

Vidgen, R., Shaw, S., & Grant, D. B. (2017). Management challenges in creating value from business analytics. *European Journal of Operational Research, 261*(2), 626-639. doi:https://doi.org/10.1016/j.ejor.2017.02.023

Virgili, J. A., & Káganer, E. (2012). *Impact of Social Media on the Financial Services Sector*. Retrieved from

Vogel, V., Evanschitzky, H., & Ramaseshan, B. (2008). Customer Equity Drivers and Future Sales. *Journal of Marketing, 72*(6), 98-108. doi:10.1509/jmkg.72.6.98

Wamba, S. F., Akter, S., Bhattacharyya, M., & Aditya, S. (2016). How does Social Media Analytics Create Value? *J. Organ. End User Comput., 28*(3), 1-9. doi:10.4018/joeuc.2016070101

Weinberg, B. D., & Pehlivan, E. (2011). Social spending: Managing the social media mix. *Business Horizons, 54*(3), 275-282. doi:http://dx.doi.org/10.1016/j.bushor.2011.01.008

Understanding Social Media

"Social is a business culture, not just tools"—**Gohar F. Khan**

Learning Outcomes

After completing this chapter, the reader should be able to:

- Understand the history and evolution of WWW and the Internet.
- Understand social media and its core characteristics and types.
- Differentiate among Web 1.0, Web 2.0, Web 3.0, and Web 4.0
- List the uses of social media for business purposes.
- Identify common social media issues.

INTRODUCTION

Social media is becoming an integral part of our lives in contemporary society and has changed the creation, sharing, and consumption of information. Billions of people are flocking to *social media platforms*, such as Facebook, Twitter, and YouTube, where they share, tweet, like, and post content. *Social media* is one of the most potent technological developments to happen in recent years, and it is almost impossible to imagine our lives without it. There are countless stories related to the role of social media in contemporary society, either in the entertainment industry where it propelled Psy (a Korean rapper) to worldwide fame through the spread of his "*Gangnam Style*" YouTube video, or in the political landscape during the period commonly called the "Arab Spring" or "Facebook revolution."

Social media growth, tools, and big data present an unparalleled opportunity to market products, enhance brand loyalty, network with customers, crowd-source ideas, drive sales, and mine business insights. Social media has been revolutionized since the beginning of it all, starting from email to internet chats to social networking and has forever changed the world and even more importantly, how we perceive the world. Let us look at some underlying tools and technologies.

THE INTERNET AND WORLD WIDE WEB

At the very core of social media is the *World Wide Web* (WWW) and the *Internet.* The Internet is the global network of interconnected devices, such as personal computers, smartphones, switches, routers, satellites, and cables. The first Internet was the Arpanet project from the US Department of Defense who funded the initial development for military purposes.

The Internet is composed of several technologies, and one of the underlying software technologies is the WWW or just the "Web." The Web in its simplest form is composed of interlinked hypertext documents (i.e., websites) that can be accessed through web browsers such as Internet Explorer and Chrome. The Web has drastically evolved since it was first created. The earliest version is referred to as the Web 1.0. In 1990, the now-famous computer scientist Sir Tim Berners-Lee created the WWW, which opened up the Internet for ordinary people—locally, nationally and internationally. Berners-Lee set out to solve that problem by creating a universal medium that could link information together. Thus, the World Wide Web was born. In November 1989, he created the three protocols—HTTP, URL, and HTML—that we now know as the "Web." With the rise of mobile devices, the WWW continues to maintain its level of significance in the modern world as it did in the early 1990s.

The Evolution of the Internet

From a humble beginning containing a couple of nodes in the 1960s, the internet has sprung into a global network of interconnected networks used by ordinary people, business, and researchers to quickly and freely communicate. Table 2.1 provides the Internet evolution timeline.

The Evolution of the WWW

Since its creation, the Web has also drastically evolved. As the Table 2.2 shows, the currently available four distinct Web phases, and we briefly cover each of them in this chapter.

Web 1.0

Web 1.0, or the "*read-only web*," was an early version of the Internet. The Web 1.0 was static. Web 1.0 allowed only one-way information flow in a one-to-many fashion. Web developers and designers would create websites and content for users to consume. The design of the site could not allow users to contribute content or respond to it; hence, the Web 1.0 users were only passive recipients of the information/content available over the Internet. In that sense, Web 1.0 was yet another channel of one-way information distribution like any other conventional one-to-many technologies, such as radio and television. Web 1.0 websites were only used for information presentation purposes, and not for generating information or content.

Table 2.1. The Internet timeline and beyond

Year	Event
1950s	After WWII, the Cold War spawns the need for new ways to communicate more quickly—hence, Arpanet originated for military uses.
1960s	Arpanet became available to researchers around the world.
1970s	Apple and IBM developed personal computers in the late 1970's, which appeal to the masses who can run simple word processing and spreadsheet applications on them.
1980s	TCP/IP was developed as a language for computers to communicate over the Internet.
1980s	Web 1.0, or the initial version of the World Wide Web, developed and was entirely made up of static, non-interactive Web pages connected by hyperlinks.
1990s	The creation of Web 1.0 led to new Internet-based business models.
1991	Gopher developed for distributing, searching, and retrieving documents over the Internet. HTML developed for creating websites.
1993	Mosaic's first browser becomes available, soon spawning Netscape.
1995	Yahoo! Search engine debuted.
1998	Google search engine founded on September 4th, 1998.
2000	dot.com business failures, which led to the disappearance of venture capital.
2004-2009	The emergence of social media and rapid growth in user-generated content and emergence of new players like Facebook, Twitter, Foursquare, YouTube, LinkedIn, Groupon—mostly all the social networks we are familiar with today.
2010-2018	The shift to increasing focus on intelligent web, internet of things, and autonomous machines (e.g., driverless cars, drones, smart robots, 3D printing, and virtual reality).
2019-??	

Web 2.0

Web 2.0 is the version of the WWW that we are the most familiar with; it is characterized by the evolution from static web pages to user-generated content and the emergence of social media along with mobile technologies.

Table 2.2. Evolution of the World Wide Web

Web 1.0	Web 2.0	Web 3.0	Web 4.0
• Read-Only • Company & Business focused • Home Page • Own your own content • Web Forms • Web Directories and Folders • Page Views • Banner Ads • Britannica Online • HTML and Web Portals	• Read-Write • Community, Social focused • Blogs, Blogging, Wikis • Share your content • Web Applications • Content Tagging • Cost Per Click (CPC) • Interactive Ads • Wikipedia • XML / RSS	• Personal, Portable, Extensible • Focused on the Individual • Streaming media, Live streaming, Data Waves • Collect & Content • Smart/Autonomous Applications • User Behavior / Quantified Self • User Engagement via collected metrics • Behavioral Ads & Targeting • Semantic Web • RDF/RDFS/OWL	• Converged • Personal Assistants (Siri/Google Now Cortona) • Bots / Intelligent Agents / Drones • Programmable Content & Content on Demand • Artificial Intelligence / Algorithms • Private Cloud, Internet of Things • Cross Channel Measurement • Programmatic Advertising • Transparent Web / WikiLeaks • Quantum Computing, AI

Source: Adapted from Web 1.0 to Web 4.0 Marshall Sponder – WebMetricsGuru INC

Web 2.0 altered the WWW landscape by turning the web into a collaborative ecosystem where users could create content, share ideas, and offer concrete products and services. Web 2.0 allows two-way and many-to-many information flows and user-generated content (Kaplan & Haenlein, 2010; Kietzmann, Hermkens, McCarthy, & Silvestre, 2011; Oreilly, 2007). The content generated by users over social media platforms is known as user-generated content (UGC). Some tools of this collaborative ecosystem are podcasting, blogging, tagging, social bookmarking, social networking, and wikis (we discuss many of these social media tools later in this chapter).

One important thing to note is that Web 2.0 is not a technical standard, or an update to the early standard (i.e., Web 1.0). However, it does reflect the changes in the way people use the web and how programmers designed websites. Due to changing societal norms, webmasters and programmers developed platforms allowing users to create quickly, present, monetize, and share their content.

Some prominent features of the Web 2.0 are:

New Business Models—the Web 2.0 gave rise to collaborative economies (or the sharing economy) business models, such as Airbnb and Uber that are beginning to threaten the survival of older business models, such as hotels and cabs.

The Long Tail—the Wired Magazine editor Chris Anderson popularized the term Long Tail in 2004. The term is used to refer to the large number of products that sell in small quantities, as contrasted with the small number of best-selling products. New platforms and revenue models are tailored to an individual's needs and desires. For example, Amazon and eBay are powered by organic and paid search engines to serve customers better. Businesses, large and small, begin to make a living by serving customers in local and global markets. Instead of the masses, companies only needed a small number of loyal supporters and customers.

Scalability of Software—this refers to the ability of the Web to track and collect the ever-growing amount of behavioral data via cookies and clickstream analytics. Clickstreams are the path/order of the pages that visitors choose when navigating through a site (Note: clickstreams, as applied to the Web, are the categories of websites that users visit on a regular basis—the clickstream is used for re-targeting purposes.) Users emerged as co-developers and software began harnessing the collective intelligence of developers and users.

Device Agnostic Software Development—Mobile Software Development Toolkits (SDK), such as the Android SDK, aid in the development of programs that run on the most significant number of devices possible.

Web Analytics—web Analytics matured as a platform to measure Web 1.0 and Web 2.0 digital traces.

Search Engines—search engines pick up specific keywords that when used in a search can narrow results down from the infinite amounts of unstructured data available on the Web. Search engines are discussed in chapter 8.

Semantic Web—this is an extension of the Web which makes the Web intuitive and intelligent by separating the presentation of content from its meaning. With the help of the Semantic Web, we can customize and personalize communications and the content available online.

Social Media—web 2.0 led to the development of social media tools and technologies which allow users to communicate and share content through social networks. Social media is discussed later in this chapter.

Anywhere Internet—between 2010 and 2018, almost half of humanity was online in one form or another. The development of the internet led to automated advertising (now called programmatic advertisement) which would have been impossible without the Web 2.0.

Geolocation—mobile devices broadcast their location to Internet Service Providers via the Global positioning service (GPS), near field communication (NFC), and Geo-fencing. GPS makes it simpler to navigate by almost eliminating the need for physical maps; it also made humanity more productive and saved us an enormous amount of time and energy.

Web 3.0

Web 3.0 is the next revolution in the WWW and alters the Web yet again. In addition to having the properties of Web 2.0, *Web 3.0* marks the era of a connected Web operating system where most software components (e.g., application programs and operating systems) and data processing reside on the Internet. The Web 3.0 is smarter, quicker, and more reliable in connecting data, concepts, applications, and people.

A critical dimension of the Web 3.0 is the Semantic Web or Linked Data. The Semantic Web is known as the "Web of data" (W3, 2015), which aims to make vast amounts of data (and the relationship among the datasets) web-available in a machine-readable format (such as Resource Description Framework [RDF] format) so that applications can query it. RDF is a general-purpose language for representing information on the web (W3, 2015). Intelligent and pervasive geo-location services, predictive analytics, and "Big Data" will power web 3.0 along with the ability to customize and personalize the web experience (for users).

As a recent example of Web 3.0 driven business acquisition, IBM purchased the Weather Company in 2015 to use changes in the weather to predict a consumers' purchasing behavior. Because of the acquisition, IBM now collects sensor data from billions of Internet of Things (IoT) sensors around the world while also serving out real-time information and insights to tens of millions of users worldwide via Watson Analytics.

Web 4.0

Web 4.0, an emerging phenomenon, will be the "ultra-intelligent" version of the Web. The technologies that will lead to the development of *Web 4.0* include the Internet of Things, Quantified Self, Private Clouds, Intelligent Computing, Embedded Intelligence, Predictive Analytics, and Artificial Intelligence. According to Daniel Burrus, a business strategist, Web 4.0 is about "the ultra-intelligent electronic agent" which will have the ability to recognize us when we get in front of it. Also, it will interact with us in the following fashion:

> *"Good morning. You are flying to Boston today. Take a raincoat; it is raining. By the way, that fight you were taking, it has already been canceled. Do not worry about it. There was a mechanical problem. I have already booked you for a new one. I will tell you about it on the way to the airport. However, remember you are going to exercise every day, and I am here to remind you that you are going to exercise." Also, you might say, "I do not know if I want to exercise today," and I will show you a nude profile of yourself. Moreover, you will say, "You know what; I think I am going to exercise today."*

SOCIAL MEDIA

Social media is built on the *Web 2.0 philosophy*, that is, to give more control to the user over the content. It can be defined as an easy-to-use Internet-based platform that provides users with opportunities to create and exchange content (such as text, videos, audio, and graphics) in a one-to-one, one-to-many, and many-to-many context. Social media and Web 2.0 are often used interchangeably, but they can be slightly differentiated (Kaplan & Haenlein, 2010). At the core of social media is the Web 2.0 concept and social media can be considered as an application of the Web 2.0 concept. In other words, social media is realized based on the Web 2.0 concept.

One important thing to note is that social media is not just limited to the popular platforms such as Facebook, Twitter, YouTube, and blogs. In this book, we consider as social media any online platform (proprietary or purpose built) that enable users to participate, collaborate, create, and share content in a many-to-many context.

CORE CHARACTERISTICS OF SOCIAL MEDIA

The best way to understand social media is through the core characteristics that set it apart from the *conventional medium*. All these properties play an essential role in creating a collaborative ecosystem.

Social Media is a Peer-to-Peer Medium

Social media enables *interaction* among users in a peer-to-peer fashion. This is unlike conventional technological media such as print, radio, telephone, and television that are based on a top-down, broadcast business communications model.

Social Media is Participatory

Unlike conventional technologies, social media encourages *participation* and *feedback* from users. Social media users can participate in online discourse through blogging, commenting, tagging, and sharing content.

Social Media is Owned by its Users

While social media platforms are provided by corporations (such as Google and Facebook), the *content* is generated, owned, and controlled by social media users. In fact, social media could not survive without its users and their content.

Social Media is Conversational

Using social media, many more people can *freely* express their views and opinions. The *ease of use* and *peer-to-pee*r conversation abilities of social media makes it possible for the people to communicate and collaborate in real-time, regardless of their location, wealth, occupation, or beliefs. This ability make social media stand out from the traditional one-to-one or one-to-many medium of interaction.

Social Media is Relationship Oriented

Most social media tools allow users to establish and maintain social and professional *relationships* easily. For instance, users can use their LinkedIn profile page to forge new business contacts and expand their professional connections. Facebook members can use their pages to gain traffic and spread the word about their personal or business project. At the same time, users express their different moods throughout the day and share what is going on/how they feel.

HISTORY OF SOCIAL MEDIA

While the first *online bulletin boards* started appearing in 1979, most of the leading social media platforms that we are familiar began to emerge around 2004, specialized analytics platforms to examine social media began to appear around the same time (see Figure 2.1). Initially, there was a small audience using these platforms. Since then, there has been a steady rise in adoption, and now most people who are online have at least one social media account.

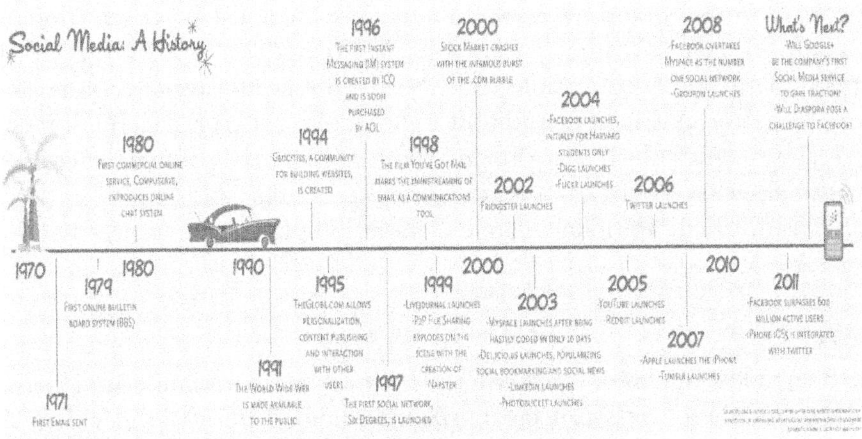

Figure 2.1 History of social media

TYPES OF SOCIAL MEDIA

Based on authentication or access mechanisms, social media tools are available in two forms: 1) Internet-based and 2) smartphone-based. *Internet-based* social media platforms are accessed through e-mail IDs. Facebook, LinkedIn, Cyworld, and Google+ are examples of Internet-based social media. Note that an Internet-based social media platform can also be accessed through any device connected to the Internet, including a smartphone application (or app for short), but the authentication mechanism is still the same. Whereas, *smartphone-based* social media platforms are accessed through mobile phone numbers; that is, users can only log in using mobile phone numbers. KaKao Talk, Tender, and 1KM are famous examples of phone-based social network services. These applications can only be installed and accessed from a phone; for example, in its current form, one cannot use KaKao Talk, 1KM, or Tender through a personal computer. Mobile applications are also an example of mobile-based social media tools (we discuss mobile apps in chapter 11).

Below, we briefly discuss different social media tools and how businesses can leverage them.

Social Networking Sites

Social networks sites or services (SNS) are types of social media platforms that are solely focused on online social relationships among users. Some examples of SNS include Facebook, Google+, and Cyworld. SNS allows users to build and maintain social relations among people who share interests, activities, backgrounds, or real-life connections. Most SNS enable users to "(1) construct a public or semi-public profile, (2) establish links (friendship) and relationships with other SNS users, and (3) view and traverse their list of connections and those made by others within the system." (Boyd & Ellison, 2007)(p. 1–2). Currently, there are two versions of SNS, a publically available one and a business SNS. For example, in addition to its public version, Facebook recently released a business social networking site, "Workplace," aimed at corporate users and allowing them to create social networks and collaborate. The workplace is primarily an online team collaboration platform that uses Facebook features for work.

Facebook

Founded in 2004 by Mark Zuckerberg, *Facebook* is an online social network service or site where users can create profiles, upload photos and video, send messages, and keep in touch with friends, family, and colleagues. As of October 2017, Facebook had more than 2.07 billion registered users. Apart from its primary function as an online social network site, Facebook has become an important marketing and outreach channel for all sorts of organizations including governments. Furthermore, there are also Facebook groups and Facebook events to advertise any potential business events.

Facebook popularized the concept of "*virtual friends.*" Facebook is now "home" for most people on social media, even if it is not always their favorite place to hang out and share information. The social network that people spend the most time on is Facebook (see Figure 2.2). Sixteen percent of college students spend 4-6 hours a day on Facebook, while another 34% spend 2-3 hours a day. When we compare those statistics with the other social networks, none of them even comes close.

Using Facebook for Business Purposes

How can a business benefit from Facebook? The answer is *Facebook pages.* Facebook pages can serve as an excellent advertisement and networking channel with customers. Facebook pages are a great way to connect and network with customers. The following questions may bring some clarity and focus to a brand's Facebook page efforts.

- What is the purpose of your Facebook page? Moreover, is the purpose aligned with the business goals?
- Who will be responsible for handling your Facebook page (e.g., posting information, responding to comments and complaints)?
- What should be the Facebook page name?

- What information should be published and what should not be posted?
- Do you have a legal mandate to establish an official Facebook page for your organization?
- Do you have a plan to collect and analyze feedback generated over your Facebook page?
- What are your security measures for possible online risks?

However, the Facebook page has a lot of rules, regulations, and laws surrounding their use for businesses. In particular, Facebook and Google have cracked down on fake news and fake news sites, and laws and regulations surrounding phony news sites are continually updated.

Daily Time Spent on Select Social Networks by US College Student Internet Users, May 2015
% of respondents

	Google+	LinkedIn	Pinterest	Twitter	Instagram	Facebook
0-1 hours	92.6%	89.5%	84.4%	73.4%	57.6%	39.3%
2-3 hours	4.9%	7.8%	11.9%	18.1%	24.1%	34.1%
4-5 hours	1.4%	0.6%	2.5%	5.3%	10.3%	15.6%
6-7 hours	0.4%	1.2%	0.0%	2.0%	3.9%	5.8%
8-9 hours	0.4%	0.6%	0.8%	0.4%	2.5%	2.7%
10+ hours	0.4%	0.4%	0.4%	1.0%	1.6%	2.5%

Note: n=514 ages 17-25 who are enrolled in a 4-year college/university; numbers may not add up to 100% due to rounding
Source: Fluent survey conducted by SurveyMonkey, Aug 25, 2015

195987 www.eMarketer.com

Figure 2.2. Social network usage statistics

Facebook Messenger

Facebook Messenger is a mobile application created for friends and family to communicate; but it is also an innovative tool for shopping, marketing, productivity, and personal improvement. Facebook Messenger now uses "bots" to automate messaging. Although bots seem to be the opposite of what social media was intended to be about, i.e., two interactions among humans, it might be a necessary evolution to deal with the massive data overload. Bots have the following capabilities:

- Send and receive application user interface (API) calls, including text, images, and rich bubbles with call-to-action statements.
- Use generic message templates.

- Create welcome screens and "get started" buttons.

To comprehend the power of *Facebooks bots*, one must experiment with them and see what tools are available to improve their use. Bots can be virtually applied to any business type and category. Common bots include Babun (for startups), GrowthBot (for marketing and sales), SurveyBot (for creating surveys on Facebook), and Kukie (recommends free tools).

Following in Twitter Periscope's footsteps, Facebook launched a new live video streaming service called Facebook Live. Facebook also launched live video scheduling, scheduled broadcast sharing, and pre-broadcast lobbies to verified Pages. By scheduling a broadcast, potential viewers get a one-time notification in their news feed reminding them that the stream is starting.

Content Communities

Content communities, such as YouTube and Flicker, are defined by "a group of people coalescing online around an object of interest held in common. The object can be just about anything, for example, photos, videos, links, topics or issues, and is often organized and developed in a way that either includes social network elements or makes them central to the content." The most popular content community site is YouTube.

YouTube

YouTube is a video-sharing website on which users can upload, view, and share videos. It was founded in February 2005 and has been owned by Google since late 2006. The potential of anyone displaying his or her talent to millions of people in almost real-time was never possible before the advent of YouTube (which is the third most visited website on the Internet). Before YouTube, whenever someone wanted to watch a video, they had to watch it on VCR, CD or DVR devices, and more recently on cable TV networks. With over 5 billion videos watched every day, it is also the second largest search engine, next to Google. The introduction of YouTube also marks the beginning of the Viral Video era. In 2016, YouTube introduced YouTube Red, a paid-for subscription service. YouTube Red is a way for people to pay for ad-free YouTube videos.

Perhaps the most significant changes have happened more recently with the introduction of streaming live video. Anyone with a mobile device can now broadcast a live video stream for free using tools, such as Twitter Periscope, Amazon-Twitch (online streaming of live games), and Facebook Live (Facebook's in-app video streamer). While other video sites (such as Facebook) are quickly gaining market share, nothing comes even close to YouTube for the sheer size of the audience, because it shares the same data as its owner, Google. YouTube is also appealing to its users because they can efficiently use its shared links to convert any songs posted on YouTube into MP3 format and store them on their smartphones.

Using YouTube for Business

An essential feature of YouTube is the *YouTube channel.* A YouTube channel is a public online space (or page) on YouTube. A YouTube channel allows users to upload videos, leave comments, or make playlists. Businesses from around the world use YouTube channels in a variety of ways. For example, it is a great way to advertise, educate customers by uploading training materials, spread awareness, and display information about product and services.

Khan Academy (https://www.khanacademy.org/) is an excellent example of the practical use of educational videos on YouTube. Before configuring a YouTube channel, the questions raised in the previous section should be reviewed and answered. Answers to most of the issues should be rooted in a brand's social media strategy. YouTube also allows users to make videos rating a product and promoting it to their channel subscribers.

Finally, YouTube is also an excellent advertising channel and has a variety of ad types and formats. In addition to advertising, educating, and placing information about products or services, businesses also utilize known YouTubers as their advertiser by using sponsorships. (i.e., sponsoring a known YouTuber to talk about their products to generate more customers and offering the YouTuber a discount code to their viewers to gain more incentive to purchase the product).

Building a YouTube Channel

Below, are some questions to ask before beginning starting a YouTube channel.

- What is the purpose of the YouTube channel? (e.g., advertisement promotes awareness, share useful content, provide training). Also, is the purpose aligned with the business goals?
- Who will be responsible for handling the channel (e.g., creating and posting videos)?
- What should be the name of the YouTube channel?
- What type of content should or should not be posted?
- Do you (or your unit) have a legal mandate to establish an official YouTube channel for your organization?
- Does your organization have a plan to collect and analyze feedback generated over the channel?
- How will the channel be secured from external and internal cyber-attacks and hacking?

Blogs

A *blog* is a type of online personal space or website where an individual (or organization) post content (text, images, videos, and links to other sites) and expresses opinions on matters of personal (or organizational) interest on a regular basis. Blogs are one of the first forms of social media that evolved; the first blogs appeared in the early 1990's and became popular after the turn of the century. Blogs are still the channel of choice for reputation and brand building. The most popular blogging platforms are WordPress, Tumblr, and Blogger. Blogging does not require technical expertise or programming skills, so ordinary users can quickly build and manage a professional-looking blog. Blogs made it easy for ordinary people to voice their opinion on any subject and to publish it online instantly.

Blogs that are consistent in their topic tend to do better in search engine results listings (which generate a substantial amount of traffic to many blogs). Blogs utilize RSS Feeds (Really Simple Syndication) alerting search engines and RSS readers of new content/posts that are being produced (search engine optimization (SEO) is covered in chapter 8).

Blog Features

Essential features of a blog include:

Interactivity—readers can leave comments in response to a blog post.

Archives—blogs provide archives of past blog entries stored in reverse chronological order (that is, the most recent appears first).

Subscription—Internet users can subscribe to blogs. Subscribed users are alerted when new content is posted on the blog.

Focused—most blogs are focused on a particular area of interest.

Using Blogs for Business Purposes

An official business blog is not just a business diary or journal, but a great way to build a community of readers, receive early and direct feedback on business issues and solicit innovative ideas. As with other platforms, before creating your business blog, review the following questions.

- What is the purpose of the official blog? (e.g., advertisement, promotes awareness, solicits ideas). Moreover, is the purpose aligned with the business goals?
- Who will be responsible for handling the blog (e.g., creating and posting content)?
- What should be the name of your blog?
- What type of content should be published and what should not be posted?

- Do you have a legal mandate to establish an official blog for your organization?
- Do you have a plan to collect and analyze feedback generated over the blog?
- How will the blog be secured from external and internal cyber attacks and hacking?

Microblogging

Microblogging is a miniature version of blogging that allows users to exchange/publish brief messages, including text, images, or links to other websites. The most popular microblogging platform is Twitter.

Twitter is an online microblogging service that enables users to send and read short messages commonly known as "tweets. A tweet is a text message limited to one hundred forty characters. Jack Dorsey, a well-known entrepreneur, was one of the founders of Twitter (he is the current CEO of Twitter as well as a point-of-sale platform called Square). At the time, Dorsey was an undergraduate student at New York University, where he introduced the idea of an individual using an SMS service to communicate with a small group. Let us spend some time to understand basic Twitter terminologies.

Tweet

A *tweet* is a one hundred forty-character message posted via Twitter; it can include a video, picture, or link. Users can also add links, photos, and videos in a tweet. Usually, a tweet is in the public domain. Twitter users, however, can set their tweets to be private, so only the audiences that they have allowed can view them.

Retweet (RT)

A *retweet* is a re-post of someone else's tweet. One way to gauge the popularity of tweets is by measuring retweets. Popular tweets can get many retweets, and many celebrities are paid for their tweets. It is important to note that only the tweets from public accounts can be retweeted.

Following

Following is a person on Twitter you follow. On Twitter, following another Twitter account means that:

- You are subscribing to their tweets as a follower (their tweets will appear on your Twitter main page).
- Their updates, retweets, and favorites will appear on your Home tab.

- That person can send you direct messages.
- Private accounts must provide their permission to be followed.

Followers

Followers are people who follow you on Twitter. If someone follows you, it means that:

- They will show up in your followers list.
- They will see your tweets in their home timeline whenever they log in to Twitter.
- You can send them direct messages

Research suggests that the number of followers and following are strongly correlated, meaning that people who follow more Twitter accounts end up getting more followers, and vice versa. One of the objectives of a Twitter user should be to increase their followers.

Direct Messages

Unlike a tweet, which is public and seen by everyone, a *direct message* is a private message seen only by the sender and the recipient. Typically, a direct message can only be sent to people following you. Anyone you do not follow can send you a direct message if: 1) you have opted in to receive direct messages from anyone, or 2) you have previously sent that person a direct message.

Mention

When another user includes your username preceded by the @ symbol in a tweet, it is called a "*mention.*" Your Mentions tab (on the notifications page) collects tweets that mention you by your username so you can keep track of conversations others are having with you. The number of mentions is an indication of influence or popularity.

Hashtags (#)

The *hashtag*(#) symbol is used to mark keywords or topics in a tweet. It is an easy way to categorize messages. Twitter shows trending hashtags in the left navigation of a member's Twitter homepage. Trends can be tailored, based on algorithms that measure the activities of those accounts whom the user is following, or it can be manually set to a locality, such as Auckland City. In short, Trends can be arranged to show either local or worldwide trends.

Hashtags are not only used on Twitter but also on Facebook and Instagram. Hashtags are one of the best ways to connect a loosely knit structure into social media interactions. Hashtags allow public conversations around the subject of the hashtag to take place in a manner that can be decoded and gleaned for insights on public sentiments. For instance, the hashtag #WikiLeaks can be collected and analyzed to investigate the recent commentary around WikiLeaks happening on Twitter.

Using Twitter for Business Purposes

Twitter is a great way to keep customers informed. Businesses around the world use Twitter to keep customers informed by disseminating news and information almost in real time. Setting up Twitter is a straightforward process. However, it should not be taken lightly, as the Twitter channel will officially represent an organization. Before proceeding to set up, do a little bit of planning and brainstorming. Twitter is a thought sharing website, but not every business can thrive there. Specific verticals such as cosmetics and real estate would be better off focusing on more visual media-sharing sites, such as Facebook or Instagram.

The following questions may bring some clarity and focus to your Twitter efforts. Twitter users can use tweets, sponsored tweets, and right-hand rail ads to communicate with customers and potential audiences.

- What is the purpose of the Twitter account? Is the purpose aligned with the business goals?
- Who will be responsible for handling it? Since it is not a one-time deal, once a social media presence is established, it needs to be sustained and appropriately managed.
- What should be the business Twitter handler or username? Be thoughtful while creating a handle; think of a name that sums up your brand.
- What information should be published and what should not be posted on Twitter? An organization's corporate level information or communication policy may provide a useful place to start.
- Do you (or your business unit) have a legal mandate to establish a Twitter account?
- Is an organizational level plan in place to collect and analyze feedback generated on Twitter?
- What strategies and techniques will be used to secure the corporate Twitter account from online security risks?

Online Collaborative Projects

Wikipedia is an example of an online collaborative project. Online collaborative projects/tools allow people to plan, coordinate, add, control, and monitor content in collaboration with others. At the core of the online collaborative projects is the concept of the wiki. A wiki is a type of online content management system that allows users to add, modify, or delete content simultaneously in collaboration with others. Famous examples of wiki-based platforms are Wikipedia and wiki-spaces. Ward Cunningham first conceived the concept of a wiki.

Using Wikis for Business Purposes

Wikis are a great way to communicate and collaboratively work on projects with other people. An excellent example of a collaborative wiki is http://www.wikipedia.com. *Wikipedia* has more than thirty million articles in 287 languages written collaboratively by volunteers around the world. However, Wikipedia is just one type of website built on the wiki model. There are several other notable wikis. Google (www.sites.google.com) provides project wikis that can be configured for business purposes. The questions discussed in earlier sections should be reviewed before setting up a business wiki. Wikis are also helpful in research ranking and SEO (a detailed discussion on SEO is included in chapter 8).

Folksonomies or Tagging

The term *folksonomy*, also known as social tagging, social indexing, and collaborative tagging, is attributed to Thomas Vander Wal. The term was created by fusing folk and taxonomy. In simple terms it is the method of organizing data and content (through tagging) from a user's perspective. For example, del.icio.us, a social bookmarking system, allows users to tag, organize, classify, and share content (web addresses or sites) in their own unique ways. These days, almost all prominent companies (e.g., Facebook and Flicker) also provide tagging services for their users. Since the contents are tagged with useful keywords, social tagging expedites the process of searching and finding relevant content.

Another example is Pinterest. Pinterest is a big, virtual Pin Board, an online scrapbook that users can stick any image or video onto, and organize in the manner they want (on a custom "board"). Pinterest makes it easy to store and embed photos, videos, and Infographics by pinning them up onto a dashboard. The main selling point of Pinterest is its addictiveness. Users spend hours searching for images and re-pinning them, and it is a useful means of generating links back to a website or blog where the content can be further built out and monetized (if desired). Another aspect of Pinterest is that it can use to search for what styles are trending and forecast future products and collections. Pinterest is an excellent resource for inspiration as well. It gives a good idea of what is immediately attractive visually, structurally, and layout-wise when creating new images and graphics. Users can follow celebrities, brands, and bloggers on Pinterest.

Virtual Worlds

Virtual worlds are computer-generated online environments. It can take the form of a three-dimensional (3-D) virtual social world (e.g., Second Life) where people digitally represent themselves in the way of avatars and interact with others through text and voice messaging. It can also take a form of virtual interactive games, such as the World of Warcraft. Mostly, the users themselves create the virtual world environment.

Virtual reality is another dimension of virtual worlds, where real and virtual are fused together. Virtual reality uses computer software and hardware tools to simulate physical presence in the virtual world. A good example of virtual reality is the Pokémon Go computer game. Some virtual worlds do not necessarily require computer software, such as Gaia Online or Club Penguin. Virtual Reality (VR) is part of a technology and lifestyle trend for creating technology that places people in a 'virtual world,' rather than using a character or avatar to represent themselves in cyberspace digitally.

Mobile Apps

Mobile apps are becoming an integral part of our lives. Mobile apps are special-purpose tools developed to perform a variety of activities we do every day while on the move, such as communicating, social networking, sharing information, and shopping. Tinder and Skout, for example, are designed to facilitate social relations, and Viber is intended to assist communication. We provide a detailed discussion of apps in chapter 11.

Reddit

Reddit is a social news aggregation, web content rating, and discussion website. The name Reddit is a play-on-words of the phrase "read it," and the website content is divided into many categories or "default SubReddits" of discussion visible on the front page to new users and site browsers without an account. Some examples include Fitness, Food, Science, Space, Art, PhotoShopBattles, DIY, GetMotivated. Users earn "Karma" on their profile. When posts and comments are up-voted, the upvotes translate into Karma, thereby boosting the user's standing within the Reddit community.

Yelp

Yelp publishes online crowd-sourced reviews about local businesses. Good reviews boost business while terrible ones can close them down. In an age when everyone is an online critic, ratings, and product/service reviews have become vital. For example, two economists at the University of California, Berkeley collected reviews and daily reservation availability for 328 restaurants in San Francisco during May 2012 using online Yelp online reviews. The results of the study found moving from 3 stars to 3.5 stars increased a restaurant's chance of selling out during prime dining times from 13% to 34%. Therefore, moving from 3.5 stars to 4 stars increased the likelihood of selling out during prime dining times by 19 percentage points. Specifically, a restaurant with a rating that improved by even a half a star, on a scale of 1 to 5, was much more likely to be full at peak dining times.

LinkedIn

LinkedIn is a business and employment-oriented social networking service. It is a handy social platform for job seekers. LinkedIn's main strength is with business-to-business marketers and job applicants. According to a study by eMarketers (2015), 87% of the US job recruiters used LinkedIn in the recruitment process followed by 55% who used Facebook, and 46% who used Twitter (see Figure 2.3).

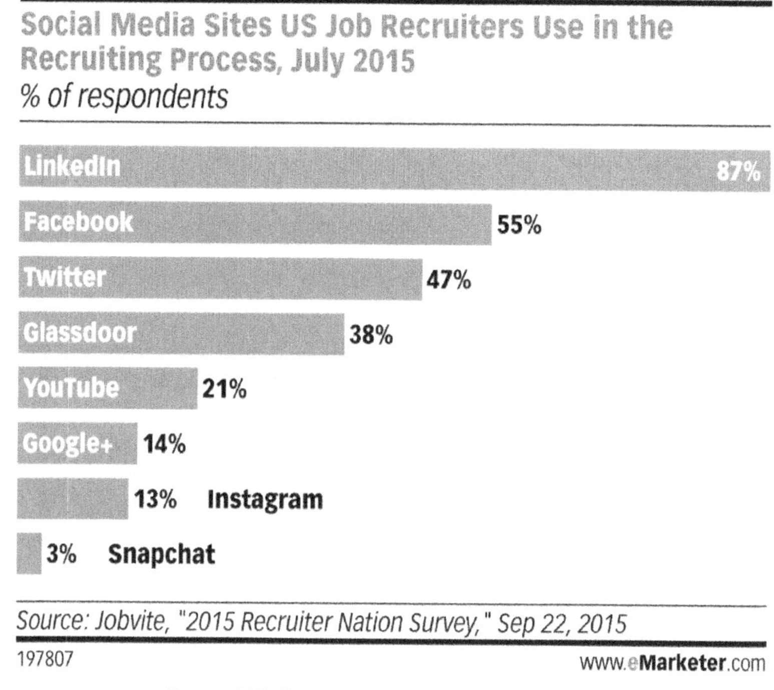

Figure 2.3. Social media sites for recruitment

LinkedIn has power network graphing capabilities and routinely shows a profile's closest connections in many of its reports. Usually, this is considered as degrees of separation. Often new opportunities are found via a friend of a friend or *weak ties* (2nd-degree connection) rather than your closest (1st-degree relationships) friends on the social graph. The idea of the value of the weak ties was first put forward by Mark Granovetter, an American sociologist, in his landmark theory on the spread of information through social networks known as "The Strength of Weak Ties" (Granovetter, 1973).

Special Purpose and Custom Built Platforms

Social media is not only limited to the types above, but it also includes an *online platform* (including purposely built in-house platforms) that enable us to participate, collaborate, create, and share content in a many-to-many context that can be called social media. Content can be anything, including information, audio/video, profiles, photographs, and text. Organizations are increasingly creating purpose-built social media platforms for inter-organizational collaboration activities.

An excellent example of such a platform is the Enterprise 2.0 (McAfee, 2006) which uses social media tools (such as blogs, wikis, and group messaging software) to allow employees, suppliers, and customers to network together and share information.

Free vs Paid Social Media

The majority of social media platforms have *free* and *paid* memberships. Creating a personal profile is usually free, and most searches and business networking can be done exclusively through a free account. However, a free account does not provide all of the privileges for searching and business networking that a paid account offers. Paid accounts (there are several tiers), offers additional search and networking capabilities to individuals and companies. For example, most LinkedIn members are using free accounts. It is estimated, based on LinkedIn Premium revenues, that only 2% to 3% of members have active Premium accounts.

REVIEW QUESTIONS

1. Why are there so many different analytics platforms for each social media channel?
2. On average how much time on a weekly basis does it take to leverage social media effectively?
3. Which social media platform is at the "center" of the Social Media Universe and why?
4. How is the exact formula for search engine ranking so hard to figure out? Be specific in your answer.
5. Which social media channel/platform best facilitates online collaboration?
6. Which platform helps members more easily find new professional opportunities? How effective is it? What other platforms that we discussed in this chapter allow us to do that?
7. What are the two most popular social media platforms discussed in this chapter?

EXERCISE 2.1: GETTING 7,000 SOCIAL MEDIA INTERACTIONS

A great way to familiarize with social media is to use it constructively. This exercise requires you to plan and execute something creative and appropriate* on social media (Facebook, Twitter, YouTube, Tumblr, Reddit, and Pinterest) and get 7,000 people to interact with you over the course of a week. The interactions can be seven thousand (7K) likes on Facebook, 7K retweets, mentions, or followers on Twitter, 7K shares/repins, and 7K views on YouTube. You may use multiple social media platform to count.

You must create something *novel.* In other words, it must be something "you" create. Note that you cannot post someone else's content and get credit for spreading that. Finally, write up a short report contain the following.

- Describe what you created and why you decided to do that. How did your choice of social media group/post/video relate to the goal of reaching 7,000 people?
- Explain your strategy for getting people to participate. How did you spread the word? Whom did you target and why?
- Analyze your success. What worked and what did not work? What could you have done differently? What were the best steps you took to get users?
- Include snapshots from your social media platform/campaign and statistics as proof.

*Appropriate means you should (1) not break the law, (2) not violate the social media's terms of service, (3) not do anything to get yourself in trouble, (4) do not harm anyone, (5) do not post pornography or seriously objectionable material (Nazis, racial threats, etc.), and (6) do not outright lie.

Track Your Results

This assignment will provide enough data and a good base for the social media analytics tools that we will learn throughout this book. Chapter 3 provides a list of the tools that you can use to track your interactions.

EXERCISE 2.2: BLOGGING

The purpose of the exercise is to introduce you to the world of *blogging*. Your task is to conceive and design a professional looking blog using https://wordpress.com/ blogging platform (or any blogging platforms of your choice). Your blog should be devoted to something of interest to you. One of the best ways to discover compelling design and rationales is to explore other blogs. The blogs hosted by the Huffington Post, Atlantic, the New Yorker, the Economist, and HBR are great places to start and look for inspirations.

Be thoughtful about how you will use color, font, images, video clips, links, etc. to convey your voice and purpose. As you plan, ask your peers for suggestions; and keep yourself open to revision.

Privacy

A blog is a genre that allows you to publicly voice your opinion, thus to engage in debate. On topics as contentious as war, this debate may get heated. While you may run the risk of offending some members of your audience, you also facilitate collaboration and discussion. Merely tread with care, considering possible counterarguments or objections to the claims you make. Here, as in all forms of writing, you are responsible for what you create. You will want to be especially careful about divulging others' private information, the opinions, for example, of friends and family members sharing their thoughts at the dinner table. To protect others' privacy, focus on the issues themselves.

The APA style blog offers general guidelines for its blogging participants that may be of use to you. Some important instructions are:

- Be critical and thought-provoking, but not malicious or degrading.
- No personal attacks, hate speech, or threats toward individuals, religious figures, or other comment posters.
- No flaming, trolling, or baiting.
- Do not post comments or images that defame or violate the copyright

or other intellectual property rights of any third party.

- To protect users' privacy, we discourage the inclusion of your or others' personal information, such as email addresses, in your comments.
- When quoting any other blog or publication, link to the original and use quotation marks or indents for longer text.

Intellectual Property

Many images, articles, and videos that you find on the web will undoubtedly inspire you. Please keep in mind that these are the work of another person and must be cited appropriately. The citation style used in blogs is a matter still up for debate. While you will find resources on how to cite a blog, you will not find definitive guidelines on how to cite all materials within a blog.

Evaluation Guidelines

Blog assignment can be graded based on the criteria provided in Table 2.3.

Table 2.3. Blog grading evaluation criteria

Evaluation Criteria	Excellent (100%~80%)	Good (79%~20%)	Poor/No Evidence (19~0%)
Look and Feel	Professionally designed with the significant use of use color, font, menus, and links.	Reasonably designed with the proper use of use color, font, images, menus, and links.	Poorly designed with bad use of color, font, menus, links.
Use of media in blog	Multimedia (video, graphic, chart, audio) use significantly improves blog presentation.	Multimedia use moderately improves blog presentation.	Multimedia use does not improve blog presentation.
Purpose	The rationale of the blog is clear and well presented.	The rationale of the blog is apparent but not well presented.	The rationale of the block is not clear.

EXERCISE 2.3: THE SOCIAL MEDIA MATURITY ASSESSMENT

When an organization or individual needs to understand whether their organization is prepared to take on a social media initiative, they run the *Social Media Maturity Assessment*. Use the provided *Microsoft Excel* sheet to measure an organization or individual's social media capabilities. This prescriptive self-assessment tool allows readers to rate their compliance with best practices across the following dimensions (see Figure 2.4):

- Senior Management Commitment
- Social Media Knowledge
- Customer Engagement
- Competitive Insight
- Staff & Resources
- Plan & Channel Selection
- Process Documentation, and
- Governance & Measurement.

This assessment also has a weighting tab that allows organizations to decide which dimensions are more critical and require a higher weighting; note that the sum of all weightings must add up to 100%. Once the assessment is completed, the reader will be provided with results and recommendations. There is a notes tab where specific information can be added.

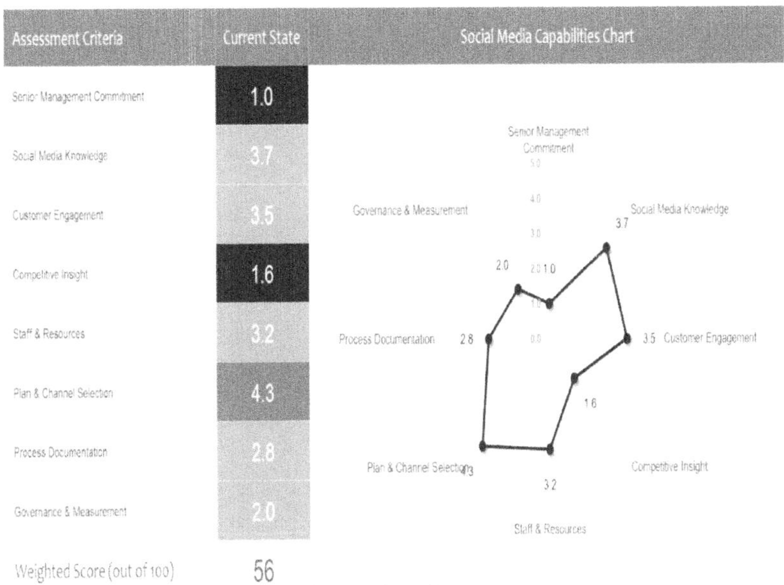

Figure 2.4. Example social media maturity assessment

The authors filled out the survey with *Social Listening Limited* (https://www.sociallistening.co.nz/) in mind and came up with a score of 56 out of 100 possible points. From the score, it is clear that there is much room for improvement on how social media is handled and tracked at Social Listening. We also changed the weightings to match better what we thought would be more relevant to the organizations we belong to (Figure 2.5).

Customize this tool by changing the weighting scale for each assessment category.

Weighting Scale								
Senior Management Commitment	Social Media Knowledge	Customer Engagement	Competitive Insight	Staff & Resources	Plan & Channel Selection	Process Documentation	Governance & Measurement	Total
5%	25%	10%	15%	5%	5%	10%	25%	100%

Figure 2.5. Example social media maturity assessment weightings

CHAPTER 2 REFERENCES

Boyd, D. m., & Ellison, N. B. (2007). Social Network Sites: Definition, History, and Scholarship. *Journal of Computer-Mediated Communication, 13*(1), 210-230. doi:10.1111/j.1083-6101.2007.00393.x

Granovetter, M. S. (1973). The Strength of Weak Ties. *American Journal of Sociology, 78*(6), 1360-1380. doi:10.1086/225469

Kaplan, A. M., & Haenlein, M. (2010). Users of the world, unite! The challenges and opportunities of Social Media. *Business Horizons, 53*(1), 59-68. doi:http://dx.doi.org/10.1016/j.bushor.2009.09.003

Kietzmann, J. H., Hermkens, K., McCarthy, I. P., & Silvestre, B. S. (2011). Social media? Get serious! Understanding the functional building blocks of social media. *Business Horizons, 54*(3), 241-251. doi:https://doi.org/10.1016/j.bushor.2011.01.005

McAfee, A. P. (2006). Enterprise 2.0: the dawn of emergent collaboration. *MIT Sloan Management Review, 47*(3), 21-28.

Oreilly, T. (2007). What is Web 2.0: Design Patterns and Business Models for the Next Generation of Software. *Communications & Strategies, 1*(17).

W3. (2015). What is Linked Data? available at: http://www.w3.org/standards/semanticweb/data.

Chapter 3

Understanding Social Media Analytics

"Analyzing is believing."—**Gohar F. Khan**

Learning Outcomes

After completing this chapter, the reader should be able to:

- Comprehend social media analytics concepts, tools, history, and industry.
- Be familiar with the eight layers of social media analytics framework.
- Understand uses of social media analytics for business intelligence purposes and distinguish between social media analytics and business analytics.
- Comprehend descriptive analytics, diagnostic analytics, predictive analytics, and prescriptive analytics.
- Understand common social media analytics limitations and issues.

INTRODUCTION

Social media analytics is the *art* and *science* of extracting valuable hidden insights from vast amounts of semi-structured and unstructured social media data to enable informed and insightful decision-making. It is a science, as it involves systematically identifying, extracting, and analyzing social media data (such as tweets, shares, likes, and hyperlinks) using sophisticated tools and techniques. It is also an art of interpreting and aligning the insights gained with business goals and objectives. To get value from analytics, one should master both its art and science.

The science part of social media analytics requires skilled data analysts, sophisticated tools and technologies, and reliable data. Getting the science right, however, is not enough. To efficiently consume the results and put them into the action, the business must master the other half of analytics, that is, the art of interpreting and aligning analytics with business objectives and goals.

Interpreting analytics results, for example, requires representing the data in meaningful ways, having the domain-specific knowledge, and training. Analytics should be strategically aligned to support existing business goals. Without a well-crafted and aligned social media strategygy, the business will struggle to get the desired outcomes from analytics. We discuss aligning analytics with business goals in a later chapter.

EMERGENCE OF SOCIAL MEDIA ANALYTICS

Social media analytics is a relatively new and emerging field. Based on Google's trends data (see Figure 3.1), the term '*social media analytics*' seems to have appeared over the Internet horizon in July 2006, and interest in it (regarding people searching for it) has steadily increased since then.

Figure 3.1. Interest in social media analytics over time

Google Trends also shows that majority of the interest in social media analytics is coming from India, Canada, United States and the United Kingdom. Moreover, the users interested in social media analytics also searched for a variety of topics including Google analytics, social media marketing, social media tools, marketing analytics, Facebook analytics, Twitter analytics, and social media management. Table 3.1 shows a full list of social media related terms. The scoring shown in Table 3.1 is on a relative scale where a value of 100 is the most commonly searched query, 50 is a query searched half as often, and a value of 0 is a query searched for less than 1% as often as the most popular query.

As social media is becoming mainstream, and people are using it to express feelings, and interests, share content, and collaborate, the social media analytics field is also gaining prominence between both the research and business communities. Businesses need to tap into the vast amounts of data produced by social media users to increase brand loyalty, generate leads, drive traffic, make forecasts, and ultimately make the right decisions. Social media data and users are of significant value to businesses. A study, for example, found that the average value of a Facebook fan was $174.17 in the considerable consumer areas (Syncapse, 2013). KINAXIS, a supply chain management company, for example, used eighteen employee bloggers and generated over forty-two million leads (Petersen, 2012). The case study included at the end of the chapter demonstrates this point; it shows how ESPN FC used social media during the World Cup. ESPN FC increased brand awareness and drove football fans to their website for the latest news, scores, and team information, all to help build the profile of the brand across the globe.

Table 3.1. Social media analytics related terms

Terms Searched	Score	Terms Searched	Score
Google analytics	100	Social media management	10
Social media marketing	40	Hootsuite analytics	10
Social media tools	40	SEO	10
Social analytics tools	35	Hootsuite	10
Marketing analytics	35	Instagram analytics	10
Facebook analytics	30	Big data analytics	10
Twitter analytics	30	Social media metrics	10
Data analytics	25	LinkedIn	5
Web analytics	20	Big data	5
Social media analysis	15	LinkedIn analytics	5
Social media tracking	10	WordPress analytics	5
Social media monitoring	10	Social media strategy	5
Social media management	10	Social media dashboard	5

PURPOSE OF SOCIAL MEDIA ANALYTICS

The central premise of social media analytics is to enable informed and insightful decision making by leveraging *social media data* (Chen, Chiang, & Storey, 2012); (Bekmamedova & Shanks, 2014). Businesses use social media for a variety of reasons including the following.

- Connecting and engaging with current customers.
- Finding and engaging with new customers.
- Getting feedback on products/services.
- Generating business leads.

- Driving traffic to business channels (Facebook pages, corporate blogs, and company website).
- Measure brand loyalty.
- Tracking products/services/campaign impact.
- Predictive business forecasting, and
- Business intelligence and market research.

The following are some sample questions that can be answered with social media analytics.

- What are customers using social media saying about our brand or a new product launch?
- Which content posted on social media is resonating more with clients or customers?
- How can we harness social media data (e.g., tweets and Facebook comments) to improve our products/services?
- Is the social media conversation about our company, product, or service positive, negative, or neutral?
- How can we leverage social media to promote brand awareness?
- Who are our influential social media followers, fans, and friends?
- Who are our prominent social media nodes (e.g., people and organizations) and their position in the network?
- Which social media platforms are driving the most traffic to our corporate website?
- Where is the geographical location of our social media customers?
- Which keywords and terms are trending over social media?
- How active is social media in our business and how many people are connected with us?
- Which websites are linked to our corporate site?
- How are our competitors doing on social media?

When it comes to social media data and using it to generate business value, the statement at the beginning of the chapter can be no more than correct. In the context of social media, seeing is no longer believing instead analyzing is. In other words, business (and social and political) decisions should be based on digging deep into the social media data rather than just by believing what we see over social media. Over the social web, each second, tons of data are generated, which may carry potential business insights; however, not all the social data is gold. A vast amount of social information is either fake or useless. To separate useful data from useless, social media analytics coupled with human judgment is the answer.

SOCIAL MEDIA VS. CONVENTIONAL BUSINESS ANALYTICS

While the premise of both social media and *traditional business analytics* is to produce actionable business insights, they do however differ slightly in *scope* and *nature*. Table 3.2 provides a comparison of social media analytics with traditional business analytics. As an emerging field, it may not be appropriate to use the term *conventional* for business analytics; we do so here for comparison purposes only.

Table 3.2. Social media analytics vs, business analytics

Social Media Analytics	Business Analytics
Semi-structured and unstructured data	Structured data
Data is not analytical friendly	Data is analytical friendly
Real-time data	Mostly historical data
Public data	Private data
Stored in third-party databases	Stored in business-owned databases
Boundary-less data	Bound within the business intranet
Data is high volume	Data is medium to high volume
Highly diverse data	Uniform data
Data is widely shared over the Internet	Data is only shared within organizations
More sharing creates greater value	Less sharing creates more value
No business control over data	Data tightly controlled by business
Socialized data	Bureaucratic data
Data is informal in nature	Data is formal in nature

Nature and Source of Data

The most visible difference between the two comes from the source, type, and kind of data mined. Unlike the traditional business analytics of structured and historical information, social media analytics involves the collection, analysis, and interpretation of semi-structured and unstructured social media data to gain an insight into the contemporary issues while supporting effective decision making (Bekmamedova & Shanks, 2014). Social media data is highly diverse, high volume, real-time, and stored in third-party databases in a semi-structured and unstructured format. Structured business data, on the other hand, is mostly stored in databases and spreadsheets in machine-readable form (e.g., rows and columns). Thus, it can be easily searched, computed, and mined. Unstructured and semi-structured social media data is not machine readable and can take a variety of forms, such as the contents of this book, Facebook comments, emails, tweets, hyperlinks, PowerPoint presentations, images, emoticons, and videos. Thus, it is not analytics-friendly and needs a lot of cleaning and transformation.

Consumption and Use

Another visible difference comes from the way the information (i.e., text, photographs, videos, and audio) is created and consumed. Social media data originates from the public Internet and is socialized in nature. Socialized data is provided for the collective good. It is produced and consumed using various social media platforms and social technologies to maintain social and professional ties (e.g., Facebook, LinkedIn), to facilitate knowledge sharing and management (Wikipedia and blogs), Socialized data creates awareness (i.e., Twitter), or to exchange information in the form of text, audio, video, documents, and graphics, to name a few (Khan, 2013). Social media data is social, informal, and not bound (i.e., the Internet is a boundary), unlike the conventional analytics data, which is bureaucratic, formal in nature, controlled by organizations, and bound or trapped within the organizational network or intranet. More importantly, the value or impact of socialized data is determined by the extent to which it is shared with other social entities (e.g., people or organizations): the more it is shared (i.e., socialized) the higher it's value.

For example, the value/effect of information can be measured regarding attracting more followers (e.g., on Twitter or Facebook). Another measure is the page views or clicks, or regarding socio-political impact (e.g., information disseminated using social media to organize political or social movements may have more effect regarding organizing the events). However, the majority of the conventional business data is confined to the organizational databases, limitedly shared, and can serve as a source of competitive advantage.

EIGHT LAYERS OF SOCIAL MEDIA ANALYTICS

Social media at a minimum has *eight layers of data* (Figure 3.2). Each layer carries potentially valuable information and insights that can be harvested for business intelligence purposes. Out of the eight segments, some are visible or readily identifiable (e.g., text and actions), and others are invisible (e.g., social media and hyperlink networks). Most of these layers can be used to develop measurable key performance indicators (KPIs). The following are eight social media data layers that will be discussed in detail in the subsequent chapters.

1. Networks
2. Text
3. Actions
4. Hyperlinks
5. Mobile
6. Location
7. Multimedia
8. Search Engines

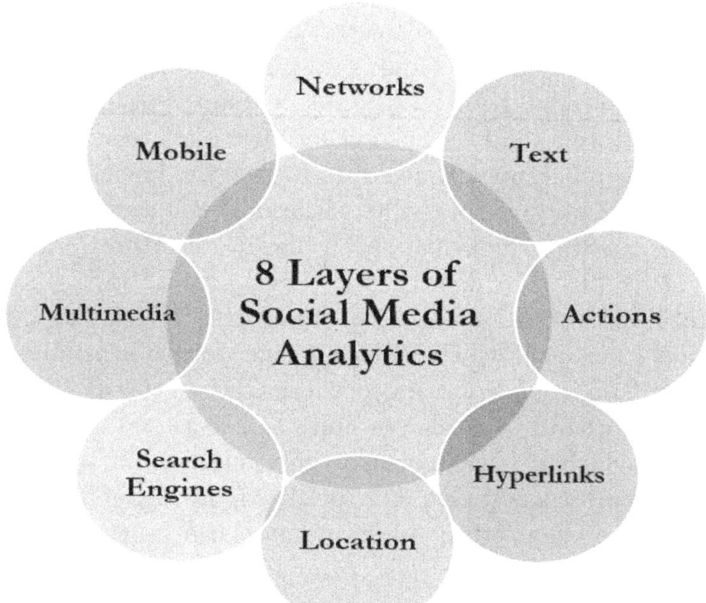

Figure 3.2. Eight layers of social media analytics

Layer One: Networks

Social media network analytics extract, analyze, and interpret personal and professional social networks, for example, Facebook, Friendship Network, and Twitter. Network analytics seeks to identify influential nodes (e.g., people and organizations) and their position in the network. Network analytics is discussed in chapter 5.

Layer Two: Text

Social media text analytics deals with the extraction and analysis of business insights from textual elements of social media content, such as comments, tweets, blog posts, and Facebook status updates. Text analytics (discussed in chapter 6) is mostly used to understand social media users' sentiments or identify emerging themes and topics.

Layer Three: Actions

Social media actions analytics deals with extracting, analyzing, and interpreting the actions performed by social media users, including likes, dislikes, shares, mentions, and endorsement. Actions analytics (discussed in chapter 7) are mostly used to measure popularity, influence, and prediction in social media. The case study included at the end of the chapter demonstrates how social media actions (e.g., Twitter mentions) can be used for business intelligence purposes.

Layer Four: Search Engines

Search engines analytics focuses on analyzing historical search data for gaining valuable insight into a range of areas, including trends analysis, keyword monitoring, search results and advertisement history, and advertisement spending statistics. Chapter 8 is dedicated to search engines analytics.

Layer Five: Location

Location analytics, also known as spatial analysis or geospatial analytics is concerned with mining and mapping the locations of social media users, contents, and data. Chapter 9 is dedicated to location analytics.

Layer Six: Hyperlinks

Hyperlink analytics is about extracting, analyzing, and interpreting social media hyperlinks (e.g., in-links and out-links). Hyperlink analysis (discussed in chapter 10) can reveal sources of incoming or outgoing web traffic to and from a web page or website.

Layer Six: Mobile

Mobile analytics is the next frontier in the social business landscape. Mobile analytics deals with measuring and optimizing user engagement with mobile applications (or apps for short). Chapter 11 discusses mobile analytics and provides a practical tutorial on analyzing and understanding in-app purchases, customer engagement, and mobile user demographics.

Layer Eight: Multimedia

Social media *multimedia analytics* is the art and science of harnessing business value from video, images, audio, and animations, and interactive contents posted over social media outlets. Chapter 12 is dedicated to multimedia analytics.

TYPES OF SOCIAL MEDIA ANALYTICS

Social media analytics help achieve business objectives through describing data to analyzing trends, predicting future problems and opportunities, and optimizing business processes to enhance organizational decision-making. Like any business analytics (Delen & Demirkan, 2013), social media analytics can take four forms (Figure 3.3 & Table 3.3):

- Descriptive Analytics
- Diagnostic Analytics
- Predictive Analytics
- Prescriptive Analytics

Descriptive Analytics (Reactive)

Descriptive analytics deals with the questions of "*what happened and what is happening?*" It is mostly focused on gathering and describing social media data in the form of reports, visualizations, and clustering to understand a well-defined business problem or opportunity. Purpose built or social media embedded platforms (such as Facebook Insights and Twitter Analytics) dashboards are used to collect and display social media metrics, such as likes, comments, tweets, and posts. Actions analytics (e.g., no. of likes, tweets, and views) and text analytics are examples of descriptive analytics. Social media text (e.g., user comments), for instance, can be used to understand users' sentiments or identify emerging trends by clustering themes and topics. Currently, descriptive analytics accounts for the majority of social media analytics.

Diagnostic Analytics (Reactive)

Also reactive in nature, *diagnostic analytics* deals with the questions of "*why something happened?*" Enablers of diagnostics analytics include inferential statistics, behavioral analytics, correlations & retrospective analysis and the outcome being a cause and effect analysis of a business issue. For example, while descriptive analytics can provide an overview of your social media marketing campaign's performances (posts, mentions, followers, fans, page views, reviews, pins); diagnostic analytics can distill this data into a single view to see what worked in your past campaigns and what didn't.

Consumers often use social media to vent frustration over various products and services. For example, by mining and analyzing social media posts by the owners of famous automobile brands, such as Honda, Toyota, and Chevrolet, researchers at Virginia Tech Pamplin College of Business were able to discover vehicle defects across the brands. The data collected could be analyzed to identify issues relating to safety and performance of their vehicles and to understand the reasons for customer dissatisfaction better.

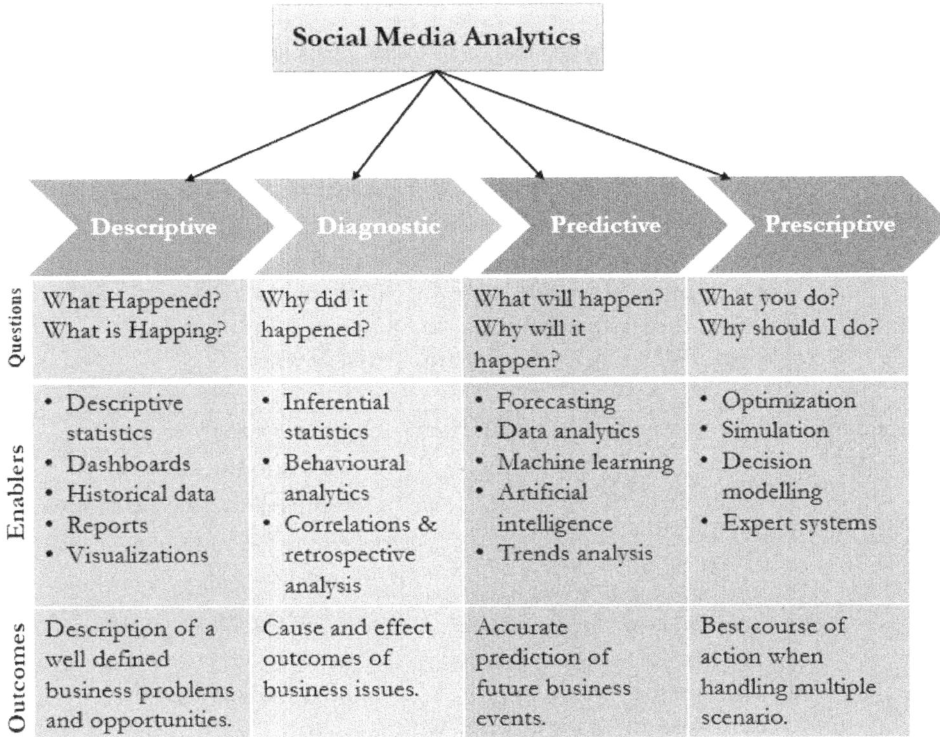

Social Media Analytics
Descriptive
Diagnostic
Predictive
Prescriptive
Questions
Enablers
Outcomes
What Happened? What is Happing?
Why did it happened?
What will happen? Why will it happen?
What you do? Why should I do?
• Descriptive statistics
• Dashboards
• Historical data
• Reports
• Visualizations
• Inferential statistics
• Behavioural analytics
• Correlations & retrospective analysis
• Forecasting
• Data analytics
• Machine learning
• Artificial intelligence
• Trends analysis
• Optimization
• Simulation
• Decision modelling
• Expert systems
Description of a well defined business problems and opportunities.
Cause and effect outcomes of business issues.
Accurate prediction of future business events.
Best course of action when handling multiple scenario.

Figure 3.3. Types of social media analytics

Predictive Analytics (Proactive)

Predictive analytics involves analyzing massive amounts of accumulated social media data to predict a *future event.* It is also a reactive type, and in essence deals with the question of "what will happen and why will it happen?" Enablers of predictive analytics include data mining, text mining, Web/media mining and statistical time-series forecasting. The primary outcome of predictive modeling is an accurate projection of future happenings and the reasoning underlying such events. For example, an intention expressed over social media (such as buy, sell, recommend, quit, desire, or wish) can be mined to predict a future event (such as a purchase).

A well-known example is the prediction of outbreaks of flu. Google used predictive analytics to collect data regarding the epidemics of influenza. By matching key search terms associated with people in different regions of the world, Google could track flu outbreaks in near real time. This data was compared with traditional flu surveillance systems and through the predictive analytics of the flu season; Google discovered a correlation with higher search engine traffic for related phrases.

Table 3.3. Business application of social media analytics

Types	Example 1	Example 2
Descriptive Analytics	Twitter Analytics, for example, provides statistics on tweet impressions, profile visits, and audience demographics. It also provides insights into content that resonate more with your audience, measure impressions, engagements, and reach (Figure 3.4).	Facebook Insights allows users to track user interaction on their Facebook pages. This descriptive analytics tool shows statistics, such as a number of likes, shares, comments, and reports on your site and your weekly reach.
Diagnostic Analytics	It can be used to determine the success of social media marketing campaigns, for example, to investigate the association between a specific event and reactions to that event on social media to tell you exactly where you went wrong. Users are then able to utilize this data to make improvements to future campaigns.	Diagnostics analytics offers insights into the behavior of consumers, such as, a customer searching for specific vehicles through Google, then clicking on a landing page of a car dealer website, but exiting without finding what they needed.
Predictive Analytics	Social media data can be used to predict future events. A study by Asur & Huberman (2010) used Tweets to forecast box-office revenues for selected movies. By tracking 24 movies, 2.89 million tweets from 1.2 million users, they predicted box-office revenues of movies before they were released.	Google used predictive analytics to collect data regarding the outbreaks of flu. By matching key search terms associated with people in different regions of the world, Google could track flu outbreaks in near real time.
Prescriptive Analytics	Netflix uses large quantities of data regarding consumer-viewing habits to optimize their processes and create recommender systems that provide users with suggestions of content they may enjoy based on their previous viewing habits.	Facebook tracks and analyzes users browsing and behavior data to recommends pages, friends, groups, games that interest them. Similarly, by using review ratings from like-minded people, it predicts your likes, interests, and prescribes items it thinks you will enjoy.

Alternatively, a business manager can predict sales figures based on historical visits (or in-links) to a corporate website. The TweepsMap tool, for example, can help us determine the right time to tweet for maximum alignment with our audience time zone. On the other hand, based on analyzing our social media users' languages, it can suggest whether it is time to create a new Twitter account for another language.

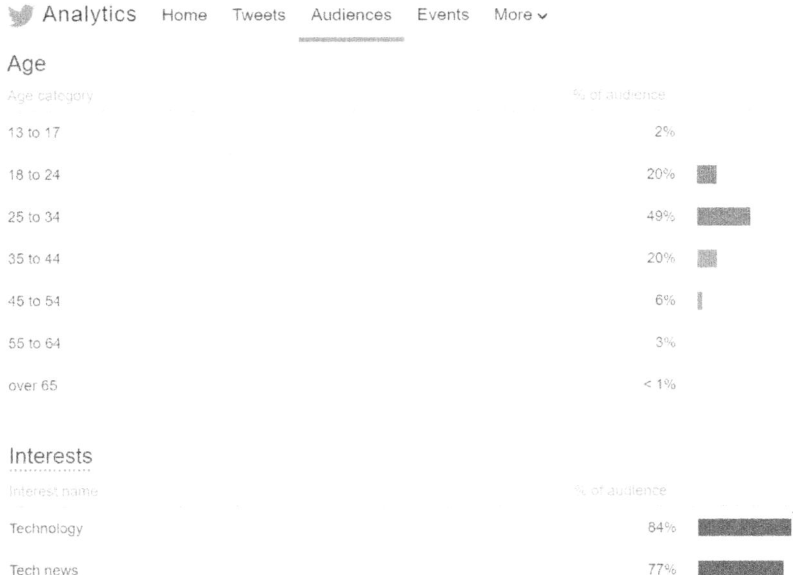

Figure 3.4. Twitter analytics audience analysis

A study conducted by Dublin University in 2011 found that social media data could be used to predict the outcome of presidential elections. They found that the number of Tweets associated with election results was the single most significant variable in predicting the presidential winner. Before the 2016 presidential election, Twitter released an "Election 2016 Candidate Buzz" tracker, which, in fact, did indicate that President Trump would likely win the election.

Elsewhere, researchers have shown that social media chatter can be used to forecast box-office revenues for movies, more accurately than those of the Hollywood Stock Exchange (Asur & Huberman, 2010).

Prescriptive Analytics (Proactive)

While predictive analytics help to predict the future, *prescriptive analytics* suggest the best action to take when *handling a scenario* (Lustig, Dietrich, Johnson, & Dziekan, 2010). For example, if you have groups of social media users that display particular patterns of buying behavior, how can you optimize your offering to each group? Like predictive analytics, prescriptive analytics has not yet found its way into social media data. The primary enablers of prescriptive analytics include optimization and simulation modeling, multi-criteria decision modeling, expert systems, and group support systems. Whereas, the primary outcome of prescriptive modeling is either the best course of action when handling multiple scenarios, or expert opinions provided to a decision maker that could lead to the best possible course of action.

Netflix collects large quantities of data regarding consumer-viewing habits including how long viewers watch, the devices they are using, what time of day they view as well as when they paused, rewound or stopped a show. This data allows Netflix to optimize their processes and create recommender systems that provide users with suggestions of content they may enjoy based on their previous viewing habits.

Collaborative filtering is a recommender system technique that assists consumers in discovering what items are most relevant to them. Within Facebook, this includes the recommendation of pages, groups, games, and pages. Facebook collaborative filters bases their recommender system on other people that have the same interests as you. By using review ratings from like-minded people, it predicts your likes and interests and prescribes items it thinks you will enjoy (Code, 2015).

Finally, predictive/prescriptive analytics models are complicated to execute and require hefty resources. However, it has the highest potential regarding business value, (Figure 3.5).

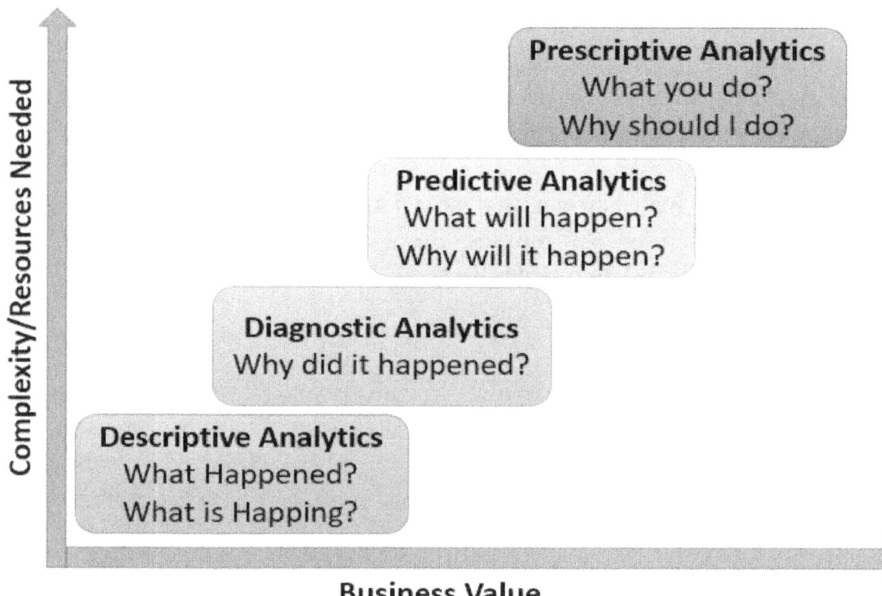

Figure 3.5. Analytics types and business value

SOCIAL MEDIA ANALYTICS VALUE CREATION CYCLE

Business *value creation* with social media analytics is a six-step iterative process (involving both science and art) of harnessing the desired business value from social media data (Figure 3.6). The value creation journey starts with the organizational *goals* and *objectives* that we want to achieve with social media analytics. The business objectives will inform each step of the social media analytics value creation cycle. Business goals are defined at the initial stage, and the analytics process will continue until the stated business objectives are fully satisfied. Note that the steps may vary considerably based on the layers of social media data mined (and the type of the tool employed).

The following are the six general steps, at the highest level of abstraction, that involve both the science and art of achieving business value from social media data.

Step 1: Identification

The *identification stage* is the art part of the social media analytics value creation process and is concerned with searching and identifying the right source of information for analytical purposes. The numbers and types of users and information (such as text, conversation, and networks) available over social media are vast, diverse, multilingual, and noisy. Thus, framing the right questions and knowing what data to analyze is crucial for gaining useful business insights. More importantly, the source and type of data to be analyzed should be aligned with business objectives.

Most of the data for analytics will come from business-owned social media profiles, such as an official Twitter account, Facebook fan pages, blogs, and YouTube channels. Some data for analytics, however, will also be harvested from other social media sources, such as Google search engine trends data or Twitter's publically available search stream data. The business objectives that need to be achieved will play a significant role in identifying the sources and type of data to be mined. We explore aligning social media analytics with business objectives in chapter 4.

Step 2: Extraction

Once a reliable and mineable source of data is identified, next comes *extraction* of the data. The type (e.g., text, numerical, or network) and size of data will determine the method and tools suitable for extraction. Small-size statistical information, for example, can be extracted manually (e.g., going to your

Facebook fan page and counting likes and copying comments), and large-scale automated extraction is done through an API (application programming interface). Manual data extraction may be practical for small-scale data, but it is the API-based extraction tools that will help businesses get the most out of various social media platforms. Social media analytics tools use API-based data mining.

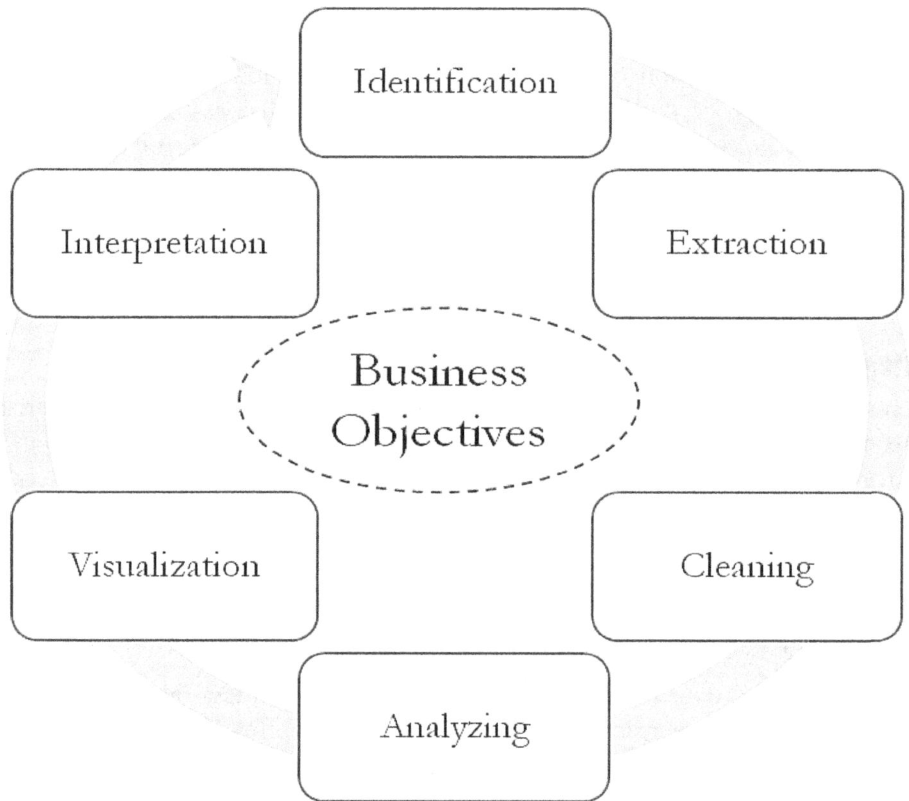

Figure 3.6. Social media analytics value creation cycle

.In simple terms, APIs are sets of routines/protocols that social media service companies (e.g., Twitter and Facebook) have developed that allow users to access small portions of data hosted in their databases. The most significant benefit of using APIs is that it enables other entities (e.g., customers, programmers, and other organizations) to build apps, widgets, websites, and other tools based on open social media data. Some data, such as social networks and hyperlink networks, can only be extracted through specialized tools.

Two important issues to bear in mind here are the privacy and ethical issues related to mining data from social media platforms. Privacy advocacy groups have long raised severe concerns regarding large-scale mining of social media data and warned against transforming social spaces into behavioral laboratories.

The social media privacy issue first came into the spotlight mainly due to the large-scale "*Facebook Experiment*" carried out in 2012. In this experiment, Facebook manipulated the news feeds feature of thousands of people to see if emotion contagion occurs without face-to-face interaction (and in the absence of nonverbal cues) between people in social networks (Kramer, Guillory, & Hancock, 2014). Though the experiment was consistent with Facebook's Data Use Policy (Verma, 2014) and helped promote our understanding of online social behavior, it does, however, raise serious concerns regarding obtaining informed consent from participants and allowing them to opt out. The social media privacy issue was further fueled by the recent *Cambridge Analytica* data scandal. Researchers at Cambridge Analytica allegedly accessed 50 million Facebook users information to build software that could target potential swing voters for President Trump 2016's election campaign.

The bottom line here is that data extraction practices should not violate a user's privacy and the data extracted should be handled carefully. The policies should explicitly detail social media ownership regarding both accounts and activities such as individual and page profiles, platform content, posting activity, data handling, and extraction. Social media privacy issues are discussed in detail in chapter 14.

Step 3: Cleaning

This step involves removing the *unwanted data* from the automatically extracted data. Some data may need cleaning, while other data can go into analysis directly. In the case of text analytics cleaning, coding, clustering, and filtering may be necessary to get rid of unrelated textual data using natural language processing (NPL). Coding and filtering can be performed by machines (i.e., automated) or can be carried out manually by humans. For example, Discovertext combines both machine learning and human coding techniques to code, cluster, and classify social media data (Shulman 2014).

Step 4: Analyzing

At this stage, the clean data is analyzed for business insights. Depending on the layer of social media analytics under consideration and the tools and algorithm employed, the steps and approach to take will vary significantly. For example, nodes in a social media network can be clustered and visualized in a variety of ways depending on the algorithm employed. The overall objective at this stage is to extract meaningful insights without the data losing its integrity.

While most of the analytics tools provide a systematic procedure to analyze social data, having background knowledge and an understanding of the tools and its capabilities are crucial in arriving at the right answers.

Step 5: Visualization

Data or information *visualization* is the process of converting numerical data into a graphical (or visual) format to reveal hidden patterns and casual relationships in the data to help facilitate business decision making. Data visualization is the use of computer-supported, interactive, visual representations of abstract data to amplify human understanding (Card, Mackinlay, & Shneiderman, 1999), thus enabling us to gain knowledge about the hidden internal structure and causal relationships in data.

The notion of using visuals to understand data and information is not new. The use of maps and graphs has been around since the 17th century. However, with the advent of computers programs and affordable tools data visualization is easy to accomplish with minimum efforts and skills. Thanks to power data visualization tools (such as Tableau, SAS Visual Analytics, Data Studio, and Power Bi) anyone can process and visualize a significant amount of data with a click of a button in no time.

When it comes to data visualization, a related concept to become familiar with is visual analytics.

Visual Analytics

Visual analytics is the science of analytical reasoning facilitated by interactive visual interfaces (Thomas & Cook, 2005).Visual analytics is becoming an essential part of interactive decision making aided by robust visualization (Wong & Thomas, 2004). The useful display is particularly helpful with complex and large datasets because it can reveal hidden patterns, relationships, and trends. Keep in mind that it is the adequate visualization of the results that will demonstrate the value of social media data to top management.

In other words, it is the science and art of employing visualization to analyze data to facilitate business decision making. According to Keim et al., (2006):

> *"Visual analytics is more than just visualization and can rather be seen as an integrated approach combining visualization, human factors, and data analysis. ... With respect to the field of visualization, visual analytics integrates methodology from information analytics, geospatial analytics, and scientific analytics. Especially human factors (e.g., interaction, cognition, perception, collaboration, presentation, and dissemination) play a key role in the communication between human and computer, as well as in the decision-making process."(Keim et al., 2008).*

Importance of Data Visualization

By nature, the human brain processes visual information more easily than numbers and spreadsheets. Thus, complex ideas and concepts can easily be conveyed using effective visuals and graphs. Useful visualization plays a vital role in decision-making; mainly it is helpful with complex and large datasets because it can reveal hidden patterns, relationships, and trends. These days visual communication is a must-have skill for managers (Berinato, 2016) because it is the effective visualization of the results that will demonstrate the value of social media data to top management.

Social Media Data Visualization

In addition to numerical results, most of the eight layers of social media analytics will also result in *visual outcomes*. Depending on the type of data, the analysis part will lead to relevant visualizations for effective communication of results. Text analytics, for instance, can result in a word co-occurrence cloud; hyperlink analytics will provide visual hyperlink networks, and location analytics can produce interactive maps. Depending on the type of data, different types of visualization are possible, including the following.

Network data (with whom)—network data visualizations can show *who is connected to whom*. For example, a Twitter following-following network chart can show who is following whom. We discuss different types of networks in chapter 5.

Topical data (what)—topical data visualization is mostly focused on what aspect of a phenomenon is under investigation. A text cloud generated from social media comments can show *what* topics/themes are occurring more frequently in the discussion.

Temporal data (when)—temporal data visualization technique slice and dice data on a *time horizon*, and can reveal longitudinal trends, patterns, and relationships hidden in the data. Google Trends data, for example, can visually investigate longitudinal search engine trends.

Geospatial data (where)—geospatial data visualization is used to map and locate data, people, and resources. Chapter 5 provides more details on location mapping.

One of the exciting data visualization techniques is *word cloud*. Word clouds are images composed of words, used in a particular text or subject, where the size of each word indicates its frequency or importance. Many text analytics platforms produce word clouds based on an analysis of the text examined. Wordle is the most well-known word cloud software and is free to use at Wordle.net. Words are stacked into a box or some other shape with the most significant words being the most prevalent though the information is mostly descriptive.

Other forms of visualizations include trees, hierarchical, multidimensional (chart, graphs, tag clouds), 3-D (dimension), computer simulation, infographics, flow, tables, heat maps, and plots.

Step 6: Interpretation or Consumption

This step relies on human judgments to interpret valuable knowledge from the visual data. *Meaningful interpretation* is of particular importance when we are dealing with descriptive analytics that leaves room for different interpretations. While companies are quickly mastering sophisticated analytical methods, skills, and techniques needed to convert big data into information, there seems to a gap between an organization's capacity to produce analytical results and its ability to efficiently consume it. For example, a study of 2,719 business executives, managers, and analytics professionals from around the world found that the most significant problem to creating business value from analytics is not data management issues or complex data modeling skills. It was translating analytics into business actions and making business decisions based on the results (Kiron, Prentice, & Ferguson, 2014).

The study also reported that there are three levels of analytical maturity in organizations:

Analytically Challenged—these organizations lack sophisticated data management and analytical skills and rely more on management experience in decision-making.

Analytical Practitioners—analytic practitioner organizations tend to use analytics for operational purposes; they have "just good enough data" and are working to become more data-driven.

Analytical Innovators—Analytical innovators organizations are strategic in their use and application of analytics, place higher value on data, and have higher levels of data management and analytical skills. These organizations are most successful in translating analytics results into business actions and decision making.

Improving Analytics Consumption Abilities

Having domain knowledge and expertise are crucial in consuming the analytics results. To enhance such abilities organizations can employ the following strategies or approaches.

Building an analytics vocabulary –while for most managers it is not necessary to understand advanced analytics topics and techniques, it is crucial to develop an analytics vocabulary and get familiar with the basics concepts such as statistics, machine learning, data management and big data, descriptive, predictive, and prescriptive analytics.

Producing easily consumable results—this approach requires training data scientists and analysts to deliver interactive and easy-to-use visual results. Managers need to talk to their data scientists to create results that they are comfortable consuming.

Improving consumption capabilities—this strategy focuses on improving management analytics consumption capabilities.

Recognizing the limitations of an analytical model—analytical models and algorithms are not perfect and are very sensitive to variation in data inputs. For effective decision-making, analytical models should be complemented with management's knowledge of changing business context. Doing so will help identify limitation in analytical models and commission additional analysis to understand the potential effects of variables not covered by analytical models.

CURRENT vs, POTENTIAL USE OF SOCIAL MEDIA ANALYTICS

As mentioned earlier, at present, the majority of the analytics industry and practice revolves around *descriptive analytics*. Moreover, if there is any use of predictive and prescriptive analytics, it is limited to structured data only. According to Garner (2013), only 3 percent of companies used prescriptive analytics, but with structured data only. However, the use of social media data for descriptive analytics is just the tip of an iceberg (see Figure 3.7). The true business potential lies in *predictive* and *prescriptive analytics*. The future of the analytics industry is in the use of predictive/prescriptive analytics, which will unleash the true potential of social media analytics.

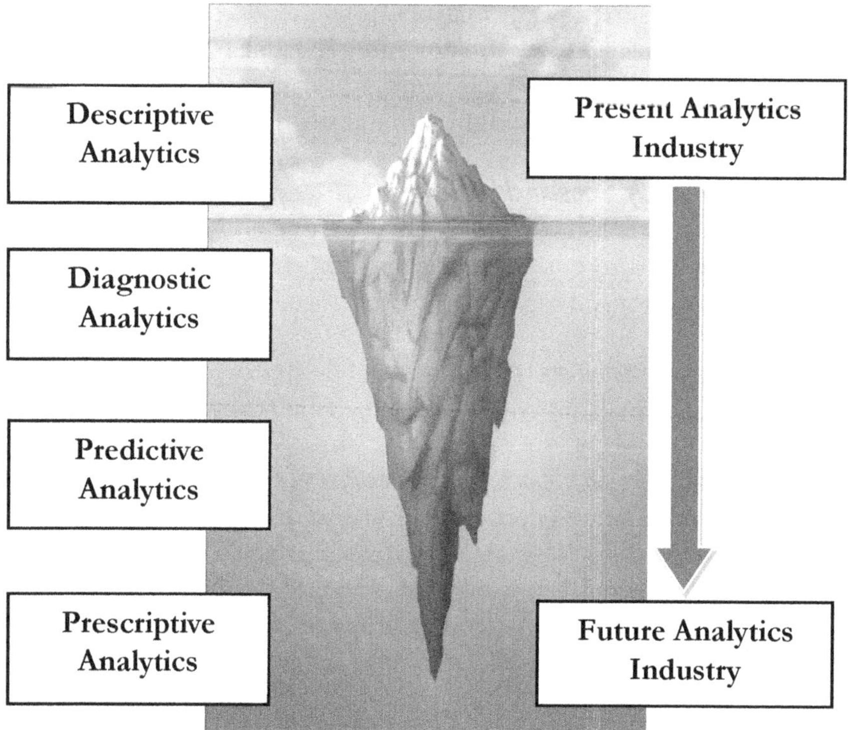

Figure 3.7. Current VS., potential use of social media analytics

CHALLENGES TO SOCIAL MEDIA ANALYTICS

Social media data is *high volume*, *high velocity*, and *highly diverse*, which, in a sense, is a blessing regarding the insights it carries. However, analyzing and interpreting it presents several challenges. Analyzing unstructured data requires new metrics, tools, and capabilities, particularly for real-time analytics that most businesses do not possess. We list some prominent social media analytics tools in a later section.

Volume and Velocity as a Challenge

Social media data is *vast* and generated *swiftly*. Capturing and analyzing millions of records that appear every second is a challenge. For example, on Twitter, three hundred and forty-two thousand tweets appear every minute, and on Facebook, one million likes are shared every twenty minutes. Capturing all this information may not be feasible. Knowing what to focus on is crucial for narrowing down the scope and size of the data. Luckily, sophisticated tools are being developed to handle high-volume and high-velocity data.

Diversity as a Challenge

Social media users and the content they generate are incredibly diverse, multilingual, and vary across time and space. Not every tweet, like, or user is worth looking at. A tweet or mention coming from an influential social media user is more valuable than a tweet from a non-influential user. Due to the noisy and diverse nature of social media data, separating relevant content from noise is challenging and time-consuming.

Unstructured Data as a Challenge

Unlike the data stored in the *corporate databases*, which are mostly numbers, social media data is highly unstructured and consists of text, graphics, actions, and relations. Short social media text, such as tweets and comments, has dubious grammatical structure and is laden with abbreviations, acronyms, and emoticons (a symbol or combination of symbols used to convey emotional expressions in text messages), thus representing a significant challenge for extracting business intelligence.

Social Media Analytics Accuracy

Owing to the challenges of volume, velocity, and diversity, the *accuracy* of social media analytics is questionable. As vast unstructured data (also known as 'dirty' data) is generated over social media, the accuracy of social listening is decreasing. For example, text analytics (one of the leading components of social media analytics) cannot capture many of the ways people use language. Western and English speaking countries have developed most of the tools. The tools often translate the text into English, apply sentiment analysis, and then assign it to the original post in its native language. This approach is problematic; if sentiment analysis is not available in the native language, it should not be offered in the first place. One has but to look at translations done by automated tools such as Babelfish to see just how mangled language translations become when processed in this manner. Similarly, many users are posting images and videos instead of text; most of this will be invisible to text-based social media analytics platforms.

Furthermore, as of at 2018, social media analytics platforms have not yet tapped into most of the new AI capabilities. There is much room for growth in this area. Hybrid Systems (usually boutique) have been developed for specialized use cases where encoded visual, auditory, and hepatic (i.e., touch sensor) data is used to provide context to Social Media, as that information is usually not present in verbatim.

SOCIAL MEDIA ANALYTICS INDUSTRY

Social media analytics is a vast and proliferating industry. According to some estimates, the global social media analytics market has grown at a compound annual growth rate of 27.6% (MarketsandMarkets, 2016). It is predicted that the total value of the social media analytics market will be USD 5.40 Billion by 2020 as compared to USD 1.60 Billion in 2015. The primary contributing growth factors of the social media analytics market are the growing number of social media users, higher spending on analytics, and more focus on market and competitive intelligence.

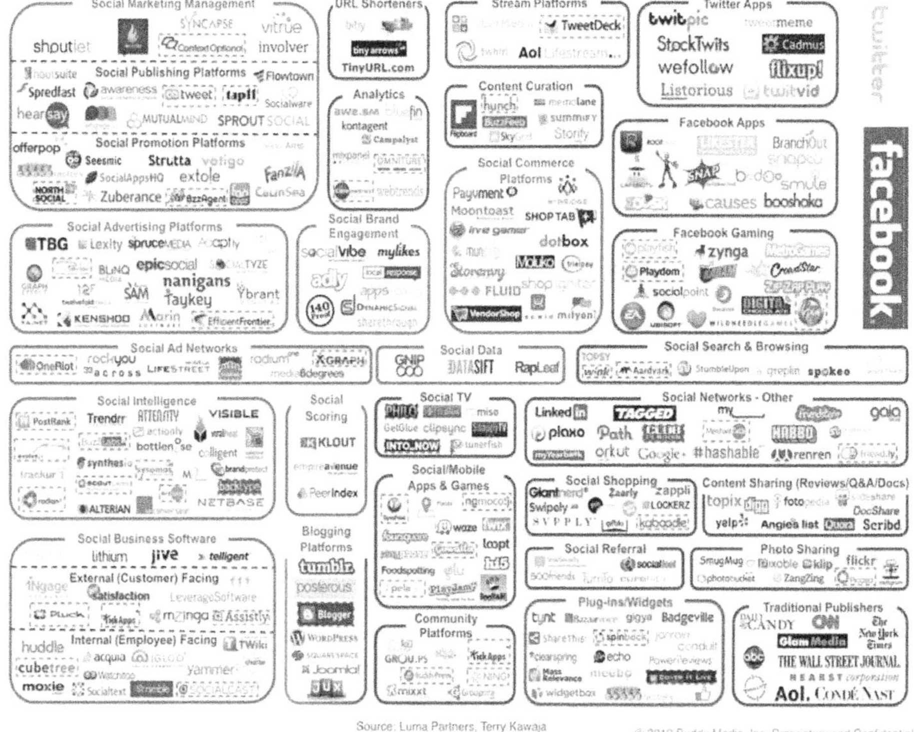

Figure 3.8. Social media ecosystem

The social media ecosystem is complex and is comprised of several players and industries. Figure 3.8 provides an overview of the social media ecosystem, containing diverse players including:

- Analytics Vendors
- Analytics Service Providers
- System Integrators
- Mobile Application Developers and Providers
- Consulting Service Providers

- IT Service Providers
- Analytics Education Providers
- Academia and Research Institutes
- Resellers
- Telecom Operators
- Enterprise Users
- Technology Providers

SOCIAL MEDIA ANALYTICS TOOLS

Social media *analytical tools* are also coming to market at a high pace to keep up with the growing need for analyzing the vast amount of data. Social media analytics tools come in a variety of forms and functionalities. Mainly they can be divided into:

1) Analytical applications that do not require programming skills, and
2) Tools/Scripts/Modules that need programming and technical skills.

We can use these tools to measure different layers of social media data, especially when aligned with an organization's business strategy. *The Digital Methods Initiative (DMI) Internet Studies Research Group* provides a comprehensive list of methods and tools for social media data (the file can be accessed using this shortened URL: goo.gl/EiTWi. Table 3.4 lists some examples of tools on each layer of social media analytics. We explore some of these tools in their respective chapters. We can use these tools to measure different layers of social media data, especially when aligned with an organization's business strategy.

Table 3.4. Examples of social media analytics tools with respect to its layers

Data	Tools
Text	Discovertext Lexalytics Tweet Archivist Twitonomy Netlytic LIWC Voyant

Data	Tools
Actions	Lithium Twitonomy Google Analytics SocialMediaMineR
Network	NodeXL UCINET Pajek Netminer Flocker Netlytic Reach Mentionmapp
Mobile	Countly Mixpanel Google Mobile Analytics Google Firebase
Location	Google Fusion Table TweepsMap
	Trendsmap Followerwonk Esri Maps Agos
Hyperlinks	Webometrics Analyst VOSON
Research Engines	Google Trends Google Correlate
Multimedia	Crimsonhexagon Image Analytics YouTube Analytics SAS Visual Analytics Google Cloud Vision API Simply Measured

CASE STUDY 3.1
THE UNDERGROUND CAMPAIGN THAT SCORED BIG

Background

ESPN is a sports television channel in the United Kingdom and Ireland owned by the BT Group under license from American sports broadcaster ESPN Inc. ESPN is a digital sports leader in the UK, operating websites, and apps that deliver a range of multimedia content to sports fans. ESPN.co.uk, the brand's central offering in the region, covers most sports, including football, cricket, rugby, tennis, golf, boxing, F1, and others. Other sport-specific websites under ESPN's stewardship include ESPN FC, which is available in app form, as is the award-winning ESPN UK app.

With a mandate to serve sports fans wherever they are, whenever they want it, ESPN's websites and apps carry the latest news, live scores, video, tables, fantasy games, and more. Featuring ESPN's global roster of talents from across the entire sporting spectrum, the brand has enjoyed significant growth in the past twelve months in the significant user engagement metrics and continues to do so.

The channel was operated by ESPN from 2009 to 2013 when it was sold to BT and became part of its BT Sports package focusing on international sporting events, predominantly American sports. Programming is available in standard definition and high definition formats.

ESPN FC is the football-dedicated division of ESPN, providing rolling coverage of the world's most famous sport. Formerly ESPN Soccernet, ESPN FC is a multimedia football website that currently has Global, UK, US, and Spanish editions. The site offers news, live scores, fantasy football, blogs, stats, interactive polls and more; ESPN FC displays the best in world football coverage. Through ESPN FC TV, the website hosts football-related video, utilizing the brand's roster of global football experts, journalists, and contributors, providing insight, analysis, and reaction to football around the globe.

The Goal

The World Cup is the most widely viewed and followed the sporting event in the world. The 2014 game held in Brazil was an eagerly anticipated event with significant sponsorship from some of the most significant organizations on the planet, including Adidas, Coca-Cola, and VISA. Teams—and fans—from all corners of the world traveled to the country. The world's spotlight was on

Brazil. ESPN FC wanted to capitalize on the mountains of excitement, enjoyment, and enthusiasm from people all over the planet to hear about the matches taking place in Brazil.

ESPN FC's primary goal over the period of the World Cup was to increase awareness of ESPN FC and to drive football fans to www.espnfc.co.uk for the latest news, scores, and team information, helping to build the profile of the brand across the globe.

The Challenge

ESPN FC likes to go the extra mile to serve sports fans, anytime and anywhere. With the World Cup being held outside the UK, many of the games were being played at inconvenient times for sports fans in the UK to watch them live on TV, as the matches were being played while people were still at work, traveling home, or very late in the evening. ESPN FC wanted to find a way to get the games to sports fans wherever they were during the World Cup.

The Solution

During the World Cup 2014, ESPN FC estimated that 100 million people would travel on the London Underground. The majority of London's Underground stations do not have Internet access, meaning fans were kept in the dark with no access to the scores during vital points in the tournament. With their mantra of 'serving sports fans anytime and anywhere,' ESPN FC had the ingenious idea of bringing the results of World Cup games to those traveling on the London Underground. Transport for London (TfL) is a local government body responsible for most aspects of the transport system in Greater London. ESPN FC collaborated with TfL to display game results on announcement boards at 150 stations across London—a media first. No brand had ever displayed messages on TfL's boards before.

Influencing the Right Demographic

The ESPN FC & TfL World Cup campaign was aimed at the commuting masses. However, ESPN FC wanted to ensure that they were also reaching the specific demographic segments relevant to their brand. Using the Brandwatch (one of the world's leading social media listening and analytics technology platforms) Demographic feature, ESPN FC were able to identify which mentions about the campaign were from Sales, Marketing, and PR professionals, a key audience they were attempting to target. Regarding all positive sentiment about the campaign, 18% came from Sales, Marketing, and PR professionals, and just 0.4% of adverse sentiment came from that industry.

Those tweets went on to help influence five other influential people in that sector, each with over 1,000 followers. Using Brandwatch, ESPN FC was able to measure that those five tweets alone reached nearly 15,000 followers.

Underground Results

Searching for the online reception of a campaign when there is no Internet reception can be tricky. Using Brandwatch, ESPN FC tracked 3,438 online mentions of the campaign in the first seven days.

However, most commuters have no access to Wi-Fi or the Internet while on the London Underground. So, many remained excited about the campaign when returning to street level—enough to share it online. "Of the mentions relating to the live coverage over 60% of them were positive a figure much higher than for most marketing campaigns." Charles Boss, Head of Marketing, ESPN FC, UK. To understand the effectiveness of this campaign, ESPN FC used Brandwatch Analytics to measure how many mentions other London Underground-based projects received over a similar period. Remarkably, the recent decision to introduce Euro cash points in London tube stations generated only 218 mentions in the first week, while commuters mentioning Virgin Media's new London Underground Wi-Fi was only slightly better with 473 mentions over seven days. When placed in this context, ESPN FC's World Cup updates were mentioned over seven times more than these similar campaigns, proving they had the loudest fans and the campaign was well received.

The Right Line

Finding out where commuters are tweeting can be just as important as what they are tweeting. ESPN FC utilized Brandwatch's advanced Boolean Queries to listen to conversation specifically from each tube line during the campaign. The Central Line proved to generate the most substantial volume of conversation of ESPN FC's World Cup updates, with 40% of tweets coming from that line, whereas the Northern and Jubilee lines followed with 27% and 23% of the chat. These insights could prove to be invaluable to ESPN FC when planning future social media advertising campaigns on the London Underground. As, Charles Boss, Head of Marketing, ESPN FC UK put it, "…Brandwatch was able to demonstrate that, using their impression score, the campaign reached a potential 2,363,921 people on Twitter…"

Commentating to Commuters

During the campaign, London commuters traveling during the World Cup final were able to follow Germany's 1–0 win over Argentina thanks to ESPN FC's live commentary and analysis at Waterloo Station. The game was relayed to the public address system at London's busiest train station by ex-Chelsea defender Scott Minto and Tottenham Hotspur Assistant Head Coach Steffen Freund. Using Brandwatch's sentiment analysis, ESPN FC was able to gauge public reaction during the commentary. Of the mentions relating to the live coverage over 60% of them were positive, a figure much higher than for most marketing campaigns. More significantly, ESPN FC did not receive a single negative mention for their World Cup Final commentary: which is impressive considering that many of those commuting during football's signature game were not the biggest fans of the sport.

Source: Brandwatch, *www.brandwatch.com*

REVIEW QUESTIONS

1. Why is it essential for business managers to understand and data-mine social media data?
2. What is social media analytics, and how it is different from traditional business analytics?
3. Briefly, explain the eight layers of social media data. Support the answer with examples.
4. What ethical issues should be considered when mining social media data?
5. What are some of the main challenges to social media analytics?
6. Compare different social media analytics tools available in the market and explain their strengths and weakness.
7. What are the limitations of social media analytics and what does the future hold?

EXERCISE 3.1: SOCIAL ANALYTICS VENDOR ASSESSMENT

Many social media analytics tools are available to extract and analyze the eight layers of social media data. However, a significant question we often stumble on is which tool is right for our organization? Deciding which platform best suits an organization's needs depends on many variables including, organizational objectives, the type of data we want to analyze, and the availability of resources (such as financial and human capital). Keep in mind that each platform captures and stores data in its own way, even when the same information is requested from similar platforms, the results will often differ. Thus, choosing the right tools and frameworks to work within an organization is crucial for creating successful social media analytics outcomes.

Your Task

Your task is to find and interview a business manager (s) (or an owner, a CEO, a consultant) to help them select a potential social media analytics vendor (s). Use the *Social Media Analytics Vendor Assessment Tool (SMAVAT)* (available from the book website) to compare social analytics platforms/vendors based on the particular requirements of an organization. To begin with, work with the manager/company to identify and define stakeholder and corporate requirements before it makes sense to use any of the assessments provided in this book. Once the requirements are drawn up, customize the *SMAVAT*, if necessary. For each requirement, your task is to rank vendors based on their ability to deliver on the organization's needs along the following criteria:

1. Does Not Support
2. Meets Requirement
3. Ideal Solution

Conducting the Assessment

Working with the business, use the Vendor Evaluation tab to answer the following questions for each vendor.

- For each parameter, rank each of the vendors based on the information that the organization or reader currently has. As every organization has different requirements, the questions can be modified to fit most decision-making criterion.
- In the "Vendor Evaluation" tab, rate each vendor based on your requirements (1-Does Not Support, 2-Meets Requirement, 3-Ideal Solution).
- View the "Scorecard" tab to see how the scores translate into a vendor's rating (% of total requirements that are ideal solutions).
- Use the data to evaluate which social analytics vendor is the best fit for a particular organization.

What this assessment allows you to do?

- A logical apples-to-apples comparison between up to 3 vendors.
- Documents requirements & necessity for each vendor.
- Provides a visual report of results in the resulting radar diagram.
- Helps the reader cut through marketing hype and negotiate with various vendors.
- Saves several hours on research & formatting and is reusable in several contexts.
- Focuses vendor demo presentations.

Finally, write a short professional report on the vendor assessment exercise that you have completed. The report should discuss which tools are right for the organization and why. Discuss the resources needed to utilize social media tools and provide recommendations professionally.

EXERCISE 3.2: NZ-SOFT NEEDS A SOCIAL MEDIA PLATFORM

NZ-Soft (not its real name), a large computer hardware manufacturer, needs to understand how their target audiences around the world perceive their brand and products. They are looking to invest in some social analytics platforms/vendors and wants to know which platform best fulfills their needs? A full list of their requirements is provided below.

NZ-Soft Business Requirements

- They need to know about conversations about their products, locations, languages.
- Which conversations are positive, neutral, or negative to their brand?
- Who are the brands' influencers and brand advocates? The platform chosen should be able to identify and track the Influencers.
- Collect problems or issues around specific products or use cases (such as pricing resistance and what to charge for their products).
- Use social data to come up with new products (market research).
- Use social media data for customer service.
- Comprehensive coverage of social media platforms that the organizations use to communicate with clients or potential customers.
- The readout from the chosen platform should be as close as possible to real-time data, actionable for employees and analysts in several lines of business (LOB) within corporate marketing.
- NZ-soft would also like to know what is happening at a retailer's locations where their products are being sold. As they sell most of their products through affiliate sales channels such as Target, K-Mart, Staples, Office Depot and Amazon.com, they do not get as clear a picture, as they would like to what is going on at the point-of-sale.
- How is the brand doing in their online marketing compared to competitors on social media?
- The brand has a significant amount of textual and image data, both internal and on the Web; they want to understand the patterns within the data by using text analytics.
- The brand uses coupons and social applications to sell their products across various channels; they would like to track the return on investment of these initiatives.
- The brand would like to understand the unique opportunities to market their products in specific locations in the primary metropolitan centers throughout the world (at the neighborhood and block level).
- The brand owns several Analytics platforms that it internally developed or bought, that are used internally to measure various use cases and desires the best integration so the data collected can be reused, if needed, in other applications.
- The Brand wants the best platform and the lowest price.

Your Task

Your goal is to use the *SMAVAT* and come up with the platform(s) that best fulfills NZ-Soft needs. Report your results explaining the choice of platforms based on the scoring and radar chart available. In your report, include a discussion on how and why the chosen platforms can best respond to the listed business requirements.

The list of stakeholder requirements is not even the entire list. What is already clear is that no single platform will meet all those needs. There are several platforms to choose from, and each has their strengths and weaknesses. Based on the requirements, customize the SMAVAT, if necessary. As a starting point, consider the social media ecosystem (Figure 3.8) for the many social media technologies available to choose from.

Conducting the Assessment

If possible, work in groups of two or three and use the SMAVAT tool to answer the following questions for each vendor.

- For each parameter, rank each of the vendors based on the information that the organization or reader currently has. As every organization has different requirements, the questions can be modified to fit most decision-making criterion.
- In the "Vendor Evaluation" tab, rate each vendor based on your requirements (1-Does Not Support, 2-Meets Requirement, 3-Ideal Solution).
- View the "Scorecard" tab to see how the scores translate into a vendor's rating (% of total requirements that are ideal solutions).
- Use the data to evaluate which social analytics vendor is the best fit for a particular organization.

CHAPTER 3 REFERENCES

Asur, S., & Huberman, B. A. (2010). Predicting the Future with Social Media *2010 IEEE/WIC/ACM International Conference on Web Intelligence and Intelligent Agent Technology* (pp. 492-499): 10.1109/WI-IAT.2010.63

Bekmamedova, N., & Shanks, G. (2014). Social Media Analytics and Business Value: A Theoretical Framework and Case Study *2014 47th Hawaii International Conference on System Sciences* (pp. 3728-3737): 10.1109/HICSS.2014.464

Berinato, S. (2016). Visualizations That Really Work. *Harvard Business Review* (June 2016)

Card, S., Mackinlay, J., & Shneiderman, B. (1999). *Readings in Information Visualization: Using Vision to Think.* : Morgan Kaufmann Publishers.

Chen, H., Chiang, R. H. L., & Storey, V. C. (2012). Business intelligence and analytics: from big data to big impact. *MIS Q., 36*(4), 1165-1188.

Code, F. (2015). *Recommending items to more than a billion people.*

Delen, D., & Demirkan, H. (2013). Data, information and analytics as services. *Decision Support Systems, 55*(1), 359-363. http://dx.doi.org/10.1016/j.dss.2012.05.044

Keim, D., Andrienko, G., Fekete, J.-D., Görg, C., Kohlhammer, J., & Melancon, G. (2008). Visual Analytics: Definition, Process, and Challenges. In J. T. S. Andreas Kerren, Jean-Daniel Fekete, and Chris North (Eds.). (Ed.), *In Information Visualization* (Vol. 4950, pp. 154-175). Berlin, Heidelberg

Khan, G. F. (2013). Social media-based systems: an emerging area of information systems research and practice. *Scientometrics, 95*(1), 159-180.

Kiron, D., Prentice, P. K., & Ferguson, R. B. (2014). Raising the Bar With Analytics. *MIT Sloan Management Review.*

Kramer, A. D. I., Guillory, J. E., & Hancock, J. T. (2014). Experimental evidence of massive-scale emotional contagion through social networks. *Proceedings of the National Academy of Sciences, 111*(24), 8788-8790. 10.1073/pnas.1320040111

Lustig, I., Dietrich, B., Johnson, C., & Dziekan, C. (2010). the Analytics Journey: An IBM view of the structured data analysis landscape: descriptive, predictive and prescriptive analytics. *Analytics-Magazine, available at: http://www.analytics-magazine.org/november-december-2010/54-the-analytics-journey.*

MarketsandMarkets. (2016). *Social Media Analytics Market worth 9.54 Billion USD by 2022.* https://www.marketsandmarkets.com/PressReleases/social-media-analytics.asp:

Petersen, R. (2012). *166 Cases Studies Prove Social Media Marketing ROI.* BarnRaisers

Syncapse. (2013). *THE VALUE OF A FACEBOOK FAN 2013: Revisiting Consumer Brand Currency in Social Media.* New York, NY

Thomas, J. J., & Cook, K. A. (2005). *Illuminating the Path: The Research and Development Agenda for Visual Analytics*: IEEE Press.

Verma, I. M. (2014). Editorial Expression of Concern: Experimental evidence of massives cale emotional contagion through social networks. *Proceedings of the National Academy of Sciences, 111*(29), 10779. 10.1073/pnas.1412469111

Wong, P. C., & Thomas, J. (2004). Visual Analytics. *IEEE Computer Graphics & Applications,, 24*, 20-21.

Part 2: Aligning the Value

Chapter 4

Analytics Business Alignment

"When what you value and dream about doesn't match the life you are living, you have pain."—**Shannon L. Alder**

Learning Outcomes

After completing this chapter, the reader should be able to:

- Understand the concept of aligning social media analytics with business goals.
- Comprehend social media alignment matrix.
- Recognize the role of CIO in aligning analytics with business objectives.
- Apprehend social media strategy.
- Understand the steps needed to formulate a social media strategy.

INTRODUCTION

It is just not enough to have a social media analytics tool ready to mine data. Analytics should be *strategically aligned* to support existing business goals. As most of the data for analytics will come from an organization's own social media engagement, without a well-crafted and aligned social media strategy, the business will struggle to get the desired outcomes from analytics. This chapter introduces social media analytics and business alignment concepts, social media alignment matrices, the role of the *chief information officer* (CIO) in facilitating the alignment, and the steps needed to formulate a social media strategy.

UNDERSTANDING SOCIAL MEDIA AND BUSINESS ALIGNMENT

As with any other technology, aligning social media objectives and goals with the objectives of the organization should be the starting point of any social media analytics initiative. The alignment of social media analytics with business objectives can be seen as analogous to the famous Chinese *Yin* and *Yang* philosophy, where two seemingly opposing forces (in this case, social media and business) complement and reinforce each other (Figure 4.1). Table 4.1 provides examples of possible scenarios for aligning social media analytics with business objectives. If the business goal is to understand customer sentiments expressed over social media, then social media analytics should be designed to facilitate this objective. It may require, for example, tools and skills for extracting and analyzing tweets or comments posted on a Facebook fan page. Alternatively, if the business objective is to identify influential social media customers and their information control ability, the focus should be on social media networks.

Figure 4.1. Aligning social media analytics with business goals (Yin and Yang philosophy)

SOCIAL MEDIA ANALYTICS ALIGNMENT MATRIX

A variety of factors determine the extent and breadth of the social media analytics alignment with business goals, including the availability of technical, financial, administrative, and leadership resources, and analytics potential to achieve business goals. Aligning information technologies with business objectives has been a widely studied field (Henderson & Venkatraman, 1993). Aligning social media analytics with business objectives may require a comprehensive approach such as the strategic alignment model suggested by Henderson and Venkatraman (1993). In this book, we use a simplified *Social Media Analytics Alignment Matrix (SMAAM)* provided in Figure 4.2. On the *Y-axis* of the matrix is the "resource availability," which refers to the availability of financial, technical, administrative, and leadership resources for social media analytics. On the *X-axis* of the matrix is the impact of social media analytics alignment regarding its potential to achieve business goals (or its potential to generate economic value and return on investment). Depending on the two variables (i.e., resources availability and its potential), your social media analytics alignment with business goals can fall into four possible quadrants.

The "*highly aligned*" quadrant (see Figure 4.2) implies that leadership, financial, administrative, and technical resources are available within the organization to leverage and (sustain) social media analytics. And the potential for social media analytics to achieve business goals is high. For instance, mining the eight layers of social media data is technically and financially demanding, but rewarding when related to the creation of economic value to the firm. Moreover, the analytics alignment efforts reside in the "*not aligned*" quadrant when its potential to achieve business goals and your resource availability is low.

Table 4.1. Aligning analytics with business objectives

Example Business Question	Layers of Interest	Data Source	Example of Tools
Is the social media conversation about our company, product, or service positive, negative, or neutral?	Text Analytics	Tweets Comments Blog posts Reviews	Discovertext Lexalytics Semanteria
Which content posted on social media is resonating more with our customers?	Actions Analytics	Likes Shares Views Mentions	Google Analytics Hootsuite
Who are our influential social media nodes, and what is their position in the network?	Network Analytics	Fan network Follower network	NodeXL Flocker Netlytic Mentionmapp
How is our mobile app performing?	Mobile Analytics	Total sessions New users Time spent	Countly Mixpanel Google Mobile Analytics
Where are our social media customers located?	Location Analytics	Geo-map IP address GPS	Google Fusion Table Tweepsmap Followerwonk
Which social media platforms are driving the most traffic to our corporate website?	Hyperlink Analytics	Hyperlinks In-links Co-links	Webometrics Analyst VOSON
Which keywords and terms are trending?	Search Engine Analytics	Trending topics	Google Trends
Is there any multimedia content related to our brand posted on social media?	Multimedia Analytics	Images Videos	YouTube Analytics Google Cloud Vision API

An organization's social media analytics efforts should focus on highly aligned and high-impact alternatives. Nevertheless, the business goals and availability of resources will play a significant role in determining the depth of the analytical efforts and resulting quadrant in the matrix. For instance, using Facebook's built-in analytical tools is financially and technically less challenging (and hence less rewarding) when compared to owning a sophisticated analytical tool, which may require technical and financial resources but will be highly rewarding regarding achieving business goals.

The SMAAM will guide us throughout the social media strategy formulation process. The alignment matrix is flexible. One can replace the variables at both the axes with any other variables of interest. For example, we can place criticality of social media analytics (the extent to which the analytics is critical to the business) on the *Y-axis* and sensitivity of the analytics (e.g., regarding security, privacy, or ethics) on the *X-axis* and determine the extent of your alignment. The social media analytics alignment, for instance, will be considered "highly aligned" if it is business critical, but less sensitive.

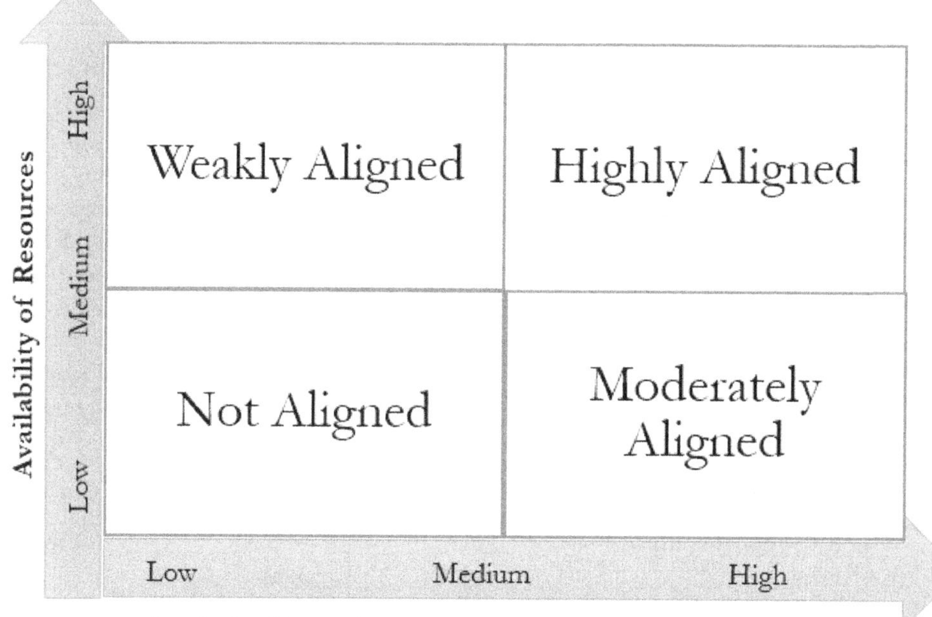

Figure 4.2. Social media alignment matrix

DIGITAL ANALYTICS MATURITY MODEL

One way to conceptualize the development of digital analytics readiness is through analytics maturity models. An analytics maturity model is essentially a framework that organizations use to assess their current state of analytics maturity and provide a structured path towards improving data analytics competence for enterprise-wide business decision-making. Digital analytics consultant, Stéphane Hamel in 2008, developed one of the useful *Digital Analytics Maturity Model* (DAMM). DAMM provides organizations with an unbiased and easy-to-understand assessment of their analytics maturity, roadmap, and strategy. Hamel's DAMM is available at https://digitalanalyticsmaturity.org/assessment and can be used free of charge.

Hamel's DAMM has six levels of maturity: initial, reactive, defined, managed, and optimized (Figure 4.34). The ultimate goal of an organization is to achieve maturity level five, i.e., optimized. Key process areas or "critical success factors" determine the maturity levels of an organization (CSF). CSF identifies the elements that are vital for a digital strategy to be successful. DAMM defines five CSF explained below.

Management, Governance, and Adoption

Organizations with *optimized maturity level* have well-defined, well-communicated roles, and responsibilities holding teams and people accountable across the full spectrum of activities required to collect, analyze, and use digital data to measure and act on business goals.

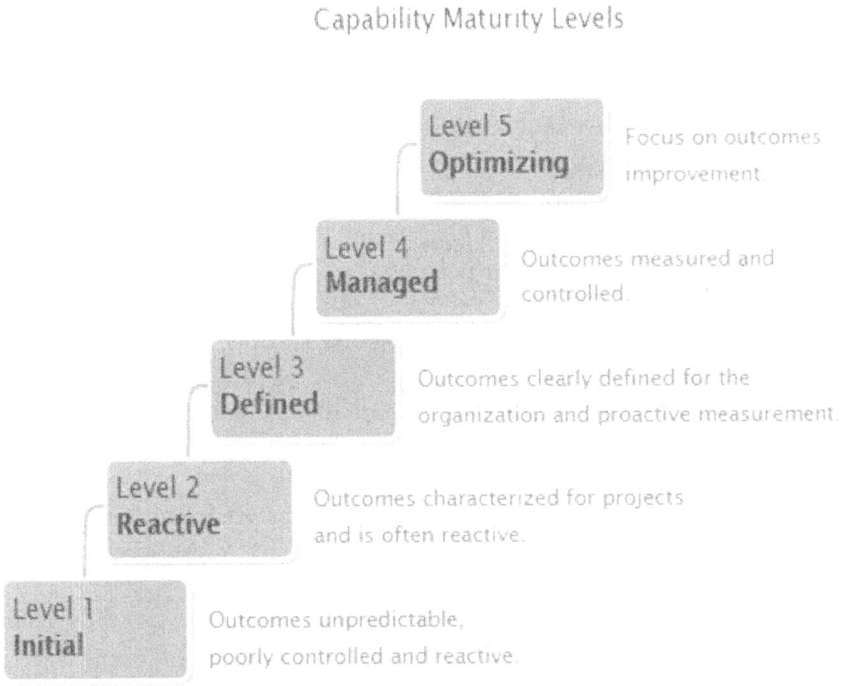

Figure 4.3. Hamel's DAMM

Objectives and Scope

Optimized maturity level organizations define very clear business objectives that are measured by structured *Key Performance Indicators* (KPIs) designed to quantify success or failure. Such organizations have extensive analysis activities throughout their entire digital ecosystem and actively leverage analytics as an organization wide program for transformational change.

Analytics Team and Expertise

Teams in organizations that have achieved the optimized level have the technical expertise to collect data, have experienced data analysts, as well as empowered business users experienced in data-driven decision-making methodologies.

Continuous Improvement Process and Analysis Methodology

Organizations with optimized maturity level leverage formal frameworks across their teams and departments and enable team members to learn and use these frameworks in a continuous improvements workflow throughout the organization.

Tools, Technology, and Data Integration

Mature organizations use relevant tools and technology to enable high-quality data-collection, intelligent reporting, useful visualizations, and advanced analysis such as statistical modeling or predictive analytics. It is not about the tools; it is about an organization's ability to leverage them. Be methodical and make sure to balance all aspects at a given maturity level.

Overall, the digital analytics maturity assessment is mostly focused on:

Accessing—this includes assigning current digital analytics strategy and capabilities to determine strengths and weaknesses.

Planning—involves aligning measurement to business goals and bridging skills and capability gaps.

Growing—this step involves change management, which is the primary obstacle for most organizations.

THE ROLE OF CIO AND IT MANAGEMENT

Senior information technology (IT) executives, particularly the CIO, play a significant role in envisioning and creating an *aligned social media analytics strategy*. The CIO is the person in charge of managing and aligning information communications technologies (ICTs) to achieve business-wide goals. The role of the CIO has evolved from a technical guru to an informed leader, communicator, and strategic thinker. For a sustained strategic IT–business goals alignment, a CIO should possess the following skills and competencies (Dawes, 2008).

Strategic Thinking and Evaluation

- Business and policy reasoning
- IT investment for value creation
- Performance assessment
- Evaluation and adjustment

Systems Orientation

- Environmental awareness
- System and social dynamics
- Stakeholders and users
- Business processes
- Information flow and workflow

Appreciation for Complexity

- Communication
- Negotiation
- Cross-boundary relationships
- Risk assessment and management
- Problem-solving

Information Stewardship

- Information policies
- Data management
- Data quality
- Information sharing and integration
- Records management
- Information preservation

Technical Leadership

- Communication and education
- Architecture
- Infrastructure
- Information and systems security

- Support and services
- IT workforce investments

FORMULATING A SOCIAL MEDIA STRATEGY

Since most of the data for analytics purposes will come from an organization's own social media profiles, having a sound social media strategy will be instrumental in supplying quality data for business intelligence. Formulating a *social media strategy* is not much different from the overall IT strategy of an organization. The purpose of formulating a social media strategy is to create rules and procedures to align the social media engagement with business goals. Planning an aligned social media strategy should follow a strategy formulation process similar to that used by IT management as suggested by Luftman et al. (2004), though some additional steps are needed to account for the unique nature of social media technologies (Luftman, Bullen, & al., 2004).

The following steps will lead to the formulation of a sound social media strategy.

Get Hold of an Executive Champion

For any organizational strategy development and implementation, the sponsorship of a *senior-level executive* is crucial. The most critical factor for success in social media analytics is not technology, but leadership and top management commitment. Success is possible only when the transformation is steered through strong leadership: setting direction, building momentum, and ensuring the disciplined execution of an inspiring vision and ambitious plans. A social media executive champion will be someone with *charisma* and the *power* to enforce social media strategy in the organization. It usually is the head of the department or the *chief information officer* (CIO). Enlisting the support of a champion is crucial for the social media efforts to be fruitful. A champion should have several attributes including, power, vision, resources, willingness to sacrifice, and persistence to support the change (Luftman et al., 2004).

Build a Cross-Functional Team

The first step in formulating a social media strategy is to create a *cross-functional team* with senior management members from all the departments, including the IT department. Ideally, a CIO should lead this team. Having a cross-functional team will make sure that all the stakeholders have their say and have the ownership of the social media initiative.

Assessing Organizational Culture

Understanding the organization's vision, values, norms, systems, assumptions, and beliefs about social media is crucial. Is the organization ready to embrace social media and social media analytics? What are the organization's assumptions and expectations about social media? Embracing social media in all aspect of the business will require organizational cultural transformation at all levels.

Change how the organization thinks about social media by first understanding the status of the corporate culture. Understanding a corporate culture and transforming it is a very complicated task and is beyond the scope of this book. A roundtable with the team members may provide some clues on the organization's social media readiness. Also, a variety of organizational culture assessment and change tools are available on the market that can be used to access and highlight the need for a cultural shift. For example, The *Organizational Culture Assessment Instrument* (OCAI) is a free tool for diagnosing organizational culture (developed by professors Robert Quinn and Kim Cameron) and Culture Builder Toolkit prepared by Corporate Culture Pros. The bottom line is that with the cultural assessment, business users and stakeholders may want to make sure that their organization is ready to embrace social media and that it has the necessary vision and will to leverage it.

Review The Current Social Media Presence

Before formulating a social media strategy, organizations need to document their current social media use and presence. Organizations may start by asking team members about their current social media status and by searching social media pages representing their organization.

The best way to do it would be to arrange small, interactive seminars. The objective is to find out all the officially sanctioned and unauthorized social media outlets, including blogs, wikis, fan pages, and Twitter pages that use the organization's name. For example, they may use https://twitter.com/topsy to search for social media profiles representing the organization.

Organizations may also employ a SWOT (Strength, Weakness, Opportunities, and Threats) analysis to determine their current social media landscape. Documenting the status will help stakeholders streamline their organization's social media presence. This activity will become a basis for the organizational baseline state and for understanding the current social media use and strategic positioning.

Determining Business Objectives

Once an organization measures and understands the baseline social media presence, the next step is to create a list of the *targets* and *goals* to achieve through that social media presence. With a clear idea of what stakeholders want to accomplish with social media, they are likely to put together a sound social media strategy. Defining business goals and objectives is essential, as different social media goals require different sets of actions and tools. Below are some commonly identified objectives by governments. Some example social media business goals are:

- To share news, alerts, and updates through mainstream social media platforms, including Twitter, Facebook, and YouTube.
- To implement a participatory platform (e.g., blog) where customers can submit ideas and suggestions, and providing them with the opportunity to participate in business strategy making.
- To increase awareness about products/services by disseminating information on social media platforms.
- To attract customers by driving traffic from social media platforms to corporate websites, and
- To network and engage in dialogue with customers.

Each department may have different goals and objectives that they want to achieve through social media, so creating a broader social media policy will make sure each department has its say. Here, we can use the social media engagement matrix introduced earlier to determine the ease of achieving an objective against its impact.

Aligning Social Media Goals with Business Goals

As mentioned earlier, aligning social media goals with business goals is vital. In addition to each goal being *specific*, *realistic*, and *measurable*, it should be in-line with the existing business goals and strategy. If the organizational goal is to network with customers via social media platforms, we can design a social media strategy to facilitate this objective.

Developing a Content Strategy

Establishing a social media presence is the easy part; *sustaining* it is the challenge. Developing a sound content strategy will make sure stakeholders know what to post when to post it, and how to post the right content. Content strategy is tied to the business goals, and only the content that supports those goals should be developed and published. At the minimum a sound content strategy should answer the following questions:

- What type of material should we post to social media, for example, news, updates, and alerts?
- How often should we post the content? Daily or weekly?
- Who will create the content?

- Does the organization approve the content?
- Who will respond to follow-up suggestions and comments?
- How will the feedback be handled?

Platform Strategy

Platform strategy should detail the type of social media platform utilized to achieve business objectives. The platform selection decision is tied to the business goals and objectives. If the aim is to share news, alerts, and updates, choose existing mainstream social media platforms, such as Twitter, Facebook, and YouTube. However, if the goal is to crowd-source ideas, we may need a custom-built Web 2.0 platform; this will determine what type of resources are required.

Resource Considerations

It is crucial to understand the desired level of social media engagement, as it will determine the kind of *resources* (technical, human, and financial) needed. For example, if the goal is to establish an idea-generation platform to solicit creative ideas, in-house, a purpose-built platform may be necessary. Bear in mind that creating and sustaining even a simple Facebook fan page requires considerable planning and human, financial, and technical resources. For example, it requires regular updates, answers to customer complaints and comments, and the extraction and analysis of the data (e.g., tweets or comments) for better decision making.

Establish a Social Media Ownership Plan and Policy

A social media *ownership plan* and policy should outline the relative rights and responsibilities of employers and employees. An ownership plan covers social media ownership regarding both accounts and activities such as accounts themselves, individual and pages profiles, platform content, and posting activity. Policies related to social media clarify issues related to personal and professional use, trade secrets, intellectual property, and confidentiality. Courtney Hunt (2014) has done a great job of providing social media ownership guidelines. The guidelines touch on the following areas related to social media ownership (Hunt, 2014).

> ***Organizations accounts and profiles***—this part of the ownership plan deals with all the social media accounts and activities, such as accounts themselves, individual and page profiles, platform content, and posting activity. Ideally, an organization should own all its social media profiles.

Individual profiles—the individuals own their social media profiles, but for the sake of organizations reputation, businesses should provide all employees with guidelines about how they should represent themselves on social media.

Contact information—social media allows people to have multiple contact addresses (e.g., e-mail), and this policy should specify which communicate with the employee should display on their profile. A good practice is that employees include both a personal and a professional address.

Contacts—this policy should specify the rules for social media contacts made during the employment period (e.g., through LinkedIn). For example, businesses may specify that the contacts made during the employment are joint property, but that employees can keep their connections after leaving the organization. However, organizations should have an internal system or mechanism to capture the valuable connections.

Comments—ownership strategy should also provide policies and guidelines on whether and how employees can comment on a variety of social media platforms. For example, when commenting, employees should make it clear whether they are discussing on behalf of the organization or expressing their thoughts.

Posting—what should and should not be posted to the social media platform is covered here. Defining posting rules can help avoid issues with trade secrets, intellectual property, confidentiality, and defamation.

Groups—organizations may establish policies and guidelines about the kind of groups employees can join or be a member. For example, allowing employees to join groups that promote the business goals is encouraged.

Privacy settings—by setting guidelines for social media privacy settings, businesses may encourage employees to set their social media privacy settings in the best interest of both individuals and the organization.

Select Success Metrics

Success metrics will help stakeholders evaluate their social media strategy's effectiveness. Defined parameters should be in place to measure the success of social media in the organization. Metrics will help determine whether social media is making a difference in the business. Depending on the type of social media engagement, success metrics may vary. For example, if the prime objective of social media use is to engage customers in a dialogue, we can utilize the number of comments as a metric. Alternatively, if it is to promote awareness, then the number of likes, shares, and page views may provide some indicators.

Use Analytics to Track Progress

Social media analytics should be used to evaluate social media presence and to see how the organization is performing. For example, *Google Analytics* can provide a variety of analytical measures. *HootSuite Pro* also offers advanced analytics and reporting for social media measurement needs. The critical thing to note is that we should adequately configure the analytical tools to match the organization's success metrics and business goals.

Organizations often have a vast amount of data, but it is not always captured in a useful or usable form. Sometimes, crucial data that should have been tracked has not been captured. It is probably best to perform a social media audit to understand better what data exists in the organization, where it is located, who owns the data, and how to access it.

Social Media Strategy Implementation Plan

Organizations carefully design information technology strategies, but rarely implement them. A *strategy implementation plan* is an essential part of the social media strategy formulation process. This plan lays out strategies and tactics to put the strategic ideas into action. The strategy implementation process can vary from organization to organization and depend on a variety of factors including support from senior executives and involvement of members from key departments. Four significant barriers to strategic implementations are (Kaplan & Norton, 2001):

- 85 percent of executive teams spend less than one hour per month discussing strategy.
- 60 percent do not link budgets to strategy.
- Only 25 percent of managers have incentives linked to strategy, and
- Only 5 percent of the workforce understands the strategy.

The best way to go is to select team members from critical departments who understand the purpose of the plan and the steps involved in implementing it. Establish a mechanism to discuss progress reports and let team members know what has been accomplished. Communicate the plan throughout the organization and clearly specify ownerships, deadlines, and accountabilities.

Periodic Review

In the face of rapid technological, business, and social changes, organizations should *periodically review* social media strategy. The review will make sure that the initial assumptions made about the external and internal factors (e.g., technology, vision, budgets) are still relevant.

CASE STUDY 4.1
CREATING SOCIAL MEDIA STRATEGY FOR SANCTUARY DESIGNS

Introduction

Brandon is the owner of an interior design studio, Sanctuary Designs, which specializes in retail and office decor. They have recently established a presence on social media and are looking to build a strategy in line with their overall company goals.

Social Media Strategy Template

In this social media creation exercise, we will use a social media strategy template by HootSuite and create a social media strategy for the Sanctuary Designs. Organizations may need to conduct a SWOT analysis and incorporate findings into their strategy. One of the prime objectives of social media strategy is to bridge the gap between where an organization currently is and where it wants to be. Using the template will help organizations create a social media strategy to guide them in their daily online activities. Readers may follow along with the example case study and answer the questions in each step for their own company's strategy. Once you answer these questions, you can put your plan into action by knowing what your goals are, how to achieve them, and how to measure your success.

Step 1: Set Business Objectives

The first step involves determining what we hope to achieve with social media and aligning social media objectives with the overall company vision, mission, and strategy.

Questions to Ask	Case Study Example
What do you want to achieve with social media?	Build trust and brand recognition within the home decor community and our customers.
Do your social media objectives align with your overall company vision, mission, and marketing strategy?	Drive traffic to our website and convert visitors to leads.
Are your objectives S.M.A.R.T: specific, measurable, attainable, relevant, and time-bound?	The objective is to increase traffic to the website via social media channels by 20% within 12 months.

Step 2: Develop an Audience Persona

Developing an audience persona can help you understand where your audience is online and what type of content is going to affect them the most.

Questions to Ask	Case Study Example
What would be a broad description of your ideal customer?	Robb is the operations manager at a restaurant chain, a customer of Sanctuary Designs. He is in charge of hiring design firms and liaising with them to complete the projects in their office on time.
What do they do and what do they care?	He cares about getting the most out of his budget as well as having excellent quality work completed according to their project deadlines.
What is important to them when conducting business with our company?	Catelyn is the owner of an up-and-coming small fashion boutique, also a customer of Sanctuary Designs. She is currently researching for inspirations to design her dream store and is very active on social media platforms like Pinterest?

Step 3: Conduct a Social Media Audit

Audits are vital for benchmarking previous efforts and planning for new ones. If you are just getting started on social media, begin with an initial kick-off review. The review will help in understanding which accounts are currently linked to your company and what they are being used for.

Questions to Ask	Case Study Example
Which accounts are currently attached to my company?	Sanctuary Designs currently has a Facebook Page, Twitter account, Google+ Page, Flickr account, and Pinterest account.
How are they currently being used?	The Facebook, Twitter, and Google+ accounts are currently used to communicate relevant interior design content. The Pinterest page is used to display projects.
Have they gone dormant/ are they being used as spam?	The Flickr account has gone dormant; no content has been posted for over six months.
Are your current messaging and social networks the best possible networks for your intended audience?	Migrating the Flickr content to Pinterest, as there is more engagement there and we have more female customers on social.
How often do you post	Most accounts are updated 1-2 times per

content to these accounts?	week.
How relevant is the content you are sharing with your audience?	Relevant, as we usually publish industry-related content and information that our customers usually seek.
What are your engagement rates like?	Followers and likes have not increased by very much since the conception of the accounts.
How does your present social media progress compare to the past?	We went from 50 likes on Facebook to 1,000 and 500 Twitter followers to 1,500 in 12 months.
How is your company's reputation online according to Google or Yelp?	Customers are delighted with their experience with us, and a number of them would hire us again.
What are people saying about your competitors?	Our principal competitors, Luxury Interiors offer lower rates, but customers feel that our work is of better quality.
What are they doing that is working for them?	They are running some contests, which are gaining them more social media traffic.

Step 4: Set Social Media Initiatives

Where are your buyers? Give your favorite customer a phone call, send them an email, or if they are concerned about their information, create an anonymous survey online for them. Find out where they are online and how best you can reach them.

Questions to Ask	Case Study Example
Which social media networks are our customers more active?	Facebook, Twitter, Instagram, and Pinterest.
Which social networks should we focus on based on our audience profile?	Facebook, Instagram, and Pinterest.
What kind of initiatives can we take based on the findings from our social media audit?	-Blogging: Guest posts on the blog by respected interior designers and happy clients. -Post behind the scenes as well as transformation photos and videos on Facebook -Have clients pin photos of completed spaces as well as inspirations. -Follow and engage with noted interior designers and customers on Instagram.
What types of content resonates	Photos, decor inspiration ideas, and

with our customers the most?	how-to blog articles.
What types of content will help our drive people to our website?	Yelp reviews, contests, Pinterest pins of completed projects with a link to the item on our website.

Step 5: Set Tactical Steps

Based on the findings from the Social Media Audit phase, create tactical steps for your business objectives as well as metrics to measure them.

Blogging	**Metric: Increase blog subscribers**
Create a content strategy. **Create an editorial calendar (monthly).** **Research guest posters.**	Monthly Success: An increase of 10 blog subscribers per month Quarterly Success: At least 40 blog subscribers by the end of Q1 Yearly Success: At least 160 blog subscribers by the end of the year

Facebook	**Metric: Increase website traffic from**
Create a content strategy. **Create a weekly content calendar.** **Post enticing photos and videos every day according to the content calendar.** **Review Facebook Insights every month, look at which posts were more engaging and build on that.**	Monthly Success: Increase traffic to the website via Facebook Quarterly Success: Increase traffic to the website via Facebook by 15% by the end of Q1 Yearly Success: Increase traffic to the website via Facebook by 20% by the end of the year
Instagram	Metric: Increase Instagram subscribers
Create a content strategy. **Follow IG accounts of noted interior designers/ clients.** **Post behind the scenes snapshots of projects.** **Engage and comment on client's IG accounts.**	Monthly Success: At least 75 new Instagram followers per month Quarterly Success: At least 250 new Instagram followers at the end of Q1 Yearly Success: At least 1,100 Instagram followers by the end of the year
Pinterest	**Metric: Increase leads from Pinterest**

Create a content strategy. **Create boards for project galleries, behind the scenes snapshots and inspirations.** **Invite clients/ influencers to pin on boards.** **Engage with clients/ community by pinning on their boards.**	Monthly Success: At least four leads on Pinterest per month Quarterly Success: At least 12 leads from Pinterest by the end of Q1 Yearly Success: At least 48 leads from Pinterest by the end of the year

REVIEW QUESTIONS

1. What is the goal of aligning social media analytics with business goals?
2. Explain the social media alignment matrix.
3. Briefly, explain the role of the CIO in aligning analytics with business objectives.
4. What is the purpose of a social media strategy?
5. Explain the steps needed to formulate a social media strategy.

EXERCISE 4.1: ANALYTICS MATURITY ASSESSMENT

The social media analytics maturity assessment provides an organization with an unbiased and easy-to-understand representation of their organization's expectations of and commitment to analytics infrastructure and initiatives.

Your task

Use Hamel's digital analytics maturity assessment tool (available at https://digitalanalyticsmaturity.org/assessment) to assess an organization's analytics maturity. Report the results while providing a critical discussion on what we can do to achieve the highest level of digital analytics maturity.

Based on your objectives, scope and resources, methodology, tools and management, Hamel's tool will illustrate whether your organization is engaged in the critical data gathering and customer insight-sharing activities required for your business' success. The maturity levels of an organization are determined by five key "*critical success factors*" (CSF) which are the elements that are vital for a digital strategy to be successful:

Management, Governance, and Adoption—Organizations with an optimized maturity level have well-defined, well-communicated roles and responsibilities holding teams and people accountable across the full spectrum of activities required to collect, analyze, and use digital data to measure and act on business goals.

Objectives and Scope—Optimized maturity level organizations define very clear business objectives that are measured by structured Key Performance Indicators (KPIs) designed to quantify success or failure.

Analytics Team and Expertise—Teams in organizations that have achieved optimized level have the technical know-how to collect data, have experienced data analysts, experienced in data-driven decision-making methodologies.

Continuous Improvement Process and Analysis Methodology—Organizations with optimized maturity levels leverage formal frameworks across their teams and departments and enable team members to learn and use these frameworks in a continuous improvements workflow throughout the organization.

Tools, Technology and Data Integration—Mature organizations use relevant tools and technology to enable high-quality data-collection, intelligent reporting, useful visualizations, and advanced analysis such as statistical modeling or predictive analytics.

EXERCISE 4.2: ANALYTICS-BUSINESS ALIGNMENT

Organizations should strategically align their social media analytics efforts to support existing business goals. Without proper alignment, a business will struggle to get the desired outcomes from analytics. The five core process areas or CSF that determine the alignment maturity of an organization and that are vital for an analytics strategy to be successful are: 1) Planning & Decision-Making, 2) Alignment of Goals & Objectives, 3) Communications, 4) Processes, and 5) Culture.

Your Task

Your task is to set up a meeting with a business Manager or CEO of an organization to complete the assessment. Use the accompanying *Microsoft Excel Analytics Business Alignment Tool* (available at the book companion site) to help the organization align their analytics efforts with business objectives. To begin with, work with the manager to identify and define stakeholder and corporate requirements before it makes sense to use any of the assessments provided in this book. Once you determine the requirements, customize the analytics-business alignment tool, if necessary. Rank the organization's analytics-business alignment based on the five CSF.

Conducting the Assessment

Before taking the assessment, the reader should look at the instructions (Figure 4.4).

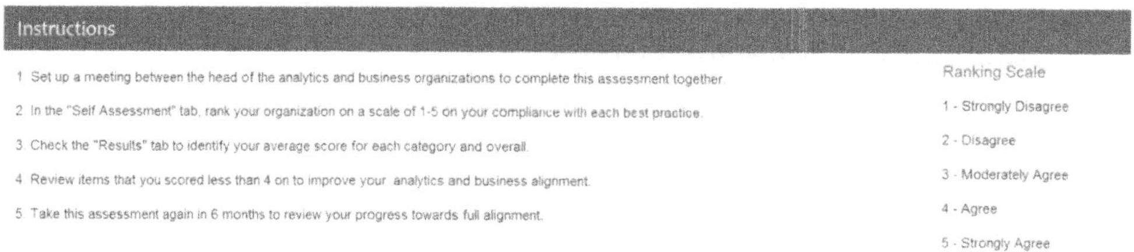

High Performance Marketing
DEMAND METRIC
Analytics & Business Alignment Tool

Instructions

1. Set up a meeting between the head of the analytics and business organizations to complete this assessment together.
2. In the "Self Assessment" tab, rank your organization on a scale of 1-5 on your compliance with each best practice.
3. Check the "Results" tab to identify your average score for each category and overall.
4. Review items that you scored less than 4 on to improve your analytics and business alignment.
5. Take this assessment again in 6 months to review your progress towards full alignment.

Ranking Scale
1 - Strongly Disagree
2 - Disagree
3 - Moderately Agree
4 - Agree
5 - Strongly Agree

Figure 4.4. Instructions for conducting the assessment

Use the "self-Assessment" tab to answer the following questions for the organization.

- In the "self-Assessment" tab, rank the organization on a scale of 1-5 on their compliance with each best practice.
- For each parameter, rank the organization based on the information that the organization or reader currently has. As every organization has different requirements, you may modify the questions to fit most decision-making criterion.
- View the "Result" tab to see how the scores translate into the organization's analytics-business alignment (Figure 4.5).
- Use the analytics-business alignment index to evaluate the organization's alignment and suggest improvements.

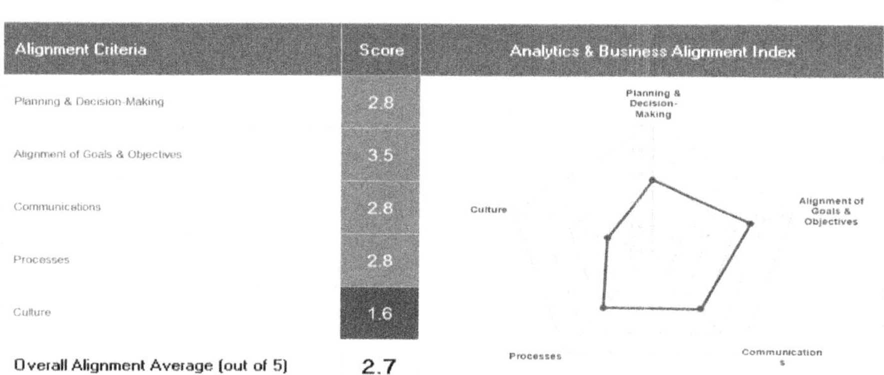

High Performance Marketing
DEMAND METRIC
Analytics & Business Alignment Tool

Alignment Criteria	Score
Planning & Decision-Making	2.8
Alignment of Goals & Objectives	3.5
Communications	2.8
Processes	2.8
Culture	1.6
Overall Alignment Average (out of 5)	**2.7**

Figure 4.5. Analytics-business alignment tool results

By taking the assessment, the reader can determine how aligned their analytics and business objectives are. We filled out the evaluation having an example organization in mind. The alignment of analytics and business are not a strong point at the origination, and our results of the evaluation show that too.

CHAPTER 4 REFERENCES

Dawes, S. S. (2008). What Makes a Successful CIO? *Intergovernmental Solutions Newsletter, GSA Office of Citizen Services and Communications, 21*.

Henderson, J. C., & Venkatraman, N. (1993). Strategic alignment: leveraging information technology for transforming organizations. *IBM Syst. J., 32*(1), 4-16.

Hunt, C. (2014). Social Media Ownership: Recommendations for Employers, available at: http://denovati.com/2014/02/social-media-ownership.

Kaplan, R. S., & Norton, D. P. (2001). *The Strategy-Focused Organization, available at: http://iveybusinessjournal.com/topics/leadership/building-a-strategy-focused-organization#.VLjEetKUd5E*.

Luftman, J. N., Bullen, C. V., & al., e. (2004). *Managing the Information Technology Resource: Leadership in the Information Age*: Prentice Hall.

Part 3: Capturing the Value

Chapter 5

Capturing Value with Social Media Network Analytics

"Pulling a good network together takes effort, sincerity, and time."—**Alan Collins**

Learning Outcomes

After completing this chapter, the reader should be able to:

- Understand network analytics theories, concepts, and tools.
- Comprehend different types of networks and their terminologies.
- Recognize uses of social media network analytics for business intelligence purposes.
- Extract, construct and analyze conventional social media networks.
- Understand network strategies.

INTRODUCTION

Networks are the building blocks of social media. Networks form as social media users make friends, follow brands, like and share content, review and rate products, and forge professional ties. Organizations can then analyze these networks to reveal their structure, size, and the critical nodes in them. *Social media network analytics* is, therefore, the art and science of extracting, constructing, analyzing, and understanding social media networks. Managers can employ network analytics to identify influential nodes (e.g., people and organizations) or their position in the network; it can also be used to understand the overall structure of a network. Businesses, for example, can use network analysis to explore their Twitter or Facebook followers and identify influential members on those networks.

Network analytics vastly shortens the amount of time it takes to research prospective customers and industry influencers while providing valuable insights to gauge marketing effectiveness within the networks being examined.

From a marketing perspective, some people on social media are more influential, as they can share information with a broad audience of followers, subscribers, and friends. Due to their vast follower base, some celebrities such as Kim Kardashian are paid to advertise products/services on social media. Humans of New York Facebook page has been very influential with over 18 million followers and over 100,000 people talking about the page at a time. Athletes like Kobe Bryant post products on their social media accounts and when people see the product being endorsed by the celebrity or athlete they are more likely to buy it. A tweet by former President Barack Obama, for example, can instantly reach several million followers on Twitter. However, it is important to highlight that on social media not only famous people are considered influencers nowadays. Many "ordinary" people are attracting millions of followers on Instagram, Twitter, YouTube, and other platforms.

Furthermore, a researcher may be interested in the overall structure of networks to see how specific social media networks differ or converge. The case study included in this chapter highlights the usefulness of social media networks and how it is employed to answer interesting real-world research questions. The case study shows how a research team used social media data and proved that the differences in cultural norms (e.g., those of the United States and Korea) influence social media use patterns in the public sector.

Overall, the purpose of network analysis is to do the following (Perer and Shneiderman, 2008).

- Understand overall network structure, for example, the number of nodes, the number of links, density, clustering coefficient, and diameter.
- Find influential nodes and their rankings, for example, degree, betweenness, and closeness centralities.
- Find relevant links and their rankings, for example, weight, and betweenness centrality.
- Find cohesive subgroups, for example, pinpointing communities within a network.
- Investigate multiplexity, for instance, analyzing comparisons between different links types, such as friends vs, enemies.

COMMON SOCIAL NETWORK TERMS

Network

At a fundamental level, a *network* is a group of nodes that are connected with links (Wasserman and Faust, 1994). Nodes (also known as vertices) can represent anything, including individuals, organizations, countries, computers, websites, or any other entities. Links (also known as ties, edges, or arcs) represent the relationship among the nodes in a network.

Social Networks

A *social network* is a group of nodes representing social entities, such as people or organizations, and the links formed by these social entities. For example, links can represent relationships, friendships, and trade relations. *Social networks* can exist both in the real and online worlds and supplement each other. In fact, the online world helps create better connections in the real world. A network among classmates is an example of a real-world social network. A Twitter follow-following network is an example of an online social network. In a Twitter follow-following network, nodes are the Twitter users and links among the nodes represent the follow-following (i.e., who is following whom) relationship among the users.

Social Network Site

A *social network site* is a special-purpose software (or social media tool) designed to facilitate social or professional relationships. Facebook, Google+, and LinkedIn are examples of social network sites. We explore different forms of social networks in a later section.

Social Networking

The act of forming, expanding, and maintaining social relations is called *social networking*. Using social network sites users can form, grow, and maintain online social ties with family, friends, colleagues, and sometimes strangers.

Social Network Analysis

Social network analysis is the science of studying and understanding social networks (Hanneman and Riddle, 2005) and social networking. It is a well-established field with roots in a variety of disciplines including Graph Theory, Sociology, Information Science, and Communication Science.

NETWORK STRUCTURES

Network structures or *topologies* exist due to degree distribution. The degree of a node measures the number of links a node has to the other nodes in a network. *Degree distribution* is the probability distribution of nodes degree over the whole network. Degree distribution tries to capture the difference in the degree of connectivity between nodes in a graph. It tells us how something will flow through it, which nodes have influence, or how quickly we can affect the entire network. For example, consider the following network (Figure 5.1) and its degree distribution where one node has 1 degree, five nodes have 2 degrees, and two nodes have 3 degrees, and one node has 4 degrees and one 5 degrees.

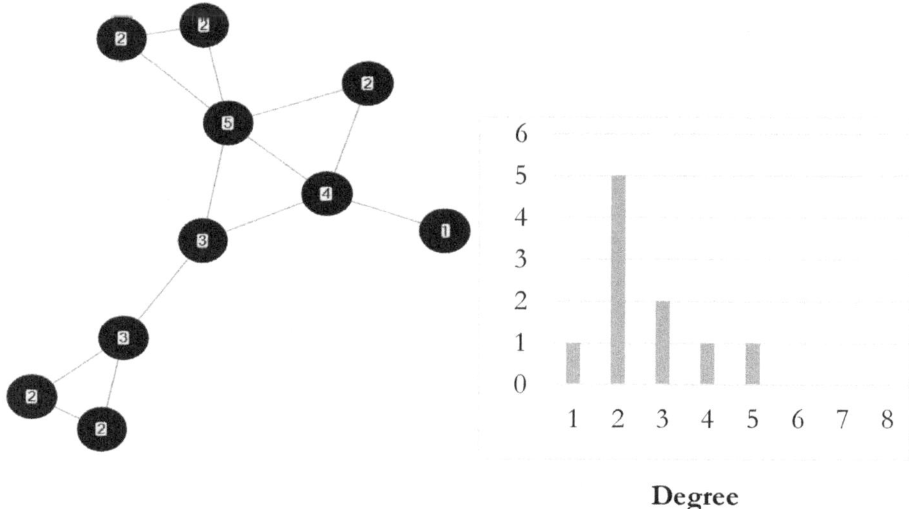

Figure 5.1. Degree distribution Example

Based on the notion of degree distribution, three major types of networks topologies are:

- Random Network
- Scale-free or Decentralized Networks
- Small World or Centralized Networks

Random Networks

A network with a normal distribution or homogeneous degree distribution is known as a *random network*. In random networks, most nodes have approximately the same number of connections or degree. In other words, such networks do not have a distinct pattern and are generated by random processes (e.g., see Figure 5.2). Most social media and real-world networks are formed to serve a specific purpose and are constrainted by limited sources to give them distinct topologies or patterns. For example, the structure and size of our friendship networks (both real virtual and real world) is constrained by a number of factors including, the cognitive limit to the number of people with whom we can maintain stable social relationships, internet connectivity, our social skills, and access to information. Hence most real-world networks are not random.

If random networks are not typical, then why bother to study them? Network scientists mostly use random networks for comparison purposes. When solving a network related hypothesis, a network scientist usually starts with a random network to understand how a network created without specific rules differ to the network that is created to serve specific purposes having distinct topologies or patterns.

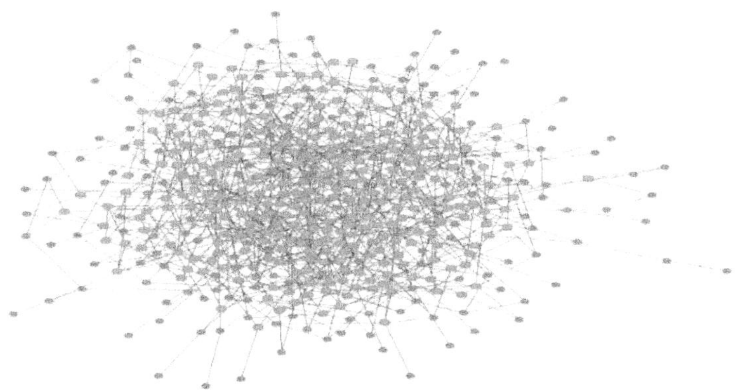

Figure 5.2. Example of a random network

Scale-Free Networks

A *scale-free network* (also known as a centralized network) is a network whose degree distribution follows a power law (Figure 5.3). In other words, in such networks, very few nodes will have a large number of connections (or links) and a large number of nodes will have very few connections. Centralised network structures imply that very few central nodes control the flow of information and resources.

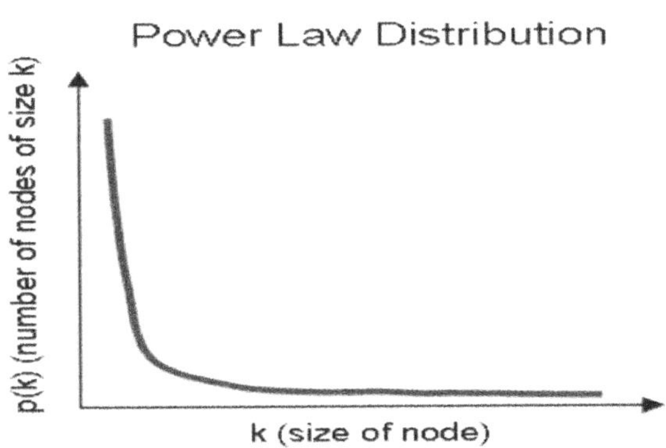

Figure 5.3. Power law distribution example

Most real world networks are scale-free. For example:

Social networks—on social networks, such as Facebook and Twitter social networks, very few people have many connections/friends/followers and many people have very few friends.

Website networks—out of billions of website available over the Internet, very few have a vast number of in-links. For example, there are millions of other website linking to Google and Yahoo.

Scholarly networks—in the academic world while there are millions of scholars publishing their work, only a handful of scholars or articles get a massive number of citations.

Small World Network

Small world networks (or decentralized networks) have one or a few dominant hubs (nodes with many links) and many nodes with a relatively low level of degree (Figure 5.4). In such networks, most nodes (people, organizations, and computers) are not neighbors, but we can reach most nodes with a few steps or nodes. An important question here is, how many steps? The network scientists believe that people are separated by six degrees. The six degrees of separation hypothesis suggests that most people in the world are six or fewer steps away from each other so that we can make a chain of "a friend of a friend" statements to connect any two people in a maximum of six steps. Some studies, however, have shown that on a social network site, such as Facebook, people are just separated by 3 degrees.

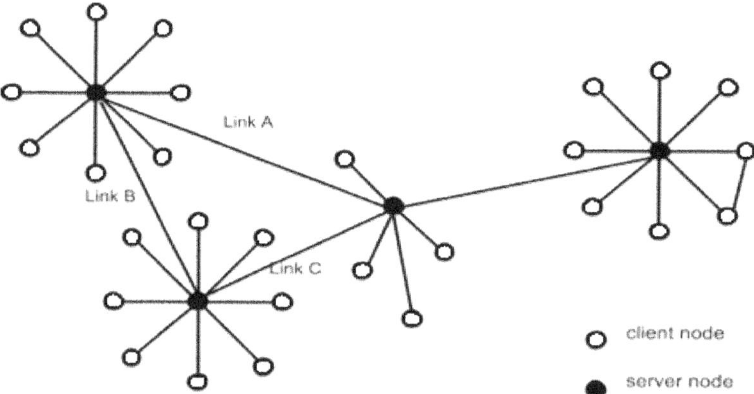

Figure 5.4. Decentralized network example

SOCIAL MEDIA NETWORK TOPOLOGIES

When people engage over social media different forms of *network structures,* and topologies emerge. A study by Smith et al., (2014) suggested that over Twitter at least six distinctive network structures arise depending on 1) the subject being discussed, 2) the information sources being cited, 3) the social networks of the people talking about the issue, and 4) the leaders of the conversation. The six network structures suggested by Smith et al., (2014) are:

- Polarized Crowd
- Tight Crowd
- Brand Clusters
- Community Clusters
- Broadcast Network
- Support Network

We discuss these briefly.

Polarized Crowd

Polarized crowd or *discussions networks* emerge when people discuss topics that are often highly contentious and political. Usually, two prominent and dense groups have little connection between them. These networks mostly develop over Twitter when there is usually little or no conversation between the two groups despite the fact that they are focused on the same topic. Polarized Crowds on Twitter do not argue but ignore one another while tweeting different web resources and using different #hashtags.

Tight Crowd

Highly interconnected people with few isolated participants form *tight crowd* networks. Tight crowd networks are formed around conferences, professional topics, hobby groups, and other subjects that attract like-minded communities. These structures show how networked learning communities function and how social media can facilitate sharing and mutual support.

Brand Clusters

A significant amount of disjointed social media users who tweet about a brand, but do not interact with one another, form *brand clusters.* The larger the number of people talking about a brand, the less likely it is that participants are connected to one another. In other words, brands mentioning or tweeting participants focus on a topic but tend not to connect to each other.

Community Clusters

Community clusters form around popular topics. These networks develop around a few dominant hubs (users) with its audience, influencers, and sources of information. These conversation networks are similar to 'bazaars' with multiple centers of activity. For example, a global news event often attracts coverage from many news outlets, each with its following. That creates a collection of medium-sized groups—and a fair number of isolates.

Broadcast Network

Broadcast network is a hub and spoke structure in which many people repeat or broadcast viral events and prominent news and media organizations tweets. Nodes in such a network are often connected only to the hub or information/news source, without connecting to one another. Hubs in these networks are agenda setters and conversation starters having a substantial impact on the conversation.

Support Network

Support networks are also a hub and spoke network, but unlike the broadcast network, in this network the hub account replies to many otherwise disconnected users, creating outward spokes. A brand's Twitter service account used in resolving and managing customer issues around their products and services is an example of a support network.

COMMON SOCIAL MEDIA NETWORK TYPES

The following are some common types of social media networks that we come across, and that can be subject to network analytics.

Friendship Networks

The most common type of social media networks are the *friendship networks*, such as Instagram, Facebook, and Snapchat. Friendship networks let people maintain social ties and share content with people they closely associate with, such as family and friends. Nodes in these networks are people and links are social relationships (e.g., friendship, family, and activities).

Follow-Following Networks

In the *follow-following network*, users follow (or keep track of) other users of interest. Twitter is an excellent example of a follow-following network where users follow influential people, brands, and organizations. Nodes in these networks are, for example, people, brands, and organizations and links represent follow-following relations (e.g., who is following whom).

Fan Network

Social media fans or supporters of someone or something, such as a product, service, person, brand, business, or other entity form *fan networks*. The network formed by the social media users subscribed to a brand Facebook fan page is an example of a fan network. Nodes in these networks are fans, and links represent co--likes, co-comments, and co-shares. A fan network can be passive (via bought subscribers) or active (organically generated followers who actively engage with your posts).

Group Network

People who share common interests and agendas form *group networks*. Most social media platforms allow the creation of groups where a member can post, comment, and manage in-group activities. Examples of social media groups are Twitter professional groups, Yahoo Groups, and Facebook groups. Nodes in these networks are group members, and links can represent co-commenting, co-liking, and co-shares.

Professional Networks

LinkedIn is an excellent example of *professional networks* where people manage their professional identity by creating a profile that lists their achievements, education, work history, and interests. LinkedIn members can also search profiles or jobs by specific keywords (e.g., analytics). Nodes in these networks can represent people, brands, or organizations. Links are professional relations. On LinkedIn, the links are called "connections" (such as a co-worker, employee, or collaborator).

An important feature of professional networks is the endorsement feature, where people who know you can endorse your skills and qualifications. Also, the recommendation feature, where unconnected members of a social network are suggested to a user, is another essential feature.

Content Networks

The content posted by social media users form *content networks*. A network of YouTube videos is an example of a content network. In such a network, nodes are social media content (such as videos, tags, and photos) and links can represent, for example, similarity (i.e., content belonging to the same categories that can be linked together).

Dating Networks

Dating networks (such as Match.com and Tinder) are focused on matching and arranging a dating partner based on personal information (such as age, gender, hobbies, shared interests, and location) provided by a user. Nodes in these networks are people and links represent social relations (such as romantic relations).

Co-authorship Networks

Co-authorship networks are two or more people working together to collaborate on a project. Wikipedia (an online encyclopedia) is an excellent example of a social media-based co-authorship network created by millions of authors from around the world (Biuk-Aghai, 2006). A more explicit example of the co-authorship network is the ResearchGate platform: a social networking site for researchers to share articles, ask, and respond to questions, and find collaborators. In these networks, nodes are researchers and links represent the co-authorship relationship.

Co-commenter Networks

Co-commenter networks are formed when two or more people comment on social media content (e.g., a Facebook status update, blog post, Yelp restaurant reviews, or YouTube video). For example, we can construct a co-commenter network from the comments posted by users in response to a video posted on YouTube or a Facebook fan page. In these networks, nodes represent users, and a link represents the co-commenting relationship.

Co-like

Co-like networks are formed when two or more people like the same social media content. Using NodeXL (a social network analysis tool), one can construct a network that is based on co-likes (two or more people like a similar content) of a Facebook fan page. In such a network, nodes will be Facebook users/fans and links will be the co-like relationship. Facebook also uses co-likes to suggest potential friends.

Co-occurrence Network

Co-occurrence networks are formed when two more entities (e.g., keywords, people, ideas, and brands) co-occur over social media outlets. For example, one can construct a co-occurrence network of brand names (or people) to investigate how often specific brands (or people) co-occur over social media outlets. In such networks, nodes will be the brand names and the links will represent the co-occurrence relationships among the brands.

Geo Co-existence Network

Geo co-existence networks are formed when two or more entities (e.g., people, devices, and addresses) co-exist in a geographic location. In such a network, the node represents entities (e.g., people) and links among them represent co-existence. Examples of geo co-existence networking are:

- Visitors to a museum (or any location) use social media applications on their mobile devices to check-in using Facebook or Swarm (Foursquare); other members who have recently checked in to the museum are shown to the member via the application (app).
- Shoppers visit brick and mortar stores and shop there using a Bluetooth enabled app that connects to an iBeacon network installed in the location.

Hyperlink Networks

In simple terms, a *hyperlink* is a way to connect documents (such as websites). Hyperlinks can be referred to as being either in-links or out-links. In-link is a hyperlink originating in other websites (Björneborn and Ingwersen, 2004), thus bringing traffic/users to your website. Out-links originate in your site, thus sending traffic to other websites. Typically, in hyperlink networks nodes are websites and links represent referral relationships (in the form of in-links or out-links). We discuss hyperlink networks in detail in chapter 10.

TYPES OF NETWORKS

From a technical point of view, we can classify the networks mentioned above in a variety of ways, including:

1) Based on Existence
2) Based on the Direction of Links
3) Based on Mode
4) Based on Weights

Based on Existence

We can classify networks based on the way the networks exist online or are constructed:

- Implicit Networks
- Explicit Networks

Implicit Networks

Implicit networks do not exist by default. Instead, we intentionally built them with the help of dedicated tools and techniques. Examples of such networks include keyword co occurrence networks, co-citation networks, co-commenter networks, hyperlink networks. Constructing and studying implicit networks can provide valuable information and insights. For example, an implicit network emerges when several Twitter users post about an event taking place using a specific hashtag. In such a network, the users (nodes) are connected to each other via the hashtag.

Explicit Networks

Explicit social media networks do exist by default. In other words, they are explicitly designed for social media users to be a part of it. Most social media networks are explicit. Examples of explicit social media networks include Facebook friendship network, Twitter follow-following networks, LinkedIn professional networks, YouTube subscribers' network, and bloggers' networks. In this chapter, we will focus on explicit social media networks.

Based on Direction

We can classify networks based on the directions of links among the nodes as:

- Directed Networks
- Undirected Networks

Directed Networks

A network with directional links among nodes is called a *directed network*. Said differently, in such networks, the relationships among the nodes have a direction. Usually, a link with an arrow is drawn to show the direction of the relationship among the nodes (Figure 5.5). For example, the Twitter following-following network is a directed network where the direction of the arrow shows who is following whom. As another example, Facebook recently added the option to "follow" certain people's posts, similar to Twitter, which is an example of a directed network.

Undirected Network

In *undirected networks*, the links among the nodes do not have any direction. A Facebook friendship network is an example of an undirected network. That is to say that the friendship ties do not have direction.

Based on Mode

Based on the composition of nodes, networks can be classified as:

- One-Mode Network
- Two-Mode Networks
- Multimode Networks

One-Mode Networks

A *one-mode network* is formed among a single set of nodes of the same nature (Figure 5.5). A Facebook friendship network is an example of a one-mode network where nodes (people) form network ties (friendships).

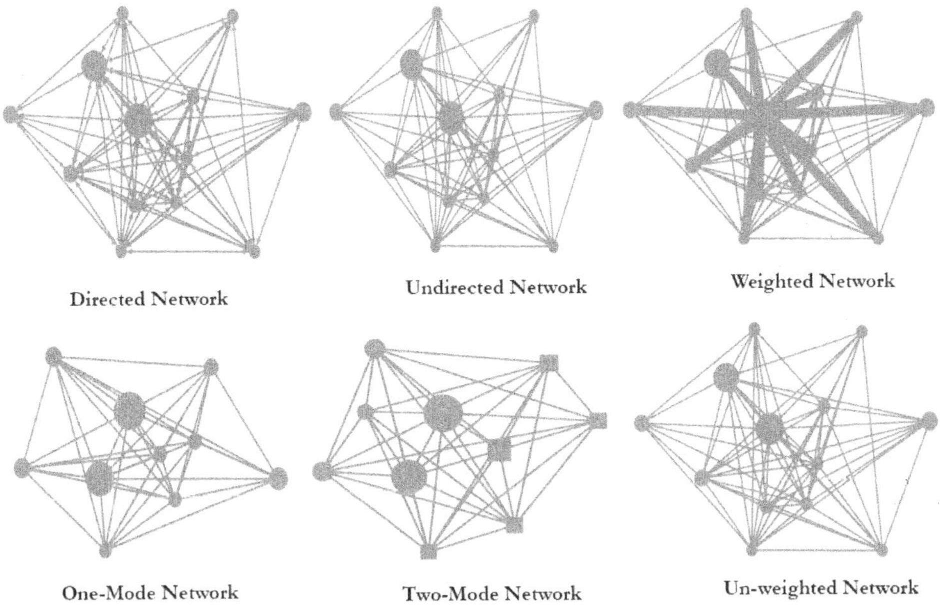

Figure 5.5. Types of social media networks

Two-Mode Networks

Two-mode networks (also known as bipartite networks) are networks with two sets of nodes of different classes (Latapy et al., 2008). In these networks, network ties exist only between nodes belonging to different sets (Figure 5.5). For example, consider the two-mode network given in Figure 5.5, where one set of nodes (circles) could be social media users, and another set of nodes (squares) could be participation in a series of events. Users are linked to the events they attended.

Multimode Network

A *multimode network* is also possible where multiple heterogeneous nodes are connected. It can be considered as an amalgam of one and two-mode networks.

Based on Weights

Networks can also be classified based on the weight assigned to the links among the nodes. There are two types of *weighted networks*:

- Weighted Networks
- Unweighted Networks

Weighted Networks

In weighted networks, the links among nodes bear specific weights to indicate the strength of association among the nodes. The link (relationship) between, for example, two Facebook friends (nodes) will be thicker if they communicate more frequently. While weighted networks provide rich information, they require sufficient historical data to construct. For example, Facebook and LinkedIn use proprietary algorithms to condense a user's news feed based on his/her interests and interaction with other users. Instagram also changed their algorithm, so images no longer appear chronologically on their news feed, but based on the interests of the user. Facebook recently changed their search tab to show pictures/videos of what the user typically clicks on/views.

Unweighted Networks

In *unweighted networks*, links among nodes do not bear weights. The links only indicate the existence of a relationship and cannot provide clues about the strength of the relationship (Figure 5.5). Un-weighted networks are easy to construct but may conceal useful information.

Keep in mind that the above-classified types are not mutually exclusive and can exist in a single network. For example, there may exist a directed weighted one-mode network. Alternatively, one could construct an undirected two-mode unweighted network, and so forth.

COMMON NETWORK TERMINOLOGIES

Now, let us look at some common network terminologies or properties. Network properties can be divided into two categories:

- Node-Level Properties
- Network-Level Properties

Node-Level Properties

Node-level properties focus on one node and its position in the network. Some essential node properties include degree centrality, betweenness centrality, eigenvector centrality, and structural holes.

Degree Centrality

Degree centrality of a node in a network measures the number of links a node has to other nodes (Hanneman and Riddle, 2005). In a Facebook network, for example, this will measure the number of friends that a member has. In a Twitter network, it will equate to the number of followers or following a user has. In a directed network, the degree can be either in-degree (followers) or out-degree (following). In a Twitter network, in-degree (followers) is a more critical measure of a node's influence than out-degree (number of individuals a person follows).

Betweenness Centrality

Betweenness centrality is related to the centrality (or position) of a node in a network. The nodes with high betweenness centrality can control the flow of information between connected nodes due to their central position in the network (Liu et al., 2005). In a Facebook network, the users who occupy the central position (have more direct connections to essential friends in the network) are better positioned to control the flow of social media content and information.

Eigenvector Centrality

Eigenvector centrality measures the importance of a node based on its connections with other vital nodes in a network. It can provide an understanding of a node's networking ability relative to that of others (Marsden, 2008)). The Google search engine has used eigenvectors to rank search results by their relevance to the searcher's query results from the very beginning.

Structural Holes

The idea of *structural holes* was first put forward by Burt (Burt, 1992) who suggested that a specific node has an advantage or disadvantage based on its location in a network (Hanneman and Riddle, 2005).

In a social media network, some nodes or users, because of their location in the network, may have an advantage or disadvantage spreading information to other nodes in the network (Nooy et al., 2005). The most useful information turns out to arise from structure holes (or loose ties) that exist in a network. As an example, in a Facebook or LinkedIn social network, new job opportunities are more likely to come from a friend of a friend, rather than someone in the individual's closer connections.

Network-Level Properties

Network properties provide insight into the overall structure and health of a network. Important *network-level properties* include clustering coefficient, density, diameter, average degree, and components.

Clustering Coefficient

The *clustering coefficient* of a network is the degree to which nodes in a network tend to cluster or group. Clustering coefficient can be either local or global. The global clustering coefficient measures the overall clustering in a network, whereas the local clustering coefficient measures embeddedness of single nodes.

Density

The *density* of a network deals with the number of links in a network. Density can be calculated as the number of links present in a network divided by the number of all possible links between pairs of nodes in a network. For an undirected network, the number of all possible links can be calculated as $n (n - 1)/2$; where n is the number of nodes in a network. A fully connected network, in which each node is connected to every other node, will have a density of 1.

Components

Components of a network are the isolated sub-networks that connect within but are disconnected between sub-networks (Hanneman and Riddle, 2005). In a connected component, all nodes are connected and reachable, but there is no path between a node in the component and any node not in the component (Wasserman and Faust, 1994). The principal or most significant component of a network is the component with the highest number of nodes.

Diameter

The *diameter* of a network is the largest of all the calculated shortest paths between any pair of nodes in a network (Wasserman and Faust, 1994), and it can provide an idea of how long it would take for some information/ideas/message to pass through the network.

Average Degree

The *average degree* centrality measures the average number of links among nodes in a network. For example, some estimates suggest that the average Facebook user has 338 friends.

SOCIAL MEDIA NETWORK STRATEGIES

Knowing an organizational social media network structure and statistics (network and individual level properties) is crucial. Based on a brand's social media network structure, a business manager may formulate some essential *network strategies*. Not many businesses create network driven social media strategies. Here we discuss three crucial network strategies.

Strategy 1: Shortest Path to Prominence Strategy

A rule of thumb is that brands should connect with the 100 most influential social media users at the cost of 1,000 non-influential ones. In other words, connecting and empowering the most influential users is the *shortest path to prominence*. To find the shortest path to prominence, a brand can use social network analysis techniques to discover and empower the most influential social media users, i.e., the users with the highest betweenness and degree centralities.

Strategy 2: Bridge Building Strategy

This strategy requires looking a network structure as a whole and selectively reshaping its structure in a way that is conducive to a brand. For example, if a brand has a polarized network, but they hoped to create a community then they have a lot of *bridge building* to do. Furthermore, a brand's network with a high clustering coefficient indicates strong local community clusters who hardly talk to each other. As a result, a brand's message is not going across the network. To address this problem, a network driven strategy will suggest introducing people (nodes) to one another to facilitate bridges among the isolated clusters. Bridge building is something scarce that brands hardly do. In fact, very few brands introduce their brand fans to one another.

Strategy 3: Smart Tweet Strategy

Smart tweet strategy is based on the idea that a brand should talk to the most influential people/nodes about the things they care about. This strategy calls for finding, connecting, and empowering the prominent nodes using text and network analytics. Brands, for example, can employ text analytics to discover what influential nodes in their network tweet. In other words, what interested them the most? Then use that information to start a conversation with the influential users. NodeXL, for instance, has "Smart Tweet" draft messages that let brands directly engage with the key influences by sending customized messages on Twitter.

NETWORK ANALYTICS TOOLS

Variety of network analysis tools are available in the market with two deployment models:

- On-Premise Model
- Cloud-Based Model

On-Premise Model

On-premise network analysis applications are installed locally on a company's computers and servers. It is a comparatively expensive option but provides extra security and control over business data. Examples of the on-premise tool include NodeXL, UCINET, and Pajek.

NodeXL—NodeXL (an add-in for Microsoft Excel) is a free tool for social network analysis and visualization. It can help brands construct and analyze Facebook networks (based on co-likes and co-comments), Twitter networks (followers, followings, and tweets), and YouTube networks (user network and comments), among others.

UCINET—UCINET is a social network analysis software application for Windows operating system. It also includes the Netdraw tool for network visualization. It can be downloaded and used free of charge for 90 days: https://sites.google.com/site/ucinetsoftware/home.

Pajek—Pajek is a software application for analyzing and visualizing large networks (http://mrvar.fdv.uni-lj.si/pajek/). Pajek runs on Microsoft Windows operating systems and is free for non-commercial use.

Netminer—Netminer (http://www.netminer.com/) is also a software application for sizeable social network analysis and visualization. Netminer offers a free license to educators and students.

Cloud-Based Model

Cloud-based network analytics applications are hosted on a vendor's servers and accessed through a Web browser. Cloud-based model is very attractive to small and medium scale businesses providing them cost-effectiveness, scalability, and lower risks solution. Since the data is processed and hosted over the cloud, there is a possibility of loss of control on one's data. Examples of cloud-based applications include Polinode, Flocker, and Reach.

Polinode—Polinode is a cloud-based network analysis application to map, visualize, and analyze relationships across organizations (www.polinode.com).

Flocker—Flocker (http://flocker.outliers.es/) is a Twitter real-time retweets and mentions networks analytics tool.

Reach—Reach is a cloud platform to map hashtag networks and identify the most influential accounts of the Twitter conversation: http://www.reach-social.com/.

Mentionmapp—this online tool is used to investigate Twitter mentions networks (http://mentionmapp.com/).

CASE STUDY 5.1
DO SOCIAL MEDIA NETWORKS REFLECT SOCIAL CULTURE?

Background

Cultural values and norms form an integral part of a society in which "every person carries within him or herself patterns of thinking, feeling and potential acting which were learned throughout their lifetime" (Hofstede, 1984)(p. 4). Research has shown that culture can have a considerable influence on the use of technologies, as people with different cultural backgrounds perceive technologies differently (Hofstede, 1991, Hofstede, 1984, Simon, 2000). For example, a cross-cultural study of knowledge workers in the U.S. and Japan found that their cultural background played a significant role in their predisposition toward and selection of technologies (e.g., telephone and fax) (Straub, 1994).

However, little is known about the effects of various cultural dimensions such as collectivism and individualism (Hofstede, 1984) on the use of social media in the public sector. This raises the question as to how differences in cultural norms (e.g., those of the U.S. and Korea) influence social media use patterns and strategies in the public sector. This was the question a research team at Cyber Emotion Research Center in South Korea was determined to investigate. The research team knew that they could find an answer by mapping and analyzing social media networks formed by organizations from different cultures, hence were looking to leverage network analytics. The hypothesis was that cultural differences might be reflected in the structures of social media networks formed among people of various societies.

What They Did

Based on previous research on cultural difference, the team decided to investigate Twitter networks of South Korean and U.S. ministries. Korea is a hierarchical, collectivistic, and matriarchal society that avoids uncertainty and collectivism, whereas the U.S. is a nonhierarchical, individualistic, and patriarchal society that accepts uncertainty and emphasizes individualism (Hofstede, 1984, Hofstede, 1991). The researchers thought that a cross-cultural comparison of social media networks between South Korean and U.S. governments might provide a better understanding of the diverse patterns of social media use in the public sector.

To this end, the research team compiled a list of Twitter accounts utilized by the 40 Korean and 32 U.S. government agencies. The data on Twitter following-followers network was collected. The data was collected using an in-house software program with a design based on the Application Programming Interface (API) provided by Twitter.com.

The program can be used to submit queries to Twitter.com and process results. Once the network data was harvested, NodeXL was used to construct and visualize the networks. Also, with the help of a research assistant, some follow-up telephone interviews were conducted with the manager in charge of the Twitter accounts in selected ministries. The purpose of the interviews was to get a first-hand account of the Twitter communication strategies in the ministries that had dedicated social media staff. As it turns out, market research of this type has many applications beyond traditional marketing.

Results

The results were surprising and showed clear structural differences between the two Twitter networks. For example, South Korean ministries were well connected in a dense network of follower-following relationships, whereas U.S. government departments tended to be loosely connected (see Figure 5.6). Regarding network density (or, the portion of the potential connections in a network that are actual connections), the South Korean network (density = 0.86) was substantially denser than the U.S. network (density = 0.26).

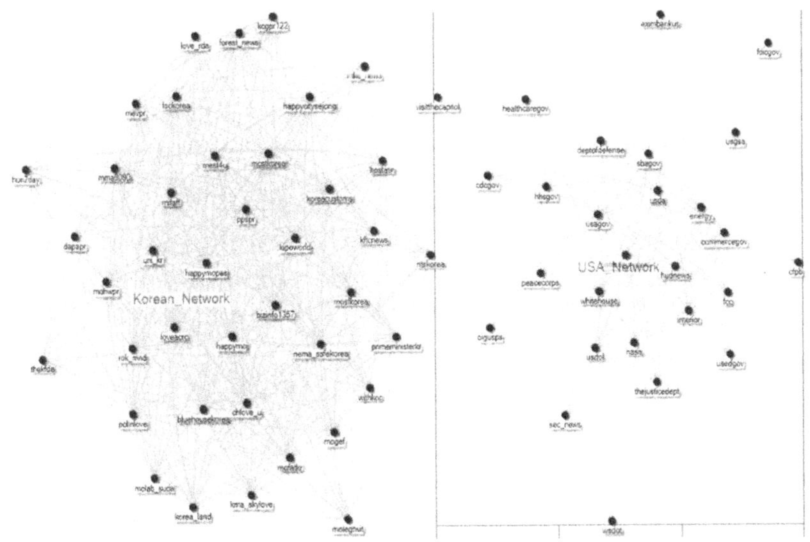

Figure 5.6. Follow-following Twitter network diagram of Korean and US public sector organizations

This density is a simple but useful measure of group cohesiveness. The Korean network had 1,348 (86%) ties, whereas the U.S. network had only 255 (26%). The clustering coefficient (i.e., the degree to which nodes in a network tend to cluster together) was higher for the Korean network (0.86) than for the U.S. network (0.50), indicating that the Korean network was more likely to form "cliques." In other words, Korean ministries tended to be locally embedded in dense neighborhoods (clusters). This was supported by the average degree (the average number of other government agencies followed by a government agency), which was much higher for Korean accounts (33) than for U.S. accounts (7.9). This indicates that, unlike U.S. government departments, almost all Korean ministries followed all other ministries.

What We Learn from the Case Study

The case study highlights the usefulness of the social media network and how it can be used to answer interesting real-world research questions. The research provided some new insights into the effects of cultural values and social norms (e.g., collectivism vs individualism) on the pattern of Twitter networks in the public sector. For example, Korea is a collectivistic society, whereas the U.S. is an individualistic one (Hofstede, 1984). In this regard, the result indicating a dense Twitter network of Korean ministries may reflect the country's collective norms in the online environment. Unlike organizations from individualistic cultures such as the U.S., who were loosely connected and tended to be interested more in engaging in individual communication (e.g., tweets) than in forming dense networks to pursue corporate agendas.

Source: The author compiled this case study from the study by Khan et al. (2014). Readers can access the complete version from Khan, G. F. Young, H., & Park, H. W. (2014). Social Media Communication strategies of Governments: A comparison of the USA and S. Korean governments, Asian Journal of Communication (SSCI), Vol. 24, No. 1, 2014, pp. 60–78.

TUTORIAL 5.1
ANALYZING SOCIAL MEDIA NETWORKS WITH NODEXL

INTRODUCTION

NodeXL is an easy and powerful tool for extracting, analyzing and visualizing social media networks. It is an add-in or template for Microsoft Excel and compatible with Excel 2007, Excel 2010, and Excel 2013. It can help you construct and analyze Facebook networks (based on co-likes and co-comments), Twitter networks (followers, followings, and tweets network), and YouTube networks (user network and comments), among others. In this tutorial, we will cover the essential features of NodeXL. A detailed tutorial on NodeXL can be found at https://www.smrfoundation.org.

INSTALLING AND RUNNING NODEXL

Step 1: Go to the https://nodexlgraphgallery.org and download the latest version of the NodeXL template, then run it. Please note that this tutorial is based on NodeXL Pro, which requires a license key. The basic version is still free but has limited functionalities.

Step 2: To open NodeXL after installation, in the Windows Start menu or Start screen, search for "NodeXL," then click "NodeXL Excel Template" in the search results.

After it is opened, you will notice that NodeXL has its menu ribbon available at the top right (Screenshot 5.1) and that the first Excel worksheet is called Edges (i.e., nodes). Other default four main sheets are "Vertices" (i.e., links), "Groups," "Group Vertices," and "Overall Metrics."

The Groups worksheet clusters the nodes by common attributes. NodeXL analyzes their connectedness and automatically groups them into specific clusters. The Overall Metrics worksheet shows the overall network measures, for example, density, degree, clustering coefficient, betweenness centrality, etc.

UNDERSTANDING NODEXL WORKFLOW

Screenshot 5.2 shows the workflow of NodeXL, which consists mainly of four steps:

- Importing data
- Cleaning data

- Calculating network analysis
- Visualizing the network

We will go through each of the stages in detail.

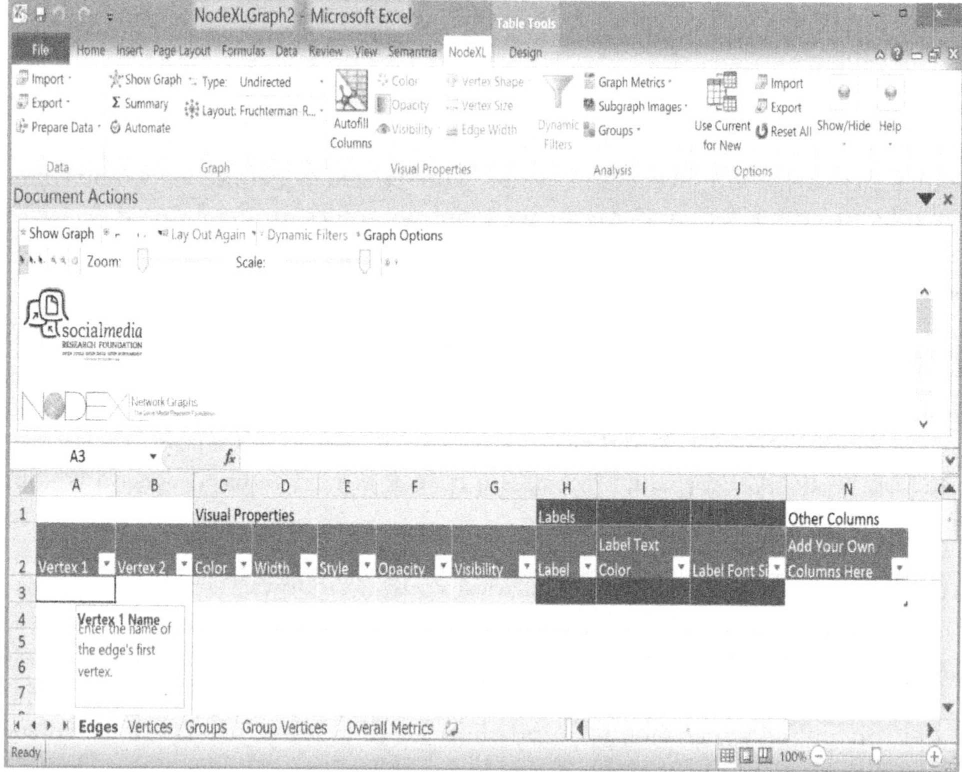

Screenshot 5.1. NodeXL template

Stage 1: Importing Network Data

The first step in analyzing networks with NodeXL is to import the network data. In NodeXL, network data can be imported from a variety of sources and formats, including Pajek files, UCINET[2], other spreadsheets, and comma separated value (CSV) files, and directly from social media sites. You can also start creating your network by manually typing a list of the edges in the network into the NodeXL sheet. With NodeXL social imports/plug-ins, data from a variety of social networks can be directly imported, including Facebook, Twitter, YouTube, Flickr, e-mail, Exchange, wikis, and surveys.

---

2 *Pajek and UNINET are social network analysis tools with their own network data formats and mechanisms.*

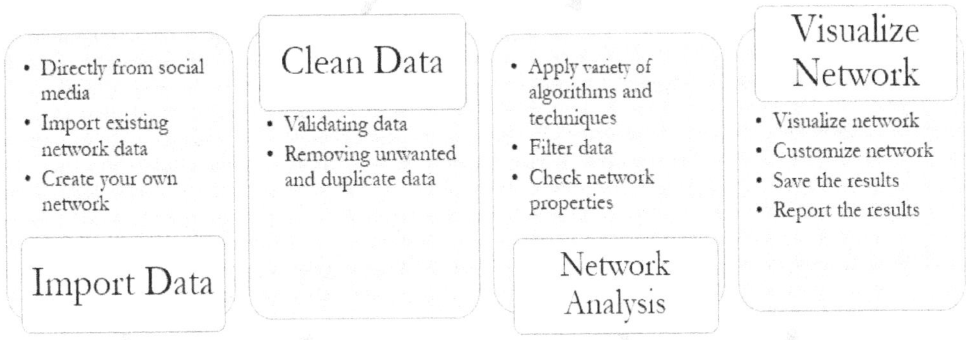

Directly from social media
Import existing network data
Create your own network
Import Data
Clean Data
Validating data
Removing unwanted and duplicate data
Apply variety of algorithms and techniques
Filter data
Check network properties
Network Analysis
Visualize Network
Visualize network
Customize network
Save the results
Report the results

Screenshot 5.2. NodeXL workflow stages

Social importers are regularly updated, and new social importers are made available on the NodeXL website. To add new social importers, use the following steps.

Importing Third-party Data Importers

Step 1: Download the installation zip file from the NodeXL social importer website: http://socialnetimporter.codeplex.com/.

Step 2: Unzip it and save it to your desktop (or any other location). After unzipping it, you will find the following four items:

FacebookAPI.DLL
FacebookAPI.pdb
SocialNetImporter.DLL
SocialNetImporter.pdb

Step 3: Now open the NodeXL template and then go to Import>Import Options>Browse. Locate and select the unzipped files you have just downloaded and then click "OK."

Step 4: Close and restart NodeXL. You should now see the "Facebook Import" option in the NodeXL> Import menu.

Note that other data importers, (e.g., e-mail, wiki, and VOSON) can be accessed and installed similarly by going to NodeXL>Data>Import menu>Get third-party Graph Data Importers.

In this tutorial, we will import data directly from a Facebook network.

Importing a Social Media Network Directly

Step 1: Open the NodeXL template and then click on File→Import**.** Note that there is a variety of options to import data. For this exercise, we will use a Facebook fan page network.

Step 2: Then click on "Import from Facebook Fan Page Networks."

Step 3: Next, you will be provided with the "Import from Facebook Fan Page Networks" dialogue box (Screenshot 5.3). To import the network, NodeXL should be authorized. Click on the "Log in" button available at the bottom of the dialogue box. Provide your Facebook username and password in the Facebook login window, and then click "Log In."

Step 4: Once you are connected to Facebook, you will be able to provide your Facebook fan page name or ID in the specified field. The ID or name of the fan page can be found in the fan page URL.

In this tutorial, we will extract data from the Centre for Social Technologies Facebook fan page. Select all the other desired options provided in the "Import from Facebook Fan Page Networks" dialogue box, such as network nodes (e.g., users will become nodes in the network), type of network relations (e.g., likes and comment will become links among the nodes), and edge creation options. You may also change the limit on the number of posts to include or specify a particular date for data extractions. Depending on the size of the activity on the fan page, choosing several options may cause it to take a long time to extract the data. Once you are ready, click the "Download" button to extract the network.

Stage 2: Cleaning the Network Data

After the network, data is downloaded, sift through the NodeXL worksheets, and verify, and clean the data if necessary. If the data looks right, proceed to the analysis stage.

Stage 3: Network Analysis

Step 1: Calculate the network properties by clicking on the "Graph Metrics" option available at the top of the NodeXL window.

Step 2: In the "GraphMetrics" window, select all the network measures of interest (e.g., overall graph metrics, degree, betweenness centrality, clustering coefficient, etc.) and then click on the "Calculate Metrics" button.

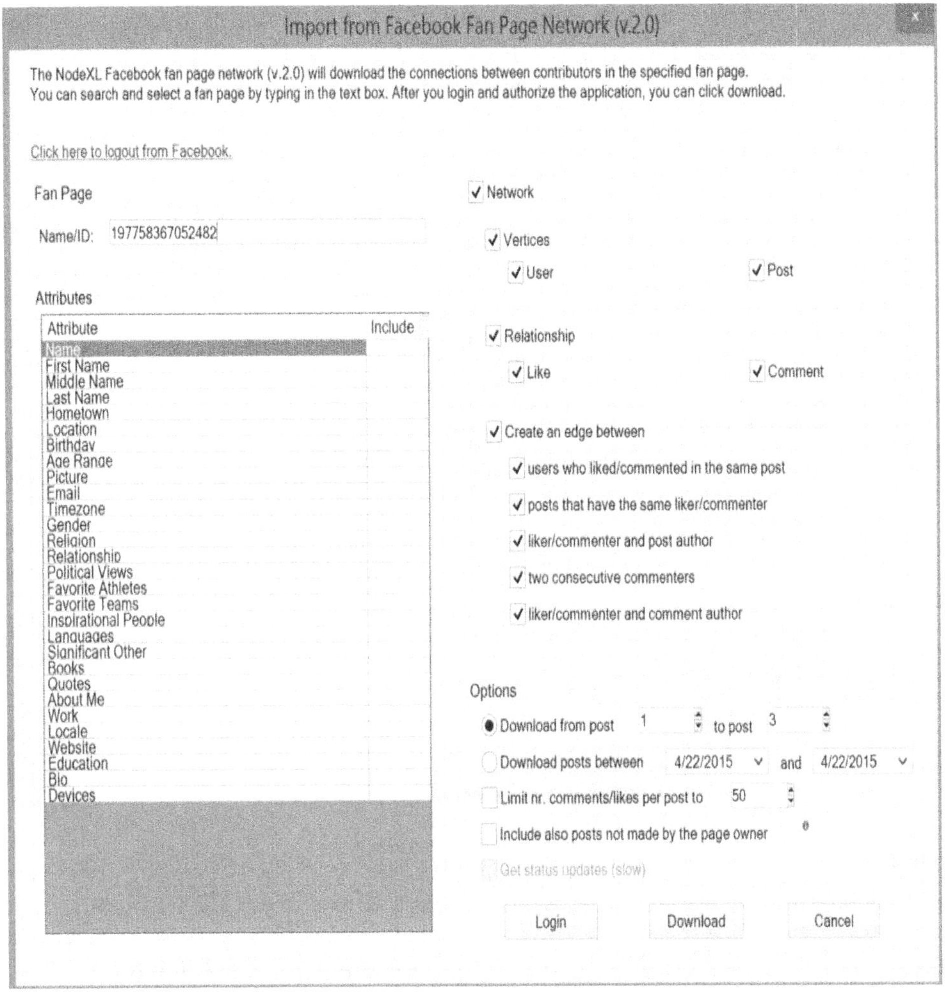

Screenshot 5.3. Import from Facebook fan page window

The network measure will be calculated and added to the NodeXL worksheets. You can explore, for example, the overall network measures in the "Overall Metrics" worksheet of the NodeXL. You can see that the network has 293 nodes and 1,216 edges (or links between the nodes). From the network density and diameter, it is evident the network is very sparse.

Step 4: Next, click on the "Show Graph" button to visualize the network.

Step 6: The constructed network will be displayed. However, the network is basic and does not carry much information (Screenshot 5.4).

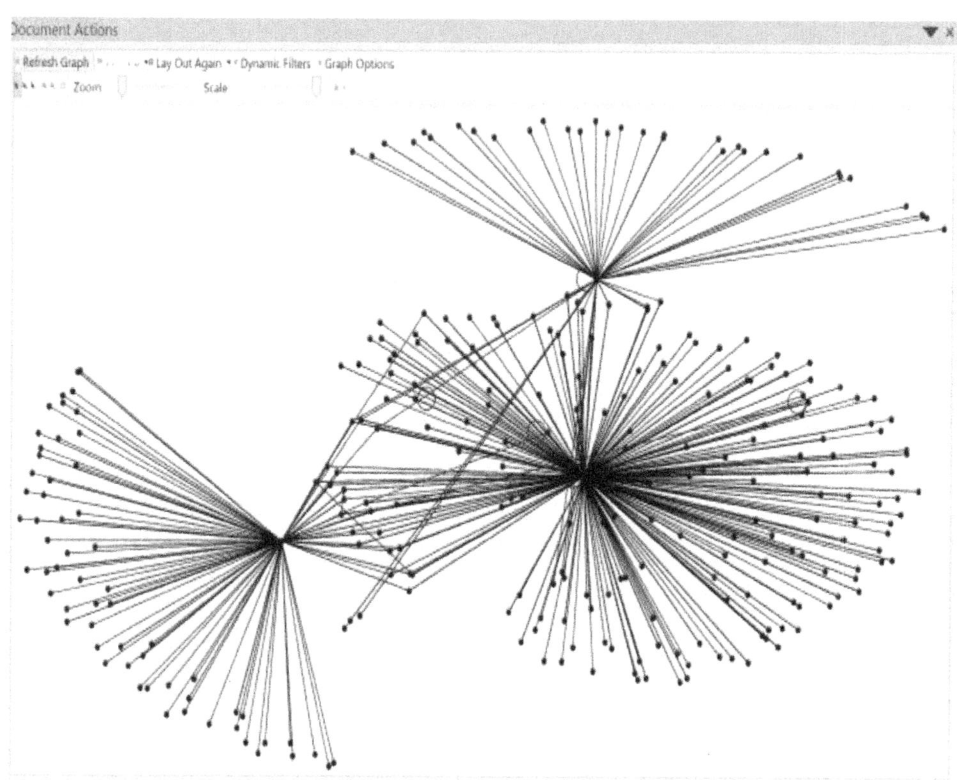

Screenshot 5.4. Facebook fan page network

Step 7: To make the network more constructive or informative, click on the "Autofill Columns" button available at the top of the NodeXL window.

Step 8: With the "Autofill Columns" functionality, you can alter the node and edge appearance (e.g., size, shape, color, opacity, or label) according to the network properties, such as degree centrality, betweenness centrality, clustering coefficient, and page rank. For example, node size can present importance (betweenness centrality), edge size can represent the strength of relationships among the nodes, and color of a node can be coded as gender.

Step 9: Click on the "Autofill Columns" and resize the vertices (fans) according to their in-degree centrality (so that the size of the node will represent importance regarding the number of connections a person has) (Screenshot 5.5). Also, set "Vertex Shape" to gender and color (in our dataset, gender is coded as 1=male and 2=female). To do so, click on the "Options" arrow and set 1= Disk and 2= Solid Squire.

Next, select the "Edge" tab, and set the width of the edge according to the number of comments/likes, so that the width of the link represents the strength of the relationships among the nodes regarding the number of comments/likes received. Set "Edge Label" to "Edge Type" to display the type of relationship among the nodes, such as Liker, Commenter, Post Author, Co-Liker, etc. Next, click the "Autofill" button to redraw the network.

Now the network conveys more useful insights (Screenshot 5.6). It is clear that there are three important male fans (circle nodes with a more significant size) in the network that drive most of the network activity, and that liking accounts for the majority of the network activity.

Autofill Columns

Edges Vertices Groups

When Autofill is clicked, fill in these worksheet columns...	...using the values in these source columns, if the columns exist	Options
Vertex Color	Gender	
Vertex Shape	Gender	
Vertex Size:	In-Degree	
Vertex Opacity		
Vertex Visibility		
Vertex Label		
Fill Color		
Vertex Label Position		
Vertex Tooltip		
Vertex Layout Order		
Vertex X		
Vertex Y		
Vertex Polar R		
Vertex Polar Angle		

Clear All Worksheet Columns Now

Reset All Autofill Settings

Autofill Close

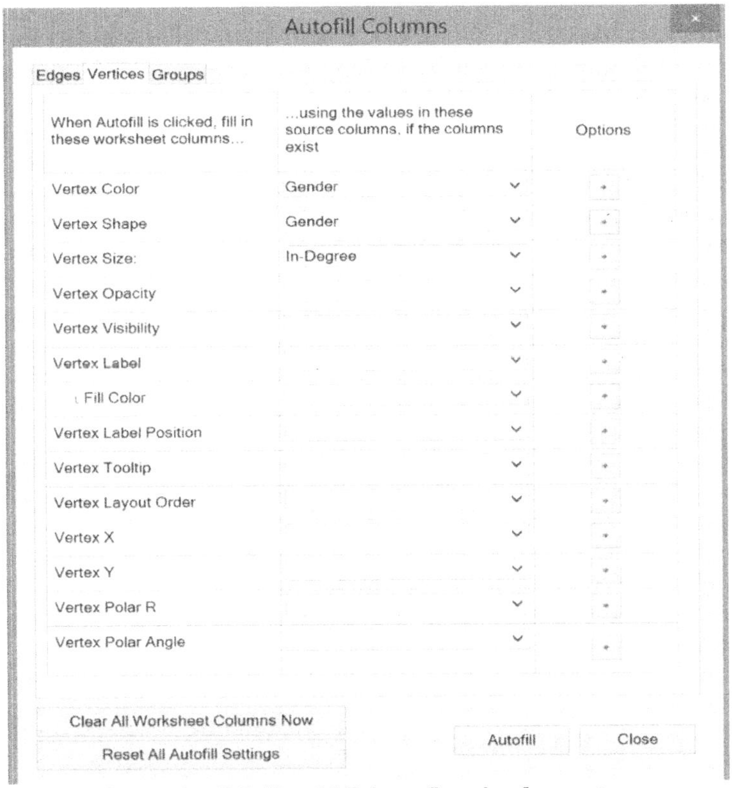

Screenshot 5.5. "Autofill Columns" window for vertices

In Screenshot 5.6 node size is proportional to node in-degree and node color and shape mapped to the Gender. Circle nodes are male, and squares are female fans. Links represent the type of relations (Liker, Commenters, and Users

Tagged, etc.) and width represents the strength of ties.

Further Adjustments

Several useful adjustments can be performed to the network with the NodeXL template. Next, we briefly discuss some of the relevant options.

Adjust Layout: with the help of "Adjust Layout," you can adjust the layout of the network (i.e., where each node in the network will be located) using a variety of different algorithms available at the "Adjust Layout" dropdown list. These include a force-directed Fruchterman-Reingold layout algorithm for automatically grouping tightly connected nodes, as well as circles, grids, and spirals.

Apply Dynamic Filters: Dynamic filters trim parts of the network and then recalculate network metrics and layout based on the remaining nodes and edges. With dynamic filters, edges, and nodes can be selectively hidden or shown, depending on the attributes of the network. For example, the in-degree filter will conceal less critical nodes.

Graph Options: **Graph** options allow further customization of the network layout, such as changing edge color, arrow size, and curvature. An updated network is shown (in the Screenshot 5.7) after the application of some these options.

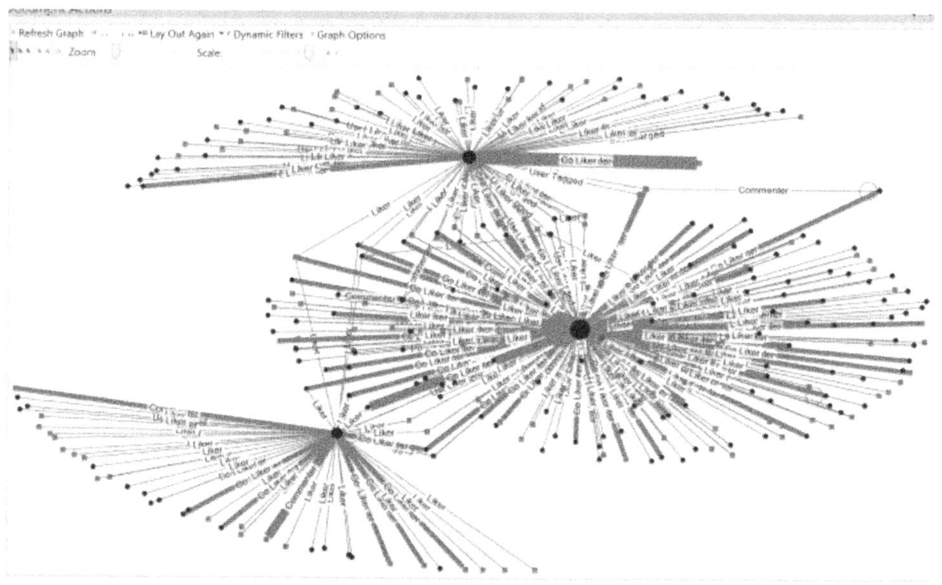

Screenshot 5.6. Facebook fan network updated

Saving the Network

Saving the diagram: To save the network diagram to your computer, right-click on the network diagram and then click on "Save Image of File→Save Image."

Saving the network data: The network data can be saved in its native NodeXL format for future use ("File→Save"), or it can be exported into a different format to be used in various network analysis tools (such as UCINET and Pajek files). The "Export" menu is available at the top left a corner of the NodeXL window (below "Import").

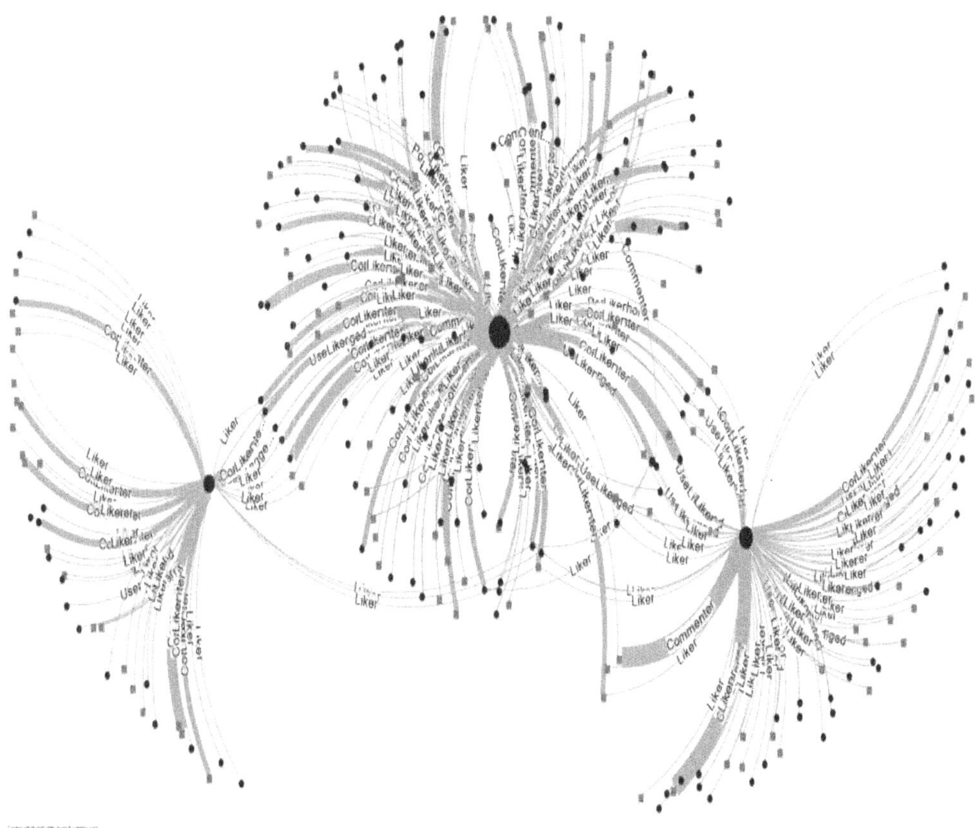

Screenshot 5.7. Facebook fan network after application of graph options

REVIEW QUESTIONS

1. What is a network?
2. What is the purpose of network analytics?
3. Briefly differentiate among social networks, social network sites, social networking, and social network analysis.
4. Briefly explain the different types of social media networks.
5. What is the difference between explicit and implicit networks?
6. What is the difference between one mode, two-mode, and multimode networks?
7. Differentiate between weighted and unweighted networks.
8. Briefly define relevant node-level properties, such as degree, betweenness, eigenvector centralities, and structural holes.
9. Briefly explain important network-level properties, such as clustering coefficient, density, diameter, average degree, and components.

EXERCISE 4.1: UNDERSTANDING NETWORK FUNDAMENTALS

Consider the following sample network:

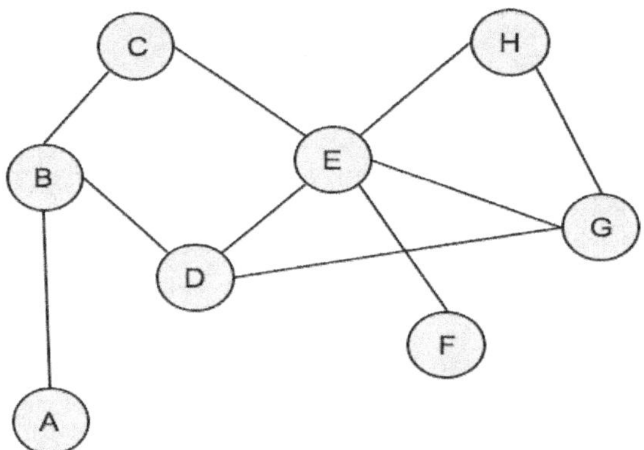

Figure 5.7. Example network

Moreover, answer the following questions about this graph.

1. How many nodes are in the network?
2. How many edges are in the network?
3. Is this graph directed or undirected?
4. Which node(s) have the highest degree? What is the degree? Which node(s) have the lowest degree? What is the degree?
5. What is the degree distribution for this graph?
6. What is the length of the shortest path from node A to node F?
7. What is the density of this graph?

EXERCISE 4.2: NETWORK ANALYSIS

This exercise will put to the test all the network analysis concepts and techniques you learned in this chapter. You will be provided with a sample network dataset to construct, analyze, and visualize a network from. Your goal is to write a 2 to 3 page single-spaced report about the network, describe its exciting features, essential institutions, and relationships.

Data Source

Download the New Zealand's knowledge network data file from the book companion site. It represents a sample of New Zealand's scholarly network based on 3,385 computer science related publications from 1972-2016. In the dataset, nodes represent authors and links represent co-authorship relations. The network data file is in the .net format, which can be opened/read by either NodeXL or Gephi (or any other tool of your choice that supports the .net extension). A tutorial on Gephi is available here: https://gephi.org/users/quick-start/.

Your Task

Your goal is to visualize the network and write a short report describing exciting features, essential institutions, and ties in the network. This is not something you can do just by looking at the network structure. You will need to analyze both the node and network level properties. You should provide an in-depth investigation into this network explaining who the central institutions/universities are. What is their role in the network (e.g., what are their Degree, Betweenness, and Eigenvector Centralities)? What are the significant clusters or groups? Besides, what does each group represent?

Figure 5.8 is an example of the network constructed from the same data using NodeXL. In the network, nodes represent institutions and links represent co-authorship ties. In this instance, node size represents betweenness centrality, and connections width portrays the intensity of the collaboration.

Your Report

It is vital to ensure that your final report is analytical rather than descriptive and should include the following analysis:

- Include a meaningful visualization of the network. Try to replicate the Figure 5.8. You should filter the network, for example, highlighting the critical nodes and show the intensity of collaboration among the institutions (e.g., with link widths and colors).

- Include network level statistics (such as the total number of nodes, clustering coefficient, average degree, density, and diameter of the network) with a brief explanation of results. What else do the statistics say about the network structure?
- Include a list of the top 10 nodes (institutions) regarding degree, betweenness, and eigenvector centralities accompanied by a concise explanation of the results. Instead of just reporting the result, give a meaningful description of who the institutions are, what their role is in the network, and how their research activities relate to that role, etc.
- Regarding e*igenvector centrality*, what is the position of Waikato University as compared to others and what does it mean?

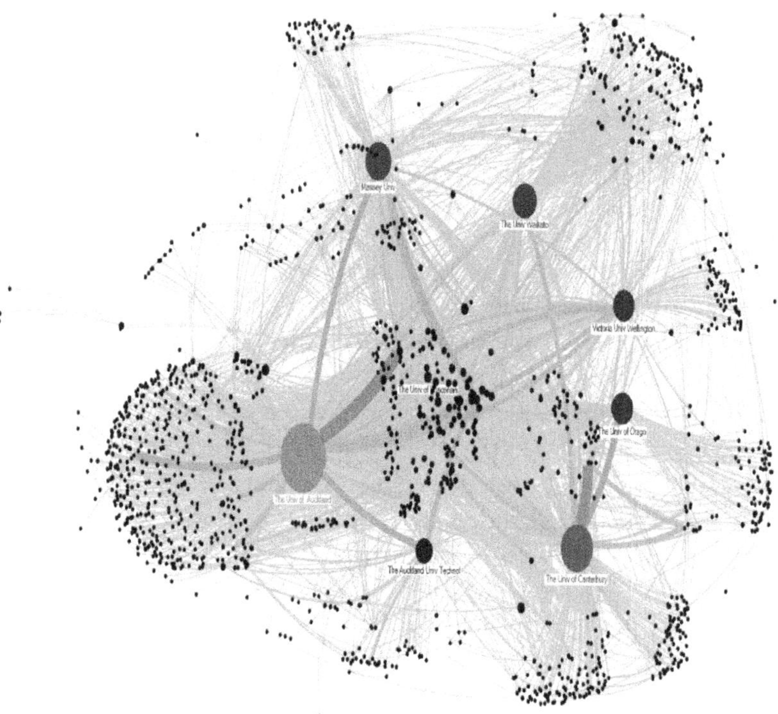

Figure 5.8. New Zealand's knowledge network (Computer Science Field 1972-2016)

CHAPTER 5 REFERENCES

BIUK-AGHAI, R. P. Visualizing Co-Authorship Networks in Online Wikipedia. 2006 International Symposium on Communications and Information Technologies, Oct. 18 2006-Sept. 20 2006 2006. 737-742.

BJÖRNEBORN, L. & INGWERSEN, P. 2004. Toward a basic framework for webometrics. *Journal of the American Society for Information Science and Technology,* 55, 1216-1227.

BURT, R. 1992. *Structural Holes: The Social Structure of Competition,* Cambridge, MA, Harvard University Press.

HANNEMAN, R. A. & RIDDLE, M. 2005. *Introduction to social network methods,* Riverside, CA, University of California. Published in digital form at http://faculty.ucr.edu/~hanneman/).

HOFSTEDE, G. 1984. Cultural dimensions in management and planning. *Asia Pacific Journal of Management* 1, 81-99.

HOFSTEDE, G. 1991. *Cultures and Organizations: Software of the Mind,* London, McGraw-Hill.

LATAPY, M., MAGNIEN, C. & VECCHIO, N. D. 2008. Basic notions for the analysis of large two-mode networks. *Social Networks,* 30, 31-48.

LIU, X., BOLLEN, J., NELSON, M. L. & VAN DE SOMPEL, H. 2005. Co-authorship networks in the digital library research community. *Information Processing & Management,* 41, 1462-1480.

MARSDEN, P. V. 2008. *Network Data and Measurement,* London, Sage.

NOOY, W. D., MRVAR, A. & AL., E. 2005. *Exploratory Social Network Analysis with Pajek (Structural Analysis in the Social Sciences)* New York, Cambridge University Press.

SIMON, S. J. 2000. The impact of culture and gender on web sites: an empirical study. *SIGMIS Database,* 32, 18-37.

SMITH, M. A., RAINIE, L., SHNEIDERMAN, B. & HIMELBOIM, I. 2014. Mapping Twitter Topic Networks: From Polarized Crowds to Community Clusters. Pew Research Center, available at: http://www.pewinternet.org/2014/02/20/mapping-twitter-topic-networks-from-polarized-crowds-to-community-clusters/

STRAUB, D. W. 1994. The Effect of Culture on IT Diffusion: E-Mail and FAX in Japan and the U.S. *Information Systems Research,* 5, 23-47.

WASSERMAN, S. & FAUST, K. 1994. *Social Networks Analysis: Methods and Applications,* Cambridge, UK, Cambridge University Press.

Chapter 6

Capturing Value with Text Analytics

"To do big data well, you need text analytics skills." –**Lori Siegel**

Learning Outcomes

After completing this chapter, the reader should be able to:

- Comprehend basic social text analytics concepts and tools.
- Understand uses of text analytics by business, government, academia, and financial institutes.
- Recognize objectives of social media text analytics for business intelligence purposes including sentiment analysis, concept mining, trends mining, and topic mining.
- Comprehend text analytics cycle and the steps required to mine business insights from the text.
- Understand different types of text analytics terms, methods, and algorithms.
- Extract and analyze social media text.
- List common text analytics limitations and issues.

INTRODUCTION

Text is one of the fundamental elements of the social media platforms. Textual elements of social media include comments, tweets, blog posts, product reviews, and status updates. *Social media text analytics*, also known as *text mining*, is a technique to extract, analyze, and interpret hidden business insights from textual elements of social media content. Organizations use text analysis techniques to extract hidden valuable meanings, patterns, and structures from the user-generated social media text for business intelligence purposes. Text Analytics is a specialized subject, and in this book, we have done our best to explain it in the most straightforward way we can.

Text analytics is something that is performed on large sets of textual social media data (such as comments and reviews), as reading large quantities of textual data is usually not feasible. Text analytics techniques turn text into numbers by applying linguistic, statistical, and machine learning techniques to get insights that we might not get otherwise. However, the danger of doing so is that the transformation of text into numbers risks losing part of the essence of the textual information being transformed.

Text analytics, for example, is useful in gaining a quick and accurate understanding of the emotion and sentiment expressed over social media channels (e.g., tweets or Facebook comments) related to a brand or a new product launch. The case study included in this chapter demonstrates this point and shows how Flyertalk.com successfully mined the textual feedback that their current and potential customers provide on their website. The volume and speed at which the comments over social media are generated do not allow for manual reading and calls for advanced text analysis techniques.

Text analytics has evolved into a well-established field with roots in a variety of domains; including data mining, machine learning, natural language processing, knowledge management, and information retrieval. Studies have suggested that approximately 80 percent of data in an organization is textual; in this book, however, we only focus on social media text analytics.

Text analytics tools, such as IBM Watson Analytics for Social Media and Lexalytics provide free trials for anyone to try out, and we provided a tutorial on these tools in this chapter. We advocate for the use of text analytics more widely, but for most organizations, it remains a "niche" activity. However, everyone in the world uses text analytics several times a day – the Google search engine is the most potent text analytics engine that exists, and Google is doing everything we discussed in this chapter for text queries and search results. This text analytics process includes activities involving no analytics such as counting words, word distance from a word of interest (such as 'wellness' or 'illnesses') and word category. In this process, sentence structure, punctuation, and word groupings are all eliminated. More profound insights can arise when different sources of data (demographics, psychographics, and customer journey) are merged with text analytics data.

TYPES OF SOCIAL MEDIA TEXT

Based on its nature, we can broadly classify social media text into two categories: 1) dynamic text and 2) static text.

Dynamic Text

Dynamic text is a real-time social media user-generated text or statement that expresses an opinion about content or information posted on social media. A social media user posts dynamic text in response to social, political, economic, personal, cultural, or business issues to express their views and feelings related to it. Dynamic text is usually smaller in length (e.g., a couple of sentences), diverse in nature, and is updated or deleted more frequently. Examples of dynamic social media text include tweets, Facebook comments, and product reviews. Below, we briefly explain the most common dynamic social media texts.

Tweet

A *tweet* is a one hundred forty-character message posted by a Twitter user. A tweet may include text, images, video, or links to other websites. A tweet may also include a hashtag (#). Hashtags are used to mark keywords or topics in a tweet and are organically created by Twitter users as a method to categorize messages. A keyword marked by a hashtag can quickly appear in Twitter search, and popular hashtags are often trending topics on Twitter. Tweets accumulate over time, carry a time stamp and user information, and mostly appear in descending order; that is, the most recent first. Tweet data provides a valuable source for mining valuable business insights, including exploring trending topics, measuring brand sentiment, and gathering feedback on products and services.

Comments

Social media *comments* are written (usually short) statements that express opinions about content or information posted on social media. While most comments are text only, it can also include images, video, or links to other websites. The ability to post comments and participate in social media discourse is the underlying characteristic that distinguishes social media from traditional media (e.g., TV and print). Like tweets, social media comments are also an excellent source for mining valuable business insights from social media. Almost all social media platforms provide commenting features. Comments accumulate over time, carry a time stamp and user information, and mostly appear in descending order; that is, the most recent first.

Discussion

Social media *discussions* take the form of textual or written conversation or debate about a particular topic, product, or service. Mostly, discussions among social media users happen through Internet forums. Internet discussion forums are treelike in structure; that is, a forum can contain other sub-forums focused on specific topics or threads. In these forums, users can post questions and reply to questions posted by other users. Discussions accumulate over time, carry a time stamp and user information, and mostly appear in descending order; that is, the most recent first. Vault Network is an example of an Internet forum that focuses on online games.

Conversation

Social media textual *conversation* (also known as chatting) is an instant exchange of short written messages between two more people. Chatting usually takes a casual form and are carried out through dedicated messaging services/tools. A variety of messaging tools have been developed for textual conversation, including desktop-based (e.g., Skype); web-based (e.g., Google Hangouts and Facebook chat) and mobile-based (e.g., Viber). Note that these services are not just limited to the textual conversation, they also support video and voice conversation. Now that all media are converging, most of the messaging services come in desktop, mobile, and web forms. For example, Skype has both desktop and Smartphone versions. An important point to note here is that most of the social media textual conversation is private and may not be subject to mining.

Reviews

Reviews are critical evaluations of a product or service performed by customers and experts. They can take both longer and shorter forms. Reviews by customers are mostly shorter when compared to formal reviews by experts. Reviews can include textual elements and ratings. ProductReview.com.au, for example, is a site devoted to product/service reviews and ratings submitted by customers. Product reviews can serve as an excellent source for mining customers' opinions and feelings about a product or service.

Static Text

Static social media text is usually abundant in length (e.g., several paragraphs) and is generated, updated, or deleted less frequently. Examples of static text include wiki content, a blog page, Word documents, corporate reports, electronic mail (e-mail), and news transcripts. At the highest level of abstraction, the purpose of static social media text is to inform, educate, and elaborate.

TEXT ANALYTICS INDUSTRY

The text analytics industry is vast and growing fast. According to some estimates, it is expected that the global text analytics market could reach $6.5 Billion by 2020 growing at a rate of ~25% from 2013 through 2020 (Figure 6.1). The primary factors responsible for the growth of the text analytics market is the big textual data being generated from various sources such as social networking sites, emails, chats, comments, documents, tweets, web blogs, and forums.

According to a 2013-2020 report by Allied Market Research, critical players in text analytics market are IBM, Microsoft, Oracle, Microstrategy, HP, SAP, Tableau, OpenText, SAS Institute, Attensity, and Larasoft.

Most text analytics tools are very costly. Depending on the version, complexity, and type of analysis, the cost may range from $500-$3500 per month. Due to high-cost considerations, many companies do not use text analytics at all which in turn negatively affects the global text analytics market.

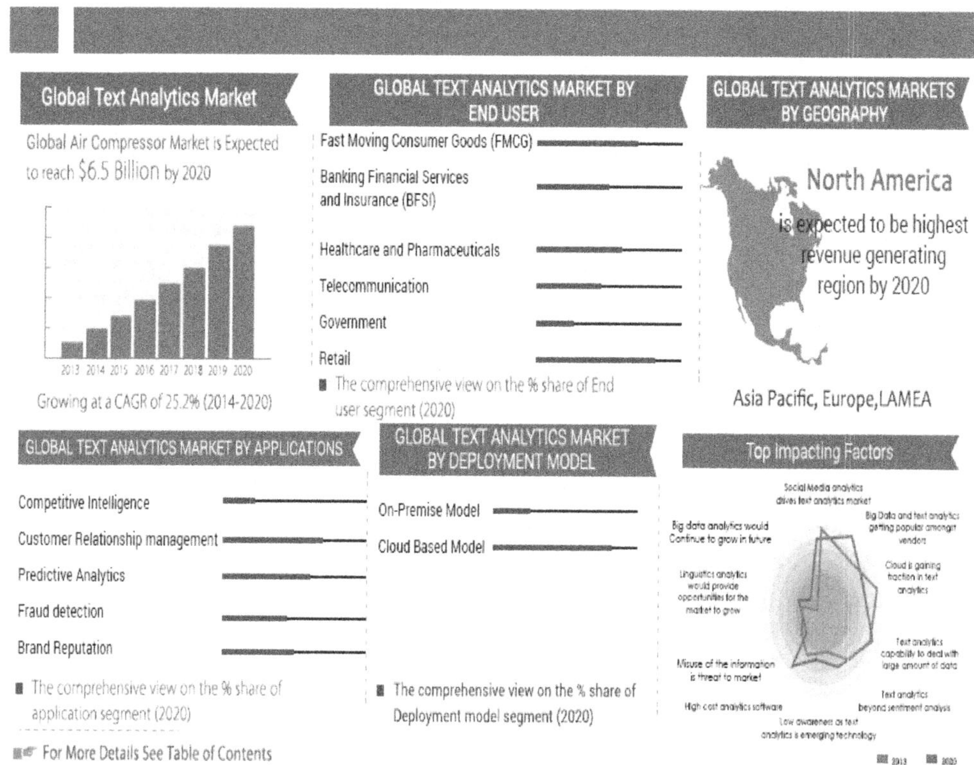

Figure 6.1. Text analytics industry
Source: http://www.datanami.com/

TEXT ANALYTICS DEPLOYMENT MODELS

Based on the deployment model, we can segment the global text analytics market into two:

- On-Premise Model
- Cloud-Based Model

On-Premise Model

This model provides *on-premise* text analytics capabilities to organizations. Typically, organizations purchase text analytics applications and use it on local servers/computers. It is a comparatively expensive option but provides extra security and control. For this reason, government agencies mostly see on-premise model as favorable compared to cloud-based models.

Cloud-Based Model

Going cloud is comparatively low cost and considered the most significant revenue-generating segment that is significantly contributing to the growth of global text analytics market. *Cloud-based models* are particularly attractive to small and medium scale businesses providing them cost-effectiveness, scalability, and lower risks solution.

PURPOSE OF TEXT ANALYTICS

Various sectors including government, telecommunications, pharmaceutical, retail, healthcare, academia, banking, financial, and insurance services employ text analytics. The use of text analytics comes from market research, competitive intelligence, and counter-terrorism/threat detection to medical research. Here we discuss some of them.

Uses by Business

Businesses use text analytics for a variety of purposes including market research, survey content analysis, social media analysis, the voice of customers, churn analysis, competitive intelligence, risk analysis, and document analysis. For example, research suggests that adding unstructured textual information into a conventional churn prediction model (i.e., models that identify those customers that are most likely to discontinue using a service or product) resulted in a significant increase in predictive performance (Coussement & Van den Poel, 2008). Such predictions can help managers identify customers at risk of switching thus organizing a pre-emptive customer retention campaigns.

Uses by Government

Application of text analytics in the government sector can vary from counter-terrorism, cyber-security, bio-surveillance, to health analytics. An increasing number of governments from around the world use text analytics, for example, for national security purposes, primarily by monitoring and analysis of social networking sites, blogs, forums, and instant messages (Zanasi, 2009). In the area of bio-surveillance, government agencies need to develop and adequately coordinate responses to potential epidemics (such as the Ebola virus) or acts of bioterrorism (such as anthrax letters). By combining social media data (such as chats and comments) with organizational data from sources such as 911 calls, poison control centers and hospitals, government agencies use text analytics to detect potential epidemics ahead of time. Such early detection enables government agencies to take proactive steps to limit the spread of disease, for instance, by providing early warnings and recommendations to citizens and health care providers. They also use text analysis to characterize the rise and decline of bio-events accurately, so resources can be efficiently allocated, resulting in substantial health care savings.

Uses by Academia

One of the critical areas where academics use text analytics is to understand important topics and patterns in research studies and how it applies to current research endeavors. Analyzing research publications also helps us understand the fading and emerging topics of interest. Such analysis also ensures that any future activities do not repeat the mistakes of the past. For example, Khan and Wood (2015) analyzed the contents of 351 information technology management (ITM) scientific publications and reported the latest emerging and disappearing topics in this research domain. The most significant keyword trends in the field of ITM included digital (from 2013 to 2016), governance (2012-2016), performance (2011-2016), value (2011-2016), adopt (2010-2016) and framework (2010-2016). These highlight potential areas of research that are very much the focus of today's contemporary research. On the other hand, the analysis also shows which areas of research are not as significant as they once were and as a result fail to be included in either titles or keyword lists; these include the likes of planning (1999–2007), innovation (2007–2010), technology(1989–2000), and strategic (1985–1998). In terms of author supplied keywords, current trends show that digital (2013-present), alignment (2013-present), cloud (2012-present), software (2012-present) and ITM (2011-present) are still very much in vogue, while system (1991–1998), planning (1992–1999), technology (1993–1996), reengineering (1995–2000), and integrate (2003–2007) are no longer as widespread as they once were (Khan & Wood, 2015).

Uses by Financial Institutes

Text analytics is useful in early warnings for financial crises and fraud. Social media data, for instance, has been used to highlight economic trends (such as severely reduced spending) as an early signal for impending job loss. Such social media monitoring also serves as a safeguard against illegal, discriminatory, and fraudulent practices, saving government and individuals countless dollars in damages.

SOCIAL MEDIA TEXT ANALYTICS FOR BUSINESS INTELLIGENCE

The following are some of the objectives of social media text analytics for business intelligence purposes (Figure 6.2).

Sentiment Analysis

Sentiment analysis examines and categorizes social media text as being positive, negative, or neutral. Social media sentiment analysis usually focuses on dynamic text. It is mostly a collection of methods used since 1995. The primary purpose of sentiment analysis is to determine how customers feel about a particular product, service, or issue. For example, as a manager of a recently launched product, you might be interested to know how your customers on Twitter feel about a new product/service launch. Analyzing a brand's tweets or Facebook comments may provide an answer to such questions. Using sentiment analysis, a brand may be able to extract the wordings of the comments and determine if they are positive, negative, or neutral.

Sentiment analysis can be used to understand how others see the world on the subject of the data being studied. Sentiment analysis works by comparing the words in documents to external tag lists of words (called lexicons) that are classified as positive or negative. The overall balance of positive to negative words determines the sentiment score of a document (this can be done on the sentence level as well). The type of list (lexicon/dictionary) is often subjective and applied arbitrarily by whoever composes the list; these definitions may or may not work well in every situation. At the end of the chapter, we list several analytical tools for semantic analysis.

A later section of the chapter provides a systematic guide to analyze social media textual data using Semantria (a text sentiment analysis tool). It will go through the following steps to extract sentiments from a document:

Step 1: It breaks the document into its basic parts of speech, called POS tags, which identify the structural elements of a sentence (e.g., nouns, adjectives, verbs, and adverbs).

Step 2: Algorithms identify sentiment-bearing phrases like "terrible service" or "cool atmosphere."

Step 3: Each sentiment-bearing phrase earns a score based on a logarithmic scale ranging from negative ten to positive ten.

Step 4: Next, the scores are combined to determine the overall sentiment of the document or sentence. Document scores range between negative two and positive two. For example, to calculate the sentiment of a phrase such as "terrible service," Semantria uses search engine queries similar to the following:

"(Terrible service) near (good, wonderful, spectacular)"
"(Terrible service) near (bad, horrible, awful)"

Each result is added to a hit count; these are then combined using a mathematical operation called "log odds ratio" to determine the final score of a given phrase.

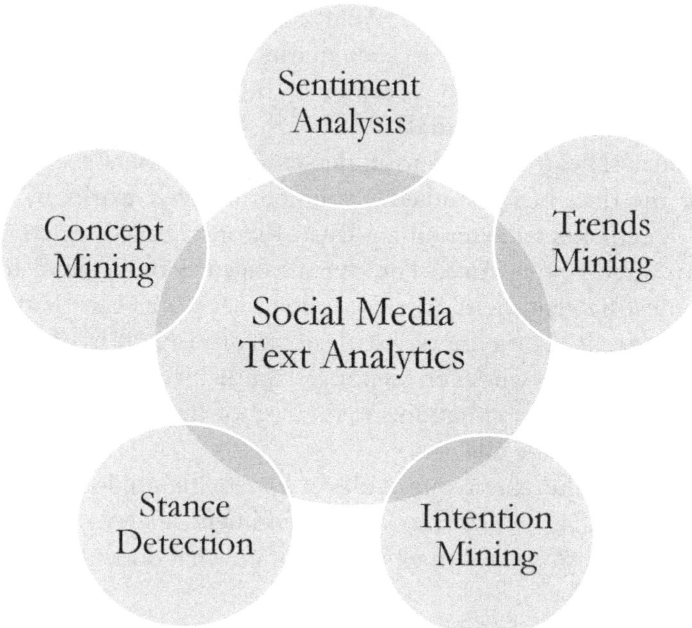

Figure 6.2. Purpose of social media text analytics

There has been a lot of misuse and misrepresentation of sentiment analysis capabilities, but there are still excellent and valid reasons to employ it within text analytics, provided there is a good set of data (sample frame) to work with.

Intention Mining

Intention or *intent mining* aims to discover users' intention (such as buy, sell, recommend, quit, desire, or wish) from natural language social media text such as user comments, product reviews, tweets, and blog posts (Chen, 2002). Social media is an integral part of our contemporary lives and is widely used by millions of customers to express desires, needs, and intention (Niven, 2013). Companies may use intent mining to find new potential customers who intend to buy a product (or services) and service existing customers who have trouble with a product. For example, an analysis of company-related tweets may detect purchase intention based on the presence of the word "buy" or "purchase." Similarly, detecting the "quit" intention may identify and service the customers at risk of leaving the company. The Semantria analytical tool discussed later in this chapter, for example, can be used to mine intentions.

Trends Mining

Trends mining, also known as *predictive analytics* uses enormous amounts of historical and real-time social media data to predict future events. For example, we can mine a vast amount of social media data (e.g., comments and tweets) to identify patterns and trends for new product or service development or to improve customer satisfaction by anticipating their needs. Trend mining exploits patterns in large amounts of data by using sophisticated statistical techniques, including machine learning, data mining, and social network analysis. Predictive analysis using conventional business data has been used in a variety of domains, including marketing, banking, telecommunication, and healthcare. However, social media predictive analytics is still an emerging practice and may take some time for sophisticated tools and techniques to emerge.

Concept Mining

Concept mining aims to extract ideas and concepts from documents. Unlike text mining, which is focused on extracting information, concept mining extracts ideas from large document sets. Thus, concept mining is useful in extracting ideas from massive amounts of static social media text, such as wiki content, a web page, Word documents, and news transcripts. Concept mining can be employed to classify, cluster, and rank ideas.

Concept analysis works best when the information is already cleaned and organized, but sometimes just running any text through topic analysis can reveal interesting patterns for further analysis, such as the content of the author's Twitter profile shown in Figure 6.3. Readers are encouraged to experiment with their tweets or websites using http://tweettopicexplorer.neoformix.com. Explore the various bubbles that are organized by the software into clusters. While the clustering is not based on the meanings of the sentences but rather the words used, it is an advance over merely looking at the text without structuring it.

Stance Detection

While sentiment analysis is used to decide whether a piece of text is positive, negative, or neutral, *stance detection*, however, determines a social media user's "favorability towards a given target and the target even may not be explicitly mentioned in the text."(Krejzl, Hourová, & Steinberger, 2017)(p.1). *Stance detection* can be formally defined as a method of automatically detecting whether the author of a piece of social media text (e.g., comments or tweets) is in favor of the given target (an entity or a topic), against it, or neither. Based on this definition, it can be considered a sub-category of opinion mining and sentiment analysis. However, stance detection techniques are used to decide a user's favorability towards an entity or a topic, and the target may even not be explicitly mentioned in the textual conversation.

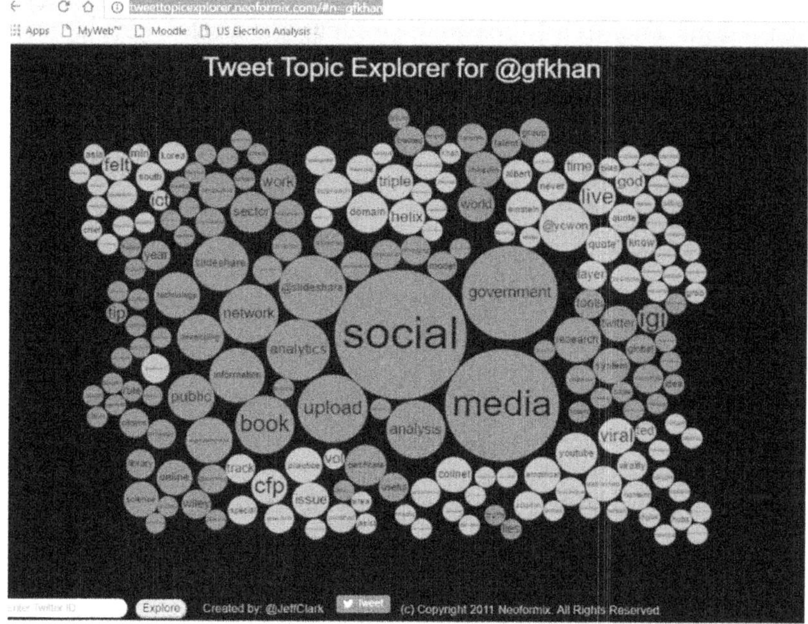

Figure 6.3. Twitter content for @gfkhan

TEXT ANALYTICS VALUE CREATION CYCLE

Text analytics, like any other form of social media analytics, is the art and science of getting the desired business intelligence from the text posted on social media. While the steps required for text analytics are mostly dependent on the type of approach and tool employed, a typical social media *text analytics value creation cycle* includes the following cyclical steps (see Figure 6.4).

Identification and Searching

The text analytics process starts with identifying the source of the text that we want to analyze. Text posted on social media is dynamic, vast, diverse, multilingual, and noisy. Thus, finding the right source for text analytics is crucial for gaining useful business insights. The genre of the source text will also determine the type of tool used to extract and analyze it. For example, extracting tweets requires different tools and approaches than analyzing a document or website text. Analyzing tweets, for example, requires API-based searching and extraction of data from the Twitter timeline based on criteria that a user specifies. A brand can choose to extract tweets that include specific keywords, such as a product and brand name. The desired business questions that a brand needs to answer with text analytics will serve as a good starting point.

Text Parsing and Filtering

The next step is to parse, clean, filter the text, and create a dictionary of words using natural language processing (NPL), which is mostly based on machine learning techniques. For computer and algorithms to extract meanings from the text, the sentence structures and parts of speech are determined, named entities extracted (people, organizations, product/service names, so forth), stop words removed, and spellings are checked. Most of these steps are automatic; however, at certain stages, human intervention is required. For example, in the filtering stage, manually cleaning (by humans with domain expertise) may be required to remove unwanted or irrelevant terms.

Text Transformation

Before the application of analytical algorithms to any text, it should be transformed into a computer-readable format (e.g., 0s and 1s) for analysis. The cleaned text is thus transformed into numerical representations using linear algebra-based techniques, such as latent semantic analysis (LSA) and vector space models (VSM).

LSA technique is a natural language processing technique for extracting and representing the contextual meaning of words and passages from a large swath of text.

VSM is an algebraic model for representing text documents used in information filtering, information retrieval, indexing, and relevancy rankings.

Text Mining

At this step, the text is mined to extract the needed business insights. Varieties of text mining algorithms are applied to the text, such as clustering, association, classification, and predictive analysis, and sentiment analysis. Text analysis employs these sophisticated algorithms to extract sentiment and meanings from the text in a similar manner to the way humans do; however, the process is thousands of times faster.

Association

Association or *association mining* is a data-mining technique used to determine the probability of the co-occurrence of items in a collection of documents. The relationships between co-occurring items are expressed as association rules. In text analytics, for example, social media text can be clustered together based on co-occurrence frequency. Alternatively, it can also be used to find that a user who liked a social media content A and B is 90 percent likely also to like content C.

Clustering

Clustering or *cluster analysis* groups objects based on similarity in non-overlapping groups. Clustering is an integral part of data mining and text analytics. Social media text, for example, can be clustered into positive, negative, and neutral categories. On the other hand, nodes in a social media network can be clustered based on importance. Clustering of words is usually based on how closely the words are related (being the most similar). There are many families of clustering methods. Some of the well-known are hierarchical clustering, k-means clustering, and distribution-based clustering.

Hierarchical Clustering

Hierarchical clustering also known as *connectivity based clustering* groups objects (for example words in a text corpus) to form clusters based on their distance. The main idea behind hierarchical clustering is that objects are more related to nearby objects than to objects farther away.

K-Means Clustering

K-means clustering, also known as *centroid-based clustering*, is a method to classify a given data set through a certain number of clusters (assume *k* clusters) fixed beforehand. When the number of clusters is fixed to *k*, the algorithm finds the *k* cluster centers and assign the objects to the nearest cluster center, such that the squared distances from the cluster are minimized. While K-Means is easy to understand and implement, the algorithm does not control for outliers, so all data points are assigned to a cluster even if they do not belong in any.

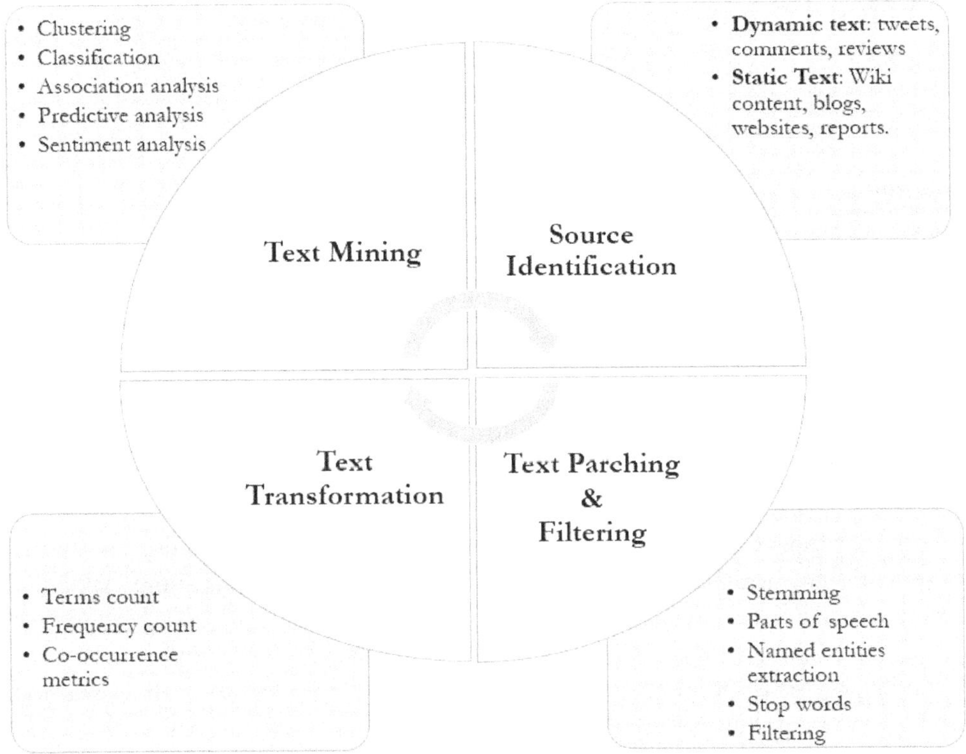

Figure 6.4. Text analytics value creation cycle

Distribution-Based Clustering

The algorithms in *distribution based clustering* define objects as belonging most likely to the same distribution. This way of clustering closely resembles the way data sets are generated, i.e., by sampling random objects from a distribution.

As a practical example, consider that Apple offers its customers a particular type of smartphone (say smartphone X). However, the sales of the smartphone are less than Apple expected. How can Apple increase the number of its customers who choose smartphone X, without undertaking a large-scale marketing campaign? One way to go about it is for Apple to use distribution-based clustering to create a data-mining model for all its customers. This model will contain one or more clusters of customers who use Smartphone X, each cluster having a specific demographic profile. Apple can then selectively target the customers of other clusters who have similar demographic profiles to those with Smartphone X, but who do not have this type of device.

Classification

From the text analytics perspective, *classification* or *categorization* is used to find similarities in the document and groups them with predefined labels based on the themes contained in the document (Chakraborty, 2013). For example, an e-mail can be classified as spam based on its contents.

SUPERVISED vs. UNSUPERVISED LEARNING

When it comes to data mining (including text mining), there are two classes of machine learning techniques: supervised and unsupervised.

Supervised Machine Learning

In *supervised* methods, a model is created based on previous observations (or datasets) as a training set (Samuel, 1959). The training data consist of a set of training examples. In other words, the algorithm is trained on the type of data it can expect to analyze. Social media analytics tools like Crimson Hexagon work in this fashion. Once the algorithm is trained, it can predict any given document's categories. Supervised machine learning uses classifiers. When a classifier is fed a new verbatim (i.e., blog post, tweet, SMS message, call center record) to classify, it predicts whether the document belongs to a particular pre-defined category. Supervised machine learning problems can be further grouped into regression and classification problems.

Classification

A classification problem occurs when the output variable is a category, such as "red" or "black" or "male" and "female."

Regression

A regression problem occurs when the output variable is a real value, such as "dollars" or "age."

Unsupervised Machine Learning

The unsupervised machine learning method tries to discover patterns rather than trying to fit the data into a predefined structure (Hinton & Sejnowski, 1999).

Clustering is an example of "Unsupervised Learning." Unsupervised data assumes that nothing is known initially, and the software learns as it runs. Unsupervised machine learning differs because it is "not supervised by a human" and does not require a training dataset. Suppose there are a large number of emails that we want to analyze as part of an eDiscovery process. We have no idea what the emails are about or topics they deal with, but we need to know what are the most common topics in the emails. In such cases, we can use clustering to automatically discover groups of similar emails within the group being examined. We can then use a clustering algorithm like K-means (discussed earlier) to group the emails into a few distinct categories or clusters. Unsupervised learning problems can be further grouped into clustering and association problems.

Clustering

A clustering problem occurs where we want to discover the natural groupings in the data, such as grouping customers based on their purchasing behavior.

Association

An association rule learning problem occurs where we want to discover rules that describe significant portions of our data, such as people that buy X also tend to buy Y.

PREDICTIVE vs, DESCRIPTIVE TEXT ANALYTICS

Earlier we discussed the differences between describing text (via word clouds) vs making *predictions* based on what is in the text. Describing relationships (a standard map) is useful, yet *predicting* which routes in a map will bring us to our destination more quickly, is far more actionable. Text analytics uses the methods discussed in this chapter such as linear regression to determine probabilities. By using probabilities, decisions can be made on the probabilities calculated from the text being analyzed.

COMMON TEXT ANALYTICS TERMS

Natural Language Processing (NLP)

NLP is a field of Computer Science and Artificial Intelligence that focuses on interactions between computers and human language. Examples of NLP applications include Siri and Google Now.

Information Retrieval (IR)

IR extracts structured information from unstructured and semi-structured data, such as text documents or web pages.

Named Entity Recognition (NER)

NER locates and classifies elements from text into predefined categories such as the names of people, organizations, and places.

Corpus

An extensive collection of documents used to infer or validate grammatical rules, perform statistical analysis and test hypothesis.

Disambiguation

Identify the meaning of words in context using computational means (software). Example: use or develop an algorithm to determine whether a reference to "Apple" in a verbatim (text) refers to the company Apple, or the fruit.

Bag of Words

Commonly used model for text classification; in this method text (a sentence or a document) is represented as a bag of words with word order and word frequency used as a feature for training a classifier.

Explicit Semantic Analysis

Understand the meaning of a text verbatim through a combination of the concepts found in that text.

Latent Semantic Analysis

Examine relationships within a set of documents along with the terms they contain; assumes that words that are close in meaning will occur in the similar text.

Latent Dirichlet Allocation

Topic modeling that is based on the idea that each text document contains a few topics such that each word in the document is attributable to one of its topics.

TEXT ANALYTICS ISSUES

In addition to the challenges of high volume, high velocity, and high diversity discussed in the first chapter, text analytics faces several other issues as well. We briefly discuss some of these here.

Lack of Business Case

Usually, companies lack a compelling business case to collect and analyze social media textual data. Regardless of the massive data "out there" to collect, unless there is a compelling reason to gather and study it, the data will not usually be collected or examined. That makes it easier to be good at finding and processing information that is valued, and not so good at collecting and examining information that is less valued (or not valued).

It is Resource Hefty

Text analytics requires a significant investment of resources, such as time, analytical capabilities, and financial commitment. For example, text analytics applications range in price from free to enterprise level, with 'enterprise level' being a secret code for 'costing lots of money. When there are significant masses of text, usually, there are also significant masses of other types of data. One may need to invest in new storage, new hardware, and new software to handle this. There may be a need to hire additional people to deal with all the resources necessary to analyze the text deeply.

It is advisable to determine a budget before embarking on any text analytics project– there are some free tools available, but they are often not that extensible or reliable. Thus, a serious effort with Text Analytics should probably rule out free or low-cost software. Once consideration in platform tool choice is the form of the data that is going to be processed as not all platforms process all file/format types.

Sentiments are Complex

Sentiment analysis aims to analyze how customers feel about a particular product, service, or issue by extracting the sentiments embedded in the social media text. However, using machines (or machine learning) to distinguish the meaning of human feeling about a topic may be problematic. For instance, "alive" is normally a positive sentiment, but maybe it is not in the context of a tweet referring to Justin Bieber: "Justin Bieber AKA the hottest bitch alive." The word "alive" here is carrying a negative sentiment. Thus, most machines learning algorithms will fail to determine the correct sentiment expressed in this tweet.

Confusion over Number of Emotions

Emotions are not standardized across different sentiment analysis software. Some vendors think people express six basic emotions (love, joy, surprise, anger, sadness, and fear); others suggest that 8 or 16 emotions will work better.

Classifying a document or sentence as positive or negative in emotion does not add much value to analysis if we cannot tell what the opinion holder feels positively or negatively about. This absence of a target for the emotion sentiment analysis would seem crippling based on common sense, yet many people who use sentiment analysis have overlooked this glaring flaw. One way to compensate is by looking at aspect analysis of the presumed target in an opinion.

Data is Raw

Most of the social media data is not normally useful information unless it is cleaned and organized first. For example, anything in the social media might be considered "data," but may or may not be useful.

Data is Contextual

Even top text analytics researchers cannot program machines to correctly tag content in a document 100% of the time. The meanings of words in a document are contextual; no matter how much software is programmed, it cannot handle the variety of ways that people say things.

Issues with International Text

Not all social media text is in English; a vast majority is in other languages, such as Chinese, Spanish, and Arabic. The problem comes from the scaling issues needed to process and respond to text in different languages. Today, companies spend millions on multilingual people who understand these languages and can respond to customers in their language. Text translation is still far too crude to replace multilingual employees. Similarly, behavior, sentiments, and opinion expressed online are shaped by where people live and which region they come from, thus complicating social media text analytics landscape.

CASE STUDY 6.1
TAPPING INTO ONLINE CUSTOMER OPINIONS

Background

Founded in 1986, Frequent Flyer Services (Flyertalk.com) has created a unique niche for itself within the travel industry as a company that conceives, develops, and markets products and services exclusively for the frequent traveler. Its focus and distinctive competency lie in the area of frequent traveler programs. Worldwide, these frequent traveler programs in the airline, hotel, car rental, and credit card industries have more than 75 million members who earn more than 650 billion miles per year.

The Problem

Flyertalk.com is one of the most highly trafficked travel domains. It features chat boards and discussions that cover the most up-to-date traveler information, as well as loyalty programs for both airlines and hotels. With millions of users generating millions of posts and comments, it wanted to tap into the explosion of customer opinions expressed online. Flyertalk.com knew that the feedback that current and potential customers provide on their website provided a rich source of feedback and was looking for ways to mine it.

The Solution

The answer to the problem faced by Flyertalk.com lies in the text analytics. The most innovative companies know they could be even more successful in meeting customer needs if they just understood them better. Text analytics is proving to be an invaluable tool in doing this. Flyertalk.com leveraged Anderson Analytics to do the job. Anderson Analytics, a full-service market research consultancy, tackles this issue using cutting-edge text analytics and data mining software from SPSS that allows the application of linguistic, statistical, and pattern recognition techniques to extensive text data sets.

Note that the text analytics techniques applied, in this case, are not limited to discussion boards or blogs but can be applied to any text data source, including survey open ends, call center logs, customer complaint/suggestion databases, e-mails, and social media data.

A text analytics project is usually part of a much larger data mining project that would typically involve the identification of some core strategic questions, the allocation of resources and the eventual implementation of findings. However, the focus of this case study is to describe the tactical aspects of a text analytics project and to delineate the three basic steps involved in text analytics:

- **Step 1**: Data Collection and Preparation
- **Step 2**: Text Coding and Categorization
- **Step 3**: Text Mining and Visualization

Step 1: Data Collection & Preparation

Having quality data in the proper format is usually more than half of the battle for most researchers. For those who can gain direct access to a well-maintained customer database, the data collection, and preparation process is relatively painless. However, for researchers who want to study text information that exists in a public forum such as FlyerTalk.com, data collection can be more complex and usually involves web scraping.

Web scraping (or screen scraping) is a technique used to extract data from websites that display output generated by another program. Many commercially available applications can scrape a website and turn the blogs or forum messages into a data table. Here is how Web Scraping works.

The Web Scraping Process

Crawl—Crawl the website and scrape for the topic, ID, and thread initiator.

Download—Use topic ID from the first step as part of the URL query string to download messages.

Store—The Web crawls and stores message display pages.

Screen Scrape—Screen scrape stored web pages and extracted data into a structured format.

Link—Link extracted posts with topics from the first step, along with other extracted fields to create the final dataset.

Even with the availability of powerful web-scraping tools and techniques, text mining a popular blog or a message board like the one at FlyerTalk.com presents unique data collection and processing challenges. The amount of free text available on such sites usually prohibits an indiscriminate approach to data scraping. A strategy with clear objectives and a well-defined data extraction method are needed to increase the reliability of data analysis in the latter stages of the research.

In this particular case, researchers at Anderson Analytics narrowed the scope to just discussion topics within a 12-month period (from August 2005 to August 2006) on the five top forums intended for discussion; the hotel loyalty programs of Starwood, Hilton, Marriott, InterContinental, and Hyatt hotels.

Specific web-scraping parameters differ depending on the structure of the target sites. In a discussion board format, the text data tend to follow a simple hierarchy. Typically, each forum contains a list of topics, and each topic consists of numerous posts. Therefore, the web-scraping process of FlyerTalk.com initially retrieves data such as the discussion topics, topic ID, topic starter, and topic start date. Then, by using the topic ID, the web-scraping application constructs and submits query strings to the FlyerTalk.com site to retrieve messages associated with each specific topic.

An excellent web-scraping tool should allow the capture of information that exists in the source data of an HTML page, not just the displayed text. Therefore, hidden information such as the topic ID, date stamp, etc. also becomes available to the researcher.

Besides making sure, the fields in the final dataset are in the correct format, another problem unique to discussion board text needs to be addressed. It is very common for posters to quote others' text within their posts. These quotes should typically be extracted from the message field and placed in a separate field to prevent double counting and inadvertently to weight specific posts.

In addition to the text messages posted on the forum, the web-scraping process should also capture the poster's ID, and 'handle,' as well as any other available poster information such as a forum, join date and forum registration information (in this case: location, frequent traveler program affiliation).

Step 2: Text Coding & Categorization

Text coding and categorization is the process of assigning each text data record a numeric value that can be used later for statistical analysis. Text coding can apply either dichotomous codes (flags & many variables) or certain codes (one variable for an entire dataset). Short answers to an open-ended survey question typically use certain codes. However, the amount of text included in most discussion board posts typically requires dichotomous codes. A typical text coding process has the following steps.

Text Coding & Categorization Process:

Preliminary Coding—Use both computer and human coder to obtain the initial understanding of the data.

Initial Classification—Use SPSS Text Mining tool to perform initial categorization on a sample data set (1/100 of the entire dataset).

Computer Classification—Information and knowledge gained from the initial concept extraction are used by the human coder to assist in computer categorization.

Coding & Classification Refinement—Categorization and coding are an iterative process. Custom libraries are created to refine the process. Text extraction is performed multiple times until the number of, and the details of categories are satisfactory.

Coding & Extraction Rules—Once the coding result becomes satisfactory, the same coding and extraction rules are used on the entire dataset.

Categorization Results—Categorization results are exported for further analysis with tools such as SPSS Text Analysis.

Text coding is usually an iterative process, and this is mainly the case for coding messages on a site such as FlyerTalk.com. Text information can be compared to survey answers. The text data on most discussion boards tend to be "user-driven" rather than "provider-driven."

Before creating categories, researchers at Anderson Analytics first randomly examined a sample of text messages to gain a basic understanding of the data. This step is required to understand the type of acronyms, shorthand, and terminologies commonly used on the forum of interest.

SPSS Text Analysis for Surveys and Text Mining for Clementine are potent tools. However, the text coding results can be significantly improved if the programs can be "trained" to understand text information better, particularly to the industry and topics of interest.

With a list of industry-specific themes, concepts, and words, the researchers at Anderson used tools such as SPSS Text Analysis for Surveys to create a custom dictionary. Then the SPSS text analytics applications can be utilized, in conjunction with an SPSS developed dictionary, to extract highly relevant concepts from the text data.

In this case, examples of some of the basic concepts in the messages that can be detected by the software include: 'rates,' 'stay,' 'breakfast,' 'points,' 'free offers.' The text extraction and categorization processes are repeated with minor modification each time to get excellent results.

Step 3: Text Mining, Visualization, and Interpretation

Depending on the needs of any given research project, the coded text data can be interpreted in many different ways. In this case, the data is examined via the following methods:

Positive/Negative Comments and Overlapping Terms

The Flytalk.com data indicate that adverse discussions among the posters are centered on the payment process, condition/quality of the bathroom, furniture, and the check-in/out process. The praises seem to be centered on topics such as the spa facility, complimentary breakfasts, points, and promotions.

Data Patterns within Different Hotel Brands

By comparing the coded text data of Starwood and Hilton forums, the researchers found that the posters seem to be relatively more pleased with beds on Starwood's board, but more satisfied with food and health club facilities on Hilton's board.

Longitudinal Data Patterns

As this study contains data from a one-year period, data can be analyzed to understand how topics are being discussed on a month-to-month basis. The data in this particular case revealed that the discussion about "promotions" on the Starwood board is especially frequent in February 2006. Crosschecking with Starwood management confirmed that special promotions were launched during that period. Text Analytics is one way to measure the impact of various communication strategies, promotions, and even non-planned external events.

Analysis of Poster Groups

Web mining may be helpful in understanding the aggregate motivation of some of the most active users of the products. Though it may be painful to segment posters with only one post, frequent posters can provide a relatively comprehensive set of segmentation variables. In this case, some general motivational themes found were the need for being 'in the know,' 'finding deals,' and the desire to "give back."

Conclusion

Companies have discovered that they can compete far more efficiently if they gain an accurate, 360 ° view of their customers. The feedback that current and potential customers provide in blogs, forums and other online spaces is a rich source of feedback. Using text analytics to monitor this information helps organizations gauge customer reaction to products and services and, when combined with analysis of "structured" transactional data, delivers predictive insight into customer behavior.

This case described how text analytics was applied to information posted by users of travel and hospitality services, but the same techniques can be applied to other industries. A company might find, for example, that when it launches a special promotion, customers mention the offer frequently in their online posts.

Text analytics can help identify this increase, as well as the ratio of positive/negative posts relating to the promotion. It can be a powerful validation tool to complement other primary and secondary customer research and feedback management initiatives. Companies that improve their ability to navigate and text mine the boards and blogs relevant to their industry are likely to gain a considerable information advantage over their competitors.

Source: Anderson Analytics, LLC.www.andersonanalytics.com

TUTORIAL 6.1
TEXT ANALYTICS WITH IBM WATSON ANALYTICS FOR SOCIAL MEDIA

IBM WATSON ANALYTICS FOR SOCIAL MEDIA

IBM® Watson Analytics™ is a cloud-based tool for social media data analysis. Watson Analytics for Social Media helps brands gain insight into social media discussions that are related to brand key focus for analysis. It helps organizations to analyze content in social media posts that are in Arabic, Chinese, English, French, German, Italian, Portuguese, Russian, or Spanish. Mostly, it helps an organization to answer the following types of questions:

- What are consumers saying and hearing about our brand?
- What are the most talked about product attributes in our product category?
- Is the feedback good or bad?
- What is the competition doing to excite the market?
- Is our employer's reputation affecting our ability to recruit top talent?
- What are the reputations of the new vendors that we are considering?
- What issues are most important for our constituency?

Before we start, go to the IBM Watson Analytics for Social Media (use this shortened URL: goo.gl/pP1yfw) and get your 30 days free trial account.

WORKFLOW OF ANALYZING SOCIAL MEDIA TEXTUAL DATA

To analyze social media text, follow the process shown in Figure 6.5.

Step 1: Create a Social Media Project

- Specify topics to analyze. You specify the keywords to include, and you can exclude keywords and define context keywords.
- Specify the date range. By default, the last four weeks are searched and analyzed.
- Specify the types of sources that you want to retrieve documents from sources that are available include Twitter, forums, reviews, Facebook pages, video descriptions and comments, blogs, and news.
- Review the suggestions for your topics, because new suggestions might appear after you specify the date range and sources.
- Optional: define themes to provide more clarity in the analysis.

Step 2: Dataset Creation

Create a dataset to retrieve documents that match the criteria that you specified. Watson Analytics for Social Media retrieves the documents, analyzes them, creates visualizations, and creates a data set.

Step 3: View and Interpret Results

View the visualizations that Watson Analytics for Social Media creates for you.

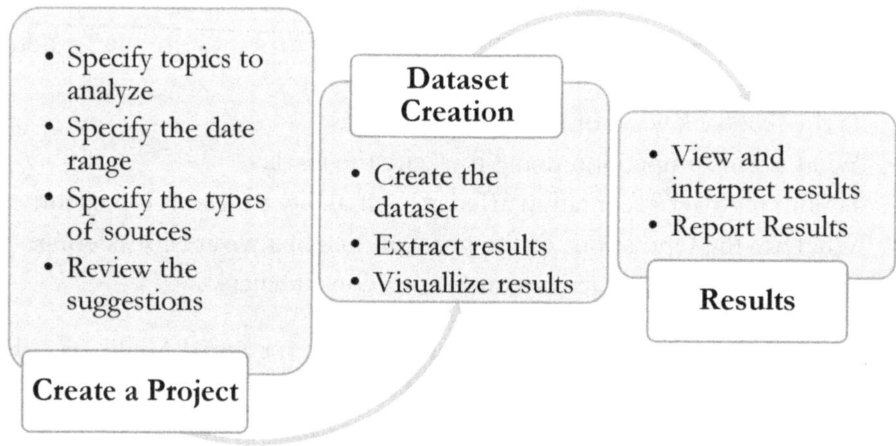

Figure 6.5. IBM Watson Analytics for social media process

STEP 1: CREATING A SOCIAL MEDIA PROJECT

To analyze social media content, you must create a project. The project contains information about the topics and themes that you want to analyze to gain insight into social media discussions that are related to your key focus for analysis. The project also contains the visual and text insights that are generated from the topics and themes.

Note: For YouTube content, Watson Analytics for Social Media can access up to 15 months of historical data. For all other content, 24 months of historical data can be accessed.

Step 1.1: In Watson Analytics, tap the arrow at the far left on the app bar.

Step 1.2: Tap IBM Watson Analytics for Social Media (Screenshot 6.1).

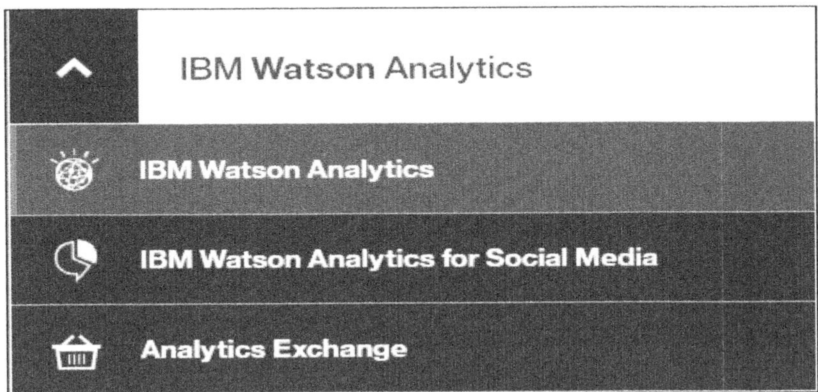

Screenshot 6.1. IBM Watson Analytics for social media

Step 1.3: Tap **New Project** (Screenshot 6.2).

Step 1.4: On the **Create** tab, provide a name for your project. Alternatively, on the **Import** tab, you can open a project file that you or someone else saved.

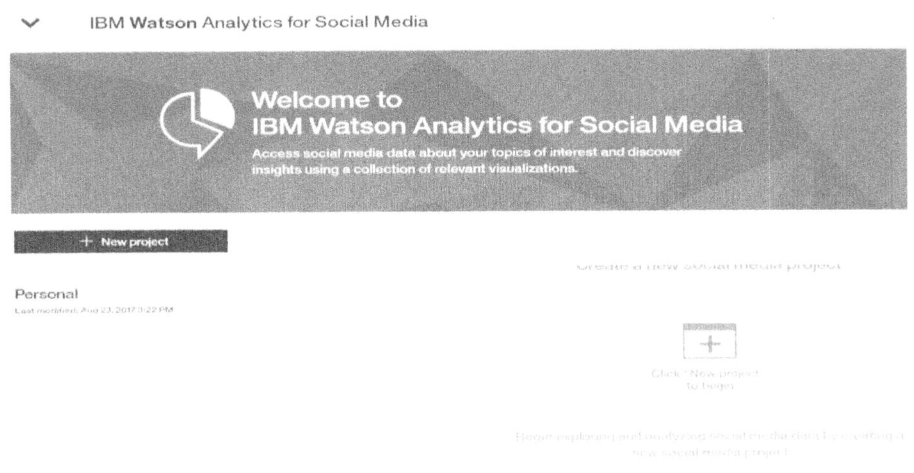

Screenshot 6.2. New project screen

Step 1.5: Tap **Next**. A new project is created. You can access it on the main page of Watson Analytics for Social Media.

Step 1.6: Enter a topic, then tap ⊕.

A topic represents a piece of social media content that you want to retrieve and analyze, for example, brands, products, services, or events. Enter as many topics as you like. You must add each topic individually. For example, you want to analyze the social media activity around three of your sporting goods company's tents. You create a topic for each of those products: Star Dome, Star Light 2, and Star Peg.

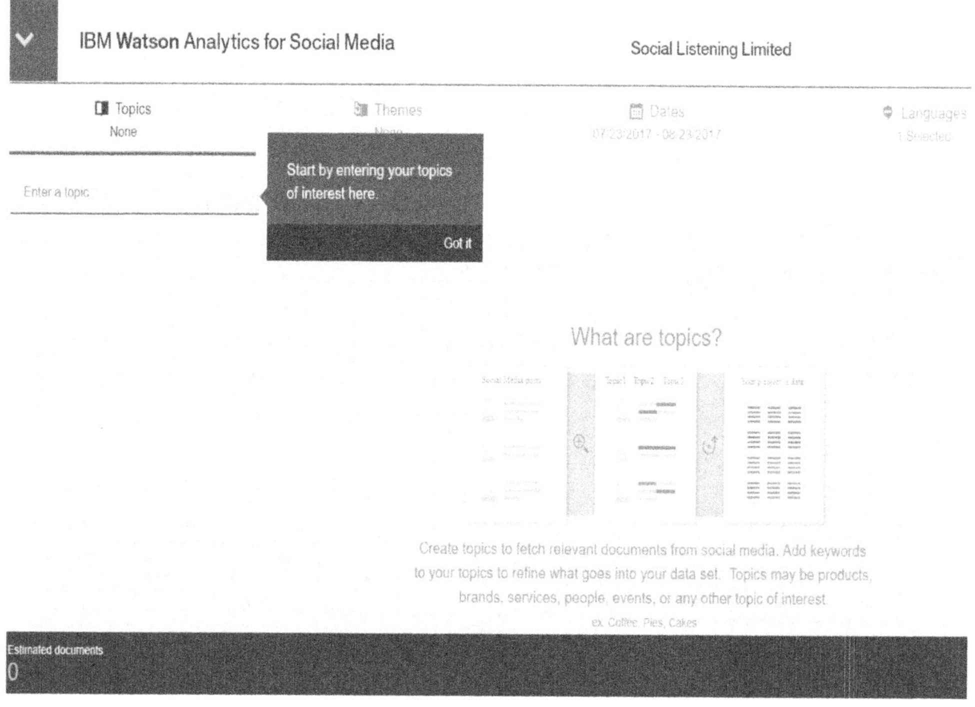

Screenshot 6.3. Topic screen

Include Keywords

Topic keywords are synonyms of your topic. At least one topic keyword must appear in a mention for it to be retrieved. *Mentions* are the parts of a document that are relevant to a topic that you want to analyze. Create topic keywords for each topic to ensure that you collect as much information as possible. Account for different spellings, alternative product names, and other variants. For a keyword that is not a proper noun, add synonyms of your keyword in multiple languages, especially for languages that you specify for inclusion in your model. For example, for three products, you create these topic keywords:

- Star Dome:
- Star Dome
- StarDome
- Star-Dome
- Star Light 2:
- Star Light 2
- Starlight2
- Starlight2
- Star-Light 2
- Star Light Two
- Star Light Deux
- Star Light Dos
- Star Light Zwei
- Star Peg:
- Star Peg
- StarPeg
- Star-Peg

Context Keywords

Context keywords must occur in the text that surrounds your topic keywords. If no context keyword occurs, a mention is not retrieved. Consider adding variants of keywords. In the example with three tents, you might want to create these context keywords, among others, for each of your topics:

- tent
- tents
- tente
- tienda
- Zelt

Exclude Keywords

Exclude keywords are keywords that must not occur in the text that surrounds your topic keywords. If an excluded keyword occurs, a mention is not retrieved. Consider adding variants of keywords. In the example, you might see a suggestion of the keyword "telescope" for the Star Light 2 topic. After you do some research, you determine that Starlight2 is the name of a telescope that is made by another company. So, you add in the keyword "telescope" as an exclude keyword for the Star Light 2 topic so that you don't retrieve irrelevant data.

- telescope
- telescopes
- télescope
- telescopio
- Teleskop

To use a negative number as an exclude keyword, you must put double quotation marks around it. For example, "-1234" and "-0.123" are both valid. You don't need to use double quotation marks around positive numbers.

To use a date as an exclude keyword, such as 2015-12-11, you must also put double quotation marks around it. For example, "2015-12-11" and "2015-12-25" are both valid.

Suggestions

When you create a topic, Watson Analytics for Social Media captures keywords and related words from a sample of documents that contain that topic. You can see the words in the **Suggestions** pane after you create a topic and view its topic keywords. You can use these suggestions as topic keywords, context keywords, or exclude keywords.

If you do not see suggestions, your topic might be too restrictive. Alternatively, your keywords might not be in a language that we support. You might need to broaden your topic in one of these ways:

- Remove context keywords or exclude keywords that might be too restrictive. For example, context keywords that are very uncommon words or exclude keywords that are ubiquitous might cause too many documents to be excluded.
- Add more variants of your topic keywords, such as hashtags or synonyms from the list of suggestions.
- Try a wider date range.
- Add more sources.
- Add more languages. You can choose to retrieve documents in Arabic, Chinese, English, French, German, Italian, Portuguese, Russian, and Spanish.

Step 1.7: In the Suggestions pane, tap Refresh, then review the suggestions for keywords that you might want to include or exclude.

Step 1.8: Optional: Tap Themes to create themes that consist of attributes on which you want to break down a topic. Example attributes are availability, loyalty, quality, and customer service.

- Create a theme, then tap ⊕.
- Enter as many themes as you like. You must add each theme individually.
- Tap a theme to add theme keywords and, optionally, context keywords and exclude keywords that apply to that theme.
- Use the same procedure that you used with topics. Keywords must be in Arabic, Chinese, English, French, German, Italian, Portuguese, Russian, or Spanish.

Step 1.9: Tap **Dates** to specify the time period that you want to retrieve social media documents from. The dates and times are inclusive and are in your local time. The earliest starting date that you can choose is restricted in the Start date calendar.

Step 1.10: Tap Languages to specify the languages of the social media documents that you want to retrieve. Available languages are Arabic, Chinese, English, French, German, Italian, Portuguese, Russian, and Spanish. By default, the English language is selected.

Step 1.11: Tap Sources to specify the sources of social media data that you want to retrieve social media documents from (Screenshot 6.4).

- **Twitter:** Retrieves 10% of the Tweets that match your criteria from Twitter.
- **Forums:** Retrieves content from message boards and forums.
- **Reviews:** Retrieves comments and reviews from review sites.
- **Facebook pages:** Retrieves data from many Facebook pages from top industries. Data is available from January 27, 2016, and later.
- **Videos:** Retrieves video descriptions and comments posted to video sites such as YouTube, Dailymotion, Snotr, 5min, and Youku. It does not retrieve the videos themselves.
- **Blogs:** Retrieves blog posts and their comments.
- **News:** Retrieves postings from major news websites and news wires.

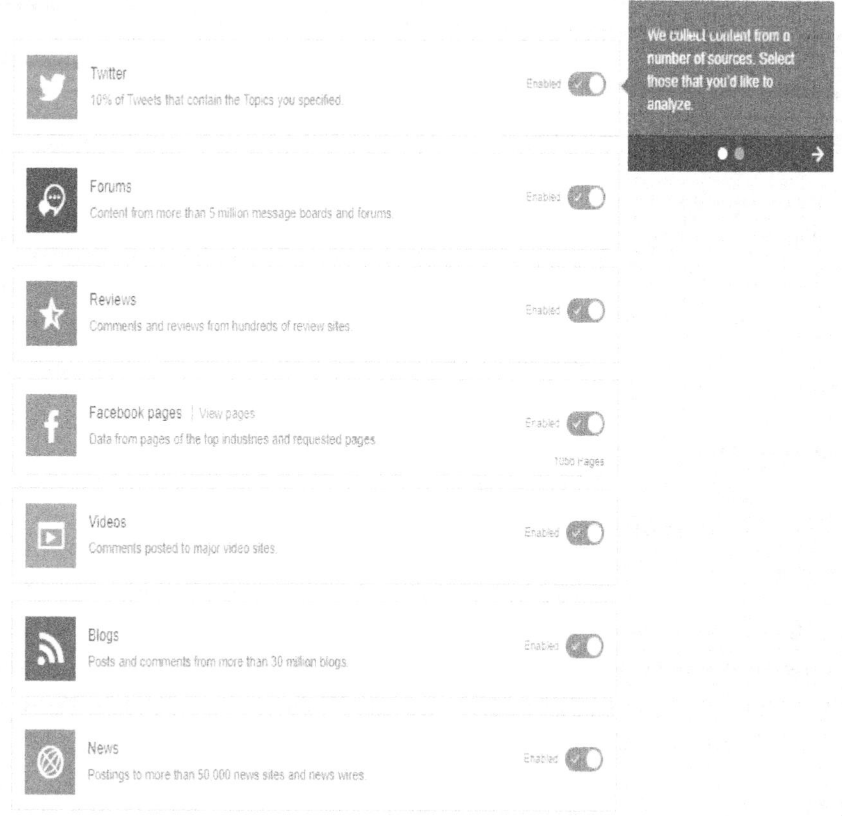

Screenshot 6.4. Social media sources to select from

Step 1.12: When you are ready to retrieve documents and view visualizations about your topics and themes, tap the Create dataset icon. It might take several minutes to retrieve the documents and do the analysis.

STEP 2: RESULTS

After the documents are retrieved, and the analysis is complete, visualizations that provide information about the documents appear in the Analysis tab. Additionally, a new social media data set is created for you. After the data set is created, you can find it on the Data page in Watson Analytics. When you create or update a social media data set in IBM Watson Analytics for Social Media, you might not receive status updates if you use a Microsoft Internet Explorer version 11 browser. Additionally, you might not see the data set on the Data page. You can make a configuration change in your browser that solves this problem.

TUTORIAL 6.2
TEXT ANALYTICS WITH SEMANTRIA

INTRODUCTION

Lexalytics is a text analytics company founded in 2003. They have two products, Salience (an on-premises text analytics engine), and Semantria, a SaaS, API, and Excel plug-in for text analytics. In this tutorial, we will configure and use Semantria for Excel for text analytics purposes. Semantria uses text and sentiment analysis techniques to analyze tweets, Facebook comments, surveys, and product reviews. This tutorial assumes that the user is using MS Windows 7, Chrome browser, and MS Excel 2010 thirty-two-bit versions. For text analysis purposes, we will use Trip Advisor's sample XLS dataset. The sample dataset contains customer comments extracted from the Trip Advisor website. You can download the XLS file to your computer from Semantria's website: https://semantria.com/support/excel/ or from the book companion website (https://analytics-book.com/). Create a folder on your computer (e.g., text analytics) and save the file to it. Before starting with Semantria, go to http://www.semantria.com/signup to get a free account.

GETTING STARTED

Semantria requires two pieces of software to run: 1) Windows XP or higher and 2) Microsoft Office Excel.

Installing Semantria is easy.

1. Go to http://semantria.com/excel and click on the download button.
2. Select your version of Excel to download the installer file.
3. Open it up when it finishes downloading.
4. Click on "Run" to activate the installer.
5. If you have not registered for Semantria, there is a link you can use to register for your free account: If you have already registered, click on "Install" to begin.

Screenshot 6.5. Installation window

6. Click "Next."
7. Read through and accept the license agreement.
8. Click "Next" again.
9. Choose your destination folder.
10. Click "Next" once more.
11. Click "Install."
12. Click "Finish."
13. Finally, click "Close" to exit the installer.
14. Startup Microsoft Excel.
15. Create a new project.
16. Click on the Semantria's ribbon and then Click on "Application Settings" button.

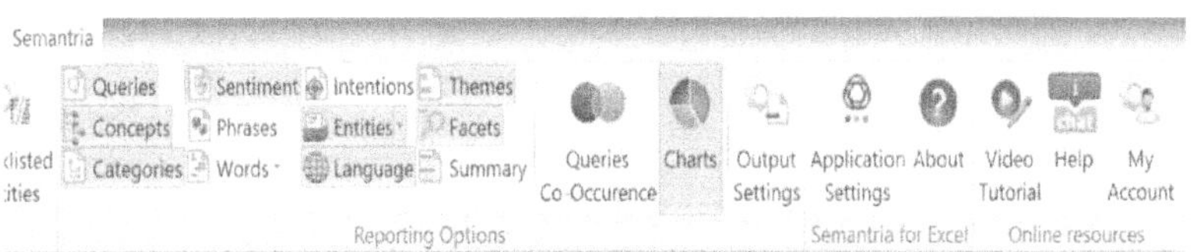

Screenshot 6.6. Semantria ribbon

17. Input your API and API Secret, which you can find in your registration e-mail.
18. Make sure to leave no spaces at the beginning or end of your credentials when copying and pasting from the registration e-mail.
19. Click "Login," and you are now ready to use Semantria for Excel.

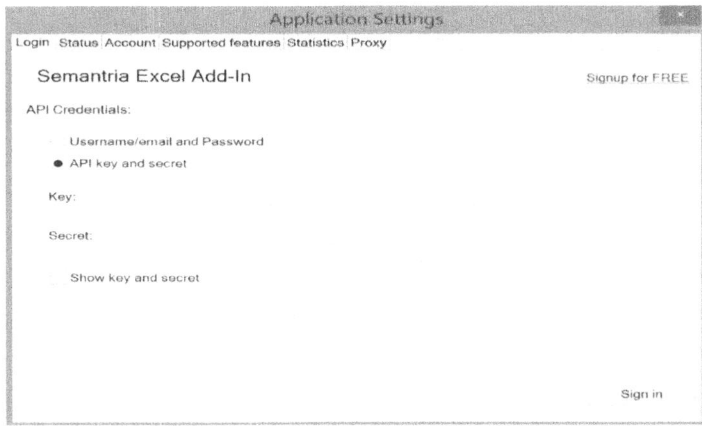

Screenshot 6.7 Semantria application settings

After this, download the sample Bellagio Hotel dataset available at semantria.com/excel/tutorial (the dataset is also available at the book companion site). The dataset contains a hundred reviews from TripAdvisor and acts as our example for this tutorial.

- **Mac users**: If you are using Parallels to run Windows, save all datasets downloaded from the web onto your Windows-side desktop. You will need to open these datasets manually in your Windows-side Excel. Opening them directly from the Internet defaults you to Mac OS-side Excel, which will not work.

RUNNING AN ANALYSIS

In order to run our first analysis, we will follow these steps:

1. Open Excel.
2. Find and open the file "Semantria Bellagio Sample Data Set.xls."
3. You should be presented with four columns: ID, Room Number, Customer Name, and Text.

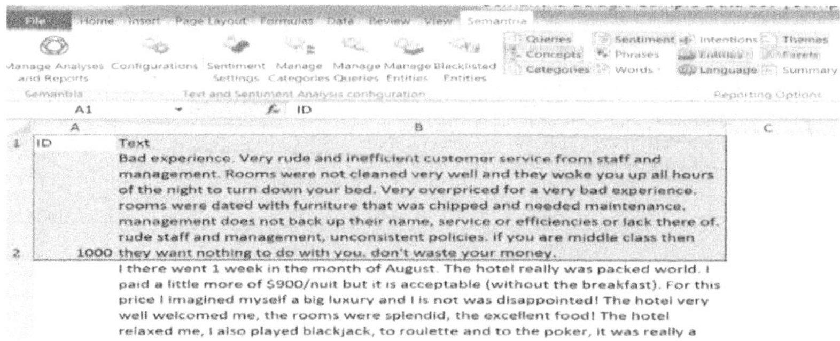

Screenshot 6.8 Sample data loaded into Semanteria

4. Before you do anything else, click the button labeled "Manage Analysis and Reports" on the top left and then click on "New."

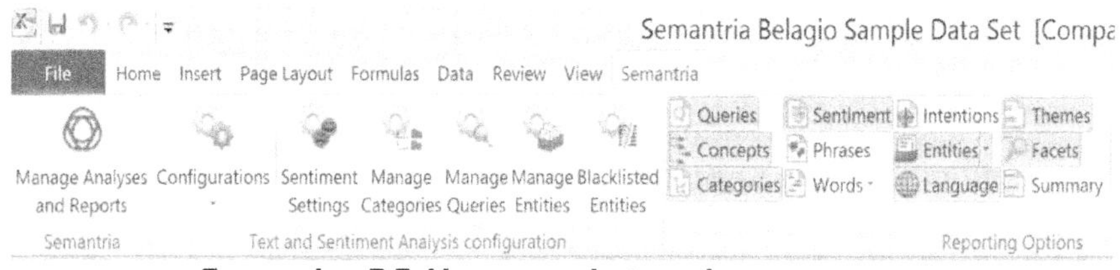

Screenshot 6.9. Manage analysis and reports option

5. For the purposes of this tutorial, we want to make sure that "Discover" is selected instead of "Detailed." This will give us a high-level overview of the data.
6. Let us label the analysis as "Bellagio2," and, because the reviews are in English, we'll leave the default language as English.
7. You will see a small button that looks like this beside the text field for "Select source text." Click it. This will allow you to select the source text manually.
8. Highlight all one hundred reviews by dragging your mouse around them. Click "OK" once you have done this.
9. Now let us analyze this data. A box will appear labeled "Start Analysis," and in it will be the analysis name ("Discovery"), the configuration (English) and the source text selected (Cells B2 to B101). It will tell you "100 documents were found from the selected range." Now click on the "Analyze" button.

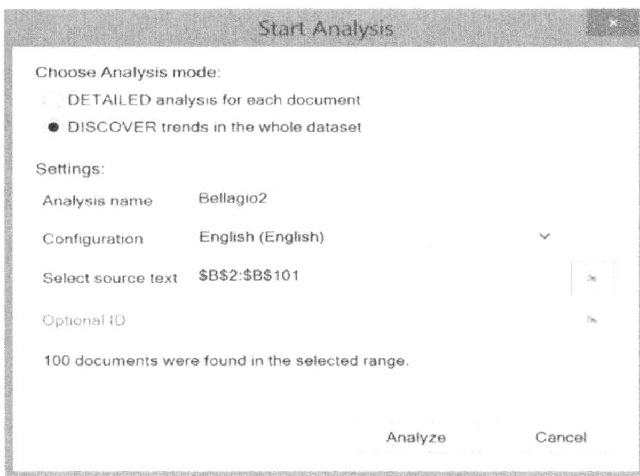

Screenshot 6.10. Analysis window

10. Look right now at the box labeled "Semantria for Excel." A yellow band will appear with your analysis information contained in it, and it will say "Receiving…" under the heading "Created."
11. Once your analysis is received, the band will turn green, and the date of the analysis' creation will appear. Double-click anywhere on this green band, and it will open up a new worksheet. This might take a moment to load. You are now viewing your analysis workbook.

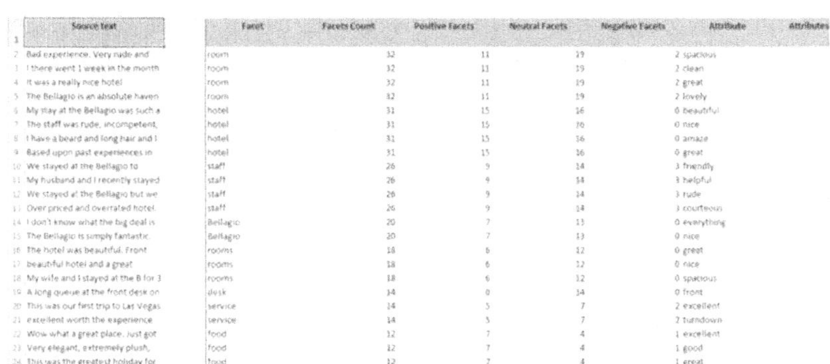

1	Source text	Facet	Facets Count	Positive Facets	Neutral Facets	Negative Facets	Attribute	Attributes
2	Bad experience. Very rude and	room	32	11	19	2	spacious	
3	I there went 1 week in the month	room	32	11	19	2	clean	
4	It was a really nice hotel	room	32	11	19	2	great	
5	The Bellagio is an absolute haven	room	32	11	19	2	lovely	
6	My stay at the Bellagio was such a	hotel	31	15	16	0	beautiful	
7	The staff was rude, incompetent,	hotel	31	15	16	0	nice	
8	I have a beard and long hair and I	hotel	31	15	16	0	amaze	
9	Based upon past experiences in	hotel	31	15	16	0	great	
10	We stayed at the Bellagio to	staff	26	9	14	3	friendly	
11	My husband and I recently stayed	staff	26	9	14	3	helpful	
12	We stayed at the Bellagio but we	staff	26	9	14	3	rude	
13	Over priced and overrated hotel.	staff	26	9	14	3	courteous	
14	I don't know what the big deal is	Bellagio	20	7	13	0	everything	
15	The Bellagio is simply fantastic.	Bellagio	20	7	13	0	nice	
16	The hotel was beautiful. Front	rooms	18	6	12	0	great	
17	beautiful hotel and a great	rooms	18	6	12	0	nice	
18	My wife and I stayed at the B for 3	rooms	18	6	12	0	spacious	
19	A long queue at the front desk on	desk	14	0	14	0	front	
20	This was our first trip to Las Vegas	service	14	5	7	2	excellent	
21	excellent worth the experience	service	14	5	7	2	turndown	
22	Wow what a great place. Just got	food	12	7	4	1	excellent	
23	Very elegant, extremely plush,	food	12	7	4	1	good	
24	This was the greatest holiday for	food	12	7	4	1	great	

Screenshot 6.11. Analysis workbook

UNDERSTANDING YOUR ANALYSIS

We will look at four major components of the structured data you are now looking at. First, you will see the Source Text listed in Column A. To the right of this column is what we will be paying attention to.

Facets Column

Each facet is a word that often occurred in your data. We can see that "room" occurred fifty times, "hotel" thirty-five times, and "staff" twenty-nine times. These are the three most common words in our data. Also, note how many times each mention of these words was positive, negative, and neutral.

Attribute Column

Attributes are adjectives that are associated with a facet. Therefore "room" has five facets here, including "nice," "clean," and "lovely." It looks as though people are happy with the rooms. The low number of negative facets confirms this.

Themes Column

Themes are noun phrases taken from individual comments and contain the main ideas of your content. To clarify, noun phrases are a word or group of words that function in a sentence as subject, object, or prepositional phrase. In this case, we find that many of the Themes are somewhat positive: "nice rooms," "excellent food," etc.

Entities Column

Entities are mostly proper nouns, like people, places, dates, companies, brands, and more. They are usually used to monitor what people are saying about your company—or your competitor's. In this dataset, most of the entities revolve around Las Vegas, the Hotel Bellagio, or Bellagio competitors like the MGM Mirage.

All of these components are also represented in graph form automatically via Discovery Mode. Here are examples of what these graphs look like.

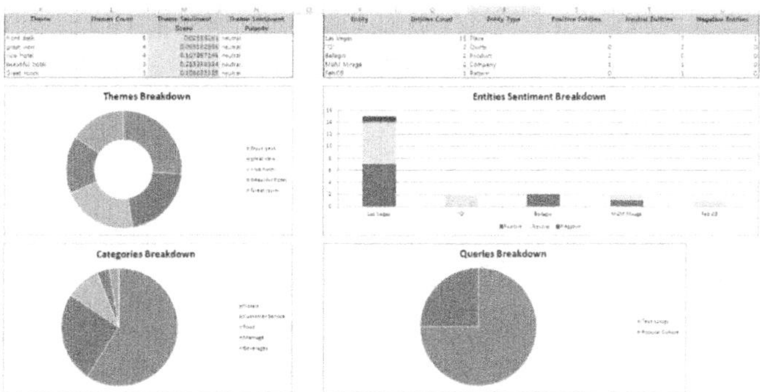

Screenshot 6.12. Results graphs

Detailed Analysis

Detailed analysis analyzes comments on an individual or "granular" level. Open the Manage Analysis and Reports tab, and click on "New."

1) Select "Detailed."
2) Name this project "Bellagio Detailed."
3) Leave the configuration as "Default English."
4) Select the source text.
5) Highlight all of the reviews and click "OK."
6) Click "Analyze."
7) Now, click the button "Phrases."
8) Double-click on the bar when it turns from yellow to green in the box labeled "Semantria for Excel." You have now opened the detailed analysis of the data in a new worksheet.

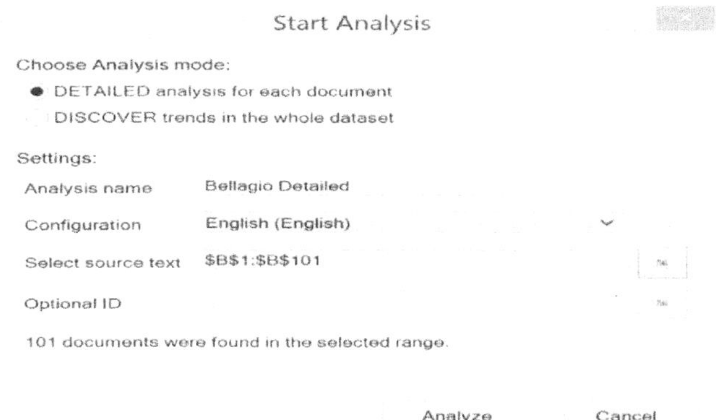

Screenshot 6.13. Analysis window

Notice that every comment has a unique ID:

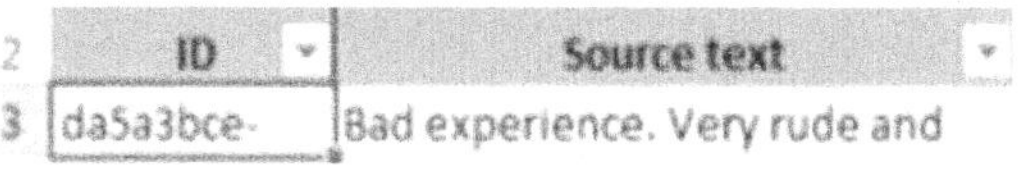

9) Semantria will assign each ID automatically, although you can assign IDs manually. The source text is the original data we analyzed—the Bellagio reviews from TripAdvisor. You will see that the first review listed has a document sentiment score of –0.32. Therefore this review is negative.
10) The document sentiment score is the score for the review as a whole. This score is made up of various sentiment-bearing phrases in the document, which are all weighted differently depending on the sentence. "Rude," "overpriced," "inefficient"—all of the phrases in this review are

negative. Each phrase is given its sentiment score. This contributes to the overall document sentiment score.

11) You can add phrases or adjust sentiment scores for any Semantria configuration by going into "Sentiment Settings."

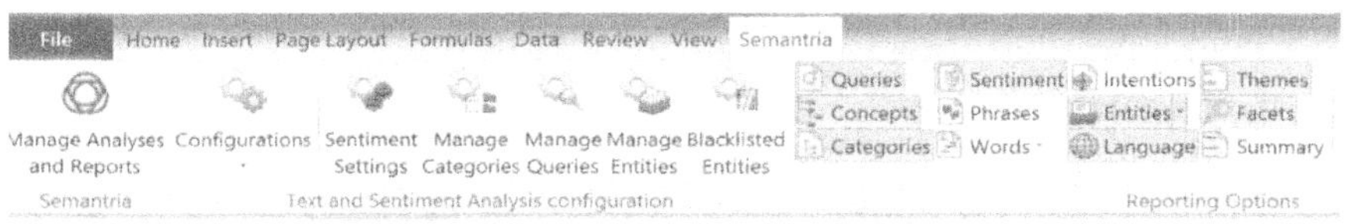

Screenshot 6.14 Sentiment settings

Semantria can also notice negators and intensifiers if they are used with phrases. It is important to note that a document sentiment score can be neutral, but contain both positive and negative phrases. Scroll down to row 49 for an example of a neutral review that contains both positive and negative feedback. This is why it is important to analyze the reviews on a granular level. Entities and themes are also assigned their sentiment score. Entities extract the proper noun from each review and assign them their sentiment score. Look at row 14. Semantria knows that "Las Vegas" is a place, and that in this review it is referred to positively.

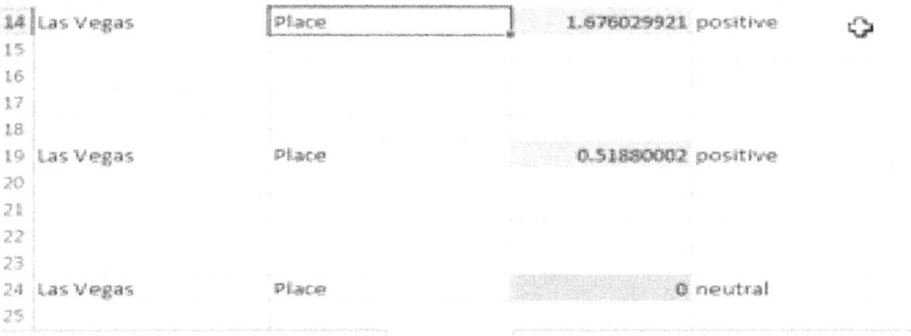

Screenshot 6.15. Row 14 to 25

Themes are noun phrases that provide the sentence with meaning using lexical chaining technology. Reading through the themes is a great way to figure out what the document is about without having to read it. Look at row 13—"Excellent food." We know the writer of this review had a good experience with the food just by looking at a few words.

Theme	Sentiment	Sentiment Polarity	Evidence
inefficient customer	-2.400000095	negative	7
rude staff	-1.200000048	negative	7
inconsistent policies	-0.906300008	negative	7
Bad experience	[illegible]	negative	7
good condition	0.99000001	positive	7
good week	1	positive	7
played blackjack	0.53828001	positive	7
big luxury	0.660000026	positive	7
excellent food	0.600000024	positive	4

Screenshot 6.16. Themes

Semantria has three methods of categorizations: 1) Auto Categories 2) User Categories and 3) Queries. **Auto Categories** will take your content and map it against over five thousand categories that Wikipedia uses to classify their own articles. **User Categories** is a similar Wikipedia-based classifier that allows you to create your categories. **Queries** allow you to classify your document using standard Boolean operators. Another benefit to the overview capabilities in Discovery mode is the graphs created automatically for **Themes**, **Entities**, **User Categories**, and **Queries**.

Creating a User Category

Creating a User Category is a way of automatically categorizing your data using the semantic knowledge from Wikipedia.

1) Click on "Manage Categories."

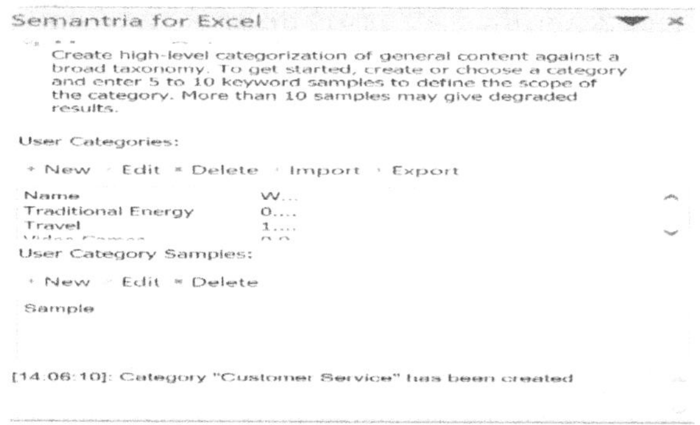

Screenshot 6.17 Creating a user category

2) Click on "New."
3) Name this category "Customer Service" and give it a default weight of "1."

4) Click "Create."
5) Scroll through the list under the box "Manage Categories" and find the category labeled "Customer Service." Click on this.
6) Now scroll down to the user category sample section.
7) Click "New."
8) Category samples are the words Semantria uses to refer to Wikipedia. As such, we want to jot down a few words that are related to customer service at a hotel.
9) Clicking "Create" after each one, jot down "customer service," "staff," and "manager."

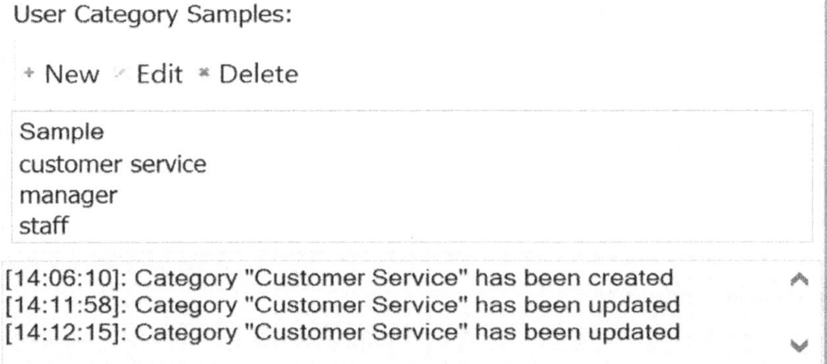

Screenshot 6.18 User category samples

10) Let us now click on the "Manage Analyses and Reports" tab with the Semantria logo on it.
11) In the right-hand pane, click the "Reprocess" button and click "Yes" when prompted.
12) Once the analysis is done processing, we can open it up and sort the reviews to see which ones are about customer service.

Understanding and Creating Queries

You might have noticed the word "rude" appeared three times as a negative attribute for the facet "staff" in our analysis. This is valuable information to know! If you were running the Bellagio, you would want to know what those reviews said, so that is what we are going to do.

1. Queries are the most specific classifier of the three. Queries are phrases that are searched against in the Semantria service. They are created using "Boolean" syntax—that means you can use "AND," "OR," "NOT," and a few others like "WITH" and "NEAR." Let us learn how to create one.
2. Log in to online.semantria.com

3. Click "Create empty configuration," type "Bellagio3" in the box, and click "Create."

Screenshot 6.19. Create empty configuration

13) Click the "EN Bellagio3" drop-down menu in the upper left (just below the Semantria logo), and select "Queries."
14) Enter a name for the query in the box where it says, "Query name." Call it "staff."
15) Click on the box right below ("type + [enter] to add terms…"), type "personnel," and hit "Enter" on your keyboard.
16) Now type "staff" in the same box as you put "personnel" and click "Enter." Now you have a query with two terms!
17) Click "Save." (This saves it while you make edits, but does not publish it.)
18) Click "Go Live." This makes your configuration active and applies it to your future analyses.

Utilizing VLookup

You can pull data from your original worksheet and add it to any Semantria analysis using the VLookup function. This is useful for deriving additional insight from your data. For example, if you analyze the Bellagio reviews to see which ones had negative sentiment, you can use VLookup to see which room numbers are associated with these negative sentiment reviews. This will show you if many negative reviews are coming from the same room.

1) Open up the "Manage Analysis and Report" tab.
2) Start a new analysis by clicking the "New" button.
3) Select "Detailed" and name this analysis "VLookup."
4) Input the source text with the icon and select all of the reviews by dragging your mouse as you did before.
5) Now we'll give a unique ID to each review by pressing the same button, , but this time beside the "Optional ID" text field.
6) Now drag the mouse over all cells in column A.
7) Each document must have a unique ID to use the VLookup feature.

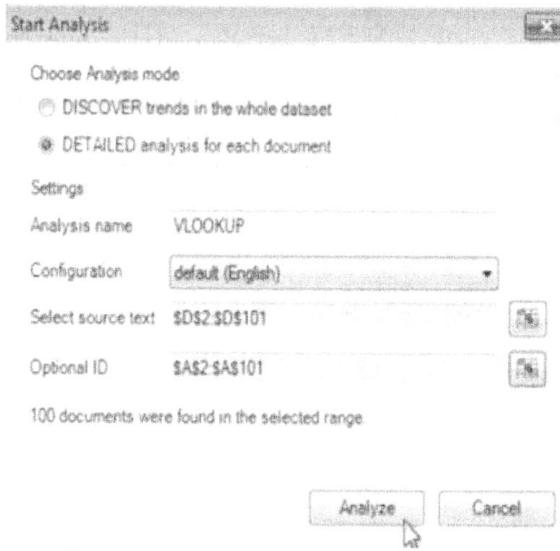

Screenshot 6.20 Vlook window

8) Now let us run our analysis by clicking the button labeled "Analyze." Wait as we did before for the bar in the right pane to turn from yellow to green.
9) Double-click the bar labeled "VLookup" as soon as it turns green. This will give us our Semantria output.
10) Now if we want to pull the room numbers to this new Semantria output (Column A), we'd drag the mouse and select the whole column, right click, select "Insert → New Column," and label it "Room Number."
11) Now click on cell A3 and input the "=" sign and select" VLookup."
12) Next click on the unique ID cell of the first review (cell B3).
13) "B3" will appear next to "VLookup" in cell A3. Add a comma after "B3." It'll look like this:

```
=VLOOKUP(B3,sentiment_bellagio!$A$1:$D$101,2
```

14) Now click back to the original worksheet tab at the bottom.
15) By dragging your mouse, select the entire table of the original worksheet.
16) To lock everything, we will put dollar signs ($) in front of the cells in the top-center text field.
17) Add a comma and after it put the number "2," because we are extracting information from the second column in our original table.
18) Close the table and hit "Enter."
19) Close the brackets in the text field and hit enter.
20) You should be on the VLookup tab once again. You will see the room number associated with the original negative complaint now listed in cell A3.

21) Just double-click the bottom right-hand corner of this cell to apply the formula to the entire column.

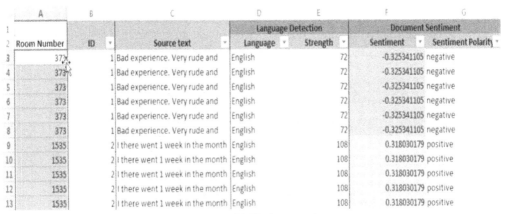

	A	B	C	D	E	F	G
1				Language Detection		Document Sentiment	
2	Room Number	ID	Source text	Language	Strength	Sentiment	Sentiment Polarity
3	373	1	Bad experience. Very rude and	English	72	-0.325341105	negative
4	373	1	Bad experience. Very rude and	English	72	-0.325341105	negative
5	373	1	Bad experience. Very rude and	English	72	-0.325341105	negative
6	373	1	Bad experience. Very rude and	English	72	-0.325341105	negative
7	373	1	Bad experience. Very rude and	English	72	-0.325341105	negative
8	373	1	Bad experience. Very rude and	English	72	-0.325341105	negative
9	1535	2	I there went 1 week in the month	English	108	0.318030179	positive
10	1535	2	I there went 1 week in the month	English	108	0.318030179	positive
11	1535	2	I there went 1 week in the month	English	108	0.318030179	positive
12	1535	2	I there went 1 week in the month	English	108	0.318030179	positive
13	1535	2	I there went 1 week in the month	English	108	0.318030179	positive

Screenshot 6.21. Vlookup results

Building Nested Queries

Building a nested query is a way to combine multiple query strings into one query. Let us build one.

1) Click on the "Manage Queries Button" in the top bar.

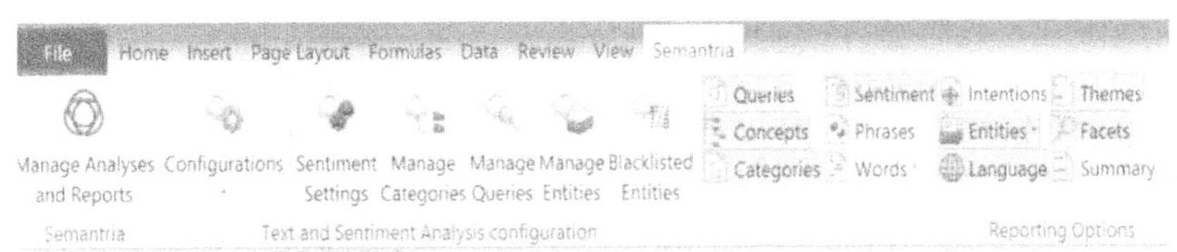

Screenshot 6.22. Building nested queries

2) In the right pane, click "New."
3) Let us build a query labeled "Poor."
4) In the text field labeled "Query," let us write down the following using Boolean logic: "poor OR rude OR bad."
5) Now click "Create."
6) Let us create one more called "Service."
7) In the Query text field, we will use the same Boolean logic, this time jotting down: "service OR staff OR manage."
8) We will also add an asterisk, or "wild card."
9) Semantria uses a wildcard to refer to an existing Query.
10) Click "Create."

11) To start our Nested Query, let us create one more Query labeled "Poor Service."
12) Under the new Query text field, we will key in an open bracket "(," a wild card, the name of the Query we want to reference ("Poor") and close of the bracket. We will now insert an "AND" operator and repeat the process for "Service," so it looks like this: (*Service).

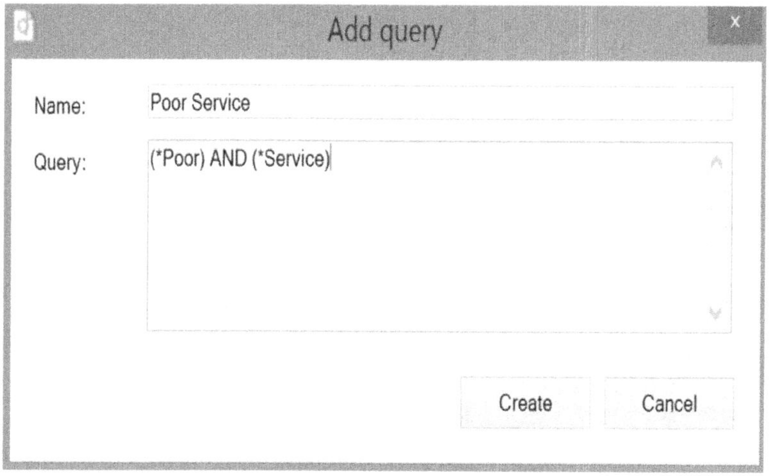

Screenshot 6.23 Add query window

Keep in mind that it is case sensitive, so if you spelled "poor" with a lower case "p" then continue using that lower case "p" for the entire process. You can only use the "AND" and "OR" operators when using Nested Queries.

13) Click "Create," and now we have a Nested Query.
14) We will now process the dataset by clicking back to the "Manage Analyses and Reports" button in the top menu. Click "New" and select "Detailed" for the analysis mode.
15) Let us call the analysis "Nested."
16) Click the "Source Text" button, , and select the entire D column (D2-D101).
17) Click the "Analyze" button.
18) Now scroll over to "Queries"(column W) and click on the drop-down menu, clicking off all check-boxes except "Poor Service."
19) Click off "Poor Service" from this drop-down menu and onto anything else, depending on the Query output you wish to see.
20) Semantria tags these Queries as "Poor Service," but it will also let us know which Sub-Queries were tagged as well.

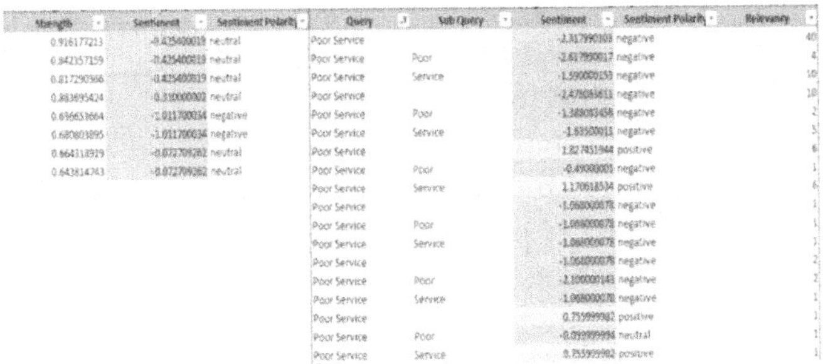

Strength	Sentiment	Sentiment Polarity
0.916177213	-0.425400019	neutral
0.942357159	-0.425400019	neutral
0.817290366	-0.425400019	neutral
0.883695424	-0.310000002	neutral
0.696653664	-1.011700034	negative
0.680803895	-1.011700034	negative
0.664313929	-0.072709262	neutral
0.643814743	-0.072709262	neutral

Query	Sub Query	Sentiment	Sentiment Polarity	Relevancy
Poor Service		-2.317990303	negative	40
Poor Service	Poor	-2.617990017	negative	4
Poor Service	Service	-1.590000153	negative	10
Poor Service		-2.478083611	negative	10
Poor Service	Poor	-1.380083458	negative	2
Poor Service	Service	-1.635000015	negative	5
Poor Service		1.827431944	positive	6
Poor Service	Poor	-0.490000001	negative	1
Poor Service	Service	1.170618534	positive	6
Poor Service		-1.068000078	negative	1
Poor Service	Poor	-1.068000078	negative	1
Poor Service	Service	-1.068000078	negative	1
Poor Service		-1.068000078	negative	2
Poor Service	Poor	-2.100000143	negative	2
Poor Service	Service	-1.068000078	negative	1
Poor Service		0.755999982	positive	1
Poor Service	Poor	-0.099999994	neutral	1
Poor Service	Service	0.755999982	positive	1

Screenshot 6.24. Nested query results

CONCLUSION

This tutorial serves to illustrate an array of basic and advanced uses for the Semantria Excel plugin. While its abilities exceed this tutorial, these are some of its most common and useful features. More information is available elsewhere on the web, including Semantria online support and a variety of other tutorials.

REVIEW QUESTIONS

1. What is text analytics? Why is it useful?
2. Differentiate between static and dynamic social media text.
3. Discuss different social media texts.
4. Explain the four primary purposes of social media text analytics.
5. Differentiate between supervised and unsupervised machine learning techniques.
6. Explain the typical social media text value creation cycle.
7. Explain what the issues of text analytics are?

EXERCISE 6.1: #HASHTAG ANALYTICS

The goal of this exercise is to apply text analytics techniques to analyze online discourse from social media about a particular event, company, product or service to:

- Identify the central topical themes and players (e.g., what customers are saying about a particular product);
- Identify the underlying sentiment (positive, negative, and neutral) contained in the tweets.
- Determine how to use the information from (1) and (2) to improve products/services under examination as well as to develop a communication strategy to influence the online discourse on this topic.

Main Steps

Step 1: Select a topic relevant to your professional interests (e.g., event, company, and product). You might choose an event and try to study how it was reacted to in social media. For example, you might study messages on Twitter (tweets) around a specific event (a conference, the Japanese earthquake, Brexit, a TV show, a new product launch, or sporting event).

Step 2: Identify the #hashtags associated with the topic. For example, a quick search on Twitter reveals the following #hashtags associated with social media analytics: #SocialIntelligence, #SocialMediaAnalytics, and #SocialListening. Hashtags (#), a part of a tweet, are used to mark keywords or topics in a tweet and are used to categorize messages. A keyword marked by a hashtag can easily appear in Twitter search, and popular hashtags are often trending topics on Twitter.

Step 3: Using a social media tool of your choice (such as Netlytics, NodeXL, Semanteria), collect and analyze the tweets associated with the #hashtags. The outcome of this step will be a set of interactive visualizations.

Step 4: Finally, use the resulting visualizations to complete objectives 1-3 and prepare a final report (~10 pages).

Step 5: Present the project results in class in the form of "lightning talk." The presentation should be based on the results to be discussed in your final report.

CHAPTER 6 REFERENCES

Chakraborty, G., M. Pagolu, et al. (2013). *Text Mining and Analysis: Practical Methods, Examples, and Case Studies Using SAS*. Retrieved from SAS Institute.:

Chen, Z., F. Lin, et al. (2002). User Intention Modeling in Web Applications Using Data Mining. *World Wide Web, 5*(3), 181-191.

Coussement, K., & Van den Poel, D. (2008). Integrating the voice of customers through call center emails into a decision support system for churn prediction. *Information & Management, 45*(3), 164-174. doi:http://dx.doi.org/10.1016/j.im.2008.01.005

Hinton, G., & Sejnowski, T. J. (1999). *Unsupervised Learning: Foundations of Neural Computation*: MIT Press.

Khan, G. F., & Wood, J. (2015). Information technology management domain: emerging themes and keyword analysis. *Scientometrics, 105*(2), 959-972. doi:10.1007/s11192-015-1712-5

Krejzl, P., Hourová, B., & Steinberger, J. (2017). Stance detection in online discussions. *Work-in-progress paper, available at: https://arxiv.org/abs/1701.00504*.

Niven, V. (2013). Does Purchase Intent Exist in Social Media? *available at: http://www.needtagger.com/does-purchase-intent-exist-in-social-media/#qHHu5pCZMYCpPP05.99*.".

Samuel, A. L. (1959). Some Studies in Machine Learning Using the Game of Checkers. *IBM Journal of Research and Development, 3*(3), 210-229. doi:10.1147/rd.33.0210

Zanasi, A. (2009). Virtual Weapons for Real Wars: Text Mining for National Security. In E. Corchado, R. Zunino, P. Gastaldo, & Á. Herrero (Eds.), *Proceedings of the International Workshop on Computational Intelligence in Security for Information Systems CISIS'08* (pp. 53-60). Berlin, Heidelberg: Springer Berlin Heidelberg.

Chapter 7

Capturing Value with Social Media Actions Analytics

"Torture the data, and it will confess to anything."—**Ronald Coase**

Learning Outcomes

After completing this chapter, the reader should be able to:

- Understand social media actions analytics.
- Understand different actions performed by social media users.
- Understand the importance of measuring actions carried out by social media users.
- Extract and analyze everyday social media actions.

INTRODUCTION

Actions are considered the cash cow of social media. Typical actions performed by social media users include likes, dislikes, shares, views, clicks, tags, mentions, recommendations, subscribing, following, commenting and endorsements.

Actions are a way to express symbolic reactions to the content posted on social media. Symbolic actions are an easy and fast way to express feelings, unlike written reactions, in the form of textual comments. Actions are not just typical responses; they carry emotions and behaviors that can be harnessed. More importantly, social media actions are social expressions. Social expressions are actions performed on social media (e.g., liking specific content) that are visible to (or shared with) other social media users, particularly to their friends. This shareable nature of the social media actions makes it very attractive to social media marketers and businesses.

Take as an example Moviefone (an American-based movie listing and information service company), which enabled logins with Facebook and Twitter credentials. Enabling such login services not only allow users to use the Moviefone service conveniently but also let them connect with their social media friends and share content over the Moviefone site.

Enabling social logins led to a 300 percent increase in site traffic, a 40,000 to 250,000 increase in referrals per month, and a 40 percent growth in click-through rate (Petersen, 2012). Also, social logins enable analysts to build better customer profiles by matching precise social actions to specific individuals via their logins.

WHAT IS ACTIONS ANALYTICS?

Social media *actions analytics* deals with extraction, analysis, and interpretation of the insights contained in the actions performed by social media users. Social media actions are of great value to social media marketers because of their role in increasing revenue, brand value, and loyalty. Organizations can employ actions analytics to measure the popularity and influence of a product, service, or idea over social media. However, actions analytics are not valid proxies for return on investment or ROI. Thus they are better suited to measuring the engagement that an audience has with the organizations' product or service.

For example, a brand marketer might be interested in knowing how widespread their new product or a competitor's product is among social media users by analyzing engagement data from social media. Analyzing the Facebook likes and Twitter mentions can provide answers to precise marketing questions.

COMMON SOCIAL MEDIA ACTIONS

Below, we briefly discuss some of the most common social media actions performed by social media users. Social media platforms used these actions as metrics. Metrics, in simple terms, are anything users, or brands want to measure. We can describe social media users as followers, fans, and subscribers.

Like Buttons

Like or "Like" buttons or like options are a feature of social media sites (e.g., social networks, blogs, and websites). These allow users to express their feelings by liking certain products, services, people, ideas, information, places, or content (Figure 7.1). These are actions performed by social media users to express a positive symbolic reaction to content posted on social media. Also, we can gauge the popularity of a person, product, or service through the number of likes they get on social media.

Figure 7.1. Facebook Like button

Facebook's "Like" button enables users to voice their feelings easily and give your product or service a virtual thumb up. In addition to the "Like" button, Facebook implemented reaction buttons so that users can express their feelings with the click of a button rather than commenting. Incorporating a "Like" button on social media platforms and websites is becoming the norm. Social media platforms display accumulated likes received by content over time. Facebook's "Like" button is the most famous one. Google+ social networking platform uses a "+1" symbol to express liking. Companies use Google+ and Facebook fan pages to receive likes from customers, but the "Like" button can also be incorporated into a company website or blog. Recently, Twitter changed their "favorite" button to a "like" button.

Dislike Buttons

Dislike buttons are included in some social media platforms (e.g., YouTube) and allows users to express their negative feelings of dislike of certain content (e.g., products, services, people, ideas, information, or places) posted on social media. Similar to the "Like" feature, it is visible to others and accumulated over time. The "Dislike" button, when it is present, is not as prevalent as the "Like" button. Perhaps, social media companies do not want people to dislike the stuff posted over their platforms. Such a practice may go against the core philosophy of advertisement, which is used to create a positive mental image of products/services offered by companies and convince them to buy them.

Figure 7.2. Facebook emoji buttons

Recently, Facebook has introduced a range of other buttons, including Love,

Sad, and Angry, to allow people to express a variety of emotions (Figure 7.2). One could argue social media creates more negativity than positivity. However, most social media platforms do not want their members to dislike user content, instead preferring to promote a positive image of the products/services offered by users and advertisers.

Share Buttons

Share or "Share" button or sharing is a feature that allows social media users to distribute the content posted on social media to other users (Figure 7.3).

Figure 7.3. Social share buttons

For example, the Facebook "Share" button lets users add a personal message and customize whom they share the content with. For example, the share button on WordPress (a blogging platform) allows users to share their blog content across a range of social media platforms. Companies incorporate share buttons into their website to boost their website traffic by channeling visitors from social media sites. Furthermore, social media Share buttons can be used to raise awareness of business and social events.

Visitors, Visits, Revisits

A *visitor* is a person who visits a particular website or blog. A single visitor may visit a page or content one or more times (revisits). Visits are also known as sessions. Other related concepts related to a visitor's visit to a website are:

Unique Visitor

A *unique visitor* is a person who arrives at a website page for the first time.

Average Bounce Rate

Average *bounce rate* is the percentage of visitors who visit a website and leave the site quickly without viewing other pages.

Session Duration

Session duration is the average length of a visitor's visit or session.

View

Views are the number of times users view social media content (a post, video, graphic, so forth). A slightly different but related concept is the page view; which is a count of each time a visitor views a page on a company website or blog. Instagram allows members to see how many views they receive on a video or a boomerang. Although members cannot see the names of all the people who viewed their Instagram content, they can still see the names of everyone who liked it.

Clicks

Clicks are the actions performed by users by pressing or clicking on the hyperlinked content of a website, image, click-ad or blog. Through clicks, users navigate the web. We can harvest click data for business intelligence purposes, such as, to reduce bounce rate and improve website traffic.

Business managers use a technique called clickstream analysis for a variety of business intelligence purposes, including website activity, website design analysis, path optimization, market research, and finding ways to improve visitor experience on the site. The clickstream is the semi-structured data trail/log (such as date and time stamp, IP address, and the URLs of the pages visited) user leaves while visiting a website.

The clickstream (of a website tracked by web analytics tool) includes every click, download, link in/out, search, keyword, time spent, and much more is recorded using programs such as Web Trends and Google Analytics.

Tagging

Tagging is the act of assigning or linking extra pieces of information to social media content (such as photographs and bookmarks, among others) for identification, classification, and search purposes. Tagging has assumed additional uses, such as tagging individuals (usually friends or connections) within a photo, tweet or post by adding the metadata of their social media account name (*which does not always correspond to their real names*).

Tagging can be used to raise users' popularity by letting users classify social media content in the manner they see fit. Tagging may take a variety of forms. For example, bloggers can attach descriptive keywords (tags) to their posts to facilitate classification and searching of content, and Facebook users can add tags to anything they post on their status, including photos and comments. Social bookmarking services (such as del.icio.us) let users organize their bookmarks by adding descriptive tags. This practice of collaborative tagging is commonly known as *folksonomy*—a term coined by Thomas Vander Wal (2005).

These days, almost all prominent companies (e.g., Facebook and Flickr) provide tagging services to their users. Because the contents are tagged with useful keywords, social tagging expedites the process of searching and finding relevant content. Tagging is also used to share interpersonal relationships and showing a user's followers who they are via tagging pictures. In fact, Instagram users are able to tag an Instagram company site, friend, follower or Instagram public page; doing so makes it easier to generate attention and user interaction on the platform.

Mentions

Mentions or *social mentions* are the occurrences of a person, place, or thing over social media by name. For example, a brand name may be referred to in a Facebook comment, blog post, YouTube video, or tweet. Mentions are significant and can indicate the popularity of a person, place, or thing. For example, a social marketer may be able to gauge the popularity of a product/service/campaign by mining Twitter mentions data. A Twitter mention is the inclusion of a "@username" in a tweet.

Hovering

Hovering is the act of moving a cursor over social media content. Capturing users' cursor movement data can help understand user behavior on a social media site. Cursor movement/hovering over an ad, for example, can be considered as a proxy for attention. Most people who view an ad do not click on it; thus if we are relying on clicks analytics only, we may lose a vital piece of information (i.e., attention). Studies have even suggested a strong correlation between hover time and purchases. Traditionally, hovering data has been used in website design and for the improvement of user experience. However, useful hovering activity may be useful to marketers for consumer intelligence; it also presents severe issues regarding user privacy.

Here we provide two examples of issues surrounding hovering and privacy:

- Collecting hovering data can infringe on a user's online privacy even when a user "knows" their online behavior is being tracked. For example, the online learning programs run by many universities are using software to verify the identity of students who are taking an online test or quiz. The verification tracks a student's cursor movement, typing pattern and gazes to build a profile of the student (via a computer cam) for test taking purposes, but it is also done for regulatory laws, and to strengthen the reputation and competitiveness of the university program. However, the adoption of such programs has turned out to be very repugnant to a number of students because of the privacy issue.

- Third-Party data providers, such as ComScore and Nielsen, employ millions of panelists that traverse the web in the course of their work or leisure, with their precise clickstream, tracked with intricate detail. However, concerns about privacy violations led thousands of individuals to sue ComScore claiming they were secretly surveilled through its proprietary tracking software. The lawsuit claimed ComScore sold panelists' private information to other parties without their knowledge or consent.

Check-ins

Check-ins are a social media feature that allows users to announce and share their arrivals in specific locations, such as a hotel, an airport, a city, or a store. Many social media services, including Facebook and Google+, provide check-in features. The location of the user is determined using GPS (global positioning system) technology. Check-in data can, for example, be mined to offer location-based services/products.

However, there are several privacy issues with sharing location data:

- Checking into a location across the country tells friends and followers that the person is on vacation, and this could be bad if the information gets into the wrong hands.
- Most mobile devices share the precise location of their device owners with the applications that are running on the device (even when the applications are running in the background). Users "passive" check-in data is routinely collected and harvested by internet service providers (ISPs), application vendors and device manufacturers for marketing and advertising purposes that are not necessarily in the interests of device owners.

In other instances, location tracking may be seen as even more invasive, such as police surveillance of public activities around protests, employee movement and activities both on and off the job. While location tracking is usually legal, many consider it unethical with many legal challenges that are yet to be resolved.

Pinning

Pinning is an action performed by social media users to pin and share exciting content (such as ideas, products, services, and information) using a virtual pinboard platform. Some leading pinning platforms include Pinterest, Tumblr, StumbleUpon, or Digg. Businesses can use these virtual pinboards to share information while connecting with and inspiring their customers. Four Seasons Hotels and Resorts, for example, use Pinterest to curate travel, food, and luxury lifestyle content to inspire customers.

Embeds

Embedding is the act of incorporating social media content (e.g., a link, video, or presentation) into a website or blog. An embed feature lets users embed exciting content into their social media outlets.

Endorsements

The *endorsement* is a feature of social media that let people share their approval other people, products, and services. Here are some examples of social media endorsements.

- LinkedIn lets users endorse the skills and qualifications of other people in their network.
- Celebrities like Khloe Kardashian command large sums of money to endorse specific products or services. Also, some platforms such as Yelp provide endorsements via a like or a positive review of a product or service.
- Twitter retweets are a form of endorsement. When a Twitter user retweets content that appears in their news feed (and it also automatically appears in his/her followers feed); it can be considered a tacit form of approval of the content of the tweet.

Uploading and Downloading

In simple terms, *uploading* is the act of adding new content (e.g., texts, photos, and videos) to a social media platform. The opposite of uploading is *downloading*; that is, the act of receiving data from a social media platform. Almost all social media content is created and uploaded by users, which is better known as user-generated content. For some companies, uploading and downloading is the single most significant action to measure. For Instagram and Flickr, which are both photo-sharing platforms, the number of photos uploaded daily matters more than anything else.

Other everyday social media actions include (Walker, 2009):

- Contest/Sweeps entries
- Coupons downloaded/redeemed

- Games played
- Invites sent
- Newsfeed items posted
- Comments posted
- Friends reached
- Topics/Forums created
- Number of group members or fans

ACTIONS ANALYTICS TOOLS

Currently, no single platform can capture all the actions discussed in this chapter. Specific platforms can be employed to measure social media actions across platforms. Here are a few leading actions analytics tools in no particular order (we could add hundreds of tools to this list but would run out of space).

Hootsuite

HootSuite is an easy-to-use online platform that enables users to manage their social media presence across the most popular social networks. HootSuite offers different plans depending on business needs and budget: free, pro, or enterprise. In this tutorial, we will employ the free version, which supports up to five social media profiles and has limited analytics information.

SocialMediaMineR

SocialMediaMineR is a social media analytics tool that takes one or multiple URLs and returns the information about the popularity and reach of the URL(s) on social media. The reports include the number of shares, likes, tweets, pins, and hits on Facebook, Twitter, Pinterest, StumbleUpon, LinkedIn, and Reddit. The tool can be accessed from here: http://cran.r-project.org/web/packages/SocialMediaMineR/index.html

Lithium

Lithium (http://www.lithium.com/) is a social media management tool that provides a variety of products and services, including social media analytics, marking, crowdsourcing, and social media marketing.

Google Analytics

Google Analytics (http://www.google.com/analytics/) is an analytical tool offered by Google to track and analyze website traffic. It can also be used for blogs and wiki analytics.

Facebook Insights

Facebook Insights (https://www.facebook.com/insights/) helps Facebook page owners understand and analyze trends within user growth and demographics.

Klout

Klout (https://klout.com/) measures your influence across a range of social media channels based on how many people interact with your posts. The Klout Score measures a users' influence on a scale from one to one hundred.

Tweetreach

This tool helps measure the number of impressions and reach of hashtags. The tool can be accessed here: https://tweetreach.com.

Kred

Kred helps measure the influence of a Twitter account: www.kred.com

Hashtagify

This tool measures the influence of hashtags: http://hashtagify.me

Twtrland

Twtrland is a social intelligence research tool (http://twtrland.com/) for analyzing and visualizing our social footprints.

Tweetstats

Using a Twitter username, Tweetstats graphs Twitter stats including tweets per hour, tweets per month, tweet timelines, and reply statistics (http://www.tweetstats.com).

CASE STUDY 7.1
COVER-MORE GROUP

Visualizing the ROI of Social

The heart of travel insurance provider Cover-More's social efforts is its Social Media Command Center, a unique way to provide customer feedback and performance metrics in an easy-to-understand visual display. Here is how the social media team took control of the cumbersome task of presenting analytics and came out looking like stars.

Cover-More Group

Cover-More Group is an Australian-owned global travel insurance and assistance group with offices in Australia, the United Kingdom, China, India, New Zealand, and Malaysia. Each year, Cover-More provides insurance policies for over 1.6 million travelers, manages more than 70,000 insurance claims, and helps more than 42,000 customers with emergency assistance.

What They Did

Cover-More had three primary objectives in building a Social Media Command Center:

- To prove the ROI on social media efforts to stakeholders;
- To provide a snapshot of Cover-More's social media presence to the board of directors;
- To give a real-time feel to reporting and automate the process.

At the board level, Cover-More needed to be able to show a snapshot of how the company's social strategy was progressing, particularly in comparison with competitors. They were also keen to show executives how social media could benefit the business and not just be seen as a risk. However, the social media and eCommerce teams wanted to know how their activities were tracking on a day-to-day basis. Reconciling the reporting needs of executives and practitioners was proving difficult.

Once a month, Lynton Manuel, Cover-More's Social Media Manager, would populate a spreadsheet with data from each of the company's social network profiles, in an attempt to put the various channels and results in context with one another. The process was inefficient and labor-intensive:

dedicating half a day each month to compile a "pseudo dashboard" became the norm. Manuel presented an overview of status, successes, and challenges to the Board of Directors monthly, but the Board was most interested in a visual snapshot. Realizing that executives—or anyone within the business that doesn't know different platforms—needed a more simplified, visually attractive way to interact with the data, the social media team decided that Hootsuite's Social Media Command Center could be the solution.

How They Did It

The Cover-More social media team needed to bring social media intelligence into the company's nerve center via a large display to inform and impress viewers. Therefore, with the help of the IT department, they set up a 60-inch television in a prominent location where employees, executives, and potential clients could see it. The team decided on what they wanted to display and set up the Command Center using some adjustable Hootsuite widgets via a simple drag-and-drop process. From there, it was just a matter of adjusting the Hootsuite Analytics, Streams, and Monitoring features to customize the display. The team picked specific widgets like Mentions, Sentiment, Exposure, and Sharing, making it quick and easy to choose what information meant the most to them, to the executives, and to prospective and current clients.

By integrating the Social Media Command Center, the social media team was able to:

- **Show the positive impact of the social media team's efforts to executives:**
- After the Command Center had gone live, a senior executive saw the most recent tweets and remarked, "I did not know we had people saying thanks on Twitter. This looks fantastic."
- **Increase employee engagement and morale:**
- Employees were able to understand quickly the real-time data, which demonstrated the company's leadership in the social media sphere.
- **Customize the Command Center screen for maximum brand visibility:**
- The company's graphic designer created a custom background image and the style incorporated elements to make sure the Command Center was visually appealing and on-brand.

The Results

Within the first few weeks of operation, the Social Media Command Centre had not only impressed the executives and colleagues at CoverMore but external clients as well. A prospective visiting client saw the display and, recognizing his company name in the feed, was impressed enough with the Cover-More's digital savvy that he signed up with the company. With relatively little set-up time and effort, the social media team had improved its efficiency (no more monthly spreadsheet updates) and had provided specific examples of how their efforts were directly impacting the business.

Source: Hootsuite, https://hootsuite.com/resources/case-study/transforming-data-into-action-cover-more-group

TUTORIAL 7.1
ANALYZING SOCIAL MEDIA ACTIONS WITH HOOTSUITE

INTRODUCTION

The tutorial assumes that you already have your social media profiles configured (such as a Twitter account and Facebook fan page). Below are the systematic guidelines to configure and use Hootsuite.

Step 1: To start using the free version, go to http://signup.hootsuite.com/plans-cc/ and click on the "Get Started Now" button available under the free version.

Step 2: Next, provide your e-mail address and name, choose a secure password, and then click on the "Create Account" button.

Step 3: Click on the "Twitter" button available under the "Connect Your Social Network" section. Note that you can choose several social media accounts to manage using Hootsuite. For now, we will only configure Twitter and Facebook.

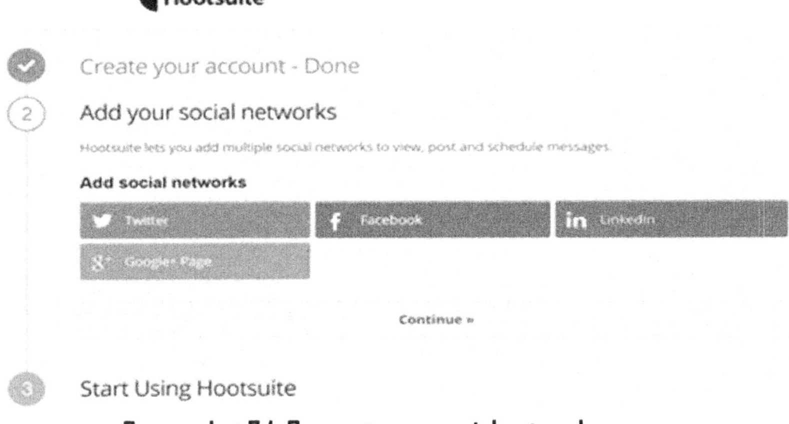

Screenshot 7.1. Connect your social networks screen

Step 4: A popup window will open asking you to authorize Hootsuite to access your Twitter account. Here, provide your Twitter username (or e-mail) and password and then click on the "Authorize App" button.

Step 5: After authorization, your Twitter account will appear in the added accounts. Next, click the "Continue" button. Note that you can add multiple accounts.

Step 6: Click on the "Get Started" button to complete the three simple steps (i.e., adding streams, creating a tab, and scheduling a message) suggested by Hootsuite.

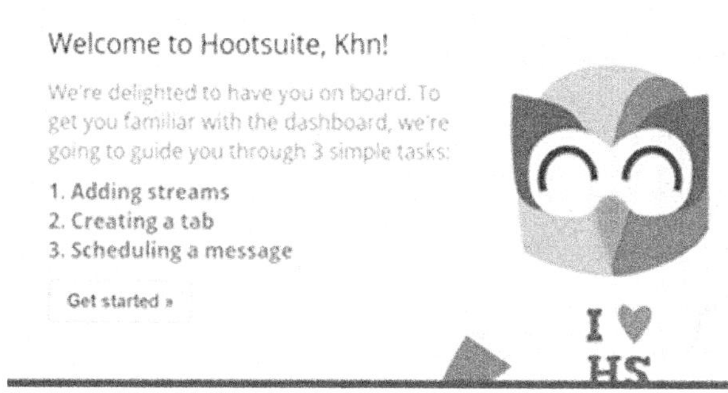
Welcome to Hootsuite, Khn!
We're delighted to have you on board. To get you familiar with the dashboard, we're going to guide you through 3 simple tasks:
1. Adding streams
2. Creating a tab
3. Scheduling a message
Get started »
I ♥ HS

Screenshot 7.2. Welcome screen

Adding Streams

Step 7: To monitor conversations and actions over Twitter, you need to add streams (Screenshot 7.3). To do so, click on all the streams you are interested in monitoring (e.g., tweets, mentions, and retweets).

Step 8: Streams will start appearing on your Hootsuite.

Creating a tab

Step 9*:* Tabs are used to group stream-based interests or similarities. To add a tab, click on the **+** icon.

Step 10: Name the new tab (e.g., Followers) and click "Next."

Scheduling a Message

Step 11: With Hootsuite, you can post messages to several social media platforms (e.g., Twitter and Facebook) either instantly or for later. To write a message, click to select the social profile(s) that will post your message (in this case Twitter). Click "Compose Message," and then type message. After writing the message, either click the "Send Now" button or the "Calendar" icon to schedule it for later. This step will complete the initial configuration of Hootsuite.

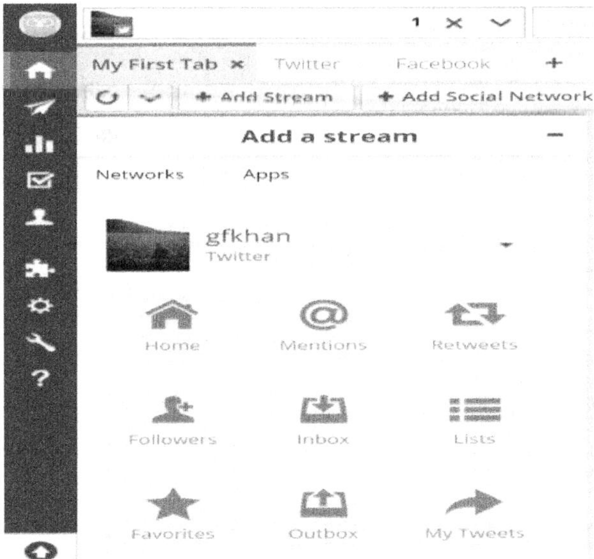

Screenshot 7.3. Adding streams to Hootsuite

ANALYTICS WITH HOOTSUITE

HootSuite provides two ways to generate analytics reports: 1) using premade templates, and 2) creating custom-made analytics reports. Note that the free version has limited analytics abilities, and you will be able to use only a limited number of templates. To use Hootsuite's pre-made templates, go through the following steps:

Step 1: Click the bar graph (Analytics) icon on the left-aligned launch menu (Screenshot 7.4).

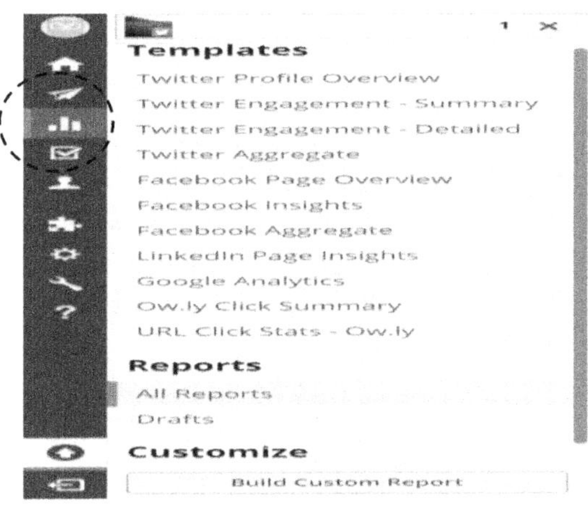

Screenshot 7.4. Bar graph (analytics) icon

Step 2: You can choose from several report templates. For example, click on the "Twitter Profile Overview" template.

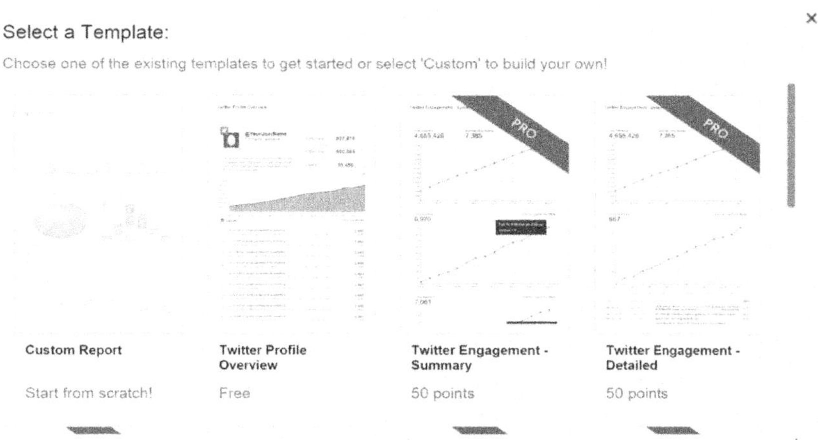

Screenshot 7.5. Selecting a template

Step 3: Click on the "Create Report" button. Note that you can have multiple social media accounts configured. You may choose them from the dropdown list.

Step 4: Next, the report will be generated.

Step 5: A report can be printed, saved as a PDF or CSV, shared with others, etc., by using the toolbar available at the top right corner of the report.

Creating Custom Reports

Step 1: Click the bar graph (Analytics) icon on the left-aligned launch menu.

Step 2: Click "Build Custom Report" (Screenshot 7.6).

Step 3: Click "Custom Report."

Step 4: This will bring you to the custom report page.

Step 5: Click "Upload Image" to upload your logo or an image to brand the report. This is done by locating the image file on your computer and clicking "Open." You can also edit the details of your organization and type of header in the report.

Step 6: Under "Details" in the top left corner, type the title of your report and a brief description. Moreover, under "E-mail and Scheduling," click the drop-down menu and select the frequency of distribution.

> **Tip:** You can also have this report e-mailed to the members sharing this report by clicking on the box, making a check.

Step 7: Next, click on "Add Report Modules" and then click to select the module, adding it to your report. Modules with ENT and PRO are only available to enterprise users.

> **Note:** Modules added to your report can be removed by clicking "Remove" in the top right corner of the module on the report.

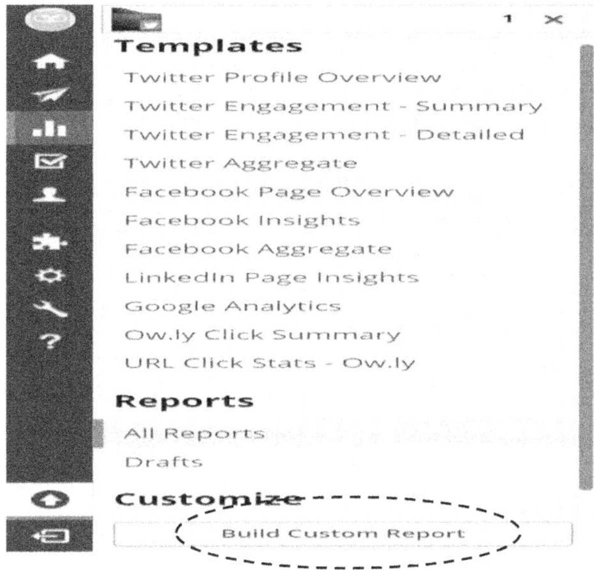

Screenshot 7.6. Creating custom reports with Hootsuite

Step 8: Complete the information requested by that module to achieve the best results. This may involve typing a title and keywords, selecting a social network profile, and so forth, and then click "Done."

Step 9: Click on the "Create Report" button available at the top right of the page. Alternatively, you can click "Save as Draft."

MONITORING AND ANALYZING FACEBOOK DATA WITH HOOTSUITE

Step 1: First, you need to add a new tab for the Facebook network. To do so, click the home (streams) icon on the left-aligned launch menu, and then click on the + icon (Screenshot 7.7).

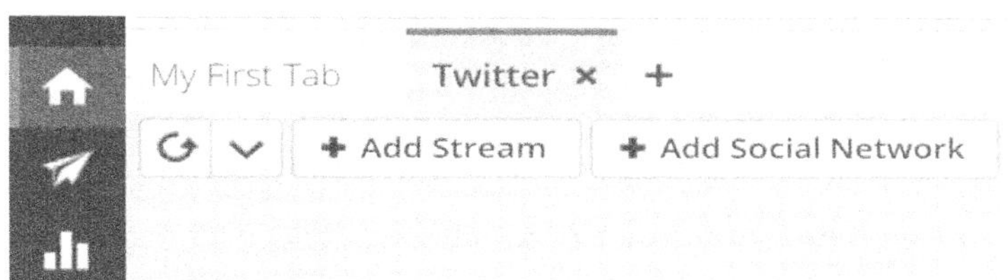

Screenshot 7.7. Creating a new stream in Hootsuite

Step 2: Name the new tab (e.g., Facebook).

Step 3: Click on the "Add Social Network" button.

Screenshot 7.8. Add a stream

Step 4: Select Facebook from the list, and click on the "Connect with Facebook" button.

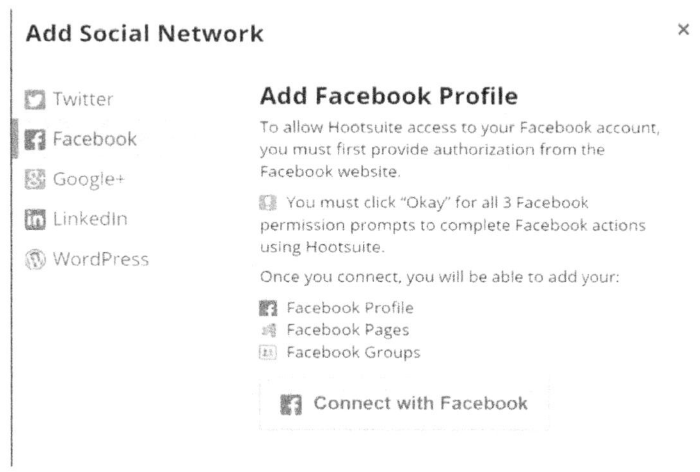

Screenshot 7.9. Add social network

Step 5: Type your Facebook e-mail (or mobile phone number) and password, and then click "Log In."

Step 6: Next, read Hootsuite's access to your Facebook account message; click to read "App Terms and Privacy Policy" in the bottom left corner, and then click "OK."

Step 7: Read posting permission note, click to select who can see the content you post to Facebook from Hootsuite, and then click "Okay."

> **Note:** Clicking "Skip" will prevent you from being able to post to Facebook from Hootsuite.

Step 8: Read the page permission note, and then click "Okay."

> **Note:** Clicking "Skip" will prevent you from being able to manage your Facebook pages from Hootsuite.

Step 9: Click to select the timeline, pages, and groups to import. A check mark indicates that the content will be imported; a plus icon indicates the content will not be imported. When done, click "Finished Importing."

Adding a Facebook Stream

Now that Facebook is added to Hootsuite, it is time to add streams to measure.

Step 1: Click the home (streams) icon on the left-aligned launch menu, then click the tab hosting your Facebook content.

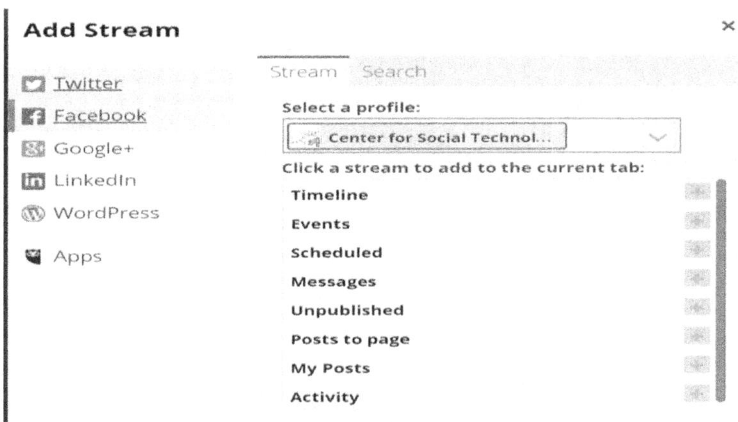

Screenshot 7.10. Adding Stream

Step 2: Next, click "Add Stream."

Step 3: Select Facebook and then select a profile that will stream content (in this case, we added a fan page).

Step 4: Click the **+** button across from the stream to add. This process can be **repeated** for multiple Facebook streams.

Similar steps can be repeated for configuring Twitter, Google+, WordPress, and LinkedIn streams for analytical purposes.

REVIEW QUESTIONS

1. Define social media actions analytics.
2. Briefly, list and define different actions performed by social media users.
3. Why is it essential to measure actions carried out by social media users?

EXERCISE 7.1: SOCIAL MEDIA CHANNEL SELECTION TOOL

Now that we have learned about the various social media actions that users, members, and followers in social media can take, it is time to determine which actions are most important for our organization, or for our personal goals.

Use the *Social Media Channel Selection* tool (available from the book companion site) to evaluate which social media channels are best suited for an audience. Use this tool to assess and rank the social media initiatives of the organization based on their strategic fit, impact, and feasibility. When done, click on the last tab of the spreadsheet to view the bubble matrix chart and communicate the findings of this analysis.

Key Benefits

- Evaluates multiple social media programs at one time.
- Allows for customized ranking of each channel.
- Includes high-quality charts that help tells stories with the data.
- Considers various components including strategic fit and cost.
- Saves several hours of visualization and formatting work.

Instructions

- In the "Selection Criteria" tab, customize weightings to match current business priorities. Be sure that the total weight equals no more or less than 100% (Figure 7.4).

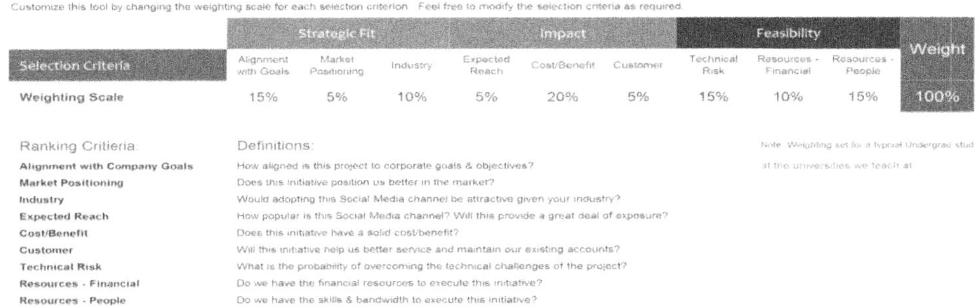

Customize this tool by changing the weighting scale for each selection criterion. Feel free to modify the selection criteria as required.

	Strategic Fit			Impact			Feasibility			Weight
Selection Criteria	Alignment with Goals	Market Positioning	Industry	Expected Reach	Cost/Benefit	Customer	Technical Risk	Resources - Financial	Resources - People	
Weighting Scale	15%	5%	10%	5%	20%	5%	15%	10%	15%	100%

Ranking Critieria:	Definitions:
Alignment with Company Goals	How aligned is this project to corporate goals & objectives?
Market Positioning	Does this initiative position us better in the market?
Industry	Would adopting this Social Media channel be attractive given your industry?
Expected Reach	How popular is this Social Media channel? Will this provide a great deal of exposure?
Cost/Benefit	Does this initiative have a solid cost/benefit?
Customer	Will this initiative help us better service and maintain our existing accounts?
Technical Risk	What is the probability of overcoming the technical challenges of the project?
Resources - Financial	Do we have the financial resources to execute this initiative?
Resources - People	Do we have the skills & bandwidth to execute this initiative?

Note: Weighting set for a typical Undergrad stud at the universities we teach at

Figure 7.4 Social media channel selection tool weightings (sample)

- In the "Channel Scoring" tab, rank each project on a scale of 1-10 based on how well it meets the selection criteria.

Rank each Social Media Channel on a scale of 1-10 for each criteria. There is a drop-down box for each Green, Amber, and Red cell

	Strategic Fit			Impact			Feasibility		
Social Media Channels	Alignment with Goals	Market Positioning	Industry	Expected Reach	Cost/Benefit	Customer	Technical Risk	Resources - Financial	Resources - People
Weighting	15%	5%	10%	5%	20%	5%	15%	10%	15%
Twitter	3	2	6	7	6	3	3	2	1
Facebook	9	7	6	7	9	9	5	5	6
Google+	1	2	1	3	2	2	1	2	1
SlideShare	10	9	7	9	8	8	1	6	2
Wordpress	9	9	7	8	5	4	3	5	3
LinkedIn	10	9	9	9	10	10	3	5	3
YouTube	3	5	6	5	5	4	5	5	2
Instagram	2	3	3	3	2	2	3	2	1
Pinterest	3	3	3	4	3	4	2	2	2
Myspace	1	1	1	1	1	1	2	1	1

Figure 7.5. Social media channel selection tool channel scoring (sample)

- Evaluate project scores in the "Rankings" tab to make resource allocation decisions.

Sort by selecting all Social Media Channels, Channel Score, Strategic Fit, Impact and Feasibility cells. Click "Data" and "Sort", and sort by Channel Score (Largest to Smallest)

Social Media Channels	Channel Score	Strategic Fit	Impact	Feasibility
LinkedIn	**7.2**	2.9	3.0	1.4
Facebook	**7.1**	2.3	2.6	2.2
SlideShare	**6.2**	2.7	2.5	1.1
Wordpress	**5.5**	2.5	1.6	1.4
YouTube	**4.3**	1.3	1.5	1.6
Twitter	**3.7**	1.2	1.7	0.8
Pinterest	**2.7**	0.9	1.0	0.8
Instagram	**2.2**	0.8	0.7	0.8
Google+	**1.5**	0.4	0.7	0.5
Myspace	**1.2**	0.3	0.3	0.6

Figure 7.6. Social media channel selection tool channel rankings (sample)

- Use the "Bubble Matrix" tab to communicate project rankings for strategic fit, impact, and feasibility. Based on the weightings, scorings and rankings in the Bubble Matrix diagram are produced that prioritize the most important channels to cultivate for our organization.

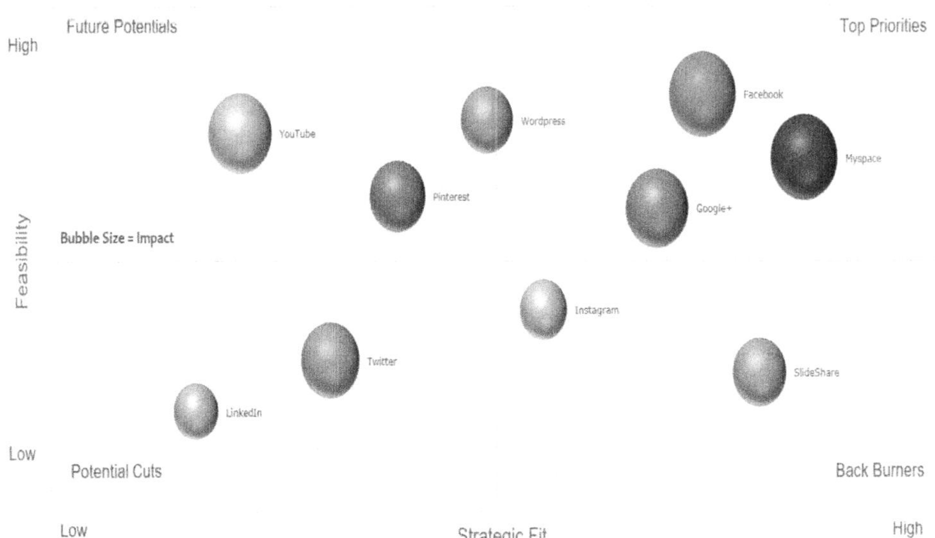

Figure 7.7. Social media channel selection tool bubble matrix (sample)

Additional Analyses

Taking the Channel Selection Analysis further, some additional steps could be added but are not currently built into the Excel Template.

- Previous return on investment by channel.
- The template could be modified to map out the most relevant channels from a cost/benefit analysis perspective.
- Competitor channel analysis
- Using what we know of our competitors or business partners and their marketing efforts, it is not very difficult to fill out the Social Media Channel Selection Tool by pretending to be that partner or competitor while using the tool.
- Using data from various University Library Databases (such as IBISWorld, or third-party analytics platforms such as ComScore MyMetrix/AdMetrix), it would be possible to come up with enough of the information needed to create channel weightings for almost any organization.

CHAPTER 7 REFERENCE

Petersen, R. (2012). *166 Cases Studies Prove Social Media Marketing ROI*. BarnRaisers.

Walker, R. (2009). *Social Media Ad Metrics Definitions, available at: http://www.iab.net/media/file/SocialMediaMetricsDefinitionsFinal.pdf*. Retrieved from

Chapter 8

Capturing Value with Search Engine Analytics

"If it is not on Google, it does not exist."—**Jimmy Wales**

Learning Outcomes

After completing this chapter, the reader should be able to:

- Understand search engines types and working mechanism.
- Develop a comprehensive understanding of search engine optimization (SEO).
- Differentiate between paid search and organic SEO.
- Understand search engine analytics and its types.
- Explain the two main categories of search engine analytics.
- Extract and analyze search engine data (using Google Trends and Google Correlate).

INTRODUCTION

Search Engines are the gateways to social media and help users search for and find information. *Search engines* are an Internet service or software designed to search information on the web that corresponds to a request (e.g., keywords) specified by the user. Considering that there are billions of websites over the web, search engines play a crucial role in helping us find the right information in a limited amount of time. In that sense, search engines have given us incredible information searching capabilities beyond our imagination. We can snip through millions of websites, documents, images, and videos with a click of a button. Before shifting our focus to search engines analytics, let us understand a brief history of search engines and its different types.

A BRIEF HISTORY OF SEARCH ENGINES

The existence of search engines date back to 1982 in the form of the 'WhOIS' search engine, which was generally used for querying Internet protocol (IP) related databases. However, mostly prior to September 1993, the World Wide Web was entirely indexed by hand. The first well-documented internet search engine was Archie used to search online content, which debuted on 10 September 1990. Alan Emtage, Bill Heelan, and Peter Deutsch computer science students at McGill University in Montreal programmed Archie. It was followed by several information searching scripts, robots (small computer programs), indexing, and crawlers tools created independently by a different computer scientist. By mid-1990s many search engines appeared in the market and competed for popularity. These included Magellan, Excite, Daum, Yahoo, and AltaVista. Yahoo! was among the most popular ways for people to find web pages of interest, but its search function operated on its web directory, rather than its full-text copies of web pages. Information seekers could also browse the directory instead of doing a keyword-based search. Currently, there are many active search engines, but there are a few that we are most familiar with such as, Google, Bing, Yahoo, and Ask. Table 8.1 shows a full list of famous search engine timeline.

TYPES OF SEARCH ENGINES

Based on the mechanisms they operate, we can divide search engines into three types:

- Crawler-Based
- Directories
- Metasearch Engines

Crawler-Based Search Engines

As the name suggests, *crawler-based* search engines create their databases or lists automatically, without any human intervention. Examples of a crawler-based search engine are Google.com and Bing.com. Crawler-based search engines are widely used to find and access content over the Internet. They operate in three steps:

- Web Crawling
- Indexing
- Searching

Table 8.1. Famous search engines timeline

Year	Engine	Current status (as of 2018)
1995	AltaVista	Inactive
	Daum	Active
	Magellan	Inactive
	Excite	Active
	SAPO	Active
	Yahoo!	Active,
1998	Google	Active
	Ixquick	Active
	MSN Search	Active as Bing
	Empas	Inactive
1999	AlltheWeb	Inactive
	GenieKnows	Active
	Naver	Active
	Teoma	Inactive
	Vivisimo	Inactive
2000	Baidu	Active
	Exalead	Active
	Gigablast	Active
2001	Kartoo	Inactive
2003	Info.com	Active
	Scroogle	Inactive
2004	Yahoo! Search	Active
	A9.com	Inactive
	Sogou	Active
2005	AOL Search	Active
2006	Ask.com	Active
	Live Search	Active as Bing
2009	Bing	Active
	NATE	Active

Web Crawling

Search engines start by collecting and storing information about web pages. This mechanism is termed *web crawling*. A web crawler (also known as a web spider or bot) is a computer program or software specifically designed to collect and store data about websites for indexing.

Indexing

Indexing helps classify a website correctly for searching purposes. The data crawled or extracted is then indexed and stored in a database for quick access.

Every search engine may follow different techniques for indexing web page data. Common indexing techniques include storing Meta tags (which are used in the header of a web page and provide descriptions of the website) and keywords related to a website.

Searching

Searching and ranking is the final step in search engine operations. When a user requests specific information by entering keywords into a search engine, the search engine queries the index and provides a list of the most relevant web pages by matching it with the indexed keywords. However, it may not be that simple; search engines use a variety of factors to rank and provide a list of matching websites (*search engine optimization is defined and discussed in more detail later in this chapter*).

Directories

The listings in *directories* are manually compiled and created by human editors. People who want to be listed in a directory submit an address, title, and brief description of their website, which is then reviewed by the editor and included in it. Some good examples of human-created directories are Yahoo Directory, Open Directory, and LookSmart.

Metasearch Engines

Metasearch engines compile and display results from other search engines. When a user enters a query, the metasearch engine submits the query to several individual search engines, and results returned from all the search engines are integrated, ranked, and displayed to the user. Examples of metasearch engines include Metacrawler, Mamma, and Dogpile. By integrating results from several search engines, metasearch engines are capable of handling large amounts of data and can help us save time by focusing on one search engine.

Local And Global Search Engines

Based on their scope, we can divide search engines into two types: local and global.

Local Search

A search engine is *local* in the sense that it is embedded within a website and only indexes and searches the content of that website. Amazon's CloudSearch or any other search engine embedded within a website is an example of a local search engine.

Global Search

Global search engines are used to search for content on the web. Google.com and Bing.com are examples of global search engines. However, note that global search engines can be localized. Google search, for example, can also embed within your website to help users find information on your website.

Other Types of Internal or Custom Search Engines

Besides popular public search engines, such as Google and Bing, there are other ways to utilize search technology to organize information. Many websites have their own search engines that enable searchers to find specific information hosted on the site. However, Google is not the only custom search engine provider around; there are other third-party vendors and types of search engines (images, videos, and even audio files). We will not go into the uses of custom search engines in depth; however, assisting searchers to find what they are searching for is win-win for site owners and searchers (and it is always a good idea to keep your searchers/customers/audience happy).

Google Custom Search Engine

Site administrators can use Google's search technology to set up their own search engines for a selected index of pages (on their website or a collection of any websites on the Web); custom search engine users can also configure how search queries are processed.

Free Third Party Search Engines

Many third-party search engines can be installed on a website (usually via a script/web API call).

Google Search Console

Formally called Google Webmaster Tools, this search engine provides information that had been, up to this point, missing from web analytics/search analytics, such as impression data from the Google search engine as well as crawling performance and/or messages from Google-bot, and other Google services. The Google Search Console must be authenticated and is the way that webmasters can communicate and receive communications from Google about the health and performance of their websites. Search Console users authenticate their accounts by uploading a specific Google supplied file to the web server, or adding a meta tag to the HTML of the website, or adding a new DNS record referring to the search console address or using their Google Analytics or

Google Tag Manager account. For more information about the Search Console including configuration and authentication search for Google Webmaster Tools.

Enterprise Search Engines

Many organizations have their industrial strength search engines; they require a different, but similar set of data algorithms than the more popular search engines have. It is important for marketers to have search queries of potential and actual customers as they navigate through their website. Armed with the information marketers can find out what customers are looking for on their sites and if they found it or not. Marketers can use this information to improve their offerings to fall in line with what customers want.

Video Search Engines

Video search engines such as YouTube and Vimeo are becoming increasingly popular and valuable as a way to glean market intelligence, and YouTube is the second largest search engine in the world, next to the main Google search engine.

Vertical Search Engines

Vertical search engines such as Career Services (LinkedIn, Monster.com, CareerBuilder) and dating search engines (Match.com, eHarmony, JDate, Plentyoffish) are customized search engines with specific listings of jobs, employers, products, partners and /or services, but the list keeps on growing. A search engine can be created around almost any subject, and depending on what the listings contain, will probably need to adapt (i.e., sound files, location files, visual files) to the time of searches that can be done and the kinds of information that searchers use the search engine to obtain.

Facts About Internet Search

- As of 2018, Google Search is the indisputable leader of the global search engine market, boasting an 86.36 percent market share. In April 2018, online search engine Bing accounted for 6.45 percent of the global search market. During the same month, Chinese search engine Baidu had a market share of 0.86 percent (source: Statistica).
- 92 percent of U.S. Internet users have used search with organic search being 'free' to use.
- As search engines are widely used by consumers continually looking for

information, businesses have realized that they need to be present and rank well in search results page.

- 29 percent of U.S. Internet users search engines daily.
- young and old use Internet search.
- all races/ethnicities use the Internet search function.
- college-educated more likely to use Internet search engines.
- Digital marketers are using search engines for everything.
- Search engines are used for branding (the awareness customers or potential customers have of a brand being seen in top search results when a branded search term, or the name of the Brand, is searched for).
- Online sales—search engines are known to be among the most efficient and cost-effective ways to drive prospects to web pages (mainly when they want to purchase a product or service).
- Lead generation—organic search is an efficient and cost-effective way to acquire potential customers, while paid search is hugely reliable and trackable for analytics, mainly search and web analytics, lending itself well for ROI (Return on Investment) calculations.
- The history of search engines is rich, but Google stole the game, and most of what is interesting in search engines has happened at Google since the turn of the century.
- Search engines evolved with the field of text analytics; as the World Wide Web evolved and spread, content was appearing with higher velocity and volume (Big Data). To create a search engine, web crawlers are needed to analyze the regularly updated version of the web within the search engine's grasp by compiling an index of the content. Web Crawlers or simplified browsers that traverse links on a web page explore a website and capture a copy of everything on it to be processed by the search engine.

HOW SEARCH ENGINES WORK

While the heavy reliance on web links seems somewhat crude and overused today, Google's *Page Rank* algorithm was revolutionary in its time for finding and ranking quality content over inferior content (websites and pages) for a specific search term or query. As time went on judging the quality of a site based on its links became much less useful as search marketers developed methods to manipulate the search results. Because of this activity, more subtle and sophisticated methods were used to determine the order of ranking of pages for a specific search term/terms.

- By the mid-1990's, the *World Wide Web* (and the Internet) quickly became crowded. The Internet routers, servers and bandwidth were being strained by the capabilities of the devices then in place, and a means to cut down unnecessary internet traffic quickly evolved to meet the need. Web caching developed as a mechanism that saves local copies of time-stamped web data (on a local server), instead of going to the source of the data, a web server connects merely with a local web cached version, which remains in place till the original data is updated at its source. Once the change is detected it propagates, and the local copies are updated, so they stay in sync with the original.

- Search indexes evolved as a sorted "master list," so to speak, of the websites and pages of each website currently available on the World Wide Web (fed by the Internet crawlers a search engine employed to get the data in the first place).
- Once a user enters a search term or phrase, it is evaluated by the search engine (which tries to understand what the term means as well as any misspellings that may be present). The most relevant pages in the search index are matched with the query and served up to the user by the search engine, operating on its unique set of search algorithms.

SEARCH ENGINE ANALYTICS

When we talk about search engine analytics, we usually mean two things:

- Search Engine Optimization
- Search Engine Data Analysis

Search Engine Optimization

Search engine optimization (SEO) are the techniques used to improve a website's ranking in a search engine result page (SERP) in order to bring more customers to a website (Davis, 2006; Malaga, 2010)(see Figure 8.1). A SERP is the list of the results returned by a search engine in response to a user's query. For example, consider a social media consulting company has a website about the consulting services they provide. When someone searches on Google or Bing, for "social media consulting," the ranking or placement of the company's website in the SERP will determine how well the website is optimized for the search engine (see Figure 8.2). The better your website is optimized for search engines, the higher will be its ranking. SERP results usually include a title, a hyperlink that points to the original website, and a short description showing where the keywords have matched content within the page for organic results. SERP results usually contain 10 organic listings and some paid listing on the top or right side.

When it comes to SEO ethics, mainly two types of SEO techniques are available:

White Hat SEO

These are the *ethical techniques* available to rank higher on SERP (Malaga, 2008, 2010). Most techniques (such as link building, social sharing, and website optimization) discussed in this book are *white hate.*

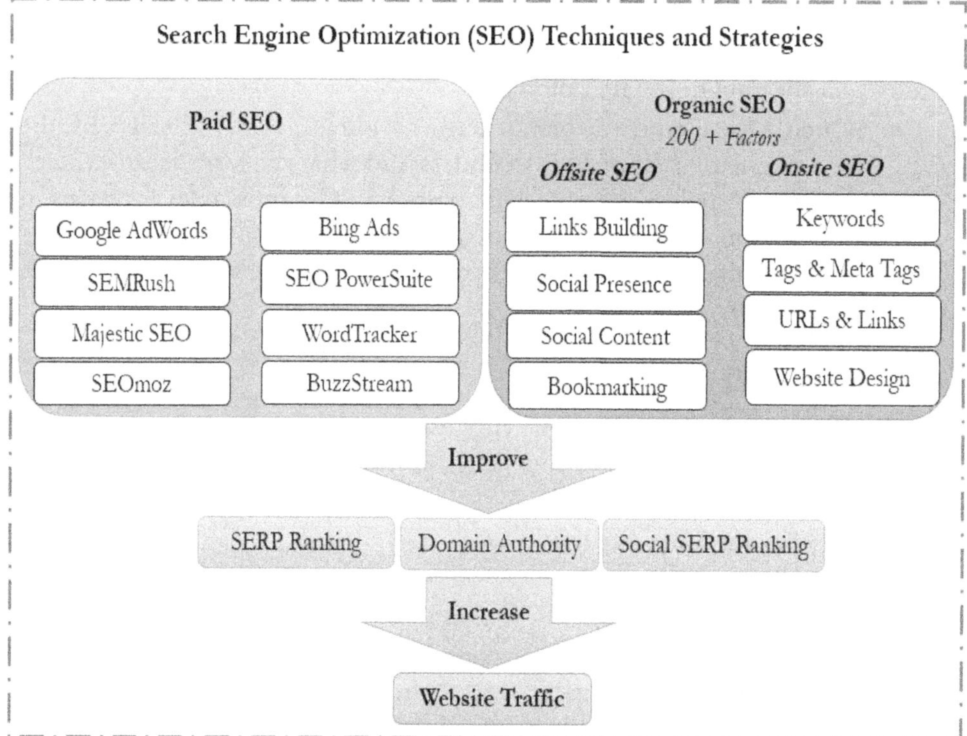

Figure 8.1. SEO techniques and strategies

Black Hat SEO

In the early days, SEO was mainly considered a shortcut to gain more website traffic and a website could easily rank high using *black-hat* SEO techniques, such as (1) stolen, duplicate, spun, thin or no content; (2) keyword stuffing, cloaking, or spamming; (3) link farms, link spam, purchased links, or link manipulation; and (4) light affiliate, top massive ad sites. However, as Google's algorithms are becoming more sophisticated and intelligent, such tactics have much less impact on search rankings. New Google algorithms such as Panda, Penguin, and Hummingbird can easily detect unethical SEO practices, and websites using such techniques are penalized or even blocked from Google SERP. Thus, unethical SEO techniques should be avoided at any cost.

Objective of SEO

The prime objective of SEO is to get more traffic (or prospective customers) to a company's website through search engines (Figure 8.1). Social media marketers strive to develop search engine strategies to make their websites appear at the top of search results. It is vital for their websites to appear at the top (e.g., in the first page of the search results) in the SERP, as users pay close attention to the top results on search engines (Pan et al., 2007). The ranking becomes more crucial when a website is commercial, that is, selling products or services. High rankings on SERP can mean more Internet traffic to a website, which in some cases converts to more paying clients and a higher return on investment (Weideman, 2009).

Types of SERPs

As you can see from the Figure 8.1, SERPs have two types of results:

- Paid Search Results
- Organic Search Results

Let us discuss these in detail.

Paid SERPs

Paid search results include paid advertisements mostly appearing at the top of the listing or the right side. Also known as "Search Engine Marketing" or SEM, paid search results are mostly determined by a combination of advertising spend (budget) and how often people click on it. Google AdWords is an excellent example of a paid SEO tool. Google AdWords search ads appear next to Google search results when people research for keywords that correspond with the products and services you offer (Figure 8.2). In order for their ads to appear in Google's SERP, advertisers bid on specific keywords that are relevant to their products/services. Advertisers are only charged when people click to visit their website.

A research study tested the effect of sponsored ad ranks on the click-through and conversion rates for an online retailer and found that top positions usually had a higher click-through rate, but not necessarily higher conversion rate

(Ashish Agarwal, Kartik Hosanagar, & Smith, 2011); however, it's not hard to see why. Conversion rates depend on the customer's experience on the landing page(s). While search engines are becoming more intelligent and successful in matching search results with a searcher's experience on landing pages via algorithms and analytics: they have not fully succeeded (yet).

Advantage and Disadvantages of Paid SEO

Paid ads have their advantages and disadvantages. Marketers can and should combine both paid and organic SEO (discussed next), as most organizations have several initiatives that can benefit from both types of strategies. The Table 8.2 lists potential advantages and disadvantages of paid SEO.

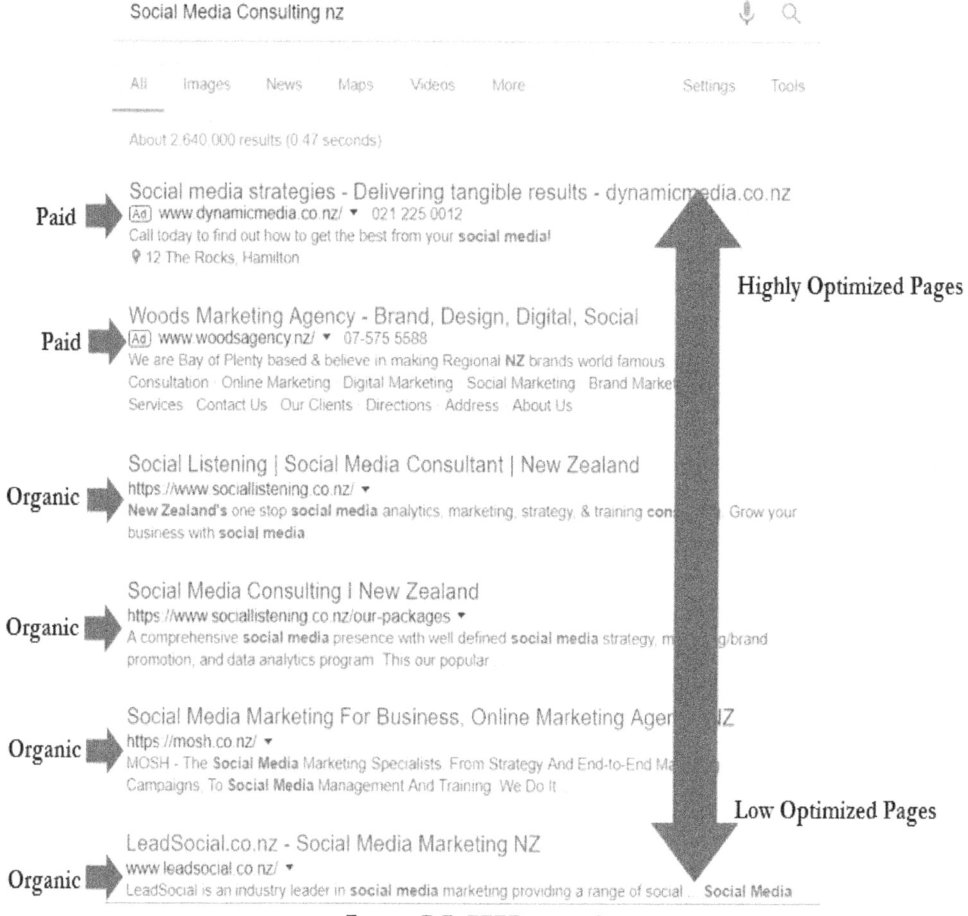

Figure 8.2. SERP example

Organic SERP

Organic or *unpaid* SERP results are automatically generated by a search engine's algorithm because of their relevance to the user's query.

How to Rank High on SERP organically?
Search engines use more than 200 factors to rank and provide a list of matching websites. However, here we discuss the most essential *onsite* and *offsite* SEO factors.

Onsite SEO Factors

Onsite SEO is the processes of optimizing the overall structure of a website to rank higher on SERP organically. Crucial onsite SEO techniques include:

- Meaningful URL structures
- Titles Tags
- Header Tags
- Alt Text
- Anchor Text
- Keywords
- Website Contents

Next, we discuss each of these briefly.

Table 8.2. Advantages and disadvantages of paid SEO

Advantages of Paid SEO	Disadvantages of Paid SEO
Very fast—get targeted visitors within hours.	Expensive.
If executed correctly, can yield highly profitable results.	Heavy competition: Competitive keywords demand higher bids.
Highly targeted—you can choose when to show your website (ad) based time of day, geographic area, or keywords and phrases searched by users.	You pay regardless of any sales: payment is based on clicks on your website address. However, more website traffic generated as a result of clicks doesn't necessarily mean more sales.
Immediate feedback.	Traffic stops when you stop paying.

Meaningful URLs

URL stands for *Uniform Resource Locator* and is used to specify addresses on the World Wide Web. A URL is the key network identification for any resource connected to the web (e.g., hypertext pages, images, and sound files). While URLs are unique to a site, they should be carefully considered before they are assigned. Consider the following two URLs:

- URL 1: https://www.sociallistening.co.nz/social-media-analytics/training-course
- URL 2: https://www.sociallistening.co.nz/44553???&&/zzddee/url$%

Compared to URL 2, URL 1 is more meaningful as it includes relevant keywords (search engines consider keywords within URLs as a ranking factor) and easy for the target audience to recall. Keywords strategically placed in the URL help search engines to understand the meaning of the content of web pages and websites. As a result, customers are provided with more relevant content, based on what they are searching for, and the same considerations impact the Title Tag, Header Tags, Body Text, Alt Text, and Anchor Text (as explained below).

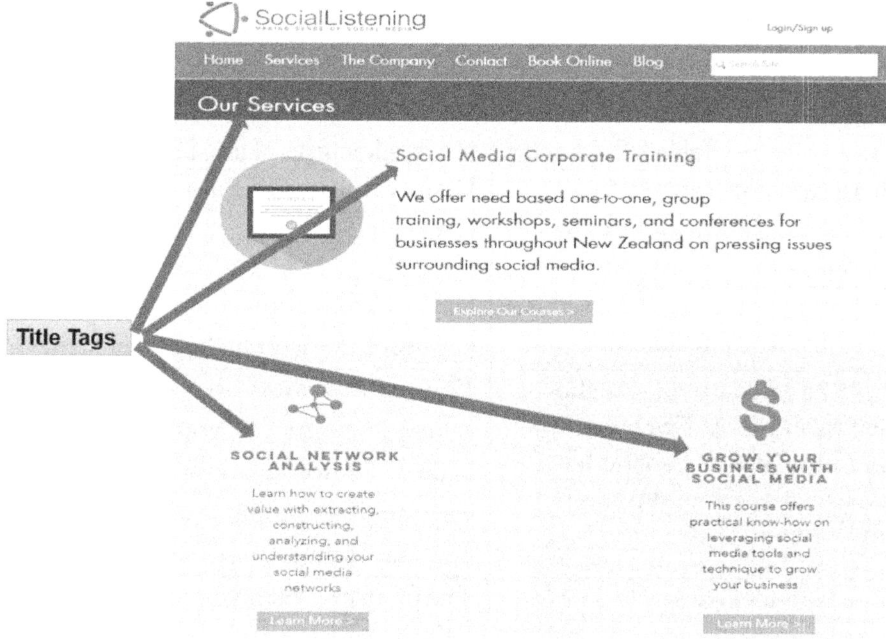

Figure 8.3. Tile tags example

Title Tag

The *title tag* is an HTML title element critical to both SEO and user experience. It is used to briefly and accurately describe the topic and theme of online documents and websites (Figure 8.3). The title tag is displayed in the top bar of internet browsers. Title tags play an essential role in onsite SEO; therefore, it should be meaningful, relevant to the content of the website, and spelled correctly.

Header Tags

The *header tag*, or the <h1> tag in HTML, will usually be the title of a post, or other emphasized text on the page. It will usually be the largest text that stands out. There are other header tags in HTML too, like h2, h3, h4, so forth. Some useful tips regarding writing your title tags:

- Place your header tag <h1></h1> at the top of the page, preferably after the <body> tag.
- Include relevant business keywords that you wish to rank higher for in SERPs. If your h1 happens to be an image, use the image alt tag to add those target keywords.
- You can have more than one header tag on the page, but one is preferred.

Main Content (Body Text)

The main content is not usually the first thing on a web page. Keyboard and screen reader users generally must navigate a long list of navigation links, sub-lists of links, corporate icons, site searches, and other elements before ever arriving at the *main content* (see http://webaim.org/techniques/skipnav/).

Alt Text

Alt text (alternative text) is a word or phrase inserted as an attribute in an HTML (Hypertext Markup Language) document to tell a website viewer the nature or contents of an image. The alt text appears in a blank box that would typically contain the picture.

Keywords

Having essential and relevant *keywords* embedded in a website enables a search engine robot to evaluate the website as being the most suitable site for the searched word. For example, a keyword density of 5–8 percent (i.e., five to eight keywords per one hundred words) is an optimal number. Other things to consider are the keyword hierarchy (alignment of keywords with specific web pages throughout the website) and keyword layout (where the keywords are located on the web page).

However, if one repeatedly uses the same keywords or definitions in page content, it may be perceived by a robot to be spamming (Yalçın & Köse, 2010). Adding keywords to the title of a page can impact web page visibility in a search engine (Zhang & Dimitroff, 2005). In addition, search visibility can be improved by increasing the frequency of keywords in the title, the full text, and in both the title and full-text. A takeaway here is that in order to achieve good search results, an organization must place keywords in section titles, images, and in the general content of its website.

Website Design

In conjunction with keywords, the overall *design*, *usability*, and *page loading speed* of a website is an essential factor that must be taken into consideration when discussing search engine optimization. For example, flash animations, while aesthetically appealing, can negatively impact the SEO evaluation results because they cannot be indexed as quickly by bots as more structured HTML content (Yalçın & Köse, 2010). For a corporation to better understand its Internet presence, its website statistics should also be checked on a regular basis so as to understand both how users access and utilize the site and also what impact site changes may have on these behaviors.

Anchor Text

The text that is displayed as highlighted in a hypertext link can be clicked to open the target web page (see https://moz.com/learn/seo/anchor-text).

Offsite SEO

Offsite SEO is the processes and strategies taken outside a company's websites to rank higher on SERP organically. Common offsite SEO techniques include:

- Backlinks Building
- Social Sharing

Backlinks Building

From a search engine perspective, *backlinks* are most commonly known as "link building" or "reputation building." For social media marketers, it is essential to understand the mechanism behind the offsite SERP ranking. The most critical factor that determines SERP ranking is the PageRank. PageRank is a mechanism (or an algorithm, to be more precise) used by Google search engines to rank websites' SERPs. The websites that rank higher are displayed on the top of the search results page. Google's PageRank algorithm predominantly relies on the number and quality of incoming hyperlinks (or in-links) to rank websites. A website, for example, with in-links from some famous websites (e.g., cnn.com) will appear on the top of the SERP if compared with a website with no quality in-links or many low-quality in-links. To understand the in-link quality and number argument, consider Figure 8.4, where nodes represent web pages and lines represent in-links (arrowhead pointing to a page) and out-links (arrowhead pointing away from a page). The PageRank algorithm will place page B higher on the SERP, even though there are fewer in-links to B when compared to D. The reason for this ranking is that in-links to website B are from a critical website; that is, A. The bottom line is that your objective is to increase the number of quality in-links to your website.

For example, by using Open SEO Stats (an extension for Google Chrome available at http://pagerank.chromefans.org/), users can determine the ranking of a website based on Google PageRank. Google PageRank uses a scale of 0 to 10, indicating the importance that the Google search engine allocates to the page. In addition to page ranking, Open SEO Stats also provides information about website traffic, hyperlink status, and speed of the page, among other things.

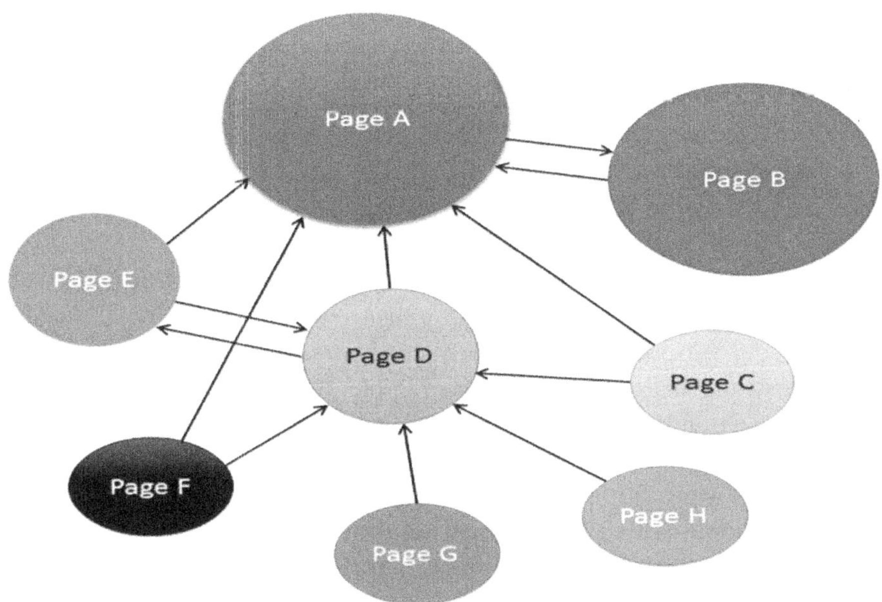

Figure 8.4. PageRank algorithm ranking example

Other core aspects of backlink building are the following:

- The greater the number of backlinks the better. However, they should be quality backlinks; otherwise, the website may be penalized. Quality backlinks are the ones coming from famous and well-known websites.
- Obtain backlinks from related/relevant websites.
- Finding links to relevant competitors.
- Giving other websites a reason to link to the site (this could be related to having compelling content on the site).
- Create new content that will hopefully attract links from other websites (Link bait falls into this category).
- Link freshness—search engines can detect abnormal linking strategies and penalize those sites that use them. When it looks like a website is getting new backlinks too quickly based on its size and update activity, it decides if the link growth is abnormal or not.
- Link diversity—it is about attracting backlinks from a variety of domains (e.g., .com, .net, .edu, and .org).

Social Sharing

Social sharing is the practice of establishing a sound social media presence. Social media presence (social media accounts, contents, engagement) do have a significant impact on your SEO rankings. In fact, social media profiles are often amongst the top results in SERP listings for brand names. When you search "Dell" in Google, the company's Twitter profiles appeared as the 2nd listings alongside other social media profiles (YouTube, LinkedIn, Facebook) on right-side of SERP(see Figure 8.5). The third listing is an article on Dell in Wikipedia (also a collaborative social media platform).

In addition to optimizing search engines, companies need to optimize social media search engines as well. Because your customers don't just use Google and Bing to find your product and services; they also use search engines embedded within social media channels to search for people, brands, product, and services. For example, if your brand has a Facebook fan page, it's entirely conceivable that prospective customers will discover your product and services after searching for relevant fan pages using the Facebook search engine. It can happen when people search your brand, relevant tweets, and #hashtags using Twitter search engines. Moreover, customers are more likely to visit your Twitter and Facebook and do a quick search to see what kind of presence you have on each channel.

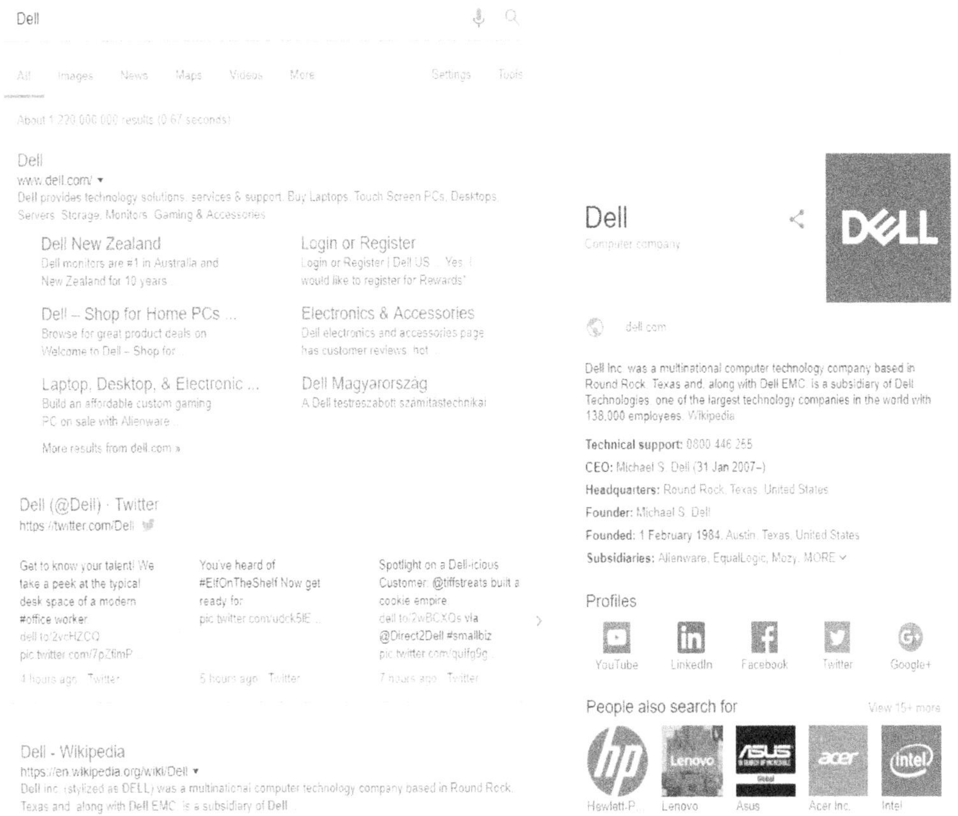

Figure 8.5. Dell's social media profiles in SERP

WEBSITE SEARCH CONSIDERATIONS

Once a visitor arrives on a specific website, they will often search within the website for specific items using the "internal search engine," when provided. Many websites have deployed internal search using Google's customized free site search services. Using internal search engine query logs, webmasters can create needs assessments and help determine areas where content is missing that would better serve existing and potential customers.

One of the significant advantages of having internal site search set up and running on a website is that the site owner can understand the unmet needs of the visitors. Because external search engine referral traffic reflects only those searchers who decided to click on a link appearing in the search engine result page that led to the website/page. In other words, all the searches that were made where the website appeared as an impression, for a searcher to click on but was not clicked on, are not usually captured in web analytics.

Understanding and Optimizing Search Engine Performance

While there are several books on this subject, performing SEO on a site comes down to having a defined need to improve the business performance of a website or group of websites and using various tools and methods employed to achieve that purpose.

- Organic search engine traffic is considered "owned media" traffic and website owners have first-party data provided by their web analytics platforms. The default data collection is often sufficient for small businesses, but it is inadequate for larger organizations with more sophisticated reporting needs.
- Organic and paid search terms and referral reports (these often work well enough out of the box, but can be customized to increase their efficiency and effectiveness, particularly for enterprise reporting).
- The third-party search engine optimization tools help website owners improve the search engine ranking and performance of their website properties. Among the capabilities of these tools is the ability to crawl a site to find out how many pages exist within it and how they appear to the more familiar search engines (thereby helping site owners to eliminate issues affecting how their websites are ranking by search engines for specific user search queries). These organic search tools help users improve the quality and number of backlinks to their sites. Some of them also provide competitive research capabilities that could be useful for website optimization and business performance.

Popularity Metrics role in Search Engine Optimization

Page Rank, *Author Rank*, *Trust Rank*, *MozRank*, and *Authority Rank* are another way of ranking content based on its quality. Page Rank is a measure of the quality of a page or site based on the number and quality of incoming/outgoing links on the page. Author Rank rates the authority of the author of the content in the search engine while Trust Rank rates the trustworthiness of the backlinks from the websites pointing to the website or web page. Authority ranking is an alternative metric calculated by Moz for Page Rank indicating how likely a domain or website will rank in Google's search results.

Popularity metrics are easy for search engines and analytics vendors to generate; they are helpful as a directional indicator that optimization changes are having a positive effect on search engine ranking. However, search engines and their continuously updated algorithms are the only real authority as they have the entire formula and decide how to rank a page. The most successful strategy for SEO is providing content that the audience finds valuable.

Additional Ways to Generate Search Engine Traffic

- Online press releases are one way to generate links and traffic that might influence the quality and popularity scores though they are not as effective as they once were.
- User engagement data ported from web analytics platforms (Google Analytics) to the search engine (Google) can influence search engine ranking.
- Sharing of photos, art, video, and music via social media can generate online discussion, engagement with the website, and ultimately, a higher quality score, if this occurs on a regular basis and search engines detect it.
- Wikis that allow users to post, edit, and organize content, as well as online ratings and reviews, can be useful tools for engaging online users.

The real issue with SEO is that it is often not applied strategically enough as shown in Figure 8.6.

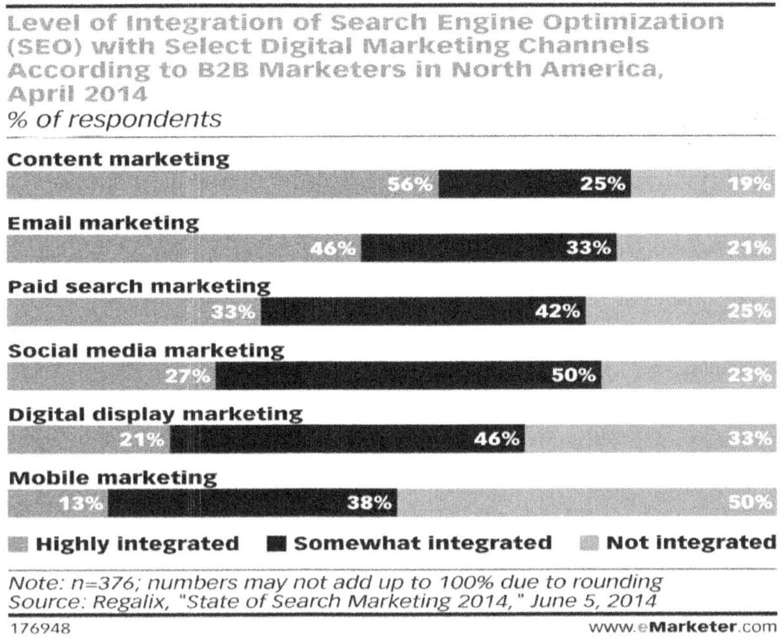

Figure 8.6. SEO integration into digital marketing

While content marketing is the most effective single thing website owners can do, it is also true that by default, optimizing content usually includes making it more SEO friendly. On the other hand, most other marketing tactics are too often not used in a strategic way along with SEO, which makes it much harder to obtain the full value of the optimization work done.

SUMMARIZING ORGANIC SEARCH ENGINE OPTIMIZATION

- Many third-party tools can be used in conjunction with Google Analytics, or other web analytics, to better understand and improve the SEO of websites or blogs.
- Organic SEO is an "owned media" acquisition and customer intelligence strategy as well as a content creation strategy.
- Success with SEO depends on upon understanding the "Voice of the Customer" and creating content that addresses what customers and potential customers search for.
- Web usability is the ease of use of a website. Search engines are increasingly assigning higher ranking in the search results to content when it has more "Web Usability" or UX.
- Every piece of data reflects an activity, and all search activity is trackable.
- Search engines are getting much better at detecting signals; they used only to look at the text in the beginning, but now they find patterns and are getting more and more intelligent.

Additional points to keep in mind about search engine algorithms:

- Search engines are an early application of document classification, and the same basic algorithmic methods applied to web documents gathered by Google off of the World Wide Web (Internet) and Internal documents, and file types gathered within organizations (intranet).
- Furthermore, the area of information retrieval and text mining are almost identical regardless of the kind of application (Internet search and retrieval, image retrieval, and classification). Sound recording information retrieval, company or subject area text indexing and retrieval, and even social media analytics require almost identical methods of processing, storage, transformation, normalization, ranking, clustering and displaying the information in some way that benefits the end user (even if the end user ends up being another computer program).
- Search engines define relevance by using classification and weighting elements within the dataset.
- Page rank was an algorithm invented to improve search results. It was a significant factor in the emergence of Google as the leading search

engine, a place it still holds today. Recently, mobile websites were strengthened as a ranking signal in Google's algorithm when mobile traffic from search surpassed desktop and laptop share. Page rank takes into account many factors, both on the page and off the page.

For Example:

- URL's could have a weight of 100.
- Title text or paragraph or section headings could have a weight of 95.
- Anchor text in a link of a URL pointing to another site could have a weight of 90.
- Anchor text in a link of a URL pointing to an internal page of a website (say the home page) could have a weight of 80.
- Plain text in a document could have a weight of 60.
- Plain text with various text sizes and italics/underlines could have various weights as well, and so on.

Ranking and classification can further be contextualized and customized depending on the purposes and needs at hand, and by doing so, these acts potentially become much more valuable. The arrangement and markup of data have turned out to be more valuable than the raw data it describes (metadata is the information that describes the data it points to). For example, when searching for a video the metadata the topic of the video and when and where it was created allows the search engine to find the video. Conversely, what is in the video would not be very helpful as search engines cannot yet understand the raw footage in the video.

SEARCH ENGINE RANKING EXAMPLE

The number of words in a search query significantly affect the *search engine rankings*. For example, a generic term with one word (like "consulting") is going to be very common in several million documents or pages and be hard to rank in the top search results in any conceivable way. On the other hand, "social media consulting," while still a difficult term to rank for, is a thousand times easier to get top ranking for than "consulting." Finally, a term such as "social media consulting New Zealand" may be very easy to get a good search ranking for because there are probably very few viable competitors for that term in the search results.

Consequently, the more words in a search query, the more likely there will be less competition for top ranking, but the audience for that result might be much smaller (perhaps only a few people will be searching for "social media consulting New Zealand." Similarly, there is less competition and less demand in a local search than the searches not restricted by location. If the audience is highly valued (and highly segmented), say a "millionaire's club" located in a town, where several of the members are looking for social media consulting, then you might have hit a valuable niche.

Paid Search Terms

Keywords—these are words & phrases triggering ads to display in the search engine results page (paid).

Ads—short sales pitches in text or images.

Bids—how much advertisers are willing to spend to show their ads, get clicks & conversions.

Landing Page—first-page people see after they click an ad (often where the conversion also takes place).

Conversions—actions that visitors take on a website such as leads, orders, downloads, phone calls.

Process—managing the tracking results, conversions, return on ad spends with testing, improving, tools & resources.

The following are terms related to paid ads.

- Pay Per Click (PPC)—an Internet advertising model in which advertisers pay to publishers when an ad is clicked.
- Search Engine Marketing (SEM)—SEM Internet marketing technique which involves the promotion of websites (or content) by increasing its visibility in search engine results pages mainly through paid listings.
- AdWords—AdWords is Google's Internet advertising service in which advertisers pay to display brief advertising in Google's ads network.
- Impressions—it is the number of times an ad is served or displayed on a platform (e.g., in Facebook news feeds)
- Click-through Rate (CTR)—CTR merely is when a user clicks on an ad and goes to the web page the ad links to. It is calculated as the number of instances an ad is clicked divided by the number of times it is displayed (also known as total ad impressions).
- Conversion and Conversion Rate—Conversion is the desired action

taken by a customer (e.g., product sales, login, download, subscription) after clicking an advertisement. The conversion rate is calculated by taking the number of conversions and dividing that by the number of total ad clicks that can be tracked to a conversion during the same time period. For example, if you had 100 conversions from 10,000 clicks, your conversion rate would be 1%, since (100 ÷ 10,000) * 100 = 1%.

- Cost Per Acquisition (CPA)—It is the cost to acquire a conversion.

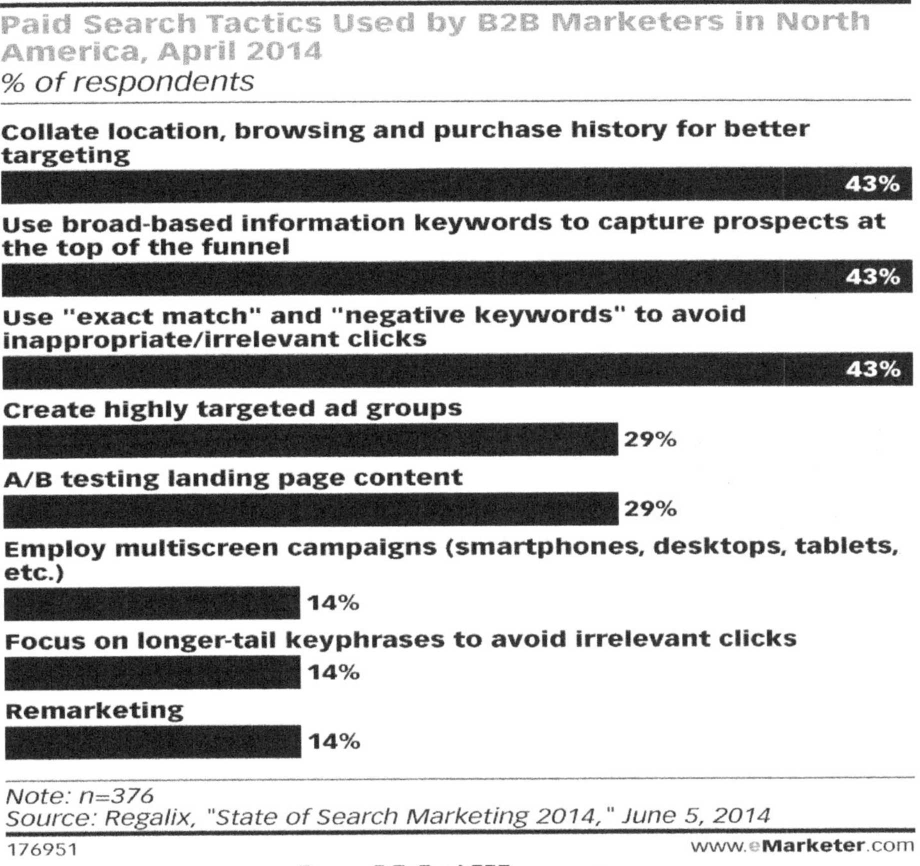

Figure 8.7. Paid SEO strategies

Text Ad Effectiveness

The *cost per click* and average position of an ad is a function of the bidding strategy along with the actual quality of the text link ad to be clicked on.

Paid search metrics are now able to be imported into a Web analytics platform or reside within the paid search campaign platform (usually Google AdWords, Bing Ads or some other third party ad network platform running the ads across ad exchanges). Text ad effectiveness depends on the advertiser and the industry; some businesses perform better than others based on Cost Per Click (CPC) and Click Through Rate (CTR) (see Table 8.3).

Table 8.3. Performance metrics of paid search text ads

Performance Metrics of US Paid Search Text Ads on Google AdWords, by Industry, 2014

	Impressions (billions)	CTR	CPC	Ad spending (millions)
Shopping and classifieds	67.27	5.36%	$0.75	$2,715.4
Financial services	12.03	6.41%	$2.83	$2,182.0
Travel	14.62	6.44%	$0.91	$858.0
Education	4.76	5.06%	$4.41	$1,060.7
Automotive	12.78	4.56%	$1.69	$985.1
Business	8.66	5.00%	$2.30	$996.0

Note: desktop/tablet only
Source: AdGooroo, "Yahoo! Bing Paid Search Performance Metrics," April 21, 2015

188794 www.eMarketer.com

Table 8.3 demonstrates that paid text ads are more effective in some industries than others. From a business perspective, it is no secret that not every transaction happens in a vacuum; there are undoubtedly buyers and sellers of a product or service, and this is often best symbolized with the "exchange" or "auction" model. Nothing in this transaction has an actual fixed price and varies based on supply and demand. In that light, it might be more illuminating to look at the number of people searching for products or services in each industry online and the value to the user of what is being offered to evaluate better whether the campaigns are profitable or not. What is more telling is that the metrics provided do not say if "targeting" or "creative" is effective or not and by how much.

Intermediate metrics such as CPC, CPA, CTR provided by the advertising platforms are unable to measure the advertising quality (though Google AdWords does have a "quality score" that is performance-based but probably does not go far enough because Google cannot yet read the mind or emotions of the viewer). If we go further down the rabbit hole, the majority of significant transactions (organizations running several thousand ads a day) are running by automation and bidding strategies along with Programmatic Advertising. Considering technology, just how accurate are metrics provided by platform vendors?

The standard metrics provided by most analytics platforms do not address "ad blocking" (and they may not be able to provide the number of blocked ads on a mobile device) which became an issue in 2015 when Apple built-in Ad Blocking to iOS 9. We can only control a part of the "equation" of search engine ranking, and at that, imperfectly, since Google and other search engines are changing the ranking factors and weightings while keeping the exact algorithms as trade secrets.

On the other hand, even of the elements we control, it is possible for malicious code to infect our websites and influence our rankings and even our inclusion in the search engine index. For that reason, it is better to keep search engine optimization as simple and straightforward as possible, perhaps even being more conservative when implementing adaptive features (such as an infinite scroll feature) because they may impact how search engines process and rank websites in search results.

DEVELOPING A SEARCH OPTIMIZATION STRATEGY AND IMPLEMENTING IT

From an analytics perspective, the best way to go about marketing campaigns is to try it first and wait a few weeks before making any changes (exploratory approach), collect the analytics and feedback, and use a "cycle of improvement" approach to understanding the gaps and strengths of your website. At a certain point, when there is enough data to know what things need to change or add, then it is time to define and implement an SEO strategy.

To run effective paid search campaigns, the majority of paid search marketers need to collect a massive amount of first-party data from their websites (usually with the help of Web analytics reporting tools, such as Google Analytics). Paid search marketers also need to generate and run several keyword variations, meaning they typically have an extensive list of keywords to run on paid search engines on a regular basis. Usually, this alone can turn out to be someone's full-time job. While paid search advertising can involve content that has images, the most common type of paid search ad is a text ad. Text ads require the advertiser to define the title, description lines, and display URL as part of the ad. Furthermore, A/B testing is an excellent way to find out the best format for the ad. A/B testing compares two versions of an ad to see which one performs better.

In general, the higher the ads appear on a web page, or the search result page, the more clicks they get, and the more advertisers pay for those ads. There are also targeting methods (broad vs narrow) in matching up keywords and phrases to searchers and what they are searching for online (based on their search queries). The overall performance of advertising campaigns has more to do with the targeting used than what is in the ad. Paid advertising is not a total marketing solution for most businesses, but advertising can be beneficial for short-term campaign events (such as a sale or time-sensitive offering) as they offer precision targeting (or at least the illusion of it). For the long-term, paid advertising can address branding needs if done within a strategic plan.

When customers view impressions of a brand ad several times, even when there is no click on the ad they will eventually be influenced by what they see. As a result, brand managers should measure branding using a more extended period than most commonly used with conversion metrics.

Using Paid and Organic Search Together

Often businesses rely on a single strategy to succeed. However, in search and social media, it is better not to. While search engine optimization is ideal for overall long-term growth, site owners cannot get consistent results that way. Consider combining paid and organic search marketing for the best marketing results.

Running a Paid Search Campaign

- Investigate Broad Search Categories and Trends
- Narrow Down Keywords
- Determine Traffic and Cost
- Select Terms and Match Criteria
- Design Ads
- Run Campaigns
- Measure and Refine

Use Keyword Research Effectively

To efficiently use keywords that are essential for effective organic and paid search, keyword research requires, at the very least, the following two objectives:

- Define the audience being targeted, and
- Decide what kind of site, or blog, to create or maintain.

Several free tools for keyword research are "good enough" such as Semrush.com or Moz.com. Google Analytics can also help with SEO/SEM traffic and research related to a website. Once results come back from the campaigns, the data should be used to improve the campaign while marketers are still running it.

SEARCH ENGINE DATA ANALYTICS

Search engine data analytics deals with analyzing historical search data to gain valuable insight into trends analysis, keyword monitoring, and advertisement spending statistics. Search engine data can be considered as a gateway into the minds of customers. Through search engines, customers search for what they want. Thus search trend analysis can provide valuable information to social marketers.

When it comes to trends analytics, Google Trends (http://www.google.com/trends/) and Google Correlate are the most convenient and comprehensive search engine trend analysis tools. Google Trends uses massive amounts of search engine data to analyze the world's interests and predict trends. For example, in the financial sector, Google Trends data has been used to detect "early warning signs" of stock market moves (Preis, Moat, & Stanley, 2013). In the health sector, Google Trends data has helped determine world flu epidemics (Ginsberg et al., 2008). Engineers at Google.org, for instance, using Google Trends data, found a strong correlation among the searches for flu-related topics and the numbers of actual flu cases circulating in different countries and regions around the world (Ginsberg et al., 2008). In this chapter, we use Google Trends for search engine analytics. From a business perspective, Google Trends can also help answer a variety of questions, including the following.

- How people search for your brand?
- When does interest spike in your products or services?
- Which keywords drive more traffic?
- Which regions are interested in your brand?
- What are the trending topics over the Internet?
- How are your competitors performing?

SEARCH ENGINE ANALYTICS TOOLS

Google Trends

Google Trends (http://trends.google.com/) is a search engine analytics tool. This chapter includes a detailed tutorial on Google Trends.

Google Correlate

Google Correlate is the inverse of Google Trends. It finds search patterns, which correspond to the real-world trends. This chapter includes a detailed tutorial on Google Correlate.

Canopy

Canopy is a multimedia analytics tool designed to support deep investigation of large multimedia collections, such as images, videos, and documents. More information on Canopy is available here: http://www.vacommunity.org/article32.

Google Alerts

Google Alerts (https://www.google.com/alerts) is a content detection and notification service that automatically notifies users when new content over the Internet (e.g., social media, web, blogs, video, and/or discussion groups) matches a set of search terms based on user queries. Users are alerted through e-mail.

Icerocket

Icerocket (http://www.icerocket.com/) specializes in blog searches and captures activity on Facebook, Twitter, and Flickr.

TweetBeep

TweetBeep (http://tweetbeep.com/) is like Google Alerts for Twitter. Choose some keywords and receive daily search results via e-mail.

TUTORIAL 8.1
GOOGLE TRENDS

INTRODUCTION

Google Trends uses percentages to analyze trend results. For example, if someone searches for the term *analytics* in New Zealand in June of 2017, Google Trends analyzes and displays the percentage of all searches for the keyword *analytics* in June in New Zealand.

TYPES OF ANALYTICS PROVIDED BY GOOGLE TRENDS

In its current form, Google Trends provides six types of analytics available in the drop-down box at the left upper corner. They are as follows.

- Year in Search
- Trending Searches
- Trending on YouTube
- Top Charts
- Explore
- Subscription

Among them, the "Explore" option is the most important from the search engine analytics perspective, and we will look at in detail in this chapter. But, first, let's briefly discuss the other analytic reports.

Year in Search

Year in Search is a short commercial video clip (with accompanying details that can be further explored) that summarizes the world's most famous searches in a particular year. Currently, a year in search video is available for the year 2014.

Trending Searches

Trending Searches provides a list of top-ten searches on a daily basis for a specific country. The search results for particular data are regularly updated. Not all countries are included in the trending searches.

Trending on YouTube

Like Trending Searches, Trending on YouTube provides a list of top-ten videos on a daily basis for a specific country. The search results for particular dates are regularly updated.

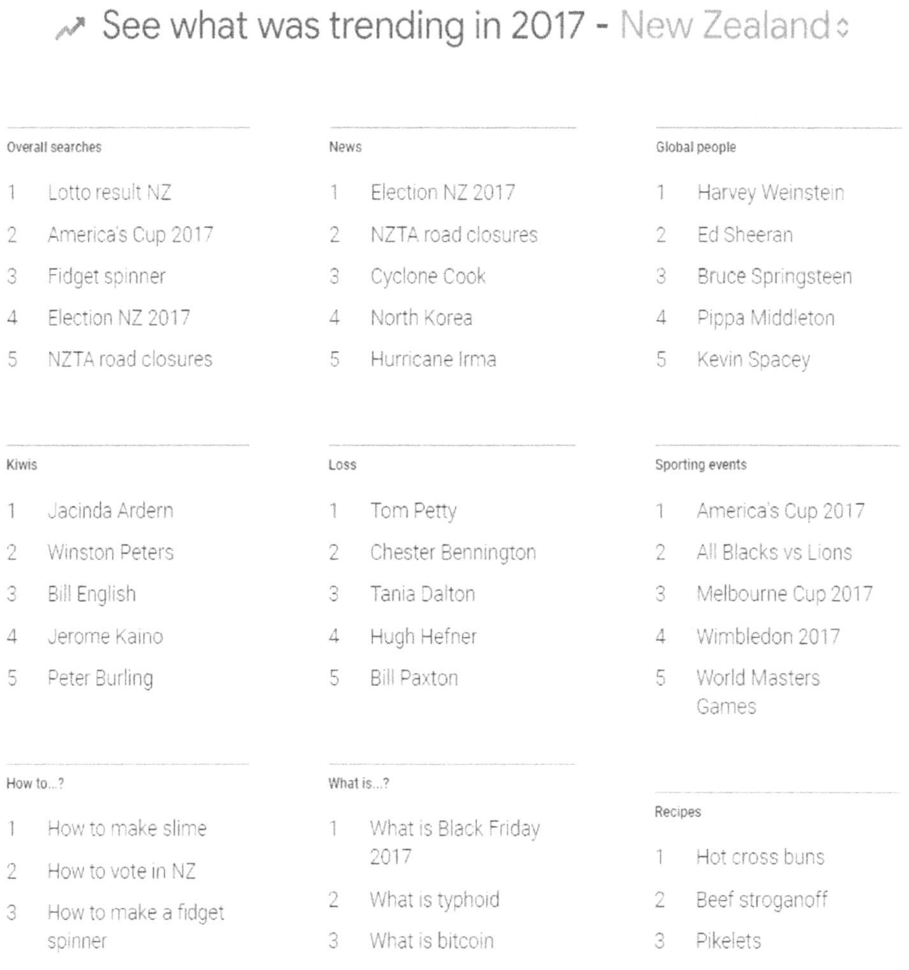

See what was trending in 2017 - New Zealand

Overall searches
1. Lotto result NZ
2. America's Cup 2017
3. Fidget spinner
4. Election NZ 2017
5. NZTA road closures

News
1. Election NZ 2017
2. NZTA road closures
3. Cyclone Cook
4. North Korea
5. Hurricane Irma

Global people
1. Harvey Weinstein
2. Ed Sheeran
3. Bruce Springsteen
4. Pippa Middleton
5. Kevin Spacey

Kiwis
1. Jacinda Ardern
2. Winston Peters
3. Bill English
4. Jerome Kaino
5. Peter Burling

Loss
1. Tom Petty
2. Chester Bennington
3. Tania Dalton
4. Hugh Hefner
5. Bill Paxton

Sporting events
1. America's Cup 2017
2. All Blacks vs Lions
3. Melbourne Cup 2017
4. Wimbledon 2017
5. World Masters Games

How to...?
1. How to make slime
2. How to vote in NZ
3. How to make a fidget spinner

What is...?
1. What is Black Friday 2017
2. What is typhoid
3. What is bitcoin

Recipes
1. Hot cross buns
2. Beef stroganoff
3. Pikelets

Screenshot 8.1. Google Top Charts for the year 2017

Top Charts

Top Charts displays a list of trending real-world people, places, and things ranked in order of search interest in a particular year. Screenshot 8.1 lists what was trending in New Zealand in 2017. With Top Charts, for example, one can see a list of the top ten most searched athletes, consumer electronics, YouTube videos, topics, and global news, among other things. Top Charts depends on

Knowledge Graph[3] technology to provide the rankings. The charts can be customized to show either global search trends or search trends in a particular country. Historical search trends going back to the year 2001 are available.

Explore

The Explore option is a vital resource in search engine analytics. The Explore option lets you analyze search engine trends related one or more search terms across time and location. Recall that some of the questions we mentioned earlier, such as, "How do people search for your brand?" "When does interest spike in your products or services?" "Which keywords drive more traffic?" "Which regions are interested in your brand?" The Explore option can help you answer these questions.

Here is how to start using the Explore option.

Step 1: Open Google Trends: http://www.google.com/trends/.

Step 2: Click on the "Trends" option in the upper left-hand corner. Next, from the drop-down menu, select "Explore" (Screenshot 8.2)

Screenshot 8.2. Google's Trends analysis menu

Step 3: Next, click on "Add Terms" to enter the search terms for what you want to analyze. Repeat this process until you have entered all the desired terms.

---

[3]Knowledge Graph is Google's knowledge base that understands facts about real-world things (e.g., people, places and things)and their connections. Knowledge Graph is used to enhance a users's search experiences by providing them structured and detailed information about the topic they are searching for. More information on Knowledge Graph can be found here:http://www.google.co.kr/insidesearch/features/search/knowledge.html

In this case, we entered three terms: "iPhone 4," "Galaxy S4," and "LG Optimus." The results are grouped into three categories: 1) interests over time, 2) regional interests, and 3) related searches (Screenshot 8.3). Below, we discuss each of the categories in detail.

Interests Over Time

Interests over time (in terms of the number of searches) are displayed in the form of a graph below the terms showing their popularity over time. The numbers on the graph reflect how many searches have been done for the terms, relative to the total number of searches done on Google over time. Note that the numbers represent search volume relative to the highest point on the graph, which is always 100. The data on the search volume is normalized and presented on a scale from 0–100, thus it does not represent absolute search volume numbers.

You can examine different points on the graph by hovering your mouse over them. The graph also displays news headlines (if available) related to the terms. The news headlines are indicated by capital letters displayed over the lines and correspond to the year of the news. By hovering your cursor over the letters, you will be able to see the detailed news. You can also see the forecasted results by checking the "Forecast" checkbox in the upper right-hand corner of the graph (forecasts are always available). You can also notice bars appearing next to the chart. The bar height represents the average of all data points on the graph for that search term.

From the graph, it is clear that interest in smartphones corresponds to their launch dates, and that interest is much stronger in the first couple of months and then declines.

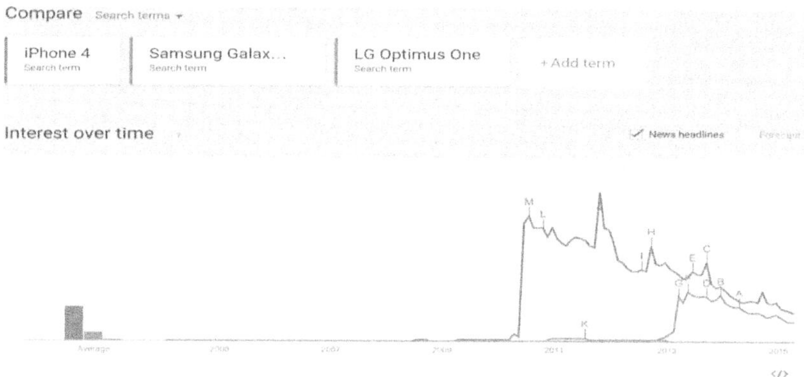

Screenshot 8.3. Interest in iPhone 4, Galaxy S4, and LG Optimus over time

Regional Interests

The "Regional Interests" section shows interest in the search terms with respect to geography (Screenshot 8.4). Note that for each search term, regional interest is shown in a separate window. In the screenshot 4, we are looking at the regional interest in the "iPhone 4" term. You can choose the "Galaxy S4" term by clicking on it. You can also switch between region and city view by the clicking the appropriate option in the top right-hand corner. From the results, it is clear that top cities interested in the iPhone 4 are Ho Chi Minh City, Hanoi, Bangkok, London, Singapore, and Manila.

Regional interest

iphone 4 samsung galaxy s4 lg optimus one

Region | City

City	Interest
Ho Chi Minh City	100
Hanoi	90
Singapore	63
Bangkok	52
Paris	51
Dallas	47
London	44

Screenshot 8.4. Regional interest in iPhone 4s

However, interest in the Galaxy S4 is coming from Jakarta, Istanbul, Sydney, Bucharest, Berlin, Munich, and Vienna (Screenshot 8.5).

Regional interest

iphone 4 samsung galaxy s4 lg optimus one

Region | City

City	Interest
Jakarta	100
Melbourne	58
Sydney	58
Bucharest	56
Berlin	50
Istanbul	45
Munich	44

Screenshot 8.5. Regional interest in Galaxy S4

You can see the detailed regional search volume by clicking on a region of interest (Screenshot 8.6).

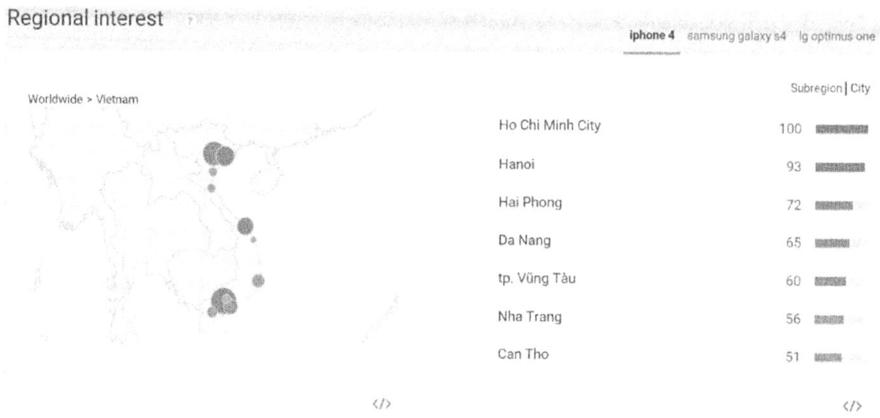

Screenshot 8.6. Vietnam cities interested in iPhone 4

Related Searches

The "Related Searches" section (available near the bottom of the page) shows the popular search terms similar to your search terms. For example, the Screenshot 8.7 shows the search terms similar to "Galaxy S4." Using this function, for example, you can find which topics will potentially drive more traffic, "smartphone," or "Galaxy S4." Knowing trending topics related to our products/services can help us optimize a campaign.

Screenshot 8.7. Galaxy S4 related search terms

Understanding the Research Function

Now that you understand the fundamental aspects of Google Trends let us focus on how to use the research function more efficiently.

USING SEARCH OPERATORS

You can use search operators to filter the types of results that you see in Trends. Use the Table 8.4 to learn about executing your search correctly.

Table 8.4. Executing your research correctly

Search Terms	The Results Displayed
Social media analytics	Results can include searches containing the terms "social," "media," and "analytics" in any order.
"Social media analytics"	Results will only include the exact search terms included inside of the quotation marks.
social + analytics	Results can include searches containing the words "social" OR "analytics."
social – analytics	Results will include searches containing the word "social," but will exclude searches containing the word "analytics."

Note that Google Trends searches ignore special characters (such as apostrophes, single quotes, and parentheses). Similarly, misspelled words and spelling variations are considered as separate words. For example, the term "analytic" and "analytics" will be considered as two separate words.

GROUPING SEARCH TERMS

Overall, you can search up to five groupings at one time, with up to twenty-five search terms in each grouping. Consider the following example:

- iPhone 2 + Galaxy S2 + LG G (Grouping 1)
- iPhone 3 + Galaxy S3 + LG Optimus F3 (Grouping 2)
- iPhone 4 + Galaxy S4 (Grouping 3)
- iPhone 5 + Galaxy S5 + LG Optimus F6 (Grouping 4)
- iPhone 6+ Galaxy S6 (Grouping 5)

CUSTOMIZING THE SEARCH

From the drop-down menu available at the top of the page, search results can be customized with respect to countries, years, categories (such as business or games), and types of web resources to focus on (such as web search, image search, news search, Google shopping, and YouTube search) (Screenshot 8.8). You can also select custom data from the date drop-down menu by clicking on the "Select Data" option. For example, in the example above, we restricted our search to January 2010–April 2018. Note that currently, trend data is only available from 2004 onward.

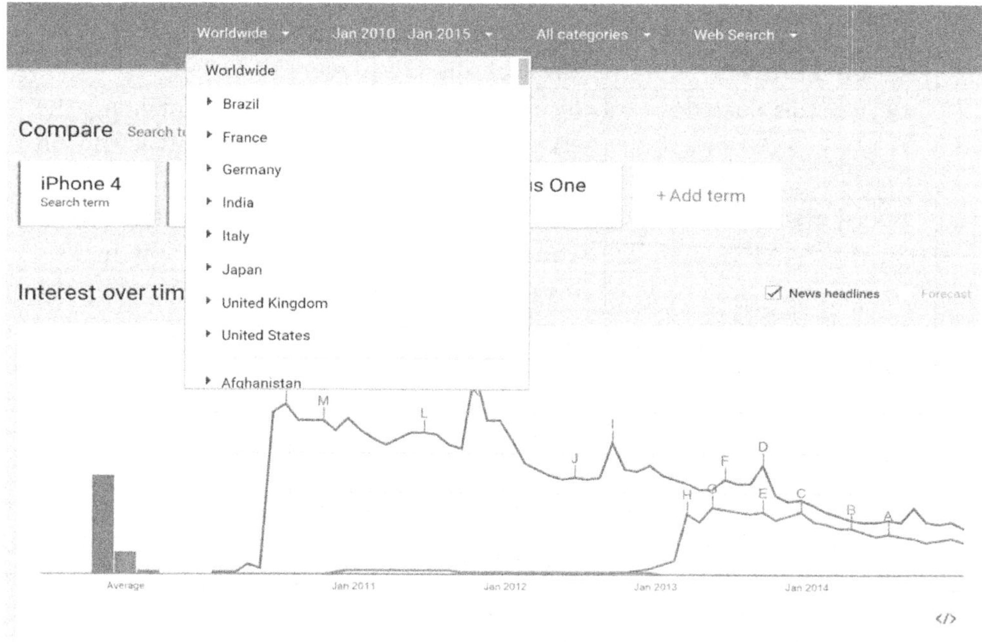

Screenshot 8.8. Customizing the Google Trends searches

TUTORIAL 8.2
GOOGLE CORRELATE

WHAT IS GOOGLE CORRELATE?

Google Correlate is an experimental tool from Google which finds search patterns that correspond with real-world trends. Google Correlate is like Google Trends in reverse. With Google Trends, you type in a query and get back a series of its frequency (over time and space). With Google Correlate, you enter a data series (the target) and get back queries whose frequency follows a similar pattern.

CORRELATED QUERIES

When you upload a dataset (or provide keywords), Google Correlate will compute the Pearson Correlation Coefficient (r) between your data/keywords and the other keywords that people search for during the same time period. Correlation coefficients range from r=-1.0 to r=+1.0. The queries that Google Correlate shows you are the ones with the highest correlation coefficient (i.e., closest to r=1.0). One thing to note is that correlation does not imply causation. Just because terms correlate (one goes up other goes up) with each other does not necessarily imply a cause and effect relationship.

GOOGLE CORRELATE FOR BUSINESS INTELLIGENCE

Imagine you are trying to roll out a new suncream, and you want to focus your marketing efforts on geographic regions, product bundling opportunities. Among other things, Google Correlate can help you find out:

Finding Geographic Areas of Interest

Which cities (note: city options are only available for the United States) to start rolling your product out.

Customer Personas

If a brand is trying to define target personas for a new product or service, they can use each correlation to get profound insights into your audience.

Product Bundling Options

What other product highly correlate with sun cream? In other words which product do people search for when they are searching for sun cream; thus offering a product bundling opportunity.

Content Strategy & Buyer Journey Mapping

Google correlate can helps brands map a customer's purchase journey from search, interest, desire, and buying decision. And it can also shed light on the type of marketing campaigns and content strategies needed to be built throughout the customers' buyer journey.

Keyword Research

Google correlate can also help find the high volume quality keywords for search engine optimization and social media marketing campaigns.

Next, we will discover each of the above business intelligence examples.

Finding Geographic Areas of Interest

Step 1: Open Google Correlate by going to:
https://www.google.com/trends/correlate

Step 2: Enter the keyword 'sun cream' and then click "Search Correlations."

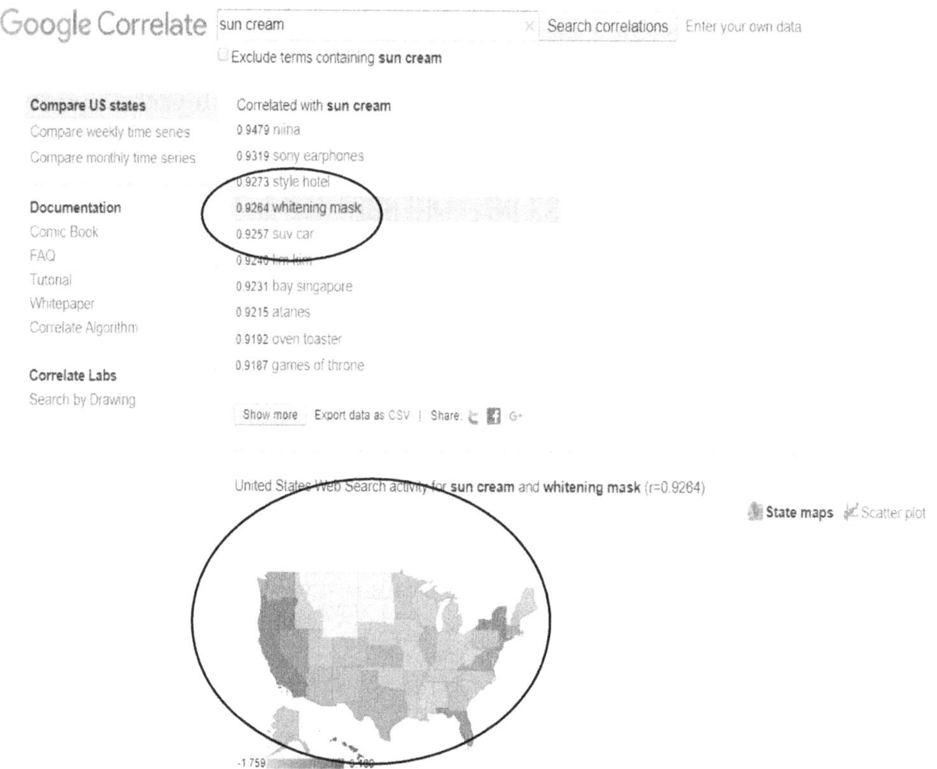

Screenshot 8.9. Google Correlate geographic results

Step 3: Select the terms that are highly relevant to sun cream (whitening mask in this case), and Google Correlate will show what states most closely correlate with those interests. From the map, it is clear that people in Hawaii, Oregon, California, and New York are quite interested in Sun-cream and whitening mask (Screenshot 8.9).

Customer Personas

Google Correlate can be used to target personas for a new product or service and get profound insights about the target audience.

Step 1: Let's expand and reconsider the sun cream research results (Screenshot 8.10).

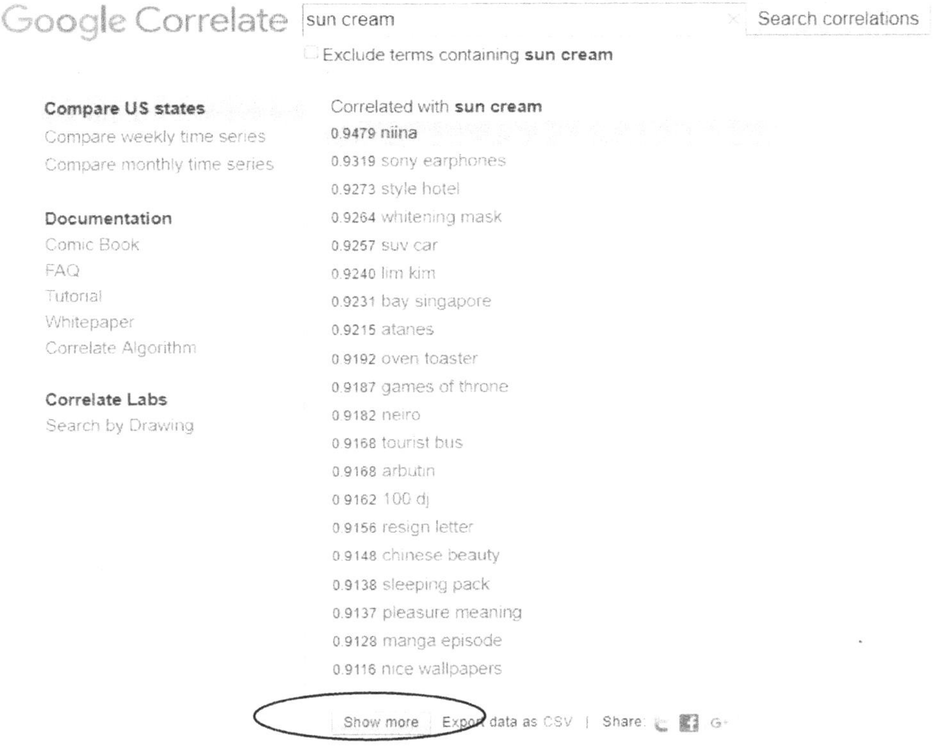

Screenshot 8.10. Google Correlate expended results

Step 2: Note how highly the terms "niina," "style hotel," "sony earphones," "style hotel," "SUV car," "Lim Kim," "Atanes," and "bay Singapore," all correlate with "sun cream." Those terms alone can define a highly specific reader persona.

Take away: If a retailer can't figure out the audience for their sun cream, it's probably a wealthy Asian person who drives an SUV, interested in travel and skin lotions/treatments (skin whiting, sleeping packs, arbutin), stays at luxury hotels (Style hotel), loves celebrities (NiinaNina, Atanes Anara, Lim Kim, Neiro, 100DJs), and Game of Tthrones. Based on this you know who your potential target customers are.

Product Bundling Options

What other product correlates highly with sun cream? In other words, which product can possibly be bundled together with sun cream?

Step 1: Let's have a look at the 'Compare US State' results again. It tells us that potential bundling options are: whitening cream, sleeping packs, arbutin based products. Moreover, perhaps bundling it with an electronic product, such as air phones, toasters, and the Game of Thrones.

Step 2: Now click on the "Compare Monthly Time Series" option available on the left side of the screen (Screenshot 8.11). This will provide country-specific results (in this case the United States). This option provides more comprehensive product bundling opportunities. Some bundling examples include hiking sandals, men's sandals, sun hats, motor batteries, rods and reels, tents, etc. You can also explore bundling opportunity in different countries by selecting them from the drop-down menu.

Content Strategy & Buyer Journey Mapping

Social media marketing and content strategies are usually made around the buyer's journey map: where customers do research before they purchase a product or service. For instance, if a brand wants to aim at customers in the 'interested phase,' then they will create marketing content that focuses on how to use a product or service. If they are aiming at customers in the 'desire phase,' then you'll create a comparison or get a deal type content.

The goal of such an approach is to help customers move down the purchase funnel. In addition, the logic is simple. When a brand is present at the time a customer becomes aware of a product through interest and desire stages, then it will be the one they purchase.

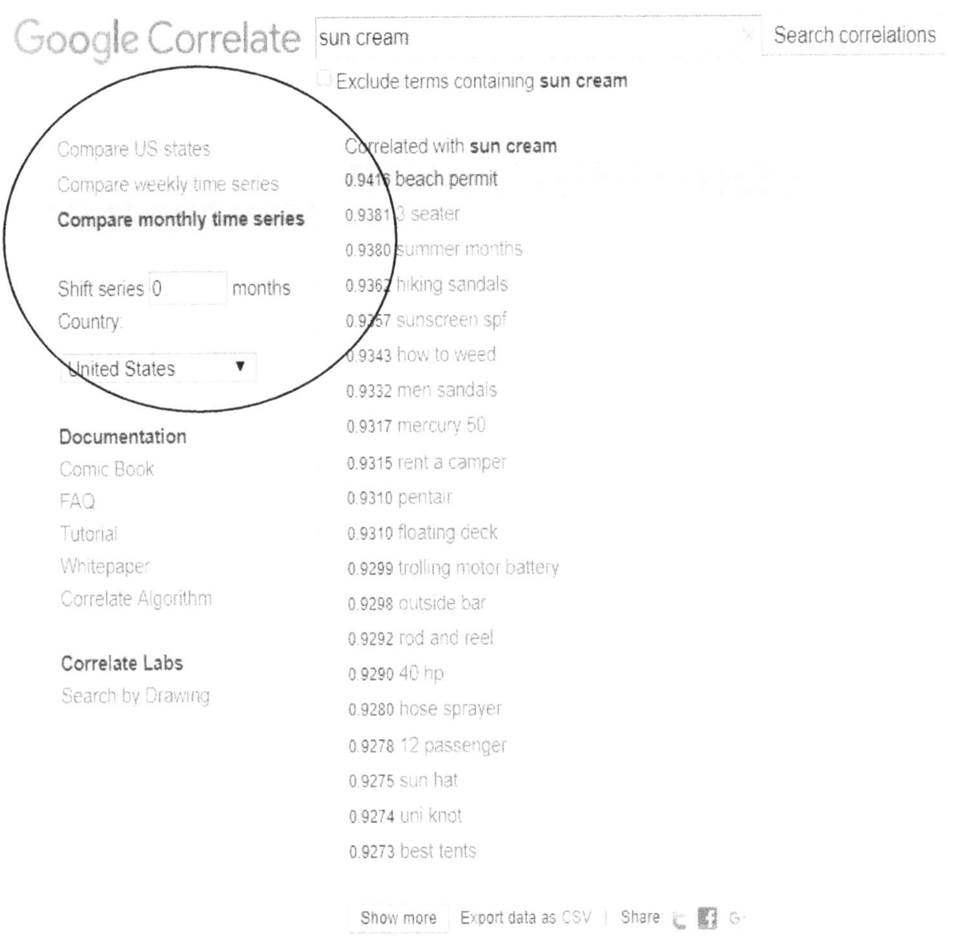

Screenshot 8.11. Shifting time series for bundling options

How can Google correlate help? Google's Correlate Time Series shift is a perfect fit for understanding and facilitating the purchase journey map. It works best for seasonal companies (such as sun cream sellers). However, any business can use it provided you have some sort of time cycle or event.

Step 1: Before we proceed, notice from the correlation results (by hovering over it) that there are spikes in searches for sun cream related products during the months of June and July (summer season in the United States) (Screenshot 8.12). With Time Series Shift, we want to know what are people looking or interested in before the summer season (or before they were looking for sun cream).

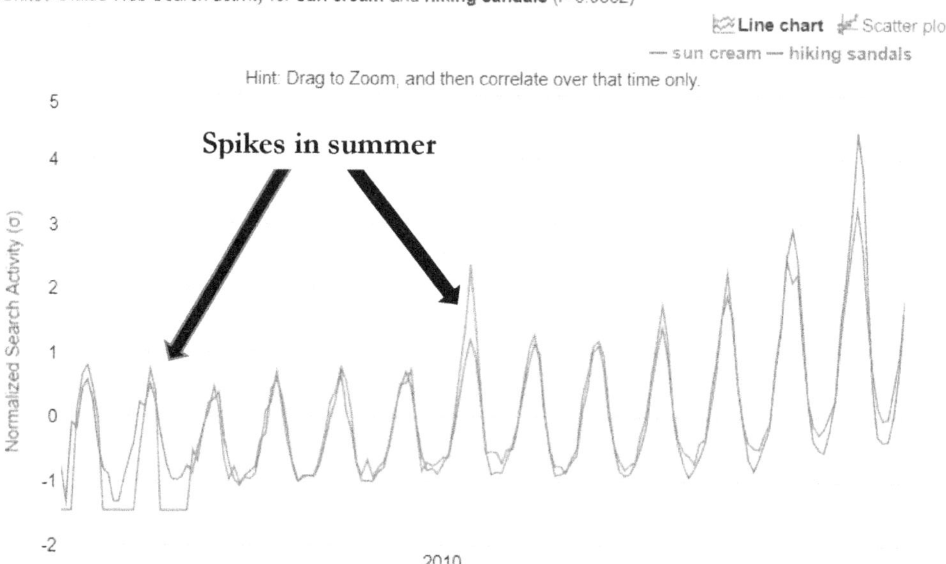

Screenshot 8.12. Correlation results

Step 2: People buy sun cream during summer. What type of content could you publish to get in front of people in the months or weeks leading up to summer (e.g., in May)? To answer this question, we will shift the time series back by 1 month (in the shift series box type '-1') (Screenshot 8.13).

Take away: Based on the results, sun scream retailers can promote content around gardening, outdoor activities, summer clothes, and then run retargeting on that audience 2 weeks later to buy sun cream. Note that Google Correlate's data is very sparse. You have to look at it as a whole to create content ideas that make sense.

Keyword Research

Keywords are the critical element of search engine marketing and optimization. When it comes to SEO and paid ads, high volume and high-quality keywords can produce fruitful results. By default, Google Correlate generates lists of keywords that correlate with your target keyword. You can take the initial "seed" keyword list, and run several through Google Correlate to see what other relevant keywords it generates. You can then export all the keywords and combine it with other sources like Reddit, Wikipedia, and others to get a giant list to edit.

Take away: In this case, if you were a sun cream retailer, you would invest in Google ads targeting summer tops and self-tanners keywords. This will allow you to get in front of customers and provide targeted ads a few weeks before the sudden rush to buy sun cream.

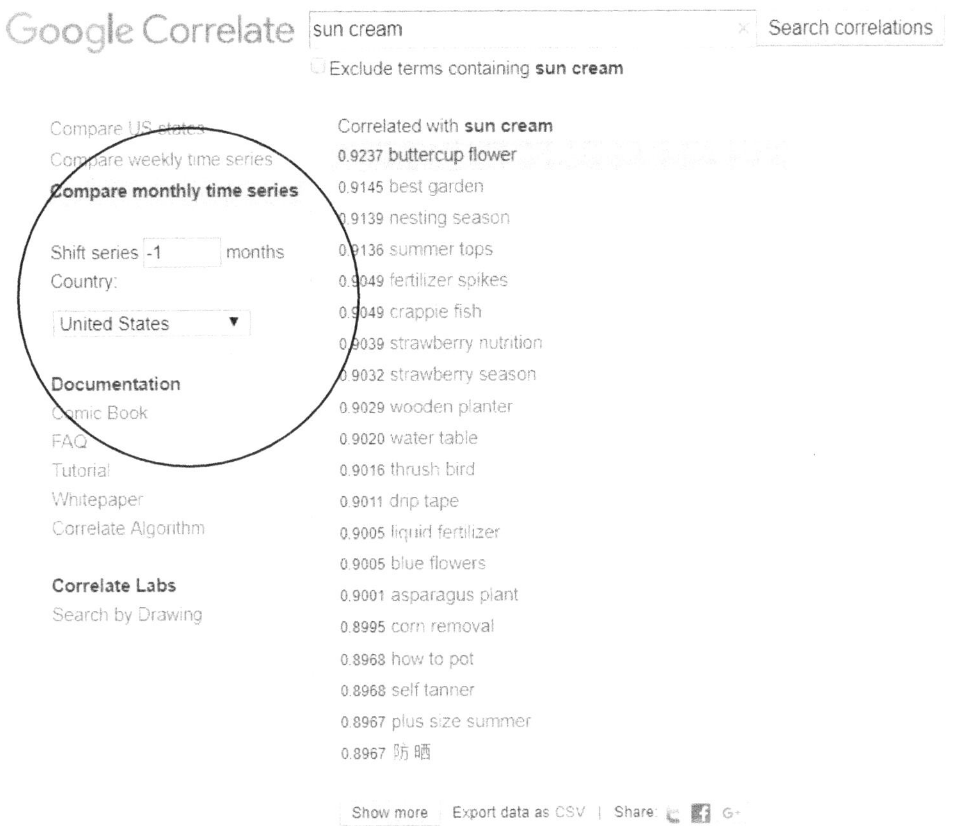

Screenshot 8.13. Shifting time series by one month

REVIEW QUESTIONS

1. What does the acronym "SEO" stand for?
2. What is the difference between paid search and organic search?
3. What are the two aspects of search engine analytics?
4. What is the function of a search engine?
5. Explain what the different types of search engines are.
6. Differentiate between local and global search engines.
7. What is search engine analytics?
8. Explain the two main categories of search engine analytics.
9. What is the purpose of search engine optimization?
10. Explain different paid and organic SEO techniques.
11. What is the purpose of search engine trend analysis?
12. What is the purpose of Google Correlate?

EXERCISE 8.1: THE SEO MATURITY ASSESSMENT

Some of the topics we covered in this chapter were an evolution of the Internet, the World Wide Web, and search engines. Ultimately, the development of the Web would be impossible for organizations to leverage without the search engines. With search engines, almost anything can be found on the Web. However, most organizations and individuals are not as easy to find as they could be and search discoverability influences the bottom line.

Evaluating Search Engine Optimization Maturity

Use this evaluation to self-evaluate an organization's *search engine optimization* (SEO) maturity. Measure an organization's SEO maturity across four key success drivers: Strategy, Buy-in, & Skills; Process Definition, Automation, & Systems; Keyword Management; and Results Reporting & Metrics.

Utilizing the Excel Spreadsheet

- Download the *SEO maturity assessment* template from the book companion site (https://analytics-book.com/) and examine the first tab (instructions).
- Next, fill out the second tab (maturity assessment); this may take up to 2 hours to complete.
- When done, an SEO maturity index diamond (radar chart) will be populated along with an SEO maturity index tabulated score (Figure 8.8).
- Use the radar chart and score to gauge one's SEO maturity; the same assessment can be adapted to gauge other websites, including competitors.

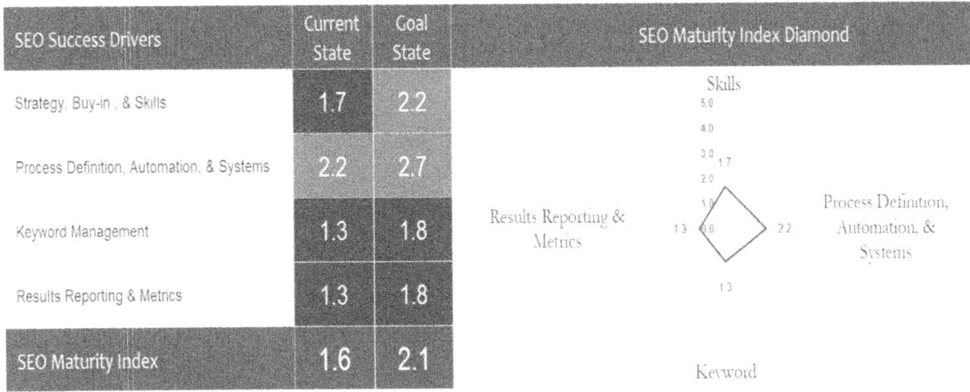

SEO Success Drivers	Current State	Goal State
Strategy, Buy-in , & Skills	1.7	2.2
Process Definition, Automation, & Systems	2.2	2.7
Keyword Management	1.3	1.8
Results Reporting & Metrics	1.3	1.8
SEO Maturity Index	1.6	2.1

Figure 8.8. SEO Maturity Assessment

Interpretation

Once the assessment is filled out, then consult the results and recommendations tab to gain insight and take action on the assessment. For example, the Success Drivers score is 1.67 out of 5.0 in this instance (Figure 8.9).

SEO Success Drivers	Scores	Recommendations
Strategy, Buy-in , & Skills		
Senior Management Commitment	2	Obtain Senior Management Commitment & use our Project Management Portfolio to create a roadmap
SEO Strategy	3	Document your SEO Strategy using our Business Strategy Template as a guideline
Financial & Human Resources	2	Obtain Senior Management Approval for the resources required to successfully complete this initiative
SEO Training & Workshops	1	Obtain Senior Management Approval for the resources required to successfully complete this initiative
Integrated Efforts	1	Identify current vs. goal state with GAP analysis, list your requirements for closed loop, and evaluate vendors
SEO Maintenance & Research	1	Create maintenance & research plan and document using Project Portfolio
Strategy, Buy-in, & Skills Maturity Average	1.67	

Figure 8.9. Digital Analytics for Marketing SEO Success Drivers

Leveraging social media analytics requires awareness of the technologies as well as an alignment with business processes. Based on the assessment the organization needs to take concrete steps to document its business strategy, define its analytics and SEO initiatives. Take the SEO Maturity Assessment on a periodic basis to observe the changes in strategy and outcomes that result from taking action on the assessment and its recommendations.

EXERCISE 8.2: GOOGLE SEARCH

As mentioned earlier, the more words in a search query, the more likely there will be less competition for top ranking, but the audience for that result might be much, much smaller. To test this assumption try the following exercise.

- Try looking at a Google search result for "social media consulting" and copying the number of search results (fill in the blank). How hard is it for *Social Listening Limited* (a New Zealand based social media consulting company) to get to the top page of search results (rate 0-5 with 0 being no chance, and five being "easy")? And at what number does it appears in the SERP?
- Try looking at the Google search results for "social media consulting New Zealand." How many search results are there (fill in the blank)? How hard would it be to get to the top page of search results (rate 0-5 with 0 being no chance, and five being "easy")? And at what number does it appear in the SERP?

EXERCISE 8.3: SERP AND WEBSITE SCORE

- Pick an exciting search query (for example "social media consulting" using Google Search), run the search and look at one of first/top SERP.
- Copy the top URL and past into the free tool called Nibbler (http://nibbler.silktide.com/) and do a website assessment.
- The result was a Nibbler overall score of 7.7 at the time the author tried this for the top website. Note some of the ratings that Nibbler reports are where the site is well optimized as well as where it is not.
- Do the same thing (step 1 and 2) for a website on the 10th page of the search results, and compare the site score differences.
- Note: Nibbler now allows users to evaluate three websites before requiring an upgrade to a paid subscription to test more sites.

CHAPTER 8 REFERENCES

Ashish Agarwal, Kartik Hosanagar, & Smith, M. D. (2011). Location, Location, Location: An Analysis of Profitability of Position in Online Advertising Markets. *Journal of Marketing Research, 48*(6), 1057-1073. doi:10.1509/jmr.08.0468

Davis, H. (2006). *Search Engine Optimization*: O'Reilly Media, Inc.

Ginsberg, J., Mohebbi, M. H., Patel, R. S., Brammer, L., Smolinski, M. S., & Brilliant, L. (2008). Detecting influenza epidemics using search engine query data. *Nature, 457*, 1012. doi:10.1038/nature07634

Malaga, R. A. (2008). Worst practices in search engine optimization. *Commun. ACM, 51*(12), 147-150. doi:10.1145/1409360.1409388

Malaga, R. A. (2010). Chapter 1 - Search Engine Optimization—Black and White Hat Approaches *Advances in Computers* (Vol. 78, pp. 1-39): Elsevier.

Pan, B., Hembrooke, H., Joachims, T., Lorigo, L., Gay, G., & Granka, L. (2007). In Google We Trust: Users' Decisions on Rank, Position, and Relevance. *Journal of Computer-Mediated Communication, 12*(3), 801-823. doi:10.1111/j.1083-6101.2007.00351.x

Preis, T., Moat, H. S., & Stanley, H. E. (2013). Quantifying Trading Behavior in Financial Markets Using Google Trends. *Scientific Reports, 3*, 1684. doi:10.1038/srep01684

Weideman, M. (2009). 2 - Elements of website visibility and research *Website Visibility* (pp. 41-58): Chandos Publishing.

Yalçın, N., & Köse, U. (2010). What is search engine optimization: SEO? *Procedia - Social and Behavioral Sciences, 9*(Supplement C), 487-493. doi:https://doi.org/10.1016/j.sbspro.2010.12.185

Zhang, J., & Dimitroff, A. (2005). The impact of webpage content characteristics on webpage visibility in search engine results (Part I). *Information Processing & Management, 41*(3), 665-690. doi:https://doi.org/10.1016/j.ipm.2003.12.001

Chapter 9

Capturing Value with Location Analytics

"The location is perfect. It's halfway to everywhere."—**Amrit Gill**

Learning Outcomes

After completing this chapter, the reader should be able to:

- Comprehend social media location analytics concepts and tools.
- Understand the uses of social media location analytics by business for business intelligence purposes.
- Understand sources of location data.
- Grasp challenges associated with location analytics.
- List location analytics privacy concerns.
- Understand application and tools of location analytics currently available in the market.
- Map location data with Google fusion table and ArcGIS Online.

INTRODUCTION

Location analytics, also known as spatial analysis or geo-analytics is concerned with mapping, visualizing, and mining the location of people, data, and other resources. All sectors, including business, government, nonprofit, and academia, can benefit from *location analytics*. The case study "Owl Bus" included in this chapter demonstrates how location analytics and social media helped the Seoul Metropolitan Government in expanding their bus routes and selecting the "Owl Bus" brand name. Thanks to the GPS (global positioning systems) embedded in mobile devices, providing location-based services, products, and information is becoming a reality. In a recent study, scientists used six million geo-located Twitter messages to observe the "heartbeat" of New York City (França, Sayama, McSwiggen, Daneshvar, & Bar-

Yam, 2016). With the dataset, the scientists were able to study and map the waking, sleeping, commuting, working, and leisure dynamics of the people living in the city during the weekdays and weekends. Such geo-analytics can be instrumental in better understanding our cities and human behaviors in space and time.

Most people are not fully aware of the extent they are being tracked within social and digital media; existing legislation to define and protect privacy has not kept pace with the technology. A majority of people who install apps on their phones mindlessly allow specific default permissions, such as location tracking. People are unaware that many of these companies mine their data as part of their business model to sell to third parties (for Third-Party Data). However, many people also just do not seem to care that third parties are mining their data. For example, according to eMarketer (based on Columbia Business School data), 80% of internet users would be OK with sharing their personal data for rewards or a cash-back offer.

The applications of location data vary by country; for example, location-based advertising is more prevalent in the USA and Singapore than Canada, the UK or Germany (because these markets are less developed in this respect, or, in Germany's case, have strong privacy laws which limit how location-based data can be harvested, shared and used)(see Figure 9.1).

SOURCES OF LOCATION DATA

Location information can come from a variety of sources, including the following.

Postal Address

Most business analytics applications rely on *address information* of their customers, including city names, locality names, and postal or zip codes.

Latitude and Longitude

In geography, *latitude* (shown as a horizontal line on a globe) and *longitude* (shown as a vertical line on a globe) are used to find the exact location on Earth.

GPS-Based

GPS is a satellite-based navigation system that can be used to find exact locations, people, and resources. Mobile analytics mostly rely on GPS-based location data. GPS-based location analytics can provide us with the most accurate location for social media users.

Note: Most GPS providers, especially those for cars, such as Garmin, are dying out because roads are always changing and providers have not been able to keep up with it. Alternatively, people prefer to use Google Maps and Apple Maps from their mobile devices because they are free and continuously automatically updated.

Location-Based Marketing Topics that Will Be of Interest to Marketing Executives in Select Countries in 2016

% of respondents

	Canada	Germany	Singapore	UK	US
Social location services	35%	40%	58%	45%	63%
Location-based advertising	33%	50%	58%	25%	51%
Internet of things (IoT)	25%	36%	46%	37%	33%
Location analytics	24%	40%	42%	22%	37%
Location-based search optimization	24%	34%	48%	25%	29%
Location-based loyalty integration	27%	14%	40%	25%	33%
Location-based privacy	22%	36%	36%	20%	24%
Merging mobile and DOOH	12%	26%	24%	12%	16%
Augmented/virtual reality	10%	18%	24%	14%	20%
Location-based gaming	14%	18%	24%	14%	16%

Note: Canada n=51; Germany n=50; Singapore n=50; UK n=51; US n=51
Source: Location Based Marketing Association (LBMA), "Global Location Trends Report," March 13, 2016

207489 www.eMarketer.com

Figure 9.1. Location-based marketing topics by country

IP-Based

Public IP (Internet protocol) can be used to determine the location of Internet users. An IP address is an exclusive numerical address (like a home address) assigned to a device connected to the Internet. Different regions of the world are assigned a specific block of public IP addresses; hence, it can be used to mine the approximate geolocation of Internet users.

iBeacons and Bluetooth

We are all familiar with the concept of AM/FM radio, but most people are just waking up to other types of broadcast networks based on different frequencies and devices. *Bluetooth* is a wireless protocol that has been around for over a quarter of a century and was used initially for wireless printing and device pairing. Bluetooth was used in personal computers and mobile devices to create small, close location radio networks. Another factoid that is commonly not known is that most smartphones have a built-in AM/FM radio though it is more commonly used for Bluetooth communications than for radio communications (but it could be and sometimes is).

In 2013, Apple developed the *iBeacon* protocol built on top of Bluetooth that allows messages to be broadcast based on proximity. One great thing about iBeacons is that the radio transmitters or beacons are inexpensive, and there is software developed by several off the shelf vendors that integrate with iBeacons and allow marketers to manage these small networks for information sharing and advertising campaigns. One of the drawbacks of the iBeacon protocol also happens to be one of its strengths. To use iBeacons (to shop in a specific location) a customer must first download an app (application) on their mobile device. The app facilitates communications between the specific iBeacons in a location and the mobile device. However, this is an action not everyone is prepared to do or even aware of, so there is often an adoption issue.

However, given that the customer must download and run the application on their mobile device first, communications are automatically "opt-in" that is often not the case with the other kinds of geological tracking we have discussed in this section.

iBeacon Case Studies

- *McDonald's tests wireless offers near stores*. McDonald's sales were up by more than 8% when using iBeacon technology in a trial run taking place in 26 stores.
- *San Francisco airport beacons help the blind get around using their phones.* The airport has teamed up with Indoo.rs to unveil a Bluetooth beacon system that helps blind passengers find their way through Terminal 2 using only their phone.
- *New York Museum Uses iBeacons to Create a 'Digital Minefield.'* The New Museum used iBeacons as part of an Art Exhibition last April. Visitors to the museum donated five dollars to help various countries

get rid of hidden landmines and helping to prevent the deaths and injuries which result from them.

- *The Super Bowl 2014 Kicks Off iBeacon Season*: Super bowl attendees got pop up messages with advertising, offers to buy merchandise and information about NFL exhibits.

Mesh Networks

iBeacons have many benefits, but they also have limitations, and it is possible and even common to install several transmitters too close to each other. When this is the case, the wrong transmitter responds nearby. iBeacons is a noisy medium if care is not taken to set up the transmitters. One solution that has recently evolved is the use of *mesh networks* of iBeacons. Mesh networks make deployments easier to manage and scale by allowing some additional ways for devices to communicate with transmitters and determine the precise location of the instrument.

Near Field Communications (NFC)

NFC is *radio-frequency identification* (RFID) technology initially developed in the 1980's allowing compatible hardware to communicate with passive electronic devices using radio waves. RFID is used for product identification, authentication, and inventory tracking. NFC creates a cell area with a 150-foot radius (geo-fencing) with mobile devices. Mobile devices that are within the radius of a "named" geo-fenced area receive communications about businesses in the location. NFC is a networking technology that several retail stores and even museums/public spaces are experimenting with, including the Brooklyn Museum of Art and the Museum of Natural History / Hayden Planetarium.

Only a few years ago near-field communication was supposed to be the technology to transform the retail shopping experience and bring it up to date with how the online shopping experience is from a data perspective. The issue with NFC technology was that it was not a widely adopted standard available in the majority of people's mobile devices until recently. Now, Android Pay and Apple Pay utilize NFC technology so that users with an Android/Apple phone can merely tap their devices to a pay screen at a store in order to pay for their goods. The Android/Apple Pay accounts are connected to the user's bank account.

MINI CASE STUDY 9.1
LOCATION ANALYTICS

Werner Enterprises GIS technology from Esri helps Werner Enterprises keep track of its fleet of more than 9,000 trucks. Using ArcGIS and a tractor-tracking device traditionally used by long-haul trucking companies, Werner can now bill mileage to customers more accurately and route its fleet more efficiently. To better manage information, Werner implemented Esri ArcGIS for Server, which integrates geographic location into business data. Werner uses the software to keep track of its huge fleet and outfits its trucks with transmitters that provide two-way text and data communications between the vehicles and Werner's headquarters in Omaha, Nebraska.

"By knowing exactly where our assets are at a given time and comparing that to the origins and destinations of loads we have in our pipeline, we can better allocate our resources and truly understand the costs of doing business."

Scott Andersen
Manager of Logistics Analysis and GIS, Werner Enterprises

Today, data is readily available by clicking a truck icon on the map to quickly access information, including where the truck is heading, the driver's name, and the hours of road time, and what type of freight is being carried. This is crucial for scheduling trucks and drivers. It is also essential for ensuring that drivers are not given too many drive hours, trucks are on time for scheduled maintenance, and routes are optimized. Consolidating all aspects of on-road operations into the visual and intuitive GIS environment has significantly streamlined Werner's workflows.

Source: The Esri Business Team.

LOCATION DATA COLLECTION

Location data is collected in a variety of ways. Here we discuss some conventional methods that are used to mine locations of people, data, and other resources.

Basic Radius Targeting

This technique captures everyone transmitting via his or her mobile devices in a specific area (e.g., through GPS Latitude/longitude). Most social media platforms that run advertisements have targeting options that include basic radius targeting including Facebook, Twitter, Instagram, and Snapchat. Low-cost tools such as Picodash.com (formerly Gramfeed.com) can geo-locate Instagram posts in a basic radius. However, the less useful aspect of basic radius targeting is that it is similar to putting out a fish net and catching everything in the area and much of what we capture we do not need.

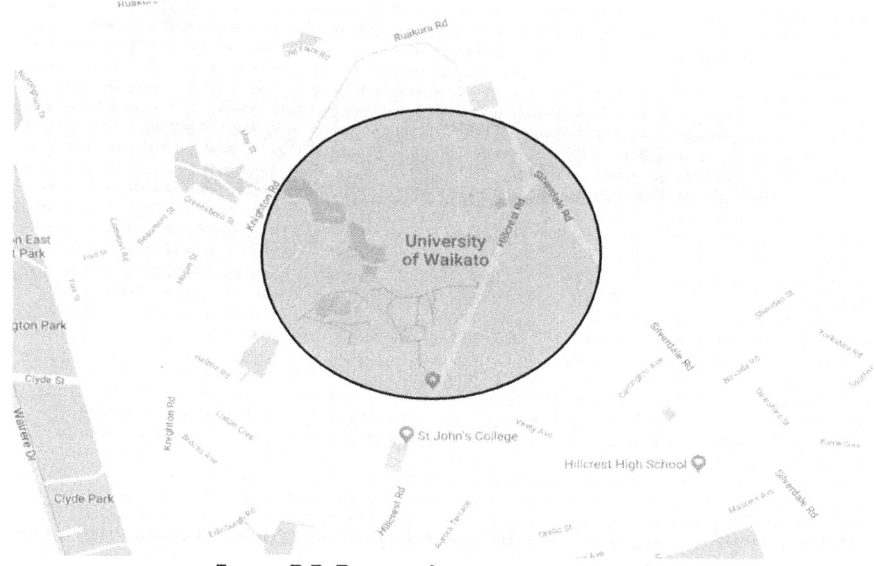

Figure 9.2. Basic radius targeting example

Retargeting with Geolocation

In the *retargeting with geolocation,* a visit to a specific location is captured, and the visitors are retargeted with messages (ads) based on their activities (when they were first acquired into the retargeting list) (Figure 9.3). For example, you physically visited a sushi shop on your campus and later in the day, the sushi shop ad appears in your Facebook news feed. If (potential) customers spent some time viewing the sushi menu or purchased a meal, the marketer (sushi shop owner), can retarget them with special discounts or menu options. Doing so reinforces the customer's earlier interest in the brand and provides an opportunity for the customer to like/share the experience with friends on Facebook. All this happens because the Facebook mobile app (if it's installed and has access to your location) is aware of your geolocation and shares this information with the marketers. Over time, geo-targeting accuracy and options have improved, and social media platforms have rich advertising offerings such as Facebook's local awareness advertising that can target potential customers within a 1-mile radius of business. This retargeting is not based on first and third-party cookies (as it is on websites), it possible due to the mobile device's unique id.

Contextual Local Targeting

The *contextual local targeting* method builds upon an existing database of locations corresponding to targeting options such as a shopping mall or school and may even be tied to the geo-demographics of a location (such as income/lifestyle and census data).

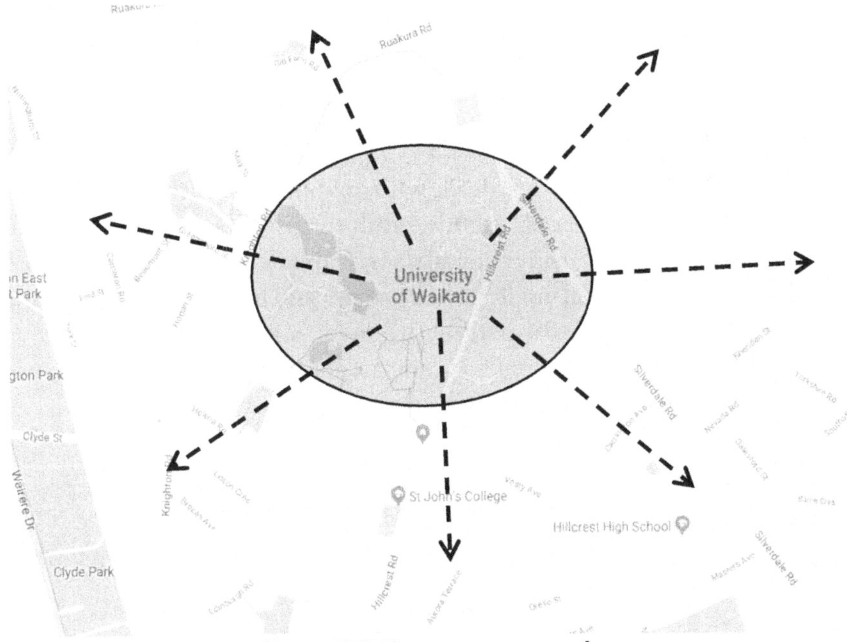

Figure 9.3. Retargeting example

There are a couple of really compelling use cases for local contextual targeting including targeting based on political affiliation within a congressional district using what is called "addressable advertising." For example, Democratic Presidential candidates for the 2016 Presidential election Hillary Clinton and Bernie Sanders used TV ads targeted at New York voters through addressable TV ads services from Cablevision and D2 Media Sales. This was all done through a partnership between DISH and DirecTV/AT&T.

Moreover, the targeting list was based on likely Democratic primary voters from voting lists during the previous elections that the campaigns provide to Cablevision or satellite providers DirecTV and Dish. That list (usually successfully matched up about 10% of the time currently) is matched against each vendor's customer database, and the desired ads are served to the matching households. While the cost of such ads is much higher, it comes with much greater certainty; the ads are reaching just the individuals who are targeted. As geolocation applications continue to improve there will be additional ways to build marketing and advertising on top of these requests, so stay tuned!

CATEGORIES OF LOCATION ANALYTICS

Based on its scope, we can broadly classify location analytics into two types:

- Business Data-Driven Location Analytics
- Social Media Data-Driven Location Analytics

Business Data-Driven Location Analytics

Business data-driven location analytics deals with mapping, visualizing, and mining location data to reveal patterns, trends, and relationships hidden in tabular business data stored within business databases. Capitalizing on the data stored in a company database, location analytics can map and capture vast amounts of geo-specific data to provide information, products, and services based on where customers are. By using a customer's location data, it is possible to recommend the nearest convenience store, coffee shop, taxi, or even probable social relations.

Applications of Business Data-Driven Location Analytics

Business data-driven location analytics has several applications, including the following.

Powerful Intelligence

Simple maps have been widely used, but they are limited in their provision of insightful details. Using sophisticated mapping techniques, such as clustering, heat mapping, data aggregation (e.g., aggregating data to regions), and color-coded mapping, can generate powerful business intelligence (Hecht, 2013).

Geo-Enrichment

Simple data maps can be enriched with customer data, including demographic, consumer spending, lifestyle, and locations (Hecht, 2013). For example, where do loyal customers spend most of their time?

Collaboration and Sharing

Maps are easy to understand and are excellent communication and collaboration tools. Location analytics can map business data for collaboration across the organization. We can also use it for information sharing purposes with customers. At the end of this chapter, we provide a systematic tutorial on how to map out sample tabular business data using Google Fusion Tables. With Google Fusion Tables, the reader can map data and display and share the results as maps, tables, and charts.

Social Media Data-Driven Location Analytics

Social media data-driven analytics rely on social media location data to mine and map the locations of social media users, content, and data; social media location information comes mainly from GPS and IP.

Uses of Social Media-Based Location Analytics

Social media location-based services are becoming an everyday reality. Geolocation data can be used to identify the real-world geographic location of objects, such as a mobile phone, automobile, ship, or Internet-connected devices and computers. Almost all social media platforms have geolocation capabilities that can bring several benefits to organizations (see Figure 9.4). We can check into locations deliberately, but what is unknown is that it is possible to be automatically checked into virtually any location as we transverse the world via our mobile devices, even when it is our desire not to be tracked that way.

Most Beneficial Features of Location-Based Marketing According to Marketing Executives in Select Countries, Jan 2016
% of respondents

	Canada	Germany	Singapore	UK	US
Ability to target	39%	44%	66%	35%	51%
Drive sales at point-of-sale	35%	44%	52%	35%	49%
Increases brand recall	27%	40%	42%	27%	20%
Proven to increase average purchase value	27%	32%	24%	20%	33%
Ability to reward loyalty	25%	32%	30%	24%	25%
Drives foot traffic	25%	20%	38%	37%	45%
Ability to enhance in-store experiences	22%	34%	40%	20%	10%
Take advantage of digital wallets	18%	24%	40%	20%	33%
Allows for meaningful personalization	12%	42%	30%	33%	25%

Note: Canada n=51; Germany n=50; Singapore n=50; UK n=51; US n=51; for their business; includes digital out-of-home (DOOH), mobile, online, print, radio and static billboards
Source: Location Based Marketing Association (LBMA), "Global Location Trends Report," March 13, 2016

207483 www.eMarketer.com

Figure 9.4. Benefits of location analytics

Until very recently, marketers usually did not know how often advertising was seen by the people for whom it was intended. However, with the latest round of targeting technology that is no longer the case, particularly in an age where most consumers have a smartphone and do much of their daily communications and media consumption on it. Marketing messages can be tuned and targeted to an audience in a precise location, perhaps even with a personalized message and then measured for effectiveness. Organizations use social media location-based services for a variety of purposes, including the following.

Recommendation Purposes

Organizations can harvest location data to recommend products, services, and social events for potential customers in real time as they approach specific localities. For example, Tinder recommends potential social relationships based on the location of users and Yelp has locale and venue recommendations that it provides to users.

Customer Segmentation

Social media location data can be used to segment customers based on their geographic location. Tweepsmap (https://tweepsmap.com/), for example, can be used to geo-locate your Twitter followers by country, state, or city.

Advertising

Location-based advertising allows targeted marketing and promotion campaigns mostly delivered through mobile devices to reach specific target audiences. Hyper-local advertising has fundamentally changed the marketing landscape. It allows marketers to use a smartphone's GPS data to target audiences for delivering relevant ads geographically.

Information Request

Based on their current location, customers can request a product, service, or resource (e.g., the nearest coffee shop, restaurant, or parking lot).

Alerts

Location data can be used to send and receive alerts and notifications. For example, mobile device users can receive sales and promotion alerts, traffic congestion alerts, speed limit warnings, and storm warnings.

Search and Rescue

Location data is vital in search and rescue operations. For example, Agos a geo-tagging and reporting platform that enables communities to deal with climate change adaptation and disaster risk reduction.

Navigation

Mobile and GPS-based navigation services and apps assist us in finding addresses. BE-ON-ROAD, for instance, is a free offline turn-by-turn GPS navigation app for Android devices.

LOCATION METRICS

In the context of retails, location analytics has two distinctive classes of real-time actionable metrics:

- Proximity Metrics
- Staying Metrics

Proximity Metrics

The idea of *proximity* is about an individual walking nearby and is drawn into action by a specialized promotion. Thus *proximity metrics* deals with connecting the geo-location of the customer and the marketing promotion or message

(Max, 2014). Draw Rate is an example of proximity metrics.

Draw Rate

The *Draw Rate* or *Capture Rate* relates to the ratio of individuals entering the store to the people passing by. Inside a store, people can get promotion or information messages as they get closer to a display or product, and therefore the *Draw Rate* relates to the ratio between people passing by close to the display and total visitors to the store.

Staying Metrics

Staying metrics relate to movements and actions by employees in a store. Staying metrics are commonly used to design a better store layout and customer service. For example, *Stay Time* and *Wait Time* metrics are used for real-time deployment of employees to particular areas inside the store.

LOCATION ANALYTICS AND PRIVACY CONCERNS

While location-based services bring ease, convenience, and safety to customers and value to businesses, they also raise serious *privacy issues* related to the collection, retention, use, and disclosure of location information (Minch, 2015). Tracking, data mining, and storing location information can endanger some fundamental human rights, such as freedom of movement and freedom from being observed. Minch (2004) raised several issues arising from location-based services, including the following.

- Should users of location-enabled devices be informed when location tracking is in use?
- Should users of location-enabled devices be permitted to control the storage of location information?
- Should location information as stored be personally identifiable, or should the user have the option to preserve degrees of anonymity?
- What legal protection should a person's historical location information have against unreasonable search and seizure?
- To what extent should users of location-based services be allowed to choose their level of identifiability/anonymity?
- What level of disclosure control should be dictated by government regulation? By the affected individual customers, users, etc.? By other parties?
- What governmental legislation and regulation is appropriate to assure citizens' rights of privacy in an era of location-aware mobile devices?

As a subject ready for legal debate on our privacy rights, Geo-Data capture has to be near the top of the list of things to be concerned about in the era of Snowden[4] along with violence and terrorism threats. Law enforcement and even schools have begun to use geolocation monitoring of localities. At universities, students have been using applications such as Yik-Yak to find out what is happening nearby on campus and send anonymous messaging (and monitoring) to nearby users.

Marketing automation is also becoming more sophisticated, and the raw data that has been collected by default from mobile devices has been surfacing in application interfaces where it can be selected and used by marketers.

Example

Myrna Arias, a central California woman, was fired after she uninstalled a working App that tracked her exact location 24/7 (even when she was not working). The app Xora StreetSmart is intended to let companies manage employees working away from the office. Its creators, ClickSoftware, stated that it lets firms "see the location of every mobile worker on a Google Map." However, ClickSoftware does not seem to envision the app as a 24-hour tracker, telling potential clients that "field employees" should launch the app "when they start their day." However, it is not hard to see how the information could be misused or abused, or just enter into a gray area where the legal precedent has not been fully mapped out.

However, there are ways to use geolocation data without giving up one's privacy. For example, users can input their zip code information into some apps rather than enabling location services and still get access to local data.

LOCATION ANALYTICS TOOLS

Google Fusion Tables

Google Fusion Tables is a web service to geotag, store, share, query, and visualize tabular business data overlaid on Google Maps. This chapter provides a detailed tutorial on Google Fusion Tables.

---

[4] Edward Joseph Snowden is an American computer professional, former Central Intelligence Agency (CIA) employee, and former contractor for the United States government who copied and leaked classified information from the National Security Agency (NSA) in 2013.

Esri

Esri's GIS (geographic information systems) is software to map, visualize, question, analyze, and interpret data to understand relationships, patterns, and trends (http://www.esri.com/). This chapter provides a detailed tutorial on Esri.

Agos

Agos is a geo-tagging and reporting platform that helps communities deal with climate change adaptation and disaster risk reduction: http://agos.rappler.com/#

Trendsmap

Trendsmap (http://trendsmap.com/) is a real-time tool that maps the latest trends from Twitter, anywhere in the world.

Followerwonk

This tool helps a Twitter user perform basic Twitter analytics, such as, who are their followers? Where are they located? When do they tweet? The tool can be accessed via http://followerwonk.com/

Geofeedia

Geofeedia is a social media location analytics platform that links social media posts with geographic locations. The tools can be accessed at http://www.geofeedia.com

Note that most location analytics software filters social media posts that are done at a particular location (latitude/longitude). The range of accuracy is approximately 20 feet; Instagram and Twitter provide a vast amount of data that can be filtered by location. Other platforms such as Facebook provide much less data because it is secured behind a membership firewall. Caveat privacy laws are beginning to constrain the capabilities of some of these platforms such as Geofeedia.

Geo-Data is considered by senior IT decision-makers to be the most actionable (and valuable) of all and is amazingly easy to collect.

Geo-Data contains the time, exact location, individuals identity (social media handle). In addition, Geo-Data often has an image of what the individual looked at or a selfie. Because Geo-Data is so specific, it is much more actionable than social media data that is not geo-specific. Enterprises with almost unlimited resources can undoubtedly scale this data more efficiently and market with it more efficiently than the author could.

CASE STUDY 9.2

"TWITTERGI": A TWITTER GEO-ANALYTICS DASHBOARD APPLICATION FOR GREEN INFRASTRUCTURE IN LONDON

Introduction

To support the need for green infrastructure in the London Borough of Barking and Dagenham (LBBD), the Sustainability Research Institute (SRI) of the University of East London (UEL) are conducting ongoing green infrastructure research in the area. To ensure that this research is implemented in the community to safeguard resilience into the future, collaboration with relevant stakeholders, partners, and networks is crucial. Thus, finding 'who is' and 'where are' the potential collaborators is essential. With limited resources and tools in hand, researchers at SRI are tasked with identifying and locating these collaborators with limited tools to assist them. This case explains the process of creating a Twitter geo-analytics and its role in pinpointing the potential collaborators.

Background Information

London is the capital city of the UK with a growing population and economy. However, London along with many other European cities is beginning to see the effects of a changing climate (Collier et al., 2016; Collier et al., 2016; Collier et al., 2013). Effects such as the enhanced risk of flooding, the heat island effect during warmer summers (Kolokotroni, Zhang, & Watkins, 2007) and imminent water shortages are looming. Along with this, heightened demand for housing and infrastructure in London has increased the volume of impervious surfaces throughout the city. This further intensifies the many effects of a changing climate in London. To counteract the increase in impervious surfaces and adapt to climate change, green infrastructure has been identified as an essential part of the London infrastructure plan (Parliament Office of Science and Technology, 2012). One area of London, which is facing the challenge of increasing green infrastructure, is the London Borough of Barking and Dagenham (LBBD). LBBD has the United Kingdom's biggest brownfield regeneration site at Barking Riverside. To support the need for green infrastructure in LBBD the Sustainability Research Institute (SRI) of the University of East London (UEL) is conducting ongoing green infrastructure research in the area(CONNOP et al., 2013). To ensure that this research is implemented in the community, identifying and collaborating with the relevant stakeholders, and forging potential partnership and networks is crucial.

Under this backdrop, the case study explores the results from the pre-design data collection, prototype development, and implementation of the Twitter geo-analytics dashboard application "TwitterGI" (Figure 9.5). The initial focus of the case is on the results from the pre-design focus groups on, 1) views on green infrastructure and collaboration, and 2) the information and functionality requirements for the application. The case then demonstrates how the information and functionality results were integrated into prototyping the TwitterGI application. The case also discusses the subsequent implementation of the application "TwitterGI" in the case study area.

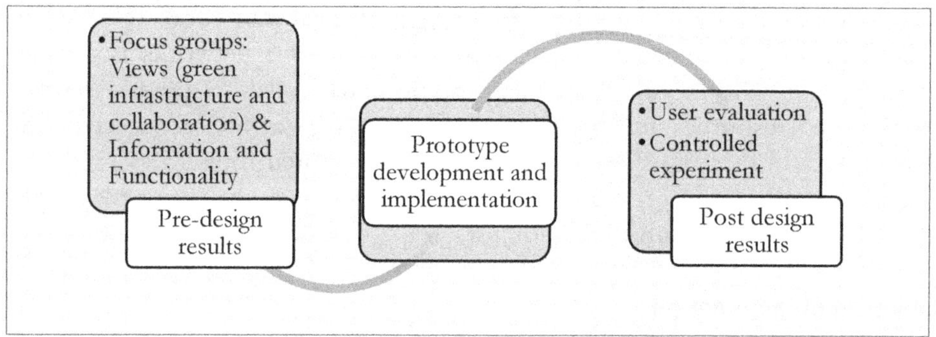

Figure 9.5. Prototyping Process

Pre-Design

This section presents the results from the pre-design focus groups. It explains how the two researchers involved in the project perceive *green infrastructure* and classify opportunities for *collaboration*. This is followed by the results of the *functionalities and information* required for the Twitter geo-analytics dashboard application needed to facilitate collaboration in green infrastructure research.

To start with, the researchers' views on green infrastructure identified during the focus groups are presented. During the focus group interview, the researchers identified five main elements of green infrastructure, namely, green structures, artificially constructed, green spaces, beneficial, not taken seriously. This was followed by the results on what the researchers constitute collaboration as, which in this case is; working with others, working together to achieve a goal, and engagement processes (Figure 9.6). The results highlight how researchers perceive collaboration as working with others as a team to achieve an end goal. Fundamental elements of collaboration for the researchers are engagement, dissemination, and communication with their networks and partnerships, this ensures their research is implemented in the real world, and they have access to research funding. Interestingly the results would indicate that the focus of the researchers is in collaboration with other researchers, policymakers, and decision-makers. The emphasis is on collaborating with those, which can help them answer questions and those who have the power to get green infrastructure into policy. There is very little focus on the collaboration with communities or citizens. It is suggested these stakeholders are the missing link in the researcher's collaboration efforts and they have an essential role to play in green infrastructure implementation. Buy in from citizens will be vital in changing attitudes towards green infrastructure not only on a local level but also will also have a crucial role in influencing policy-makers of the value of GI.

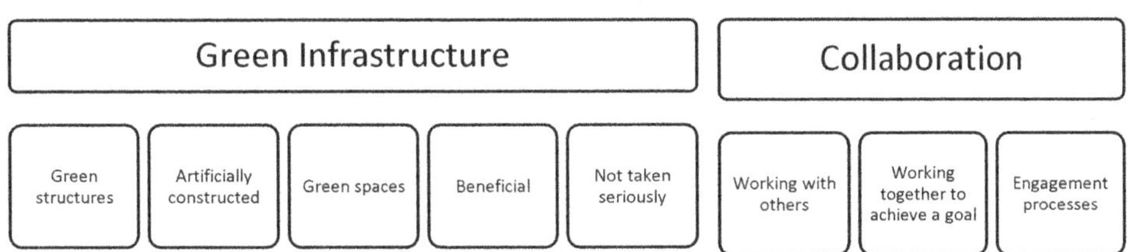

Figure 9.6. Views on green infrastructure and collaboration

With regard to information requirements, the researchers who took part in the focus group identified three categories as necessary for a Twitter geo-analytics dashboard application for collaboration on green infrastructure. The three categories were: professional details, research interests, and location (Figure 9.7).This information allows the researchers to make a quick assessment of the potential for turning those interested in the research into possible collaboration opportunities. This information is also useful for understanding what type of engagement is required from the research institute, who best to engage, and what elements of the research are most appropriate to the potential collaborators. It is suggested this information provides an initial overview of the collaborators from which the researchers can make the decision whether it is worth pursuing further.

Information required		
Professional details	**Research interests**	**Location**
Who they are?	What research they are interested in?	Where they work
Role /profession	What information they are looking for?	Where they are geographically located
Institution / organisation	The purpose of the information they require.	

Figure 9.7. Information required Twitter geo-analytics dashboard application

In considering the functionality requirements, the researchers identified three main functionalities for the application: *searching functionalities*, *analytics functionalities,* and *mapping functionalities* (Figure 9.8). These functions provide a method by which the researchers can access and visualize the information, which they outlined as crucial for gathering information about potential collaborators for green infrastructure research. These functions should begin to reveal the 'who,' 'what' and 'where' of potential collaborators. It also provides them with a way of investigating who is engaging with green infrastructure and the relevant areas in which they are interested. This, in turn, shows 'who' they are not engaging with through this method highlighting that a different approach may be required to target other potential collaborators who may be interested in working with them.

Functionalities Required		
Searching Functionalities	**Analytics Functionalities**	**Mapping Functionalities**
Search keywords	Statistics	Geographical reach
Search hashtags	Data analytics	Geographical selection
Search followers	Data visualisation	Interactive map

Figure 9.8. Functionalities required for Twitter geo-analytics dashboard application

The results on *Information and Functionality* from the focus groups were integrated into the development of the Twitter geo-analytics dashboard application for green infrastructure in London. These results were complemented by precedents for dashboard applications identified during the desktop research phase of the project. Based on the results a prototype application was developed, named, and registered. The development process for the prototype is outlined below (Figure 9.9).

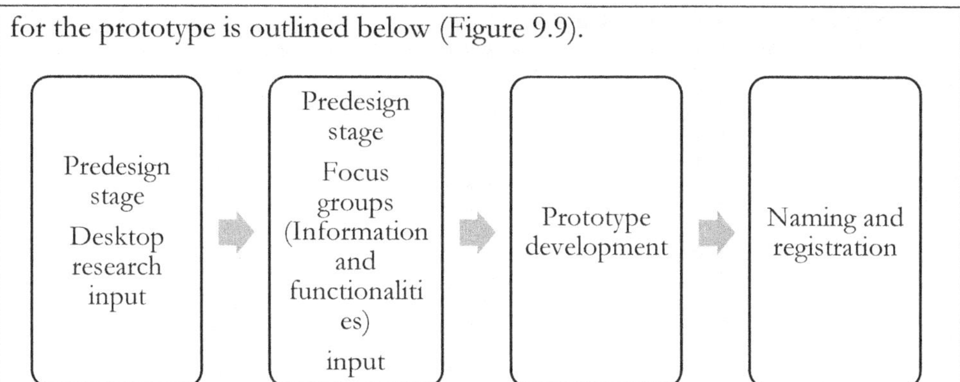

Figure 9.9. Development process: Twitter geo-analytics dashboard application

Desktop Research Input

Basic user requirements for a geo-analytics dashboard were gathered during the desktop research stage of the pre-design data collection stage. Different types of dashboard precedents were examined; twitter dashboards, city dashboards, and social media dashboards. Some of the precedents which guided the initial development of the geospatial analytics dashboard were "The London Dashboard," the Twitter Analytics dashboard and Edmonton's citizen dashboard. This provided the initial conceptualization of the geospatial analytics dashboard application.

Three essential design elements were taken from these precedents and used in the initial development stage (Table 9.1):

a) multiple page design,
b) ability to view and analyze information relating to tweets
c) good graphics

Table 9.1. Essential design elements for Twitter geo-analytics dashboard

Application	Developed by/for	Main Features
The London Dashboard	**Developed by**: CASA research at University College London. **Developed for**: providing access to City of London data	▪ Twitter trends ▪ City Statistics ▪ Multiple pages ▪ Mapped data ▪ Traffic cameras ▪ Weather station ▪ Transport information

<table>
<tr><td>Edmonton Citizen Dashboard</td><td>Developed by: City of Edmonton
Developed for: providing public access to government data</td><td>▪ Graphical interface
▪ Multiple page design
▪ Visual statistics
▪ Interactive</td></tr>
<tr><td>Dublin Dashboard</td><td>Developed by: National Institute for Regional and Spatial Analysis (NIRSA).
Developed for: providing citizens, public sector workers, and companies with real-time city data, time series indicator data and interactive maps about the city.</td><td>▪ Multiple page design
▪ Overview page
▪ Graphical interface
▪ Links to traffic cameras
▪ Visual statistics</td></tr>
</table>

The Input of Information and Functionalities

The next step involved encompassing the feedback from the *Information and Functionalities* requirements into the development of the application. To do this, the requirements were analyzed in terms of what was possible to achieve. The information requirements were analyzed in terms of what information would be possible to gather and display using the dashboard. The functionality requirements were analyzed in terms of what would be feasible to develop based on the timeframe and budget of the project. In terms of information, it was anticipated that only who the followers were and their geographic location could be gleaned from Twitter analytics and therefore displayed on the dashboard. The dashboard had three information sections on the dashboard; *presence, engagement,* and *geo-reach.* The engagement section provided information on the followers and the geo-reach section provided information on their location. The next step was to improve the functionality of the application and to address the functional requirements outlined by the researchers. The functions which were deemed possible to develop within the scope of the research project were developed (Table 9.2).

Table 9.2. Functions which were developed as part of the application

Function	Developed
Seach Keywords	No
Seach hashtags	Yes
Search followers	Yes
Statistics	Yes
Data analytics	Yes
Geographical Reach	Yes
Geographical selection	Yes
Interactive map	Yes

Based on the results from the information and functionalities pre-design data collection the following functions were added to the application: Twitter presence, Twitter analytics engagement, Hashtag tweets, Most retweeted, Followers, Reach and exposure, and Twitter geographic reach (Table 9.3).

Setting up the Twitter account and naming of the application

After the Twitter geo-analytics dashboard was developed a Twitter account and associated hashtags were created. Setting up the account involved selecting an appropriate Twitter handle for the account. The researchers in UEL chose UELSRI (University of East London, Sustainability Research Institute) as their Twitter handle. When the development of the prototype application was complete and the account set up the application was named. The name for the application was chosen by the UEL researchers who thought it was essential to incorporate the Twitter element of the application, but also its purpose for green infrastructure which is known in their research field as GI. The application was then appropriately named "TwitterGI" (Figure 9.10). The application was not registered as the application was not for public use online.

Table 9.3. Functionalities added to the geo-analytics dashboard

Function and description	Elements	Description	Type of function	Info. category
Twitter Presence This tracks Twitter through the Twitter API account. The Twitter presence page has four primary functions: shows the number of followers, number of tweets, followers and tweet tracker, live Twitter feed. The main aim of the Twitter presence function is to	Twitter followers	Shows the number of twitter followers for the account	Analytics	Who
	Number of tweets	Shows the number of tweets which have been tweeted from the account.	Analytics	What
	Follower and Tweet tracker	Shows the rise and fall of Twitter followers and tweets through a simple diagram	Analytics	Who
	Live Twitter feed	Provides a live Twitter feed as so all tweets can be searched	Searching	What
	Twitter followers	Shows the number of twitter followers for	Analytics	Who

reflect the presence of the account on Twitter		the account		
Twitter Engagement The Twitter engagement page gives an overview of the engagement with the Twitter account. The Twitter engagement page has six main functionalities: Hashtag tweets filter tweets by date, most retweeted tweet, estimated reach, estimated exposure, and followers. The main aim of the page is to provide information on who is engaging with the account	Hashtag tweets	The user can see all tweets which have used the assigned TURAS hashtag #turasGI. This allows the user to see who is posting about the research.	Searching	What
	Filter tweets by date	This allows the user to filter the tweets by date.	Searching	What
	Most retweeted	The page also shows the most retweeted tweet attributed to the account. This allows the user to see where the interests of most of the followers lie.	Analytics	What
	Estimated reach:	The reach shows the total number of estimated unique Twitter users that tweets about the search term were delivered to.	Analytics	Who
	Estimated exposure	Exposure is the total number of times tweets about the search term were delivered to Twitter streams or the number of overall potential impressions generated.	Analytics	Who
	Followers	The Twitter analytics engagement page also shows the Twitter account followers. Thus allowing the user to see whom they are engaging with.	Analytics	Who
Twitter Geo-Reach	Geographic overview	It provides an overview of the	Mapping	Where

<table>
<tr><td rowspan="3">This page shows the geographical reach of the data. The Twitter geo-reach page has three primary functions: geographic overview, interactive map, select location by tweet. The main aim of the page is to shows the locations of the Twitter followers who have engaged with the account.</td><td></td><td>geographic reach of the Twitter account through a mapping interface.</td><td></td><td></td></tr>
<tr><td>Interactive map</td><td>This allows the user to click on the map and to visualize the percentage of visitors to the page from each country.</td><td>Mapping</td><td>Where</td></tr>
<tr><td>Select location by tweet</td><td>This allows the user to click a tweet which was sent from the account and visualize on the map where the people who are interested in this tweet are located.</td><td>Mapping</td><td>Where</td></tr>
</table>

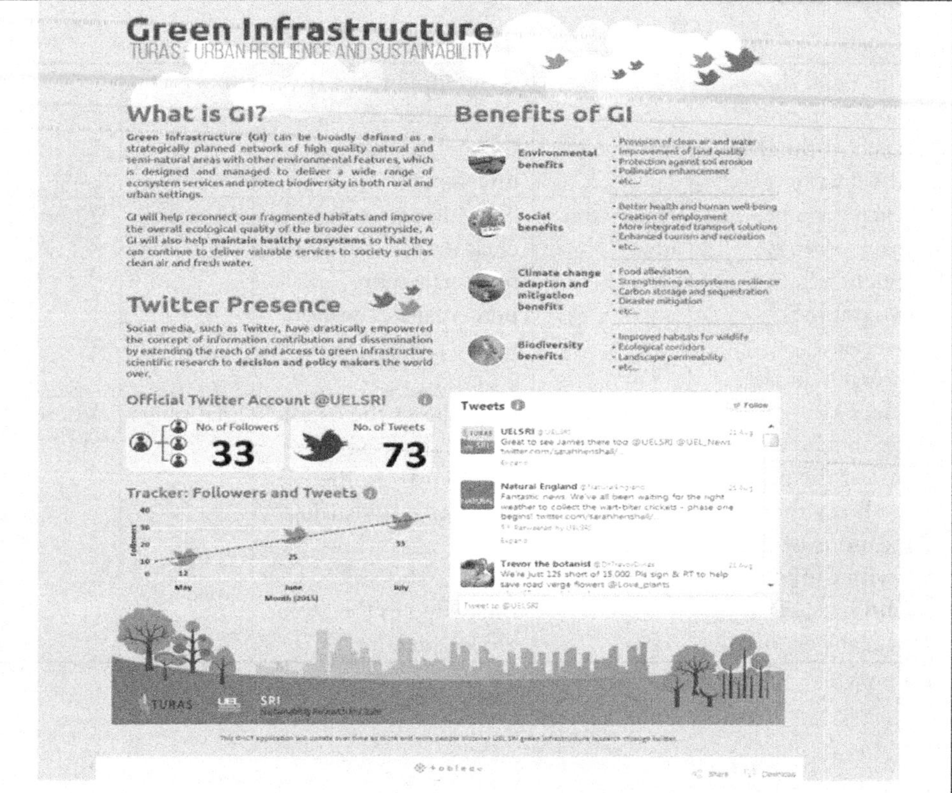

Figure 9.10. TwitterGI user interface

Implementation

TwitterGI was implemented in the case study area for a total of 12 weeks. The implementation strategy focused on the development of the Twitter account and building on the associated Twitter followers which involved curation of the account by the researchers at UEL. This implementation strategy was based on passive rather than active participation (

Table 9.4), unlike the case studies of crowd-sourcing on underutilized central-city sites in Dublin and community geo-timeline in Nottingham, which included the launch of the application, the use of social media, mentioning in the traditional media (e.g., radio and newspaper) and workshops. Overall, seventy-two Twitter followers were gained during the 12-week period. The implementation was moderately successful, and there were several key lessons learned from the implementation process.

Table 9.4. TwitterGI implementation strategy

Type	Description	Responsible party
Twitter account curators	Two researchers at the University of East London agreed to curate the Twitter account for the 12-week period. They were provided with an overview of how to use the Twitter account and some basic tips on how to gain followers. The curators also agreed to create content for the account, so the followers had information to interact with. It was also the role of the Twitter account curators to identify and follow other green infrastructure related accounts to drive some traffic to the UELSRI Twitter account.	Researchers (UEL)
Hashtags	As part of the implementation, plan two hashtags were created for the research project #twitterGI and #turasGI. These hashtags allowed for those interested in the UEL green infrastructure research to be able to find it quicker on Twitter. The aim was also for the UEL hashtags to become popular hashtags when searching for information on green infrastructure.	Researchers (UEL)
Creating content	The Twitter account curators also had to create content to populate Twitter with, but also so, the information relating to those interacting with the Twitter account could be scraped and fed to the geospatial analytics platform. This content was created mainly from the green infrastructure research, which was being undertaken in the	Researchers (UEL)

	case study area of the London Borough of Barking and Dagenham as part of the resilience research.	

Summary

Lessons were learned from the development and implementation of the Twitter geo-analytics dashboard which may prove useful in informing future Twitter geo-analytics dashboard developments and implementations. During the development phase of the project, two issues were identified. Firstly, scraping the location-based data from the Twitter API proved difficult, this was because many Twitter users do not display their locational data as part of their Twitter accounts. Secondly, the identification of the role or associated institution/ organization of the followers was beyond the scope of this prototype application development. Personal information is difficult to capture from Twitter. For this information to be revealed the user must access individual Twitter accounts. In terms of implementation, the success of a Twitter analytics geo-spatial dashboard relies on the number of Twitter followers the Twitter account gathers. It was evident from the case study that a traditional implementation plan was not suitable for this type of G-ICT application. The success of the implementation was related to those curating the Twitter account and challenging for the thesis researcher to control. The researcher provided some initial early-stage guidance on how to use Twitter but left the researchers to look after the account. The researcher could have intervened in the implementation, but it was felt it would be more useful if the UEL researchers curated their own account and therefore the dashboard would be an accurate reflection of their own efforts. The researchers were also more informed as to what followers to target and what type of information to tweet. It was found that the more time and effort put into Tweeting the more traction the account got, resulting in more followers and potential collaborators.

Acknowledgment: This study was financially supported by the European Union FP7-ENV.2011.2.1.5-1 (TURAS Project) Grant Agreement no. 282834.

CASE STUDY 9.3
THE "OWL BUS"

Background

The Seoul Night Bus, also known as the "Owl Bus," is the brand name of the Seoul (South Korea) city's intracity buses that run nine routes exclusively from midnight to 5:00 a.m. Like an owl, animated in the dark with its glowing yellow eyes, the "Owl Bus" was born to make Seoul's public transportation service ceaseless, carrying the city's late-night commuters. As the service is the first of its kind in Korea, policymakers struggled to shape action plans in detail. In particular, the biggest task was to address issues such as the selection of the routes, ensuring efficient operation, passengers' safety, and convenience. Location analytics and social media helped Seoul Metropolitan Government (SMG) to realize the "Owl Bus" project and overcome these challenges.

The Problem

Since subway line No. 1 opened in 1974 through to the transformation reform carried out in 2004, the Seoul Metropolitan SMG has steadily introduced measures to ensure greater convenience and better mobility of the citizens. However, students and workers such as sanitary workers or small business owners, who return home late at night, found it hard to benefit from the pre-existing systems. Most of them suffer from poor working conditions and low salaries, yet they still had to pay the late night extra charge when taking taxis to return home.

The second issue was the growing inconvenience due to late-night taxis refusal to take passengers and illegal operation. During late night and dawn hours, there are far less available taxis than people who are trying to hail a cab. Thus, illegal operations are prevalent with taxi drivers demanding extra fares, causing severe inconvenience to citizens. Additionally, there are practical limitations in controlling such irregularities. Firstly, there is a shortage of police officers responsible for preventing such violations, and even if the police catch an offender 'red-handed,' it is hard to obtain evidence to prove the driver's act of refusing passengers or demanding illegal excess fares.

The third issue was related to the public-private consensus on the need for new means of transportation to support urban dwellers" economic activities. Seoul, transformed into a global city in just 50 years, and is emerging as a prime location in the world economy. As the city's industrial, economic, and cultural activities expand in size and scope, the citizens reached a consensus on the need for a bus service that operates from midnight to dawn. It was also considered that advanced nations such as Germany and the U.K. have already run such services to promote the safety of the citizens and their rights to mobility.

Private bus companies' selective operation on profitable routes was a long-running concern for SMG. Thus, it shifted from private to a quasi-public bus operation system. In the new system, Seoul manages the bus routes and revenues while the private companies operate buses.

The Solution

Test Operation of Night Bus at the Request of the Citizens

Since 2012, the SMG has operated the 120 Dasan Call Center and the official blog to listen better to the voices of the citizens and has developed various policy measures based on the information collected through these channels. Along the way, an opinion was received that the late night taxi service is not only difficult to use but also imposes substantial financial burdens on users. An on-site survey conducted for about six months from October 2012 found it necessary to operate a late-night bus service. As a result, starting from April 19, 2013, the city government began operating two pilot routes exclusively for an after-midnight service.

The role of location analytics and social media

Social media and location analytics played a crucial role in expanding the bus routes and the selection of the "Owl Bus" brand name. For three months following the launch of the test operation, the service was extremely well received by 220,000 people, making it justifiable to raise the number of service routes. The seven new lines were determined by taking into consideration the heavy concentration of individuals on the move during late night hours. During the initial stages of mapping out how to operate the Seoul Night Bus, the issue of selecting bus routes emerged. The municipal government color-coded regions by call volume based on the location data provided by a private communication service provider, KT. Then, it analyzed the number of passengers who get on and off at each bus stop in the massive call volume regions and connected the dots to lead to the most appropriate routes. The data was used to construct a radial shape network linking outer districts of the city with the hub areas such as Jongno and Gwanghwamun.

With news regarding the Late Bus spreading over SNS channels, citizens voluntarily suggested naming the late-night bus. Thus, the city government invited public ideas for the naming of the service and, as a result, the brand name "Owl Bus" and "N (Late Night)," and the character that portrays an owl operating a bus were selected. These symbols have been used to mark bus stop signs, bus route map, and numbers and distinguish the late-night buses from ordinary ones. With the letter "N" in the bus number, the service began its full operation on September 16, 2014.

Results

Real-time Operation Information

The service provides citizens with real-time operation information. Anyone who wants to take the "Owl Bus" can check the arrival time and location of the bus stop in advance through the website or smartphone apps. Meantime, given that the service operates late night, safety measures were critical to protecting citizens. Besides the protective partition and speeding prevention device, it was made mandatory to inspect the vehicle before driving. The drivers with proven qualifications are also well remunerated so that they do not have to take on other vocational activities during the daytime hours and can fully concentrate during nighttime driving.

Safe and Affordable Means of Transportation for Citizens

The numbers of "Owl Bus" passengers are constantly rising. A total of 1,735,000 people have taken the buses from September 2009 to June 2013, making the average daily passengers stand at around 7,000. As for economic aspects, passengers are expected to save approximately KRW 6,000 as the "Owl Bus" charges KRW 1,850 per trip while the average taxi fare in the same timeframe costs KRW 8,000. Given that the most of the passengers are students, self-employed small business owners, or workers, the service is expected to help stabilize their household finances.

In the meantime, most passengers are concentrated in the timeframe from midnight to 03:00, when students and workers return home completing their after-school self-study, and night duties. As the less busy time tends to leave them more vulnerable, the "Owl Bus" is considered to help them move more safely. Notably, the "Safe returning-home service" provided in cooperation with the nearby police stations reinforces the safety.

Income Redistribution For The Economically Disadvantaged

Before the operation of the "Owl Bus," one had to pay up to tens of thousands of WON to go from the city center to a residential district outside the city. However, they can now complete their journey with just 1,850 WON. As the savings will lead to higher disposable incomes, income redistribution effects are expected, too. As of 2013, the SMG estimates nearly KRW 14.1 billion worth of economic benefits has been redistributed.

Distribution of the Manual for Other Local Governments to Benchmark

As residents of other cities express their interest in the "Owl Bus," through SNS channels, local governments and research institutes have inquired about the process in the run-up to the introduction and requested lectures on the "Owl Bus." With many municipal governments expressing their interest, the Busan Metropolitan Government extended the late night service. In fact, the operational hours of existing intracity buses and other cities such as Ulsan and Daejun are planning to extend their operation hours, as well.

Resources

Budget

To finance the operation of the "Owl Bus," budget provision was needed to pay for the labor costs and the installation of safety facilities such as protective walls for drivers and a speeding prevention system. However, these expenses were covered by the joint management funds for the shift from private to quasi-public bus operation. Consequently, additional costs were not incurred.

Technology

Information systems connected inside the vehicles such as the Bus Management System, the Bus Information Unit, and Bus Information Tool enable comprehensive control of the bus operations, and efficient adjustment of intervals while providing users and drivers with real-time operation information.

Human Resources

The "Owl Bus was introduced without incurring additional costs and increased operation revenues too. The allocated resources are 45 vehicles and a total of 54 workers; 36 for driving and 18 for management.

Source: Bus Policy Department, the Seoul Metropolitan Government, South Korea.

TUTORIAL 9.1
MAPPING WITH GOOGLE FUSION TABLES

GOOGLE FUSION TABLES

Google Fusion Table is a web service to store, share, query, and visualize tabular business data overlaid on Google Maps. Tabular data can be visualized and shared in a variety of ways, including charts, maps, network graphs, or custom layouts. California State, for example, shares government datasets using Fusion Tables (http://data.ca.gov) where the data can be viewed, filtered, and downloaded by citizens. In addition, to cope with Hurricane Irene in August 2011, WNYC (public radio) created an evacuation zone map for New York City area residents.

The data formats supported by Fusion Tables include spreadsheets, CSV files, and Keyhole Markup Language (KML, a file format used to display and map geographic data). Google also provides an example library of Fusion Tables:

https://sites.google.com/site/fusiontablestalks/stories

In this tutorial, we will learn how to configure Fusion Tables to map and share location data online.

GETTING STARTED WITH FUSION TABLES

Step 1: Go to https://www.google.com/fusiontables/ and click on the "Create a Fusion Table" button. For this exercise, we will use Victoria's police stations location data downloaded from https://data.gov.au in the KML format (the data file and up-to-date tutorial are available on the book companion website).

Step 2: Next, the reader will be asked to upload their data into the Fusion Table. To do so, the reader has four options:

- Upload from a computer
- Upload from Google Spreadsheets
- Create an empty table (for manipulating data later)
- Search other online publicly available data

In this tutorial, we choose the "from this computer" and click "Browse File" to upload the data. Locate the data that will be uploaded and click the "Next" button.

Step 3: Next, choose the format (i.e., comma separated, tab, colon, or another type) of data being uploaded (in this case KML). Leave the other options in their default settings and click the "Next" button.

Step 4: After the data is loaded (Screenshot 9.1), make sure that the correct row is selected for the column names (which is usually row 1) and click "Next."

Column names are in row 1

1	descr...	name	Station	Region	Divisi...	PSA	Local Govt. Area	No
2	<div class... info-window" style=... family...	Alexa...	Alexa...	Eastern	3	BENA...	MUR...	33
3	<div class... info-window" style=... family...	Altona North	Altona North	North... Metro	2	HOBS... BAY	HOBS... BAY	72
4	<div	Angle...	Angle...	Western	1	SURF	SURF	55

Rows before the header row will be ignored.

Screenshot 9.1. Data loaded into Fusion Table

Step 5: Once the data is imported, provide the following details and click "Finish" (Screenshot 9.2)

Table—provide a meaningful table name.

Allow export—if the reader checks this, other users will be able to export their data into a CSV file.

Attribute data to—here the reader can write a message that will be displayed when people view or use their data.

Attribution page link—provide the attribution page URL or link, if any.

Description—Provide a meaningful description here that may help the reader remember what the data is about.

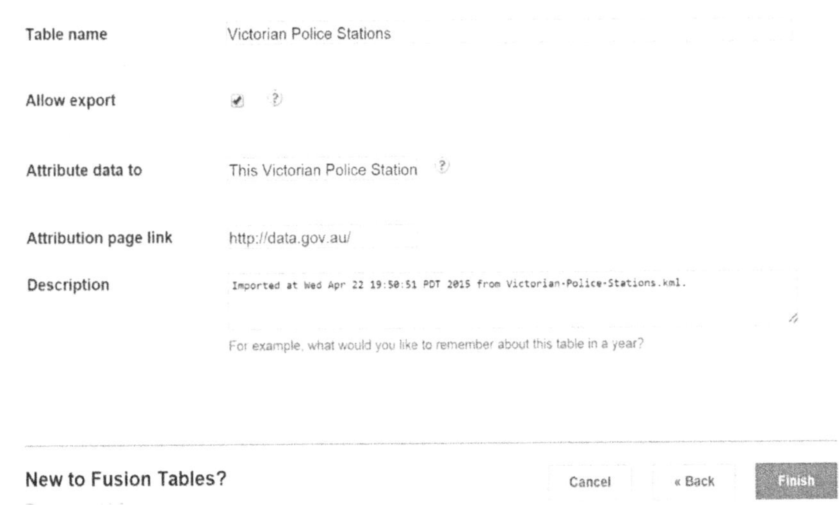

Screenshot 9.2. Fusion Table description

Step 6: Now the data is uploaded into the Fusion Table, and the reader is ready to process, visualize, and share it (Screenshot 9.3).

Screenshot 9.3. Data loaded and ready

Step 7: Fusion Tables auto-detect location data and display a tab called "Map of <location column name>." In this case, the "Map" tab is titled "Map of geometry." Click on "Map of geometry" to see a map of the police stations (Screenshot 9.4).

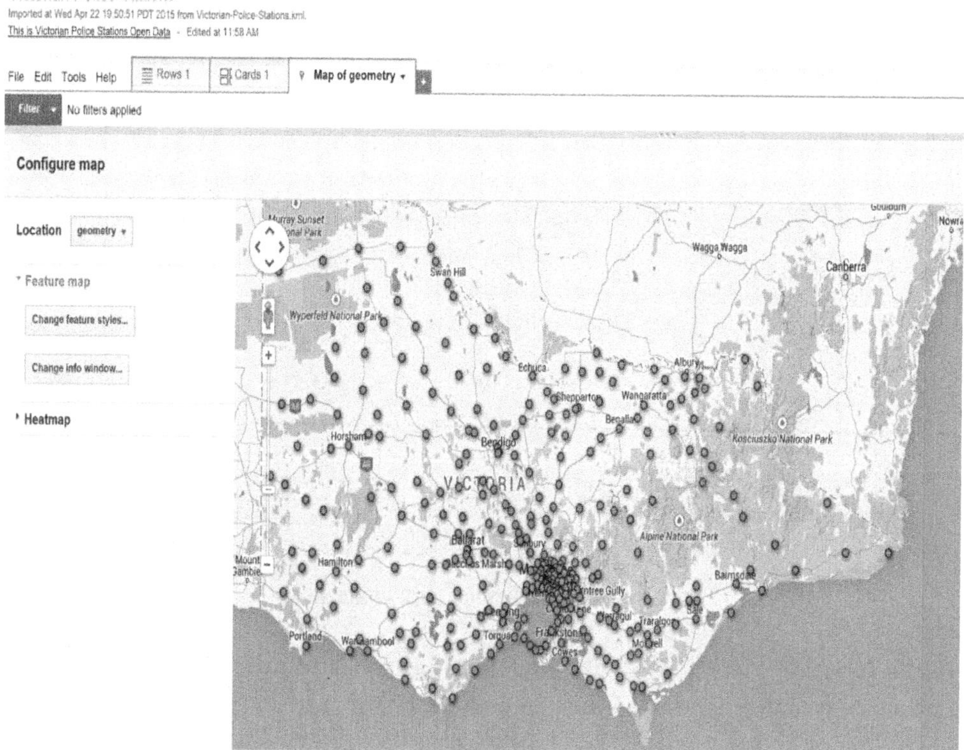

Screenshot 9.4. Google Fusion map of police stations

If the Fusion Table does not automatically detect location information, then the reader needs to configure it manually through the following steps:

- Click on the "Rows" tab and find the column name that has the location data and clicks on the downward pointing arrow.
- Next, click on "Change."
- On the page that opens up, choose "Location" for the type and then click on the "Save" button.

Step 8: Next, double-click on a red placemark to view more information about a police station (Screenshot 9.5).

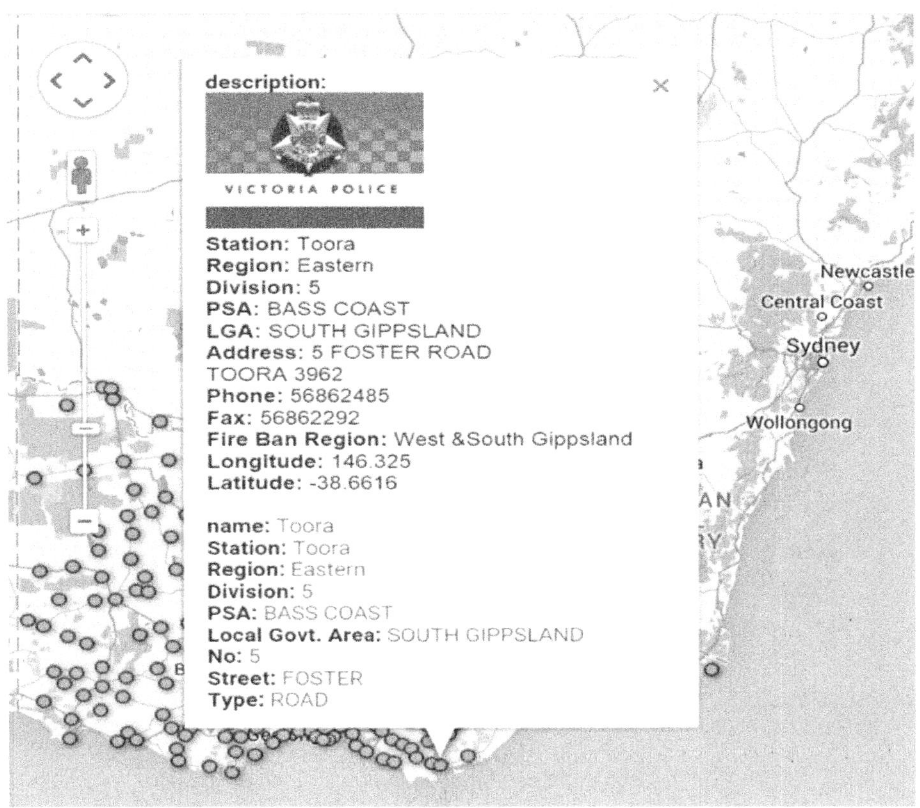

Screenshot 9.5. Detailed information about the police station

Step 9: Once you have created a map, the reader can customize different aspects of it, including creating and customizing charts, creating custom cards, changing marker styles, and applying filters to their data.

Changing marker styles—to modify the marker style (the red dots), use the following steps.

- Ensure that you are on the "Map" tab. Click "Tools→Change map→Change feature styles."
- Click on the "Marker" icon in the left panel and "Fixed" in the right panel.
- Choose a different marker style from the drop-down menu and click "Save" (Screenshot 9.6)

- The reader can also assign different marker icons to various types of variables by using the "Bucket" option. For example, police stations in the different regions can be marked with different icons.

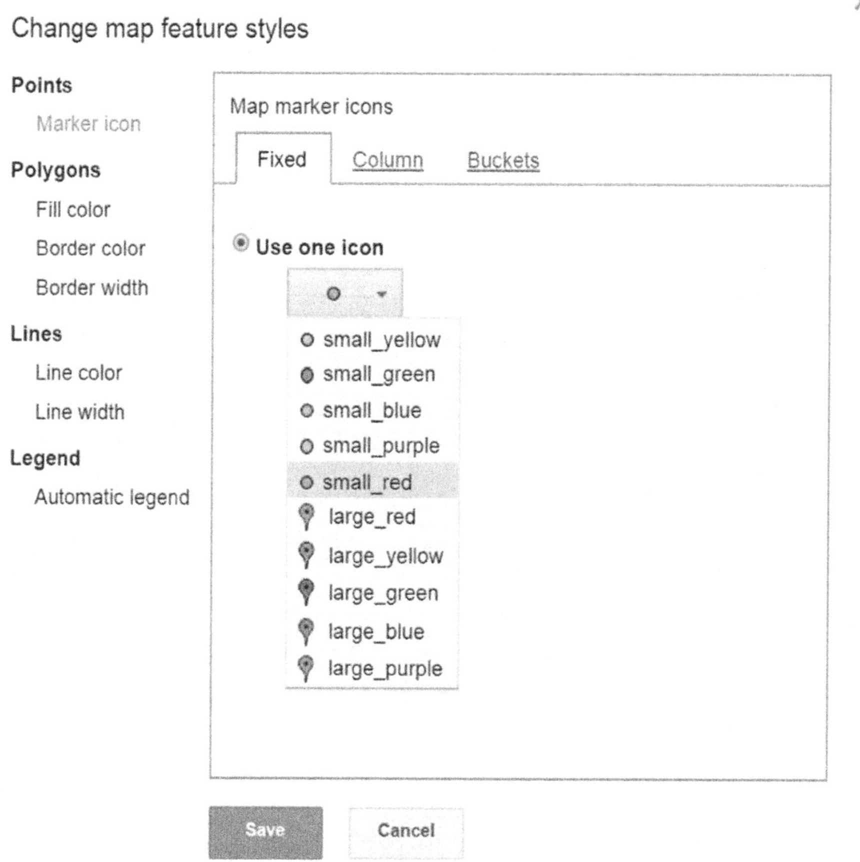

Screenshot 9.6. Changing map features

Filtering data—Filters are variables from the table/data that will be used to filter out data for display. To apply filters to this data, use the following steps.

- Make sure that you are on the "Map" tab. Click on the "Filters" button available at the upper left side of the map (Screenshot 9.7).
- Select a filter to apply from the drop-down list (e.g., we chose "Region").

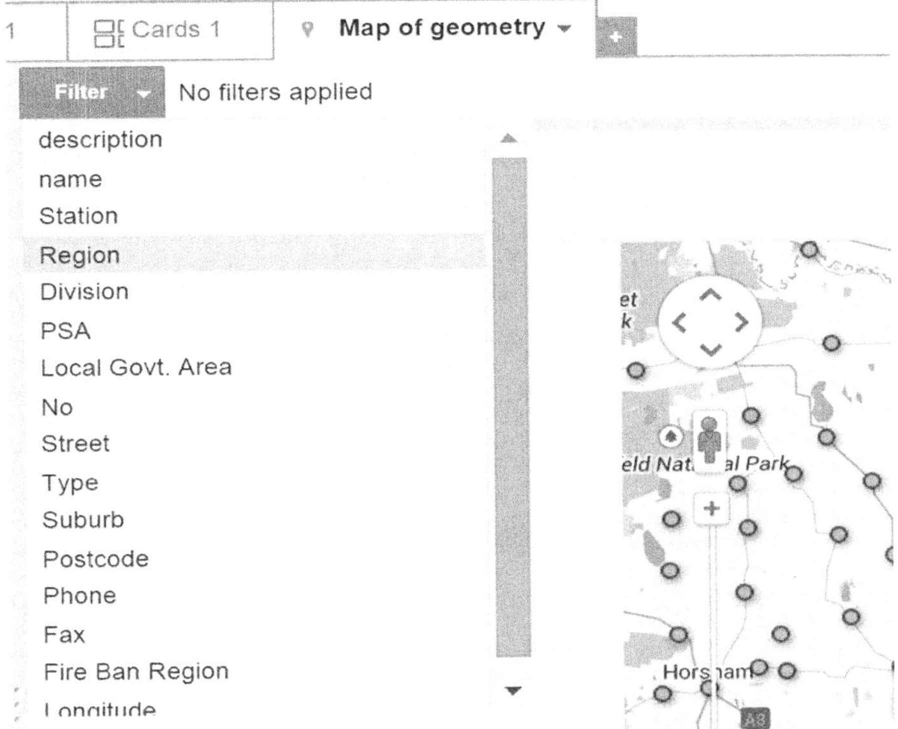

Screenshot 9.7. Data filtering

After applying the filter, the reader will be offered all the distinct values for regions (in this case, four regions are displayed). We choose to display police stations from only one region (i.e., Northern Metro). Now only data about police stations from Northern Metro is displayed (Screenshot 9.8).

Customize the info window—the default information window that appears when clicking on a red dot only uses the first ten columns from the data table, but can customize which data appears and how it is displayed.

- Ensure you are on the "Map" tab. Click on the "Tools→Change map," then click the "Change info window" button.
- Click on the checkboxes to add or remove information from the automatic info window template.
- The reader can also customize the overall style and content of the info

window template by clicking the "Custom" tab. Once done, click on the "Save" button.

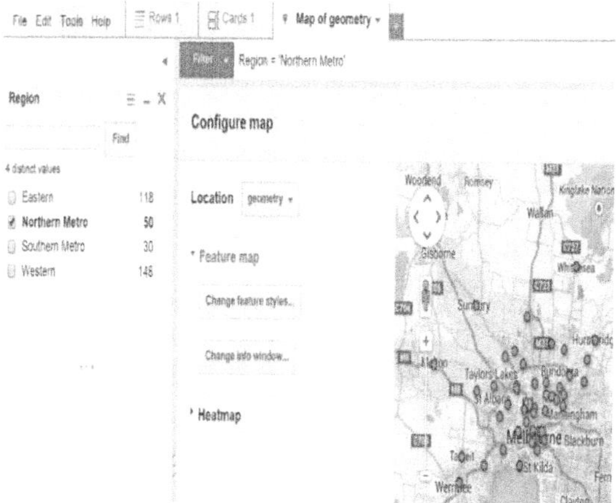

Screenshot 9.8. Results after application of filtration function

Adding charts—Fusion Tables lets the user add charts to their data so that they compare and contrast multiple values at a glance.

- To insert a chart, click on the red plus (+) sign and then click on "Add Chart" from the drop-down menu.

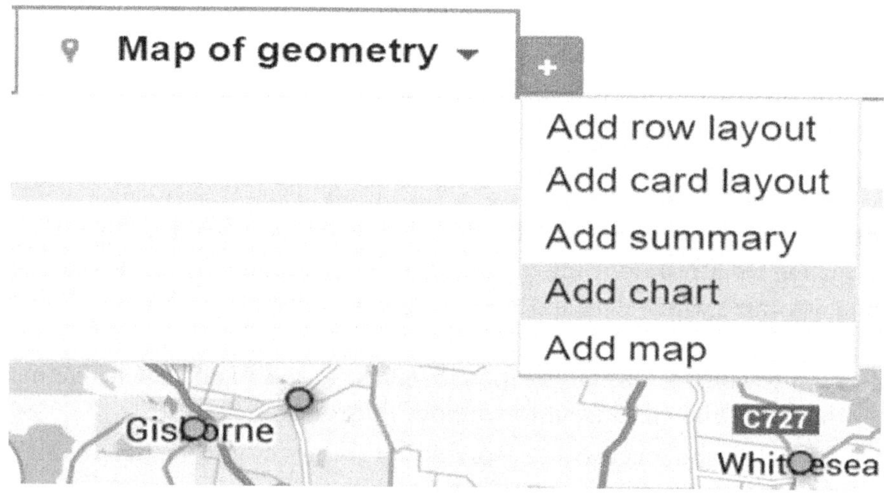

Screenshot 9.9. Adding chart

- Once a chart is added, users can choose different variables (e.g., continuous or categorical) to the chart depending on the type of chart you selected (e.g., pie chart, bar graph, line chart, or network chart). A chart type can be changed from the left panel.

- Once the user selects the right type of chart, click on the "Done" button in the upper right-hand corner.

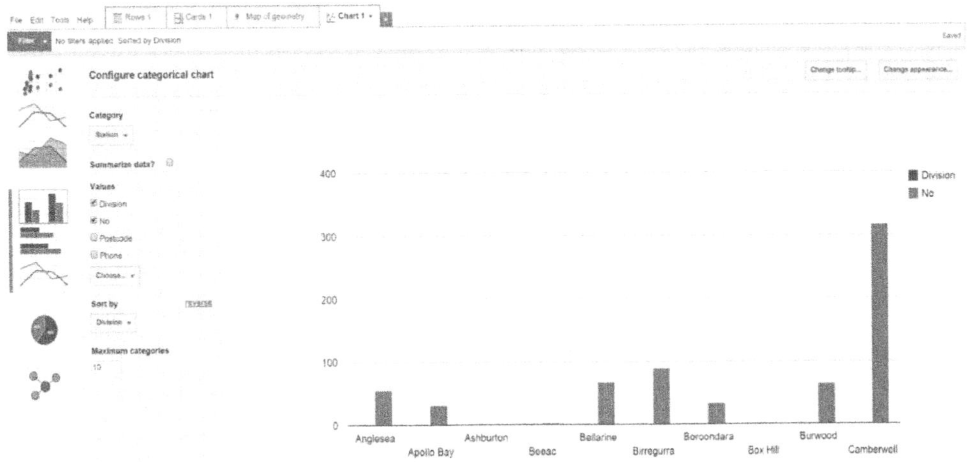

Screenshot 9.10. Google Fusion charts

Sharing data—one of the main reasons to use Fusion Tables is to make data available for others to see and download. To share a map, use the following steps.

- Make sure that reader is on the "Map" tab. Click on the "Tools" menu and then click on "Publish" (Screenshot 9.11).

- The reader can either share it with a limited number of people through e-mail. Alternatively, the reader can make it available over the Internet for everyone to see. In this exercise, we will make it accessible to the public.

- Click on the "Change" option under "Who has access." A new window will appear. Select the "public on the web" option and then click "Save."

- Next, the reader will be provided with a link and an HTML code for sharing the data. Copy it and click "Done." The code and the link can be embedded into a blog, website, or social media platforms. One can always get the link and code by clicking “Tools” and then “Publish.”

- In a similar way, the charts that have been created can be shared. Note that to share a chart, the reader must be on the “Chart” tab and then click “Tools→Publish.” The reader will be provided with a code and link to share.

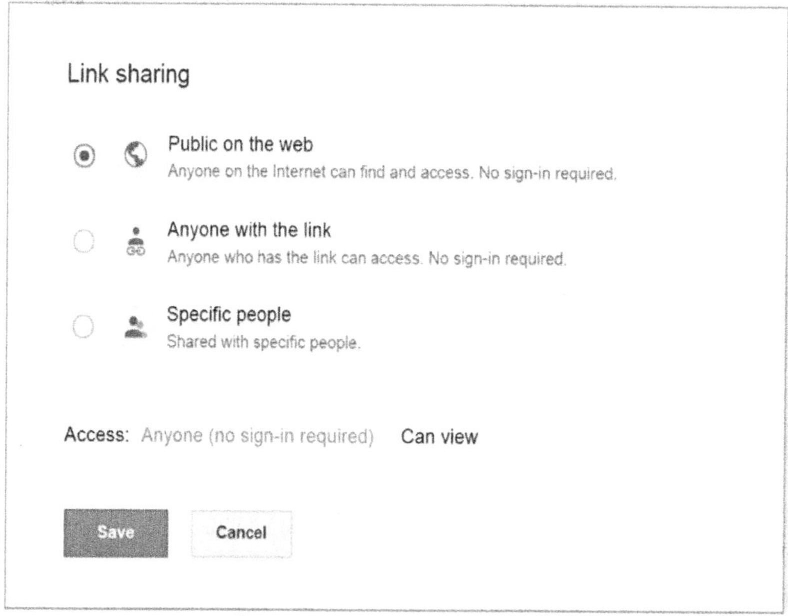

Screenshot 9.11. Sharing the data

TUTORIAL 9.3
ARCGIS ONLINE

INTRODUCTION

Developed by Esri, *ArcGIS Online* is a cloud-based application that allows the mapping, sharing, and searching of geographic information and maps. We can use it for creating and using maps, mapping and analyzing location data, sharing and discovering geographic information, and handling geographic information in a database.

Before starting with this tutorial, go to and signup for a 21 day ArcGIS Online trial account. https://www.arcgis.com/features/free-trial.html.

Note that Esri provides several other location mapping and analyzing tools, in this tutorial we only cover ArcGIS online.

In this lesson, you will re-create a new map from existing data and add the layers you need. Every new map starts with a basemap. In an ArcGIS organization, the administrator chooses the default basemap and sets its extent. This lesson assumes that your default basemap is the Topographic basemap and that its default extent is the world. If your settings are different, you will make changes as needed in the first section.

CREATE A NEW MAP

1. After you register, Login into the ArcGIS Online will load your account homepage (Screenshot 9.12).

Screenshot 9.12. ArcGIS Online user home page

2. Click on the '**Map**' menu available at the top left side of the page. This

should load your default map (Screenshot 9.13).

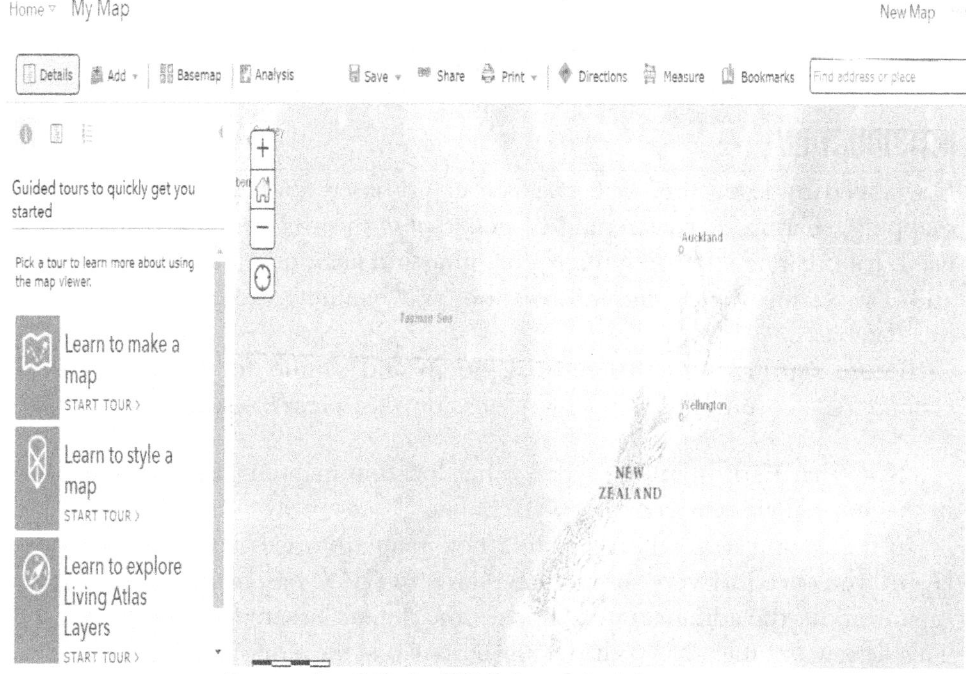

Screenshot 9.13. ArcGIS Online default base map

3. If a map is already open in your browser, click Modify Map in the upper right corner of the page. Then, click New Map and choose **Create New Map**. In the Open map window, click Yes, Open the Map.

4. If a map is not open in your browser, go to ArcGIS Online and click Map at the top of the page.

Tip: If you are in a new session, clicking **Map** will open a new map. Otherwise, it will open an existing map (the last map you were using). If an existing map opens, click **New Map**, and choose **Create New Map**.

5. The new map opens to the extent of the world.

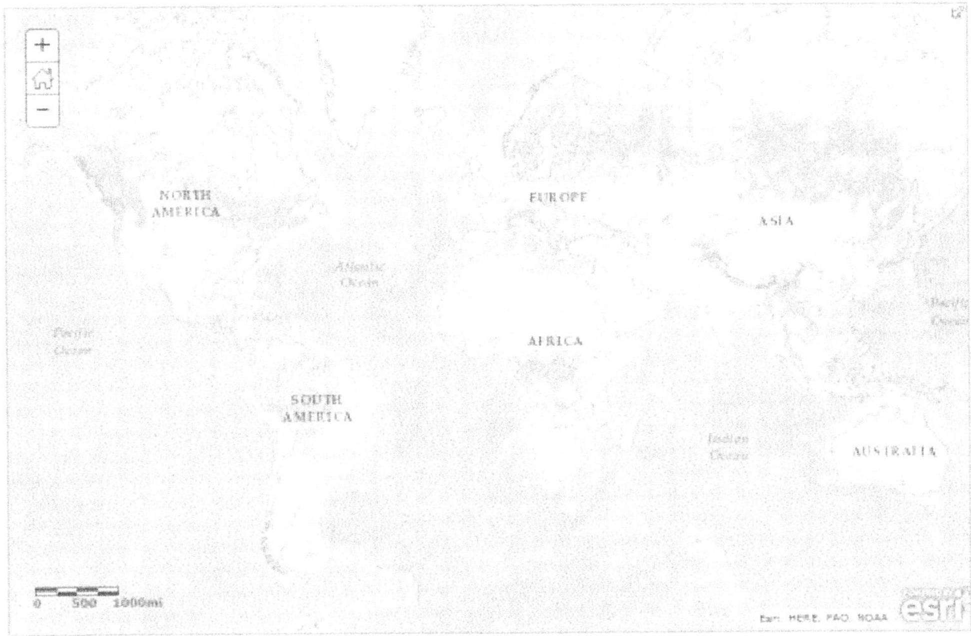

Screenshot 9.14. New map

6. On the ribbon, in the **Find address or place** box, type Island of Hawaii. In the list of suggested locations, choose the **Island of Hawai'i, United States** (Screenshot 9.15).

Screenshot 9.15. Finding an address

7. The map zooms to Hawaii (Screenshot 9.16).

Screenshot 9.16. Map zooms to Hawaii

8. Close the Search result pop-up.
9. Zoom in on the island. If necessary, pan (drag) the map to center Hawaii in the view.

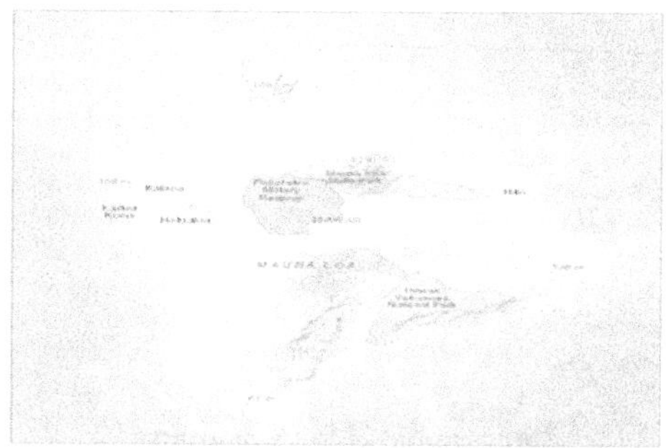

Screenshot 9.17. Hawaii map in full zoom

If you save the map, the map extent at the time of saving will become the extent used by the **Default extent** button. It can also be useful to add spatial bookmarks to navigate to particular map locations.

10. In the upper right corner, click Modify Map. (If you are already signed in, skip this step.)
11. On the ribbon, click the Bookmarks button. In the Bookmarked places list, click Add Bookmark.
12. Type Island of Hawaii and press Enter.

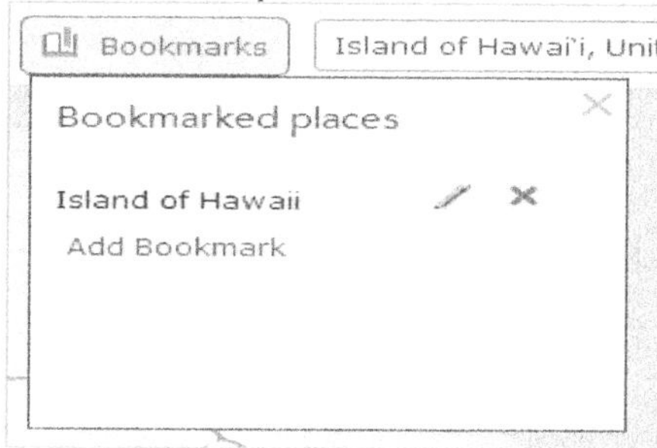

Screenshot 9.18. Adding bookmarks

13. Close the list of bookmarked places.

14. At the top of the Details pane, click the Content button.

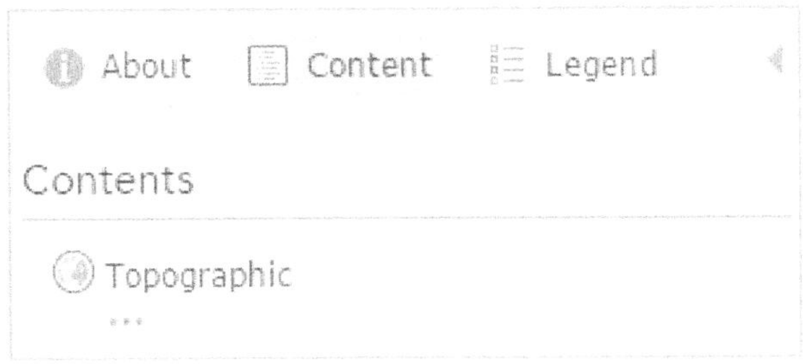

Screenshot 9.19. Selecting topographic

15. If necessary, click the **Basemap** button on the ribbon and choose **Topographic**.

Add Layers to the Map

You are ready to start adding layers to the basemap.

16. On the ribbon, click the **Add** button and choose **Search for Layers**.

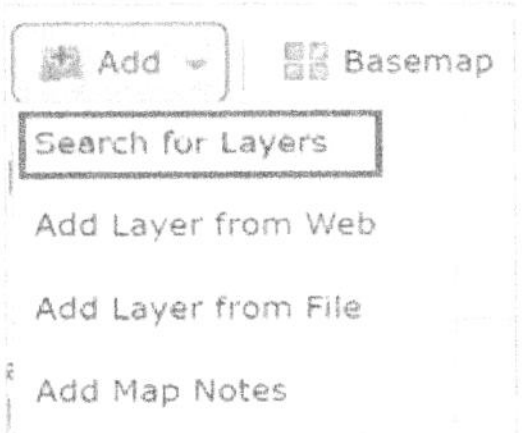

Screenshot 9.20. Searching for layers

In the **Search for Layers** pane, a default list of search results appears. You see layers that are shared with the organization and that have some geography in common with your map view.

17. If necessary, click the arrow next and choose ArcGIS Online.
18. In the Find box, type Hawaii. To limit the search results to layers owned by the Learn ArcGIS administrator account, add owner: Learn_ArcGIS to the Find box and click Go.

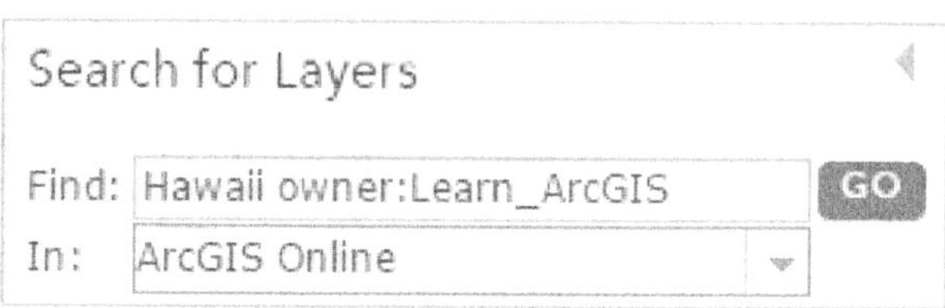

Screenshot 9.21. Searching for layers

The search results are narrowed down to a more relevant list.

19. In the list of results, locate HawaiiTerrain by Learn_ArcGIS. Click Add to add the layer to the map.

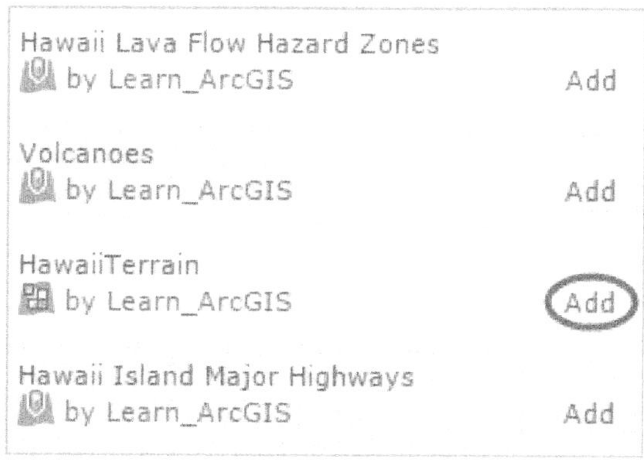

Screenshot 9.22. Add the layer

Note: The layers available in the organization are subject to change, so your search results may look different than those shown.

20. In the same way, add the following layers from the search results to the map (all layers are by Learn_ArcGIS):

- Volcanoes
- Hawaii Lava Flow Hazard Zones
- Hawaii Island Major Highways

21. At the bottom of the Search for Layers pane, click Done Adding Layers.

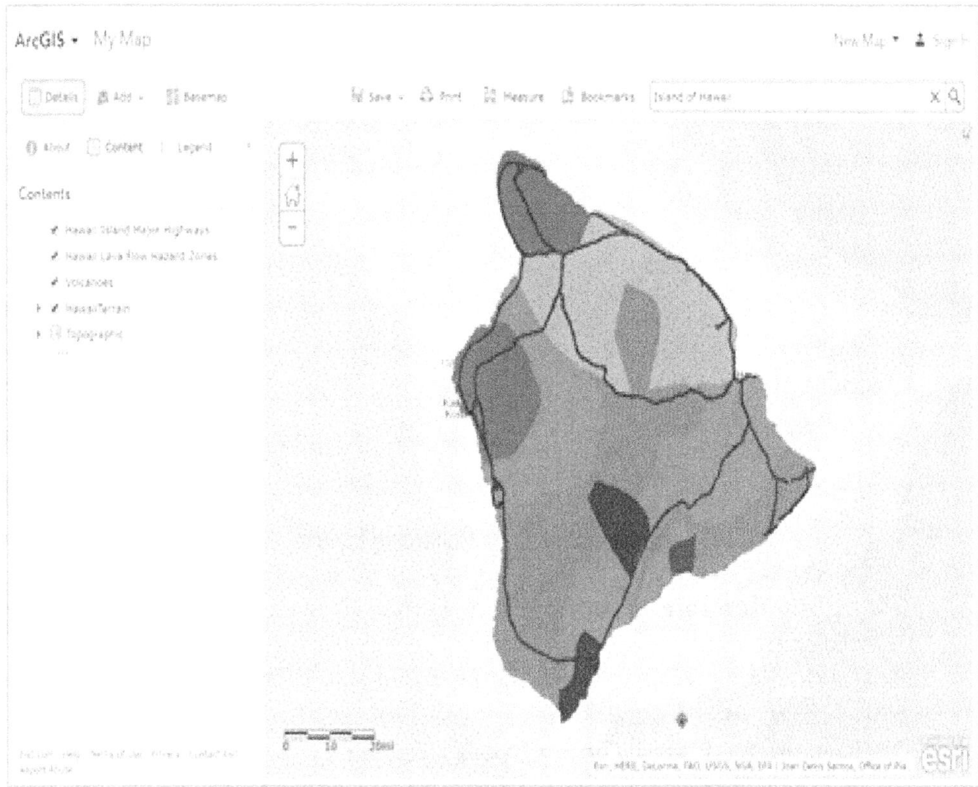

Screenshot 9.23. Map with layers added

The layers are drawn, with their default symbols, in the order in which they were loaded into the map. (This is usually, but not always, the same order in which you add them.) You do not see the volcanoes on the map because they are underneath the lava flow hazard zones.

Set Layer Properties

In this section, you will change some of the properties of the layers. You will give them shorter names, change their position in the list of layers, add labels, and adjust transparency. Layer properties are always accessed in the same way: by pointing to the layer name and clicking an appropriate button or clicking the **More Options** button and choosing the property you want to change.

22. In the **Contents** pane, point to the **Hawaii Island Major Highways** layer. Click the **More Options** button and

choose **Rename**.

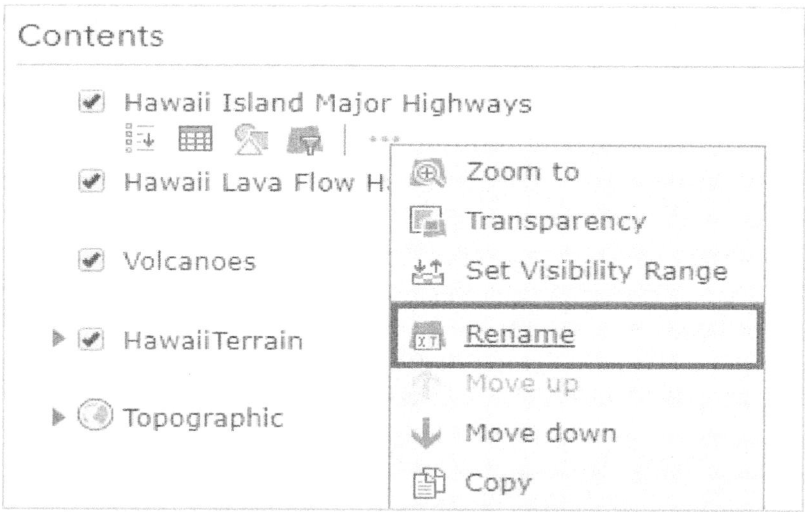

Screenshot 9.24. Renaming layers

23. In the **Rename** window, change the layer name to Highways and click **OK**.
24. In the same way, rename the Hawaii Lava Flow Hazard Zones layer to Lava Flow Hazard Zones.
25. Rename the HawaiiTerrain layer to Terrain.
26. In the Contents pane, point to the Volcanoes layer. Click the More Options button and click Move up.

The layer moves up one position, above the Lava Flow Hazard Zones layer. The volcanoes are now visible on the map.

27. Move the Volcanoes layer up again.

Now the Volcanoes layer is at the top of the list. The usual practice is to put points (such as volcanoes) above lines, and lines (such as highways) above polygons. Points, lines, and polygons are all feature layers: they usually represent discrete geographic objects that have more or less precise locations and boundaries.

Screenshot 9.25. Moving layers

The Terrain layer, like the Topographic basemap, is a tile layer. Tile layers are images and cannot be manipulated in the same ways as feature layers. They typically represent large, continuous surfaces rather than discrete objects. Tile layers cannot be moved above feature layers in a map.

1. In the Contents pane, point to the Volcanoes layer. Click the More Options button and choose Create Labels.

Each volcano is labeled with its name.

2. In the Label Features pane, change the label size from 13 to 14 and click OK.

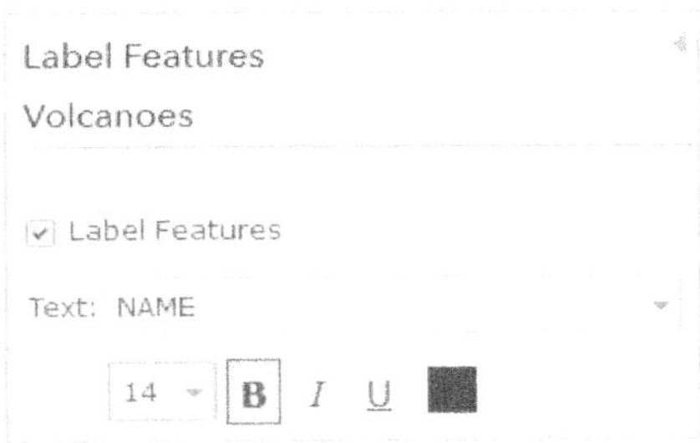

Screenshot 9.26. Changing label size

3. Open the properties for the Lava Flow Hazard Zones layer and choose Transparency. Make the layer about 40 percent transparent, or

whatever looks right to you.

4. In the same way, make the Highways layer about 50 percent transparent.

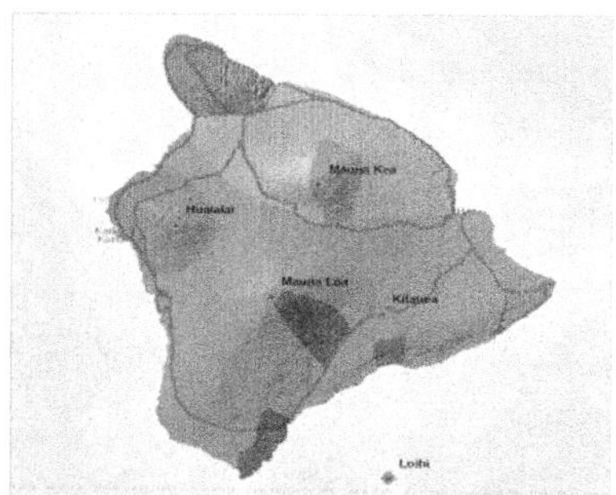

Screenshot 9.27. Map with updated information

You have re-created the appearance of the map you explored in the last lesson, except for the emergency shelters.

Define the Map Legend

When you start a new map or open a saved map of your own, it opens with the **Contents** pane showing. When anyone else opens your map, however, it opens with the **Legend** pane showing. You should think about how you want the legend to look.

5. At the top of the **Contents** pane, click the **Legend** button. Legend entries are created for all layers except the basemap. The entry for the Terrain layer (which shows grayscale values) is not useful for interpreting the map.

6. At the top of the Legend pane, click the Content button.

7. Open the properties for the Terrain layer and choose Hide in Legend.

8. View the legend again to see the effect, and then go back to the Contents pane.

Change a Symbol

You were able to re-create the map's appearance without too much effort because the symbols, such as yellow diamonds for volcanoes and shades of red and orange for hazard zones, were already set when you added the layers. A layer's default display settings, including its style and pop-up configuration, are made by its owner. Once you add a layer to your own map, however, you are free to change those settings.

9. In the **Contents** pane, point to the **Highways** layer and click the **Change Style** button.

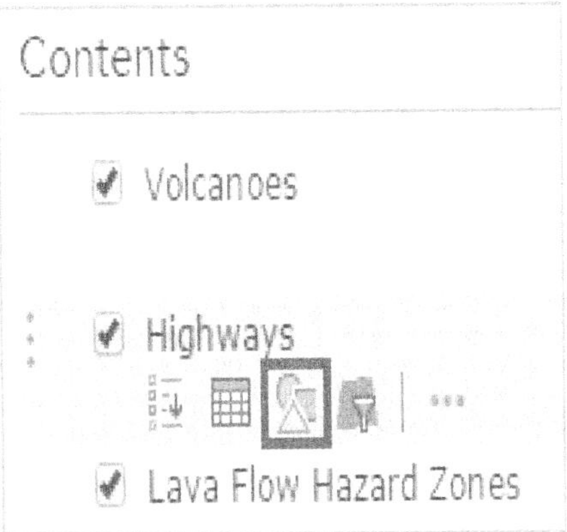

Screenshot 9.28. Changing style

10. In the Change Style pane, the currently selected style is Location (Single symbol), which is indicated by the check mark.

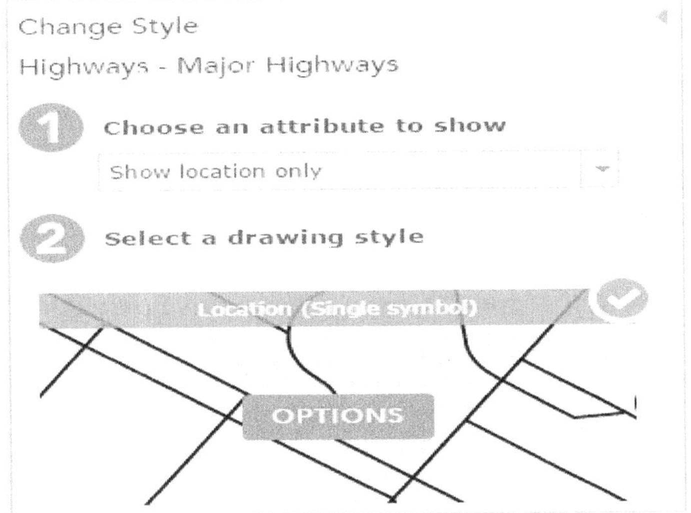

Screenshot 9.29. Choosing an attribute

In this style, all features in the layer are drawn with the same symbol. The Location style is appropriate when you want to see the features on the map, but you are not interested in their particular characteristics, such as names or speed limits.

11. For a drawing style, under Location (Single symbol), click Options.
12. Under Showing Location Only, click Symbols to change the symbol.
13. On the color palette, choose a color that you think will look good and click OK.

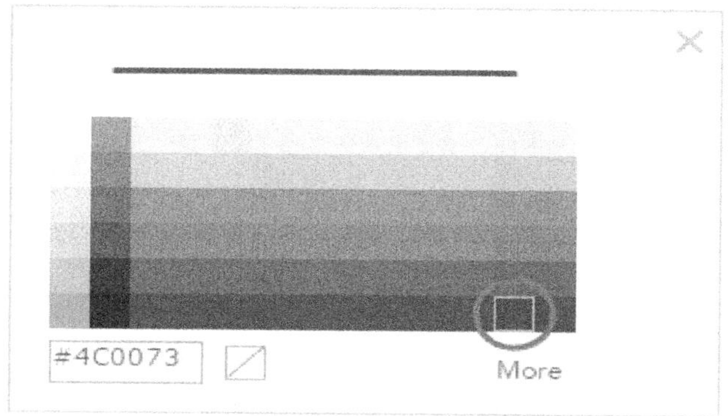

Screenshot 9.30. Changing color

The new color is applied to the map. (If you don't like it, click **Symbols** again to open the color palette and choose a different color.)

14. At the bottom of the **Change Style** pane, click **OK** and click **Done**.

Caution: Remember that you have not saved your work for this lesson. If you are continuing to the next lesson, be sure to keep the map open. Otherwise, to save your work with the appropriate details, go to Save the map.

CONCLUSION

In this lesson, you added several layers to the map and changed their properties. You have almost re-created the appearance of the map you explored in the first lesson. Several other tutorials on ArcGIS Online are available at https://learn.arcgis.com/en/projects/get-started-with-arcgis-online/

REVIEW QUESTIONS

1. Define location analytics.
2. Explain the two main categories of location analytics
3. What are the sources of location data?
4. What are the primary applications of business data-driven location analytics?
5. What are the primary applications of social media data-driven location analytics?
6. Discuss privacy concerns related to location analytics.

CHAPTER 9 REFERENCES

Collier, M., Connop, S., Corcoran, A., Crowe, P., Nedović-Budić, Z., Pichler-Milanović, N., . . . Varghese, J. (2016). European university-community partnership-based research on urban sustainability and resilience. *Current Opinion in Environmental Sustainability, 23*(Supplement C), 79-84. doi:https://doi.org/10.1016/j.cosust.2016.12.001

Collier, M. J., Connop, S., Foley, K., Nedović-Budić, Z., Newport, D., Corcoran, A., . . . Vandergert, P. (2016). Urban transformation with TURAS open innovations; opportunities for transitioning through transdisciplinarity. *Current Opinion in Environmental Sustainability, 22*(Supplement C), 57-62. doi:https://doi.org/10.1016/j.cosust.2017.04.005

Collier, M. J., Nedović-Budić, Z., Aerts, J., Connop, S., Foley, D., Foley, K., . . . Verburg, P. (2013). Transitioning to resilience and sustainability in urban communities. *Cities, 32*(Supplement 1), S21-S28. doi:https://doi.org/10.1016/j.cities.2013.03.010

CONNOP, S., GEDGE, D., KADAS, G., NASH, C., OWCZAREK, K., & NEWPORT, D. (2013). *TURAS green roof design guidelines: Maximising ecosystem service provision through regional design for biodiversity*. London University of East London.

França, U., Sayama, H., McSwiggen, C., Daneshvar, R., & Bar-Yam, Y. (2016). Visualizing the "heartbeat" of a city with tweets. *Complexity, 21*(6), 280-287. doi:10.1002/cplx.21687

Hecht, L. (2013). Location Analytics: The Future is Where. Available at: http://insights.wired.com/profiles/blogs/location-analytics-where-the-future-will-be#axzz4z9QZBRpZ.

Kolokotroni, M., Zhang, Y., & Watkins, R. (2007). The London Heat Island and building cooling design. *Solar Energy, 81*(1), 102-110. doi:https://doi.org/10.1016/j.solener.2006.06.005

Max, R. (2014). In Store or Location Analytics: The Hydra of Metrics, available at: http://www.behavioranalyticsretail.com/location-analytics-store-analytics/ (accessed on 22/11/2017).

Minch, R. P. (2015, 5-8 Jan. 2015). *Location Privacy in the Era of the Internet of Things and Big Data Analytics*. Paper presented at the 2015 48th Hawaii International Conference on System Sciences.

Chapter 10

Capturing Value with Social Media Hyperlink Analytics

"That idea of URL was the basic clue to the universality of the Web. That was the only thing I insisted upon."—**Tim Berners-Lee**

Learning Outcomes

After completing this chapter, the reader should be able to:

- Understand hyperlinks and their different types.
- Understand hyperlink analytics and its underlying assumptions.
- Understand website hyperlink analysis.
- Understand link impact analysis.
- Understand social media hyperlink analysis.
- Extract and analyze website hyperlinks.

INTRODUCTION

Hyperlinks are the pathways of social media traffic. *Hyperlinks* are references to web resources (such as a website, document, and files) that users can access by clicking on them. Hyperlinks can link resources within a document (inter-linking) and among documents (interlinking). Here are a few examples of Hyperlinking:

- Hyperlinks (usually shortened URLs) within a tweet that link to other resources (e.g., websites) available over the Internet.
- Hyperlinks within a website that link to internal resources such as the homepage, contact us page, and about us page.
- Graphics that have embedded hyperlinks.
- QR Codes that contain a link to the website page.

Hyperlinks are not merely technical links between two websites but serve a more symbolic means (Kim & Nam, 2012; Park, 2003). As a website is an official and unique entity representing an organization itself (Garrido & Halavais, 2003); therefore, embedding hyperlinks in an organization's website can be considered an official act of communication between two organizations. Hyperlinks to websites represent not only a reasonable approximation of a social relationship (Jackson, 1997) but also serve as validation or endorsement of the linked organization (Vreelnad, 2000). In addition, incoming links serve to increase the page authority, which helps SEO page rankings.

In conjunction with this, hyperlinks that exist between two organizational websites reflect a sense of validation, trust, bonding, authority, and legitimacy (Kim & Nam, 2012; Park, 2003; Vreelnad, 2000). Websites mostly link to other websites of similar nature, so hyperlinks can also serve as indicators of content similarity (Chakrabarti & M. M. Joshi, 2002).

TYPES OF HYPERLINKS

From hyperlink analytics point of view, there are mainly three types of hyperlinks:

- In-Links
- Out-Links
- Co-Links and Co-Citations

In-Links

Incoming hyperlinks are *links* directed towards a website originating from other websites (Lennart Björneborn & Ingwersen, 2004). For example, consider the top left image in the Figure 10.1, page A is receiving two in-links coming from pages B and C. Internet marketers want to get more in-links to their websites because they correlate with higher web traffic and popularity of the websites. In-links also play a significant role in website analytics, as both the quality and number of in-links can affect the search engine ranking of the website.

In-links are also the measure of a site's popularity, and the Google PageRank algorithm has been the primary mechanism employed to measure it. A study on YouTube viral videos, for instance, found that among other things, in-links play crucial roles in the viral phenomenon, particularly in increasing views of videos posted on YouTube (Khan & Sokha, 2014). Studies have also shown that in-link counts strongly correlate with measures describing business performance (Vaughan, 2004).

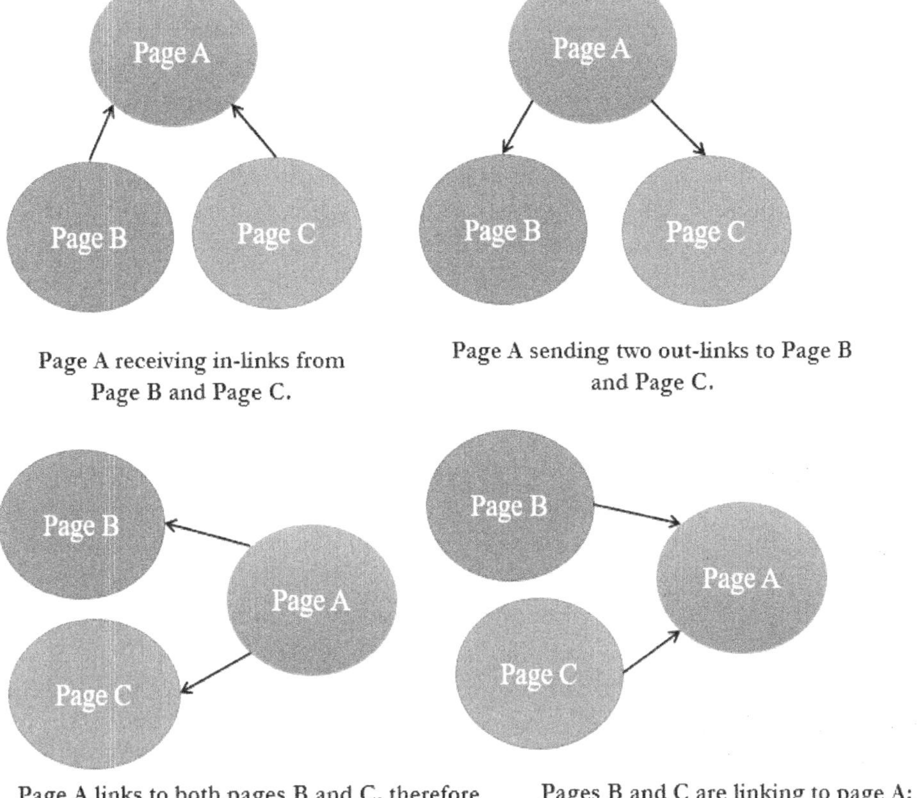
Page A
Page B
Page C
Page A receiving in-links from Page B and Page C.
Page A
Page B
Page C
Page A sending two out-links to Page B and Page C.
Page B
Page A
Page C
Page A links to both pages B and C, therefore B and C are considered to be co-linking.
Page B
Page A
Page C
Pages B and C are linking to page A; therefore, B and C are connected indirectly.

Figure 10.1. Different types of hyperlinks

Out-Links

Out-links are hyperlinks generated out of a website (Björneborn, 2001). As shown in the top-right image in Figure 10.1, page A is sending two out-links: one to page B and one to page C. Website out-links are tracked in the same way as in-links. A website's out-links become the in-links of the websites they point to. Out-links attract essential, relevant, and valuable eyeballs.

In the past, out-links (outbound links) were not considered an important factor in SEO ranking, but that position has changed. Now the consensus is that out-links may count for search engine ranking almost as much as in-links. For example, when a website or page out-links to an authoritative site it has a positive impact on rankings according to a recent study by the marketing firm, Reboot (Aharony, 2016).

Some people fear that out-links can damage a website's reputation, drop their search engine rankings, and create exit portals where customers will drop off (Fishkin, 2009). According to experts, however, out-links are very unlikely to harm a website. If appropriately used, organizations, in fact, may benefit from outbound links in many ways. Regardless of the quality of a website, it is impractical to include all the valuable information people seek on the website. Out-linking to valuable content that aligns with a website's business objectives is a great way to improve a visitor's experience on the site.

Co-Links and Co-Citations

Co-links is the interconnectivity created by two or more websites (or web pages) that link to a joint website (or web page). Co-links have two dimensions. First, if two websites receive a link from a third website they are considered to be connected indirectly. Second, if two pages link to a third page, they are also considered to be co-linking. As shown in the bottom-right corner of the Figure 10.1, pages B and C are linking to page A; therefore, B and C are connected indirectly. For example, page A links to both pages B and C; therefore, B and C are considered to be co-linking or connected indirectly (bottom-left image in the Figure 10.1). For example, when the New York Times and the Wall Street Journal both link to the Wikipedia Twitter account page in various articles, the Wikipedia Twitter page becomes a 'co-link' to both websites.

Co-links are similar in concept to the idea of "co-citation." Essentially, co-links and co-citations are used by search engines to rank pages based on the words they contain (and the keywords they do not contain, but are related based on other "common" web pages the pages link to). Search engines have evolved, via co-linking and co-citations, to rank websites for highly competitive keywords regardless of the presence of website copy containing these keywords anywhere in the title tags, metadata, or in the content of the page. For instance, for the query "cell phone ratings," consumerreports.com gets a first-page ranking in Google though it does not contain the word "cell phone" or the word "ratings," except in some of the text on the website. Cell phone ratings are not even in the page title, yet they rank well on a competitive query. Co-links and co-citations are difficult for humans to keep track of, but search engine algorithms do an excellent job on topic relationships and rank search result pages based on this information. In fact, co-links have been used to compare and map competitive similarity among organizations (Vaughan & You, 2006).

Because of the evolution in the application of search engine algorithms, optimizing web copy for optimal search ranking has become much more complicated to achieve than it once was. Great websites link to other great websites, and the search engines know this. Search engines developed algorithms that reward searcher/user behavior. There are hundreds of signals that search engines use to determine the quality of website/page for a searcher's query or search term. Most of these signals are based on the way people process text and images, attention span, and clickstream behavior.

HYPERLINK ANALYTICS

Hyperlink analytics deals with extracting, analyzing, and interpreting hyperlinks (e.g., in-links, out-links, and co-links). Hyperlink analytics reveal the internet traffic patterns and sources of the incoming or outgoing traffic to and from a website. Hyperlink analysis has been used to study a variety of topics. The case study included in this chapter demonstrates the importance of hyperlinks in viral phenomena and shows the valuable insights they carry for viral marketers in formulating viral marketing strategies. That being said, by studying hyperlinks, researchers have been able to observe linking patterns and gain new insights in a number of areas.

Link Analysis Examples

- Hyperlinks analytics has been employed to study university rankings, blogosphere interconnections, and scholarly websites (Vaughan & Thteelwall, 2003).
- It is also used to investigate political networks: political communication expressed by links connecting politicians' websites with the sites of other political actors (Park & Thelwall, 2008).
- And business competitiveness: the use of co-link to map competitive business positions (Vaughan and You, 2006).

Hyperlink Analysis Limitations

While hyperlinks analytics is a useful tool, it also has some limitations, listed here:

- It fails to provide any real insight into the type or amount of web traffic flowing among sites (Ackland, 2011).
- Usually, hyperlinks analytics does not examine internal links within a website between pages.
- It does not measure the effectiveness of navigation within a website, and
- Hyperlink analytics ignores or give low importance to internal linking

within a website (Thelwall, 2014).

TYPES OF HYPERLINK ANALYTICS

Hyperlink analytics can take several forms, including:

- Website Hyperlink Analysis
- Link Impact Analysis
- Social Media Hyperlink Analysis

Website Hyperlink Analysis

Website hyperlink analysis examines the in-links and out-links of a particular website or set of websites (as shown in Figure 10.2). Hyperlinks (i.e., out-links, in-links, and co-links) of a website are extracted and analyzed to identify the sources of Internet traffic. Website hyperlinks networks take two forms:

- Co-links Networks
- In-links and Out-links Networks

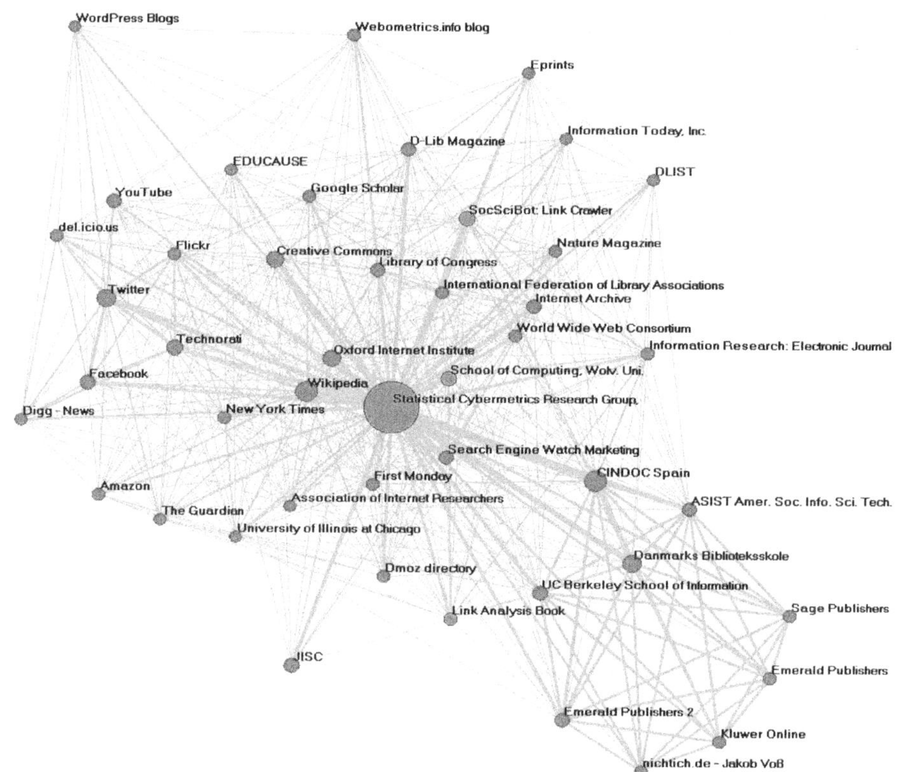

Figure 10.2. The Web Environment of the Statistical Cybermetrics Research Group Blog
(source: http://lexiurl.wlv.ac.uk/examples/cybermetrics.htm)

Co-Link Networks

In *co-links environment networks*, nodes are websites and links that represents a similarity between websites, as measured by co-link counts. With the Webometric Analyst tool, one can construct a co-link network diagram among a set of websites (Thelwall, 2014).

In-Links and Out-Links Networks

In-links and *out-links website networks* are built based on in-links and out-links from a website or set of websites. In such a network, nodes will be websites and links will present as in-links and out-links. The VOSON tutorial provided in this chapter demonstrates how to construct such a network using the VOSON hyperlink analysis tool.

Link Impact Analysis

Link impact analysis investigates the popularity of a website address (or URL) regarding the citations or mentions it receives over the internet. In a link impact analysis, statistics about web pages that mention the URL of a given website are collected and analyzed (Thelwall, 2014). URLs (or website address) that are frequently cited on the web are considered to be more popular and topical. As a result, measuring the popularity of URLs is a measure of the importance of a website, page, hashtag, or a social media account (user handle).

Social Media Hyperlink Analysis

Social media hyperlink analysis deals with the extraction and analysis of hyperlinks embedded within social media texts (e.g., tweets and comments). These hyperlinks can be extracted and studied to identify the sources and destination of social media traffic. An excellent example of the usefulness of the hyperlink embedded in the social media text is the study by Khan et al., (2014), in which they extracted out-links from Korean and US government agencies' tweets (see Figure 10.3). By extracting out-links and tracing them back to their sender, the authors were able to construct a map of the out-link structure (Figure 10). According to a comparison of out-links between tweets of the Korean and US governments, there were some differences in citation (i.e., out-link) patterns. The Korean government tended to cite domestic portals' news services and their blogs (i.e., self-citation).

Although there were social networking services and newspaper sites, most of the related out-links were for portals. On the other hand, the US government showed a more diverse pattern regarding out-link destinations. US out-links were not concentrated in specific sites and tended to go directly to news agencies, not to secondary sources such as portals. These comparisons between the US and Korean governments suggest that social media out-links can carry valuable information and can help explain real-world phenomena and shed light on the disparities in social media use among different cultures (Khan, Yoon, & Park, 2014).

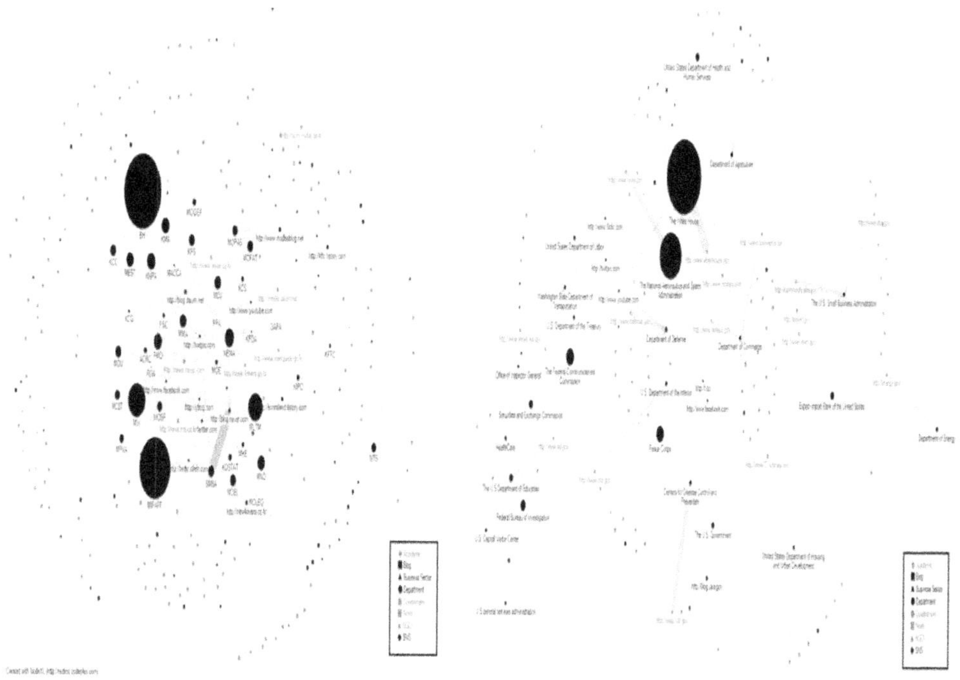

Twitter out-link diagram for Korean government agencies   Twitter out-link diagram for US government agencies

Figure 10.3. Twitter networks for Korea (left) and the US Governments (right)

HYPERLINK ANALYTICS TOOLS

The following are some popular hyperlink analytics tools.

Webometric Analyst

Webometric Analyst is a web impact analysis tool and can conduct a variety of analysis on social media platforms including hyperlink network analysis and web mentions: http://lexiurl.wlv.ac.uk/.

VOSON

VOSON (http://www.uberlink.com/) is a hyperlink analytics tools for constructing and analyzing hyperlink networks. More details on VOSON are provided in the hyperlink analytics chapter. This chapter includes a detailed tutorial on using VOSON for hyperlink analysis.

Open Site Explorer

Open Site Explorer is a link analysis tool to research and compare competitor backlinks, identify top pages, view social activity data, and analyze anchor text: https://moz.com/researchtools/ose/.

Link Diagnosis

Link Diagnosis (http://www.linkdiagnosis.com/) is a free online tool for analyzing and diagnosing links.

Advanced Link Manager

Advanced Link Manager (http://www.advancedlinkmanager.com/) provides a variety of link analysis capabilities, including the ability to track link-building progress over time, quality domain analysis, backlinks evolution, and website-crawling abilities.

Majestic

Majestic (https://majestic.com) provides a variety of link analysis tools, including link explorer, backlinks history, and link mapping tools.

Backlink Watch

Backlink Watch (http://backlinkwatch.com/) is a free tool for checking the quality and quantity of in-links pointing to a website.

CASE STUDY 10.1
HYPERLINKS AND VIRAL YOUTUBE VIDEOS

Background

Do hyperlinks play a role in the popularity of a video posted on YouTube? YouTube popularity was one of the questions that a research team at Social Listening (https://www.sociallistening.co.nz/) set out to explore. The research team knew that the answer lay in extracting and visualizing hyperlinks (particularly in-links pointing to a video) network and was looking for ways to get hands-on YouTube videos data.

What They Did

At the first stage of the quest, the research team identified the 100 most viewed YouTube videos. Every video posted on YouTube is automatically assigned a unique ID embedded within the URL of the video. For example, this 'www.youtube.com/watch? v=kffacxfA7G4' is the URL of a video posted by the user "Justin Bieber" having an ID "kffacxfA7G4." The data was collected for all 100 videos and saved in a text file with one ID per line.

At the second stage, to explore the effects of hyperlinks on the viral phenomenon, the team turned to Webometrics Analyst (http://lexiurl.wlv.ac.uk/)—a well-established tool for measuring different aspects of the web, such as web impact analysis, hyperlinks analysis, and the web search engine results. Using the IDs text file as an input, through Webometrics Analyst, the search team harvested the number of external links and Internet domains pointing to a video. This data was used to construct a two-mode network diagram (see Figure 10.4) for better understanding using UCINET social networking tool.

In Figure 10.4, the squares indicate unique videos IDs and circle nodes indicate the domain names. The links among nodes are URLs (in-link) received by the videos and users from a specific domain (arrowheads pointing from a domain toward a video or user are removed for the sake of clarity). In the case of the videos IDs, the size of a node indicates the number of URLs (in-links) received by the videos. In fact, the size of a node is more prominent when it received more URLs. In the case of the domain names, the size of the node means the number of out-link the domains are sending to the videos. The node size is bigger when a domain sent more URLs. The width of the links among the nodes indicates the number of URLs sent by a domain to a video: width is bigger when more URLs are sent by a domain.

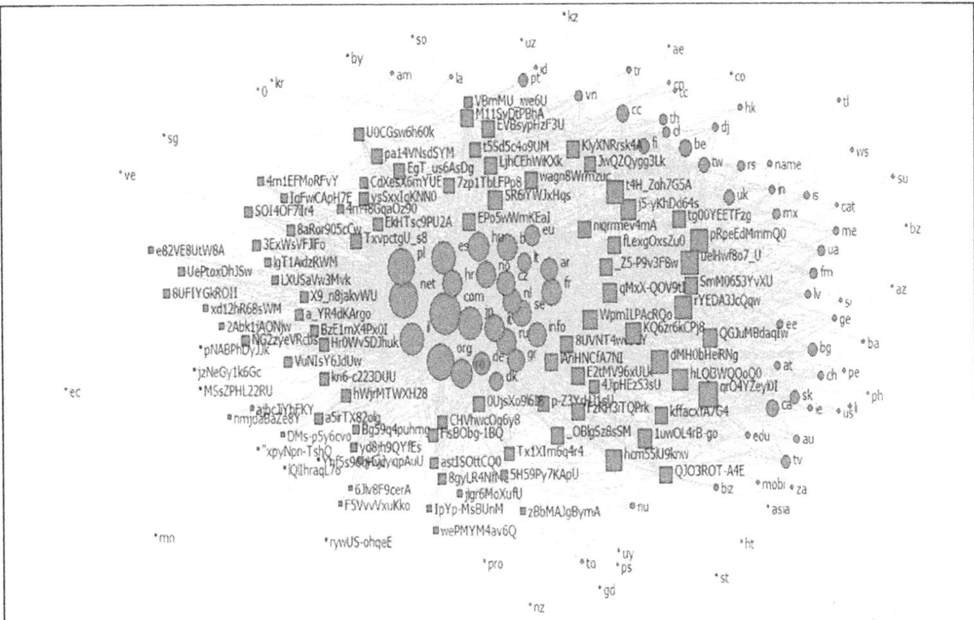

Figure 10.4. Viral Videos hyperlink network

Results

It is evident from the Figure 10.4 that most of the videos received URLs from a common set of domains (as shown by the circle nodes in the middle of the figure). However, the number of URLs received is different, i.e., some videos received more URLs than others with some domains sending more links compared to others.

The critical point to note is the diversity of domains received by some videos (as shown on the right side of the Figure above). For example, the videos on the right side of the diagram have not only have attracted URLs from the standard set of domains (such as .com) but also from several other diverse domains (e.g., tv, ca, SK, the UK, be, tw, fi, cc). The difference among the videos receiving several domains and links (as indicated by the size of the nodes on the right side of Figure 10.4) vs, the videos receiving a limited number of links (shown on the left side of Figure above) is quite visible.

Conclusion

This analysis shows that apart from their popularity inside the Youtube platform, the viral videos had a strong in-links network (links received by videos and users) originating from diverse domains on the Internet. This case study demonstrated the importance of hyperlinks and the valuable insights they carry. The necessary implication for viral marketers here is that in-links may be a factor influencing the viral potential of a video. For example, linking a videos/contents posted on YouTube on several external platforms (e.g., blogs, social network sites, and online discussion communities) may increase the chance of the video going viral.

Source: compiled from Khan, G. F., Sokha, V., (2014), Virality over YouTube: An Empirical Analysis, Internet Research, Vol. 24, Issue 5.

TUTORIAL 10.1
HYPERLINKS ANALYTICS WITH VOSON

INTRODUCTION

VOSON is a web-based tool for collecting and analyzing WWW hyperlink networks and social media networks, and their associated website/social media text content. To construct and analyze hyperlink networks, VOSON relies on web mining, data visualization, and traditional social science techniques, such as social network analysis (Auckland, 2011). VOSON is freely available to academics, researchers, consultants, government entities, and others outside of academia. This tutorial is based on the free version.

CREATE AN ACCOUNT

Before you continue, we suggest you review the underlying social network concepts discussed in the network analytics chapter.

Step 1: To access the VOSON, you must first create an account by visiting this link: http://www.uberlink.com and click on the "create a new account" option available at the top of the page.

Step 2: Once you have created a username and password by filling in the appropriate form, log in to the system. After your account is approved, you will be able to start using the tool.

Step 3: You can log in to VOSON from Uberlink's website (by following the 'Access VOSON' button along the top menu bar) or directly at https://voson.uberlink.com. You will be presented with a window where VOSON authenticates against your Uberlink account (Screenshot 10.1). When you press the "Sign In with Uberlink" button, you will be redirected to http://uberlink.com to enter your login information. When you have successfully authenticated, you will be returned to VOSON. Note that if you are already logged into Uberlink.com in another tab/window of your browser, it will not be necessary to log in again and VOSON will start automatically. You can use VOSON from any computer operating system, as it is a web service and operates through a web browser. VOSON works with various web browsers, including Firefox, Google Chrome, and Apple

Safari. Although you are able to access VOSON via mobile browsers (and we support Mobile Safari in iOS), we still recommend accessing VOSON from a desktop/laptop to enjoy the full potential of all features. After entering your user account information, you will see the Welcome Page for VOSON in your browser tab (Screenshot 10.2).

Screenshot 10.1. VOSON Authentication

VOSON MENUS

After logging into VOSON for the first time, you are presented with the default active menu items (there are many other menus that only become active when they are needed) (Screenshot 10.2). Details on the description of all menus can be found in the VOSON documentation available here: http://www.uberlink.com/services/voson

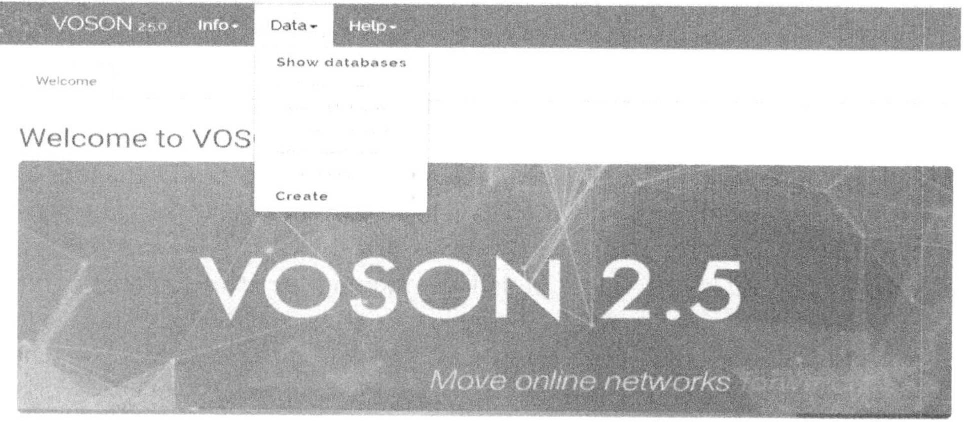

Screenshot 10.2. VOSON's user interface

Info Menu

User—this sub-menu gives information on your access privileges and the

projects that you belong to (and therefore what data are available to you). Initially, you should have access to two projects: "tutorial" and a project named after your VOSON username. In Screenshot 10.3, the user "khan" is able to connect to the VOSON server and create *www-hyperlink databases* (these were previously called 'voson' or 'voson-analysis' databases in VOSON 2.0 and earlier). This user has access to the datasets in two projects (tutorial, and a project under its username "khan").

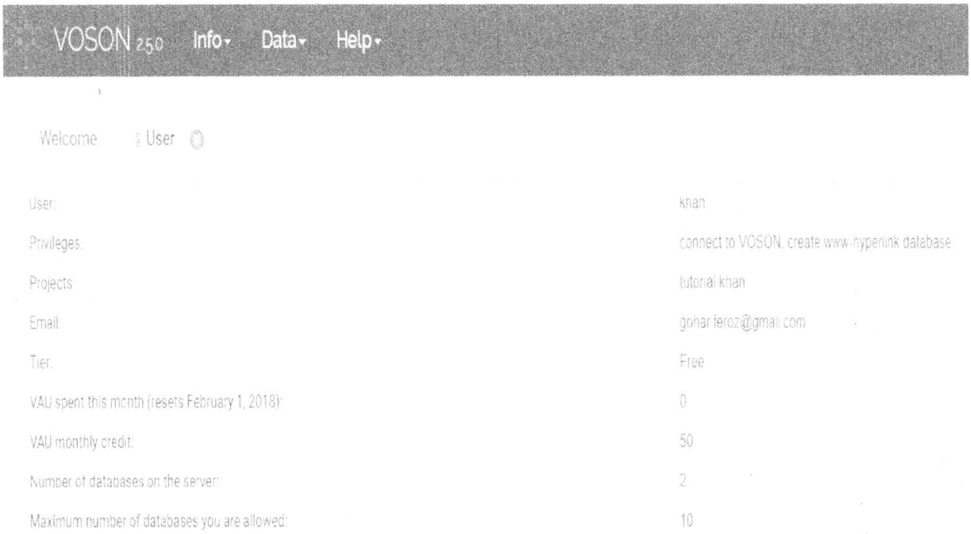

VOSON 2.5.0 Info▾ Data▾ Help▾

Welcome User

User:	khan
Privileges:	connect to VOSON, create www-hyperlink database
Projects:	tutorial khan
Email:	gohar.feroz@gmail.com
Tier:	Free
VAU spent this month (resets February 1, 2018):	0
VAU monthly credit:	50
Number of databases on the server:	2
Maximum number of databases you are allowed:	10

Screenshot 10.3. User info window

In the User window, there is also information on your VOSON Service Level or "Tier." This determines the maximum number of databases you can create, as well as specifying your monthly (or plan) limit of VOSON Activity Units (VAU). VAUs are spent on most aspects of VOSON, such as collecting Twitter data, creating databases, and performing analysis

Data Menu

Show databases—this sub-menu lists all the databases that you can access. As mentioned earlier, initially, there are only two databases available to you: *www-hyperlink* and *Twitter* databases (Screenshot 10.4). You can use these databases to get familiar with the tool. Note that VOSON+Twitter is a different product from a standard VOSON Plan (subscription, single plan, etc.). In order to access VOSON+Twitter, you will need to ensure that your existing plan contains Twitter access–you can verify this on your account page, and can purchase VOSON+Twitter access on the product page. Next to the name (which is a hyperlink) of each database is the following information:

Project: Databases are arranged according to various research activities or projects. Each user is entitled to access databases within the project(s) to which they have access privileges.

Author: Indicates your VOSON username as the author of the database.

Type: VOSON supports two database types namely www-hyperlink and twitter.

Rows: This reports the number of rows in the database, or when monitoring an ongoing Twitter collection, the number of activities (Tweets, Retweets, etc.) that have been collected.

Last modified: This shows when the database was last modified.

Lock/collection status: A database's 'lock' status is usually 'unlocked,' which allows fields to be modified in the DataBrowser. When monitoring a Twitter collection, this column displays its collection status (such as "pending" or "active").

Freshness: This only applies to www-hyperlink subset databases. If this indicates "out-of-date," then it means that there has been a change to the parent database after the creation of a subset database–there will then be an 'action' button available to refresh the subset database (see below).

Parent: This shows the name of the database from which the new database was created, or 'n.a' if no such 'parent' database exists.

Tie indicator: This column displays the type of tie or 'edge type' between nodes. The type of tie can be modified via the "Database schema" menu option. You can select either hyperlink or reciprocated hyperlink for www-hyperlink databases; for twitter databases, the edge types are a reply, mention, and retweet.

Node type: For *www-hyperlink* databases, you can select either "pagegroup" (default) or "page" (where individual pages will be nodes) via the "Database schema" (node schema) menu option. For *twitter* databases, there is only the Tweet author node type.

Action: 'Selection Info': Press this button to see the SQL code that indicates how a subset database has been constructed–note that this will be empty if the subset database is a copy of the database.

Action: 'Delete': Press this button to delete a database. Note that deleting a 'parent' database, when subset databases were created from it, will also delete those subset ('child') databases.

Comment: When you create a new database, you will be prompted to enter anything you'd like to use as a description or purpose of the database. After the comment is created, it is displayed here.

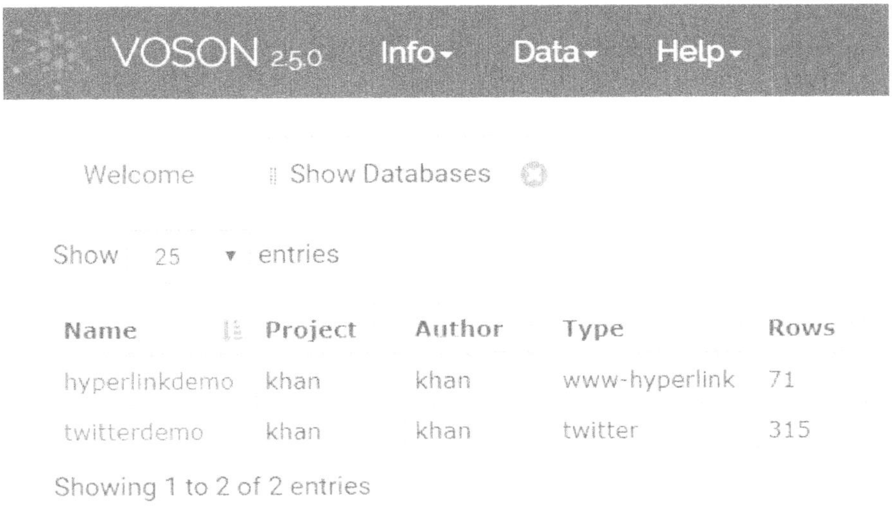

VOSON 2.5.0 Info▾ Data▾ Help▾

Welcome Show Databases

Show 25 ▾ entries

Name	Project	Author	Type	Rows
hyperlinkdemo	khan	khan	www-hyperlink	71
twitterdemo	khan	khan	twitter	315

Showing 1 to 2 of 2 entries

Screenshot 10.4. VOSON default databases

Open a Database

To open a database, first, open the Show databases window (*Data →Show databases*) and then click on the name of the database that you want to open. Once a database (either a www-hyperlink or a twitter database type) has been selected to work with, the database name, the number of nodes in the database, and the edge type will appear on the upper-right-hand side of the menu bar. The Show databases Window will display the total number of rows of a given database, with www-hyperlink databases presenting variations based upon the selected node schema.

With a database loaded up and ready to use, you will notice that the menu items change (Screenshot 10.5). Now the menu items will read as follows:

DataBrowser
This allows you to see the data, where each row is a web page.

Save database
Use this to save copies of the database.

Add seed sites
Use this to add more seed sites to the database (seed sites are used to create hyperlink networks).

Download
Use this to access the data for viewing in other software; for example, Excel and Pajek.

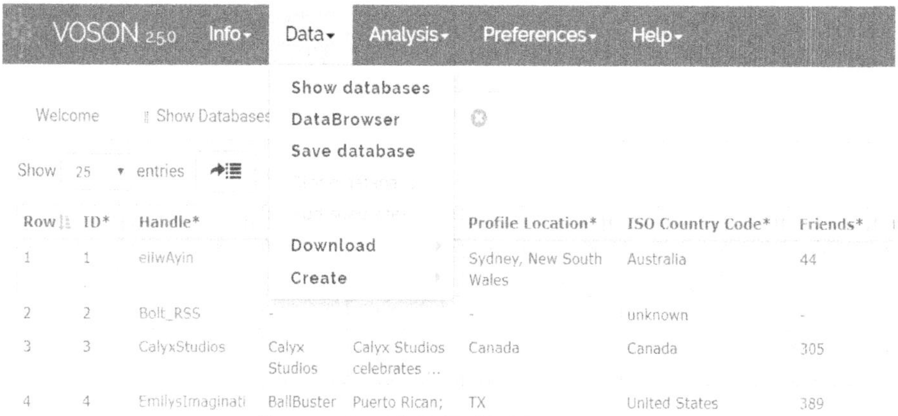

Screenshot 10.5. VOSON Data menu

Create
Www-hyperlink—use this menu to create a hyperlink database.

Twitter—use this menu to create a Twitter database. For Twitter networks, VOSON uses the collected data to create up to three different kinds of networks based on edge type: a "reply" network, where a tie denotes a user's reply to another user; a "mention" network, where a tie denotes a user's mention of another user; and a "retweet" network, where a tie denotes a user's retweet (direct or quoted) of another user.

CREATING A HYPERLINK NETWORK

Now let us shift our focus to creating a hyperlink network. The reader may also play with the existing database instead of creating one.

Step 1: To create a database, click on the "Data" tab, click "Create" and then click on "www-hyperlink database" (Screenshot 10.6).

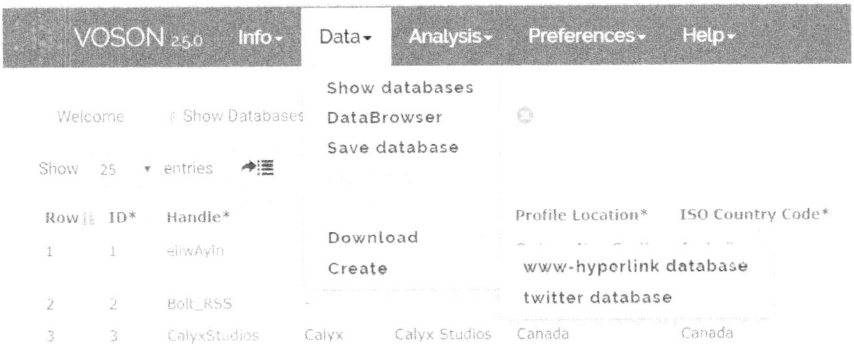

Screenshot 10.6. Creating a www-hyperlink database

Step 2: Provide the requested information (e.g., database name and description) (Screenshot 10.7). Leave the other options in their default setting. The default options will perform the following tasks:

- The crawler will look for inbound links.
    - For each seed, the crawler stops when it discovers one thousand in-links.
    - The crawler will not look for inbound links to each internal page.
- The crawler will look for outbound links.
    - For each seed, the crawler will stop when it discovers one thousand out-links.
- It will crawl twenty-five pages without finding a new outbound link (the maximum number of unproductive pages).
- It will crawl only fifty pages (the depth of crawling pages).
- It will crawl two levels (the depth of crawl in levels).
- The text content will not be parsed.
- The "Parse text content" feature captures keywords contained in the websites for text analysis.

- If you activate the option "Automatically create seeds and seeds+important subnetworks," VOSON will automatically produce two frequently used subnetworks and will make them available via the Show databases window. To illustrate, when the crawler runs for a www-hyperlink database named "test" then VOSON will create three databases: (1) The parent database "test", (2)"testSeeds" which is a subset containing just the seed sites; and (3) the "testSeedsImp" database, a subset database containing just the seed sites plus "important" sites, where a site is vital if it connects to two or more seeds.

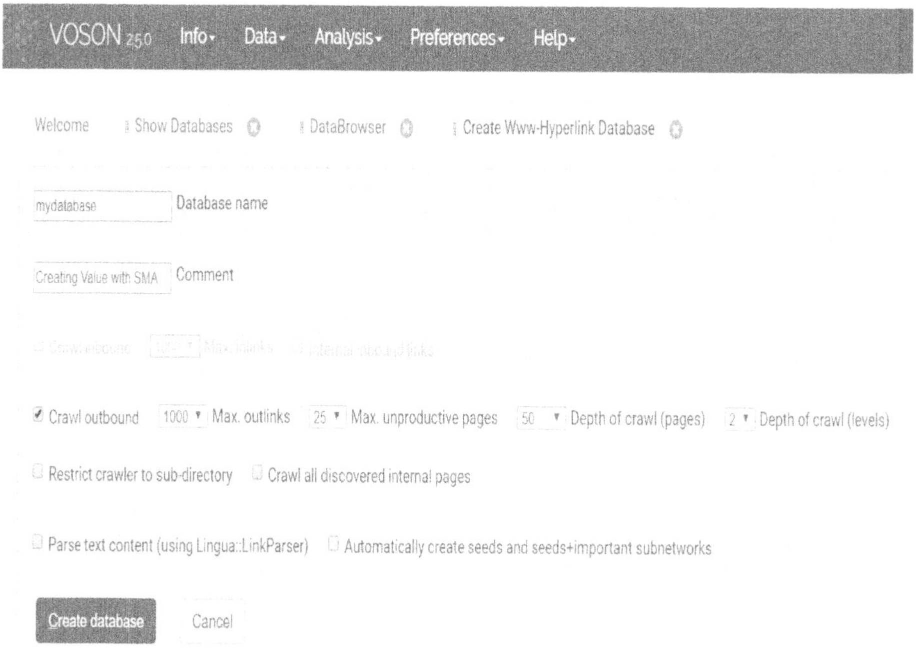

Screenshot 10.7. Interface for creating a database

Note: The "Crawl all internal pages" feature may significantly increase the length of the crawl, potentially running through your available VAU at an alarming rate. We recommend against using it unless you are absolutely certain you are not getting enough links from the crawl when this box is not checked, and you have enough VAU available.

Step 3: The database is now created (Screenshot 10.8). You will then need to add seed sites to the database (see the next step with details on how to do this).

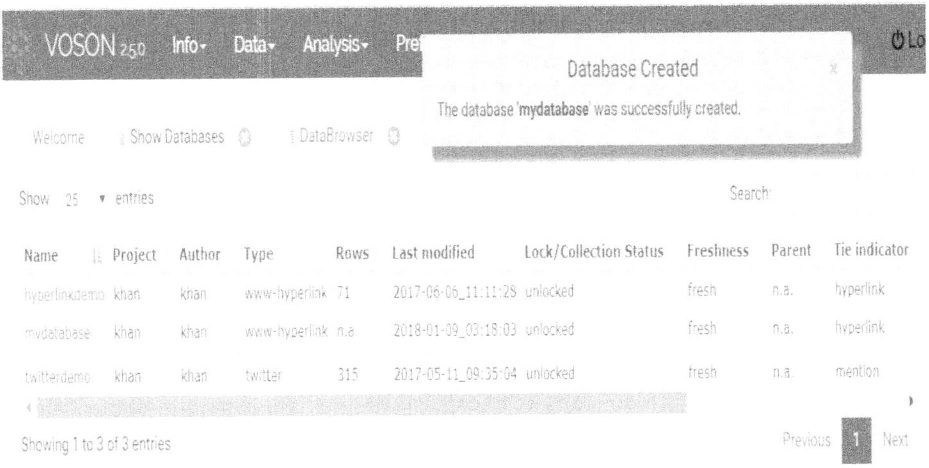

Screenshot 10.8. VOSON database window

Step 4: Now is time to add seed sites that will be used to create the hyperlink network. For this tutorial, we used http://www.uberlink.com/ as the seed site, but you can use the website address of your company. You can add several seed sites, but the total number of seed sites you can add depends on your subscription plan. To add the site, first, click on your newly created database to activate it. Then click on "Data," then on "Add Seed Sites" (Screenshot 10.9)

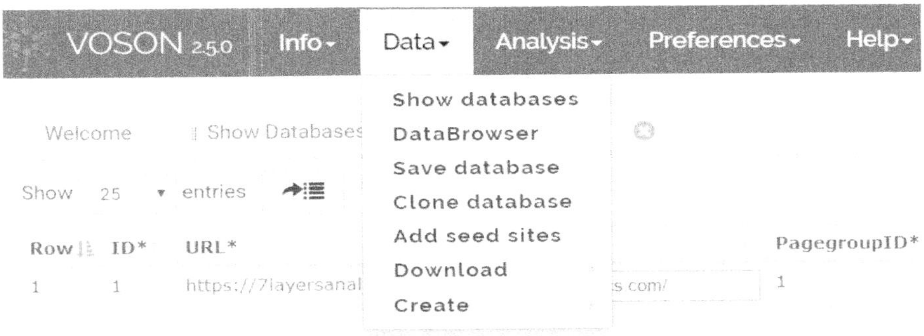

Screenshot 10.9. Adding seed site

Step 5: A new window will be opened (Screenshot 10.10). Type the URL of your company's website in the box provided. Leave other options on their default settings and click on the "Add" button next to the comment box (which you can use to add comments if you have any).

Note: To get the best hyperlink return from a given crawl, it is recommended you select the URL that represents the main page of a given site. Doing so will give the crawler the best chance of being able to traverse the site.

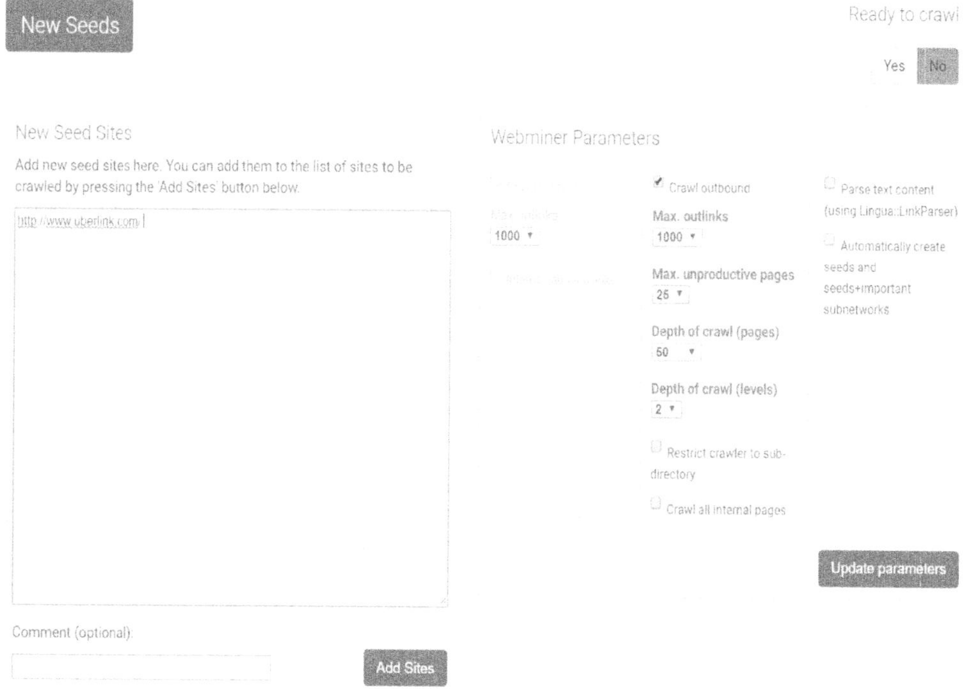

Screenshot 10.10. VOSON window for adding seeds

Step 6: When you have finished entering seed sites and are ready for the crawl to start, click "Yes" under "Ready to crawl," in the top-right of the Add seed sites window. A pop-up window will alert you to the status of credit and number of credits needed to perform the crawl. Click "X" to start the process (Screenshot 10.11).

Note: Users are assigned a certain number of "VOSON Activity Units" (VAU) credits per month, and these get used up during crawls. You can check your current VAU credit on your user account page at Uberlink.com, and by selecting the Info →User menu item.

Also, note that the sites will not be crawled immediately; you will receive an e-mail when the crawling has finished.

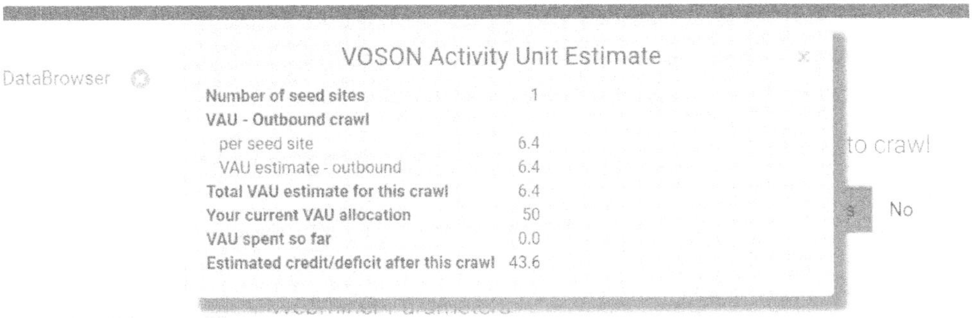
DataBrowser
VOSON Activity Unit Estimate
Number of seed sites 1
VAU - Outbound crawl
per seed site 6.4
VAU estimate - outbound 6.4
Total VAU estimate for this crawl 6.4
Your current VAU allocation 50
VAU spent so far 0.0
Estimated credit/deficit after this crawl 43.6
to crawl
No

Screenshot 10.11. The Voson Activity Units (VAU) calculation screen

Step 7: After you have received the e-mail from VOSON informing you that the data set is ready, click on "Data>Show databases." Now your database has been populated with data (e.g., thirty-one rows).

Step 8: To check the network properties of your hyperlink network, first click on the database (VOSON-analysis type) to make it active. Then, click on the "Analysis" tab and then click on "SNA" (Screenshot 10.12).

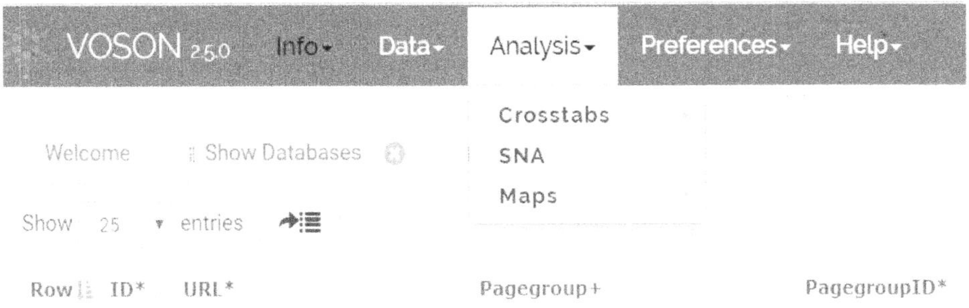
VOSON 2.5.0
Info
Data
Analysis
Preferences
Help
Crosstabs
SNA
Maps
Welcome
Show Databases
Show 25 entries
Row
ID*
URL*
Pagegroup+
PagegroupID*

Screenshot 10.12. VOSON menu for checking network properties

Step 9: A new window will open summarizing in detail the properties of the network, including the following (most of these concepts were discussed in the network analytics chapter) (Screenshot 10.13).

Size—the total number of websites (or nodes) in the network.

Number of edges—the total number of hyperlinks (in-links and out-links) among the websites.

Components—the isolated sub-networks that connect within, but are disconnected between networks (Hanneman & Riddle, 2005).

Density—the *density* of a network deals with a number of links in a network.

Number of isolates—the number of nodes that have no connections to other nodes.

Inclusiveness—the proportion of the nodes in the network that are connected.

SNA

Network size	30
Number of edges	21
Number of components	1
Number of isolates	8
Smallest component size	22
Largest component size	22
Average component size	22
Number of connected nodes	22
Inclusiveness	0.733333
Network density	0.0241379
Total number of dyads	435
...number of mutual dyads	0
...number of asymetric dyads	21
...number of null dyads	414
Dyadic reciprocity 1 (ratio mutuals to all)	0
Dyadic reciprocity 2 (ratio mutuals to nonnull)	0
Edge reciprocity	0
Centralisation (indegree, unnormalised)	9
Centralisation (indegree, normalised)	0.0107015
Centralisation (outdegree, unnormalised)	609
Centralisation (outdegree, normalised)	0.724138
Centralisation (degree, unnormalised)	588
Centralisation (degree, normalised)	0.362069

Screenshot 10.13. Hyperlink network properties

Step 10: To visualize the hyperlink network, click on the "Analysis" tab, and then "Maps," and then select one of the three available options: "Minimum spanning tree," "Complete network" or "Hierarchy" (depending on the version of VOSON you are using, you may see more options). These are in fact network visualization algorithms, and each one will visualize the network differently. We selected the "Complete Network," which show all links and nodes simultaneously (Screenshot 10.14).

Screenshot 10.14. VOSON menu for checking hyperlink network properties

Step 11: The hyperlink network will appear in a separate window (Screenshot 10.15). You can quickly notice the out-links and in-links by looking at the arrowheads. If the arrowhead points to the seed site, it is an in-link, and if it points away, it is an out-link from the seed site to another website. The countries where the hyperlinks are coming from are shown on the right-hand side. You can redraw the network based on several parameters shown in the upper part of the window. For example, we configured the node size based on the in-degree (i.e., the number of incoming hyperlinks). The node size will be more prominent if a website has more in-links. Clicking on a specific node will display more details about the node.

Step 12: To save the network diagram, click on "download map PNG" (available at the left side of the image) and save it on your computer.

Step 13: You can also export the network data to be used with other network analysis software (e.g., Pajek and GrapML). To do so, click on "Data," then "Download" and then select the format you want to download the data in.

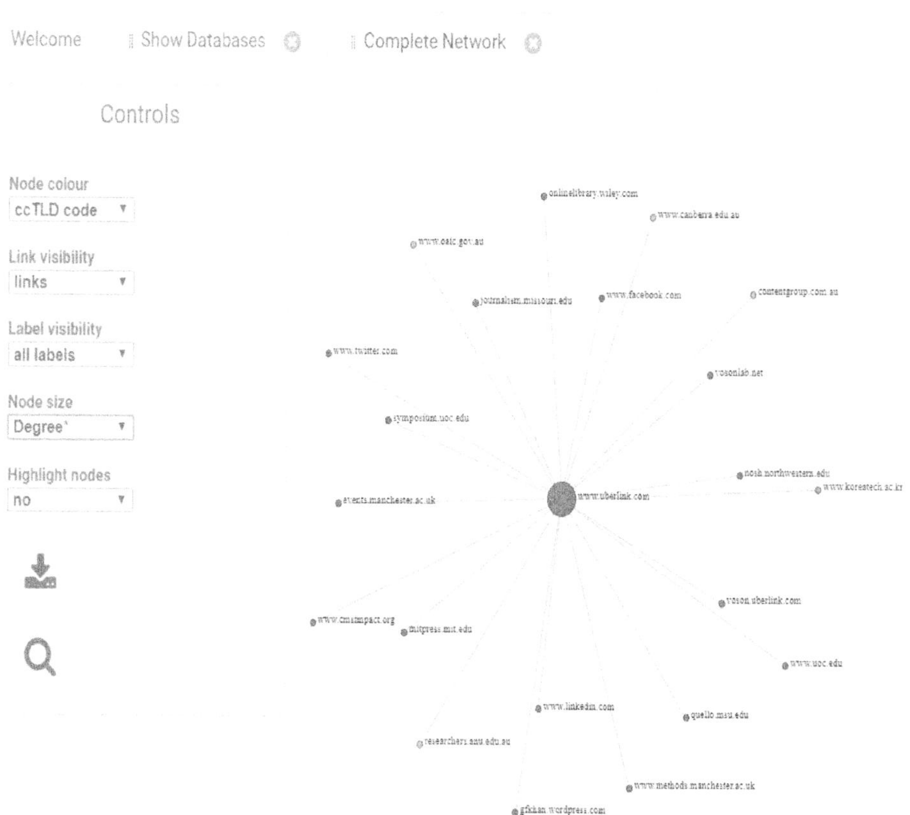

Screenshot 10.15. Hyperlink network

REVIEW QUESTIONS

1. What are hyperlinks, and why they are essential?
2. Briefly discuss in-links, out-links, and co-links.
3. What are hyperlink analytics and its underlying assumptions?
4. What is website hyperlink analysis?
5. What is link impact analysis?
6. What is social media hyperlink analysis?

EXERCISE 10.1: MENTIONMAPP

1. Sign up for a free account on MentionMapp.com.
2. Enter your own Twitter account (or a celebrity).
3. According to MentionMapp, who is the most important node(s)? Who is the least?

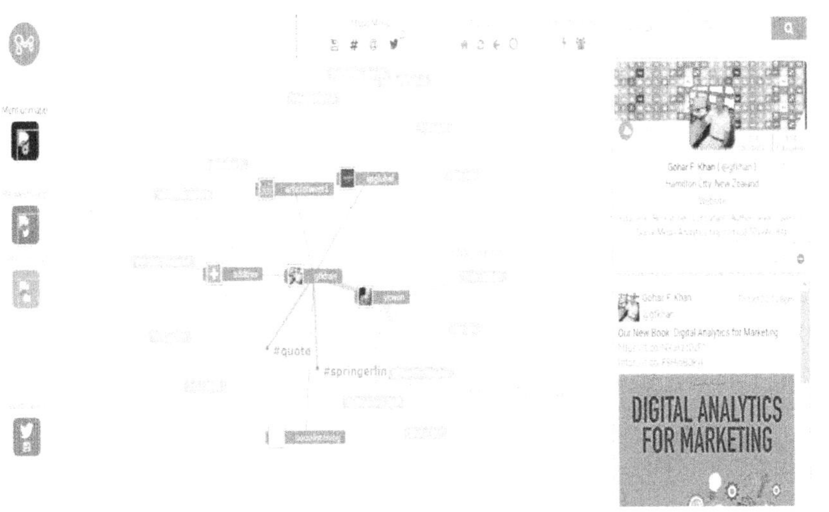

Figure 10.5. Author's own Twitter account MentionMapp

CHAPTER 10 REFERENCES

Ackland, R. (2011). Chapter 12 - WWW Hyperlink Networks *Analyzing Social Media Networks with NodeXL* (pp. 181-199). Boston: Morgan Kaufmann.

Aharony, S. (2016). Outgoing Links Used As Ranking Signal.

Björneborn, L. (2001). *Small-world linkage and co-linkage.* Paper presented at the 12th ACM Conference on Hypertext and Hypermedia New York

Björneborn, L., & Ingwersen, P. (2004). Toward a basic framework for webometrics. *Journal of the American Society for Information Science and Technology, 55*(14), 1216-1227. doi:10.1002/asi.20077

Chakrabarti, S., & M. M. Joshi, e. a. (2002). The structure of broad topics on the Web from http://www2002.org/CDROM/refereed/338.

Fishkin, R. (2009). 5 Reasons You Should Link Out to Others From Your Website.

Garrido, M., & Halavais, A. (2003). Mapping networks of support for the Zapatista movement: Applying social network analysis to study contemporary social movements. In M. M. M. Ayers (Ed.), *Cyberactivism: Online activism in theory and practice.* London, UK: Routledge.

Gohar Feroz, K., & Sokha, V. (2014). Virality over YouTube: an empirical analysis. *Internet Research, 24*(5), 629-647. doi:10.1108/IntR-05-2013-0085

Hanneman, R. A., & Riddle, M. (2005). *Introduction to social network methods.* Riverside, CA: University of California (published in digital form at http://faculty.ucr.edu/~hanneman/).

Jackson, M. H. (1997). Assessing the Structure of Communication on the World Wide Web. *Journal of Computer-Mediated Communication, 3*(1), 0-0. doi:10.1111/j.1083-6101.1997.tb00063.x

Khan, G. F., Yoon, H. Y., & Park, H. W. (2014). Social media communication strategies of government agencies: Twitter use in Korea and the USA. *Asian Journal of Communication, 24*(1), 60-78. doi:10.1080/01292986.2013.851723

Kim, D., & Nam, Y. (2012). Corporate Relations with Environmental Organizations Represented by Hyperlinks on the Fortune Global 500 Companies' *Journal of Business Ethics, 105*(4), 475-487.

Park, H. W. (2003). Hyperlink network analysis: A new method for the study of social structure on the web. *Connections, 25*, 49-61.

Park, H. W., & Thelwall, M. (2008). Link analysis: Hyperlink patterns and social structure on politicians' Web sites in South Korea. *Quality & Quantity, 42*(5), 687-697. doi:10.1007/s11135-007-9109-z

Thelwall, M. (2014). Big Data and Social Web Research Methods University of Wolverhampton, available at: http://www.scit.wlv.ac.uk/~cm1993/papers/IntroductionToWebometricsAndSocialWebAnalysis.pdf.

Vaughan, L. (2004). Exploring website features for business information. *Scientometrics, 61*(3), 467-477. doi:10.1023/B:SCIE.0000045122.93018.2a

Vaughan, L., & Thelwall, M. (2003). Scholarly use of the Web: What are the key inducers of links to journal Web sites? *Journal of the American Society for Information Science and Technology, 54*(1), 29-38. doi:10.1002/asi.10184

Vaughan, L., & You, J. (2006). Comparing business competition positions based on Web co-link data: The global market vs. the Chinese market. *Scientometrics, 68*(3), 611-628. doi:10.1007/s11192-006-0133-x

Vreelnad, R. (2000). Law libraries in cyberspace: A citation analysis of world wide web sites. *Law Library Journal, 92*, 49-56.

Chapter 11

Capturing Value with Mobile Analytics

"There's an app for it"—**Apple Inc.**

Learning Outcomes

After completing this chapter, the reader should be able to:

- Explain the two main categories of mobile analytics.
- Comprehend the purpose of app analytics.
- Understand different classes of mobile apps.
- Recognize key features of mobile apps.
- Explain the different app development options.
- Analyze app data.

INTRODUCTION

Mobile applications are becoming an integral part of our lives. *Applications* (or apps) are special-purpose software developed to perform specific tasks on the go. Each app has a precise function and runs on specific mobile devices, such as smartphones, tablet computers, and smartwatches. Mobile devices use a particular type of operating system called a mobile operating system (or mobile OS). Popular mobile OSs are Android (from Google), iOS (from Apple computers), Windows Phone (from Microsoft), and BlackBerry 10 (From BlackBerry).

Specific apps are developed for each mobile OS. Most apps (but not all) are made available online for download through application distributors (or app stores), such as the Apple Store, Google Play, and the Amazon apps store. According to http://www.statista.com/, as of June 2017, there were 5 million apps available for download in the Apple Store and Google Play alone. App stores also provide opportunities for users to comment on and rate apps, as well as create them.

WHAT IS MOBILE ANALYTICS?

Generally, mobile analytics may refer to two things:

1) Mobile Web Analytics
2) Apps Analytics

Mobile Web Analytics

Mobile web analytics is focused on characteristics, actions, and behaviors of mobile website *visitors*; that is, the visitors to the mobile version of a company's website. It is very similar to the conventional website analytics in scope and methodology. Organizations collect and analyze a variety of mobile user data, including views, clicks, demographic information, and device-specific data (e.g., the type of mobile device used to access the website).

All websites should be mobile compatible for a couple of reasons.

- Search engines rank mobile compatible websites more highly in search results than websites that are not mobile compatible. Since 2015, mobile compatibility has been a Google search engine ranking factor, and the majority of referral traffic arriving on websites now originates from mobile devices.
- Many websites have been designed to work on desktops or laptops rather than mobile devices, creating a frustrating experience for mobile visitors to the website.
- There is mounting evidence that mobile searches are highly correlated to potential customers who are willing to transact or make a purpose right away.

As a result, when a business fails to create a mobile-friendly website experience for visitors, they are most likely leaving money on the table and losing business they could have.

Mobile App Analytics

Mobile app analytics focuses on the understanding and analysis of mobile application users' characteristics, actions, and behaviors. Today, most organizations, big or small, are using mobile apps to drive sales, improve brand affinity, and make purchases possible with a few swipes. Virgin Atlantic allows customers to search, book, and board their flights with swipes on their smartphones. Companies also need to have a thorough understanding of their customers and their characteristics.

Purpose of Apps Analytics

The primary purpose of *apps analytics* is to measure and analyze user behavior, improve user experiences, and drive revenue, engagements, and loyalty. Some sample questions that can be answered with app analytics are provided below.

- Who are our users?
- Which countries are they coming from?
- What actions are they taking?
- How do our customers navigate the app?
- What are our in-app payments and revenue?
- How long do they stay on our app?
- How many daily active users (DAU) do we have? Note: DAU is considered a fundamental business metric because it provides better insights related to how well the app is performing.
- Which operator, operating system, and devices do they use?
- What item is purchased the most?
- Which countries were top performers regarding in-app purchases (IAP)?
- Which application version leads to more sales?
- How often do our users open the app?
- How many users started a specific number of sessions?
- How do our applications versions compare to one another?

Based on the types of questions being asked, the answers will vary depending on what app analytics is being performed.

TYPES OF APPS

Apps can be mainly classified in two ways:

- Through a development and deployment perspective
- Though a purpose-oriented view

FROM THE DEVELOPMENT PERSPECTIVE

There are three classification methods that mobile apps are developed and deployed across (Korf & Oksman, 2014):

- Native Apps
- Web-Based Apps
- Hybrid Apps

Native Apps (Mobile Apps)

Mobile, or *native apps*, are specially created for and installed on mobile devices by downloading them from the iPhone or Android app store. Naturally, as native apps are executable code, they can only run on compatible devices. For example, apps for Android-based mobile devices are created in Java programming language, and iOS apps are developed in Objective-C and Cocoa programming (a programming language native to Apple devices).

When a business wants to create an app that can run on both Android and iOS, they may need to develop two separate versions of the app. As previously, mentioned, Native apps are made available for download in apps stores (such as Google Play and the Apple Store). One way to distinguish Native apps from the other types is that these apps can only be accessed through specific mobile devices. Tinder (a social networking app) and Uber (a taxi-sharing app) are examples of native apps whose program must first be downloaded and installed from the app store.

Both Apple and Google run their own app stores and keep track of the most recently updated version of the app. App users are notified when a new version of the app is available in the app store. Frequently, updated apps are automatically downloaded and installed on mobile devices where the app is installed.

Web-Based Apps

Web-based apps look like native's apps, but in reality, they are websites optimized for mobile access. For example, TouchStyle (a fashion design app) is a web-based app for iPad that is accessed with Safari. Web-based apps are created using standard web coding techniques (such as JavaScript or HTML5) and are accessed using Internet browsers, and are hence not available in app stores. The advantage of developing web-based apps is that they can be accessed from any mobile device and are less costly to establish and maintain. However, regarding performance, web-based apps are not as fast and usable as the native apps. Moreover, web-based apps are merely mobile-friendly HTML 5 code that is executed by a web server. As a result, they are not distributed in an app store, and it is hard to monetize them.

Hybrid Apps

A *hybrid app* combines the functionalities of both native and web-based apps. Like native apps, they are available in app stores, and like web apps, they are developed using standard web programming languages (e.g., HTML) and then packaged up into native applications. Packaging or wrapping it into a native container makes it possible for a hybrid app to access native platform features (Korf & Oksman, 2014). The Facebook app, for example, was initially a hybrid app, but later was changed to a native app. The advantage of hybrid apps is that they can be used on any mobile device, including Android, iOS, Windows Phone, and BlackBerry. This way business can get the advantages of native applications while keeping the cost of development lower.

CLASSIFYING APPS BY THEIR PURPOSE

Mobile apps have been created to assist users in pursuing many different types of activities and purposes, and there are dozens of possible categories that apps fall under. For example, the Google Play store lists at least twenty-seven different app categories, but we only discuss some prominent ones here.

Transaction-Oriented Apps

Transaction-oriented apps are designed to carry out virtual business transactions (such as purchasing a product or depositing money into an account) with customers. For example, eBay's app allows the user to buy, sell, and manage products using their mobile devices.

Transaction-enabled apps provide functionality similar to an electronic commerce website shopping cart system. Mobile transaction applications such as Vemno and Square fall into this category. Vemno is a free digital wallet that lets users make and share payments with their friends; users can easily split most bills, cab ride fares and other types of bills or payments. Square helps millions of sellers run their business including secure credit card processing and other point of sale solutions.

Ads-Oriented Apps

Ads-oriented apps are designed to generate revenue using advertising banners that are embedded in the app. Owners provide the app for free in hopes of generating revenue by linking the user to the advertiser's website. However, it should be noted that advertising could appear within any of the types of apps listed in this section. The YouTube app requires users trying to watch a video to view several seconds of advertising before proceeding to view the content. Finally, apps such as Pandora and Spotify have a free version that requires users to view advertising and premium versions that are free of advertising.

Information-Oriented Apps

These apps are designed primarily for *information purposes.* Companies, organizations, and sometimes ordinary people deploy these apps to help users find information about things like products, services, and facilities. These apps do not have virtual transaction abilities. Examples of information-oriented apps include Find-My-iPhone (locate an iPhone), Toilet-Finder, MyCar (for locating cars), and MapFactor (a navigation app).

Networking-Oriented Apps

Networking-oriented apps such as Instagram, Twitter, and Tinder are designed to make it easier for users to connect with each other. These apps may have a common purpose, but they often appeal to different demographic groups. Millennials tend to use Instagram, Tinder, and Snapchat while older people are more accessible to reach on Twitter and Facebook, etc. Meanwhile, organizations can use these apps to generate more attention by using selected features such as hashtags.

Communication-Oriented Apps

Communication-based apps are used to facilitate communication among users. Users can exchange text messages, pictures, and carry voice and video communication. WhatsApp, Snapchat, Group Me, and Facebook Messenger are examples of communication-oriented apps.

Entertainment-Oriented Apps

Entertainment-oriented apps such as Netflix and Hulu are created for entertainment purposes such as watching popular network programming. Gaming apps such as Angry Birds and Candy Crush are free but are monetized through in-app purchases.

Education-Oriented Apps

There are many apps that are created for *educational purposes*, such as learning a new skill, language, or subject. Quizlet is an app that allows users to use commercially available study sets, or create their own study plans.

Self-Improvement Apps

Self-improvement apps are used to track or monitor oneself for a variety of purposes, including improvement of health, habits, skills, and abilities. Nike+, for example, is an app for tracking users' workouts and fitness progress, and My Fitness Pal is a free online calorie counter, and diet plan that has millions of users.

CHARACTERISTICS OF MOBILE APPS

The best way to differentiate mobile apps from desktop-based applications is through its *features*. The following are some main features that distinguish mobile apps from desktop-based applications.

Always On

An app is *always on* and connected to the Internet; this makes it possible to push information and content to users the moment it becomes available.

Moveable

Unlike the desktop applications, mobile apps go where the user goes. Thus, it stays with the user 24/7, and users can access it *anywhere* and *anytime*.

Location Awareness

Thanks to the GPS (global positioning system) embedded in mobile devices, apps are always *aware of the user's location*. The location awareness ability of apps is of great interest to social marketers, as it can be used to send targeted ads and promotions based on users' current location.

Focused

Being *focused* on one theme/issue is one of the critical features of mobile applications that distinguish it from the desktop-based applications or websites, which have a more extensive scope. There are always a narrow set of activities that apps are designed to carry out. For example, the Google Maps app is a subset of Google (and is fully integrated into Google's desktop website), but it is presented as a standalone application for mobile devices.

Personalization

Mobile apps can provide *personalized experiences* based on a user's preferences. Users get to control which content they see and how it is shared.

Short-Term Use

Unlike desktop applications that are used for more extended sessions, mobile app usage is characterized by frequent but *short-term use* ranging from several seconds to several minutes.

Easy to Use

Last but not the least, mobile apps are straightforward to use and navigate.

DEVELOPING AN APP

App development is beyond the scope of this book. However, when it comes to developing a mobile app, organizations have three options:

Do-It-Yourself

The best strategy would be to hire a programmer/developer to *develop* an app for the organization. Google's software development kit (SDK) for mobile analytics is a great place to start: https://developers.google.com/analytics/solutions/mobile. This way the user can cut costs; however, it requires a lot of technical resources.

Outsource App Development

If it is beyond the programming skills of an organization or individual to create an app, they can hire a company to develop a custom app for the user. However, by *outsourcing* app development, users lose control over the app and increase the development costs.

Go Open Source

Users can also create the business app through *open-source* platforms. For example, OpenMEAP™ is an open sourced mobile application platform that enables businesses with no technical skills to quickly create, manage, and deploy mobile apps. Alternatively, you could deploy the PhoneGap (http://phonegap.com/) open source platform to create your app for free.

MOBILE ANALYTICS TOOLS

Some leading mobile analytics tools are listed below.

Google Mobile Analytics

GoogleMobile Analytics (www.google.com/analytics/analytics) is a mobile analytics platform for analyzing and tracking mobile application data.

Countly

Countly (https://count.ly/) is a mobile application analytic tool.

Mixpanel

Like Google Mobile Analytics and Countly, Mixpanel (https://mixpanel.com/) is a mobile analytics platform that is favored by developers for mobile clickstream analysis.

Flurry (Yahoo!)

Flurry by Yahoo (https://developer.yahoo.com/analytics/), measures and analyzes activity across an app portfolio to answer marketing questions and optimize a user's mobile app experience.

CASE STUDY 11.1
MOBILE ANALYTICS TO OPTIMIZE PROCESS

About Airbnb

Airbnb is a trusted community marketplace for people to list, discover, and book unique accommodation around the world—online or from a mobile phone. Whether an apartment for a night, a castle for a week, or a villa for a month, Airbnb connects people to unique travel experiences, at any price point, in more than 33,000 cities and 192 countries. Airbnb is succeeding in the collaboration economy because they provide more affordable prices than most hotels. In addition, Airbnb provides a variety of rental properties that appeal to many different types of travelers. Airbnb collaborated with social influencers like the Kardashians, by giving them complimentary homes to rent when they travel and in return have them promote/advertise Airbnb to their massive number of followers on social media.

The Problem

Travelers love Airbnb for the high number and wide variety of exciting spaces available to rent. Airbnb needed an analytics solution to help them optimize the process host properties go through as their rental spaces are listed.

Solution

Airbnb built their web analytics tool from scratch when they developed their website. However, when it came time to launch their iPhone app they turned to Mixpanel (https://mixpanel.com/) to develop the app. Airbnb had Mixpanel set up and track the events taking place on their iPhone app in just a couple of hours by importing Mixpanel's iPhone library into their app. Finally, Airbnb added custom tracking calls to all of the events they wanted to analyze.

Outcome

Airbnb did not just optimize their first time listing and booking flows; they used Mixpanel to measure where their customers spent the most time within the app, their most frequent actions, and the percentage of people who passively browsed vs, managed a booking. Airbnb used Mixpanel's event tracking and funnel analysis to optimize the listing process for first-time hosts. Funnel analysis involves tracking a series of events that lead towards a defined goal. Based on the drop-offs they found in the Mixpanel funnel analysis, Airbnb revamped the host listing process on their app, resulting in a 400% increase in conversion rate.

Source: Mixpanel, https://mixpanel.com/

TUTORIAL 11.1
APPS ANALYTICS WITH COUNTLY

INTRODUCTION

Countly is an innovative, real-time mobile analytics software, focusing on ease of use, extensibility, and feature richness. Countly includes a server and a mobile component, both of which the reader can freely use in their company for their applications under license terms. Installation of the server application and using SDK is explained in documents users can find on the navigation bar on the left, and is beyond the scope of this book and further information can be found on Countly's resources page: http://resources.count.ly/.

Before running this tutorial, please request an online 30-day trial of Countly Enterprise Edition at https://count.ly.

DASHBOARD OVERVIEW

Countly provides a dashboard for a quick glimpse of the latest status of application usage. In the dashboard, the reader will notice the following. The options vary based on the version a user is subscribed to. Currently, Countly is available at three levels:

1. professional
2. business
3. enterprise

Below we explain common options accessible on the dashboard.

Navigation Bar

At the top of the navigation bar, readers see a list of applications. Each can be selected at once, and the dashboard will adapt itself showing numbers for the selected application. "Dashboard" is the initial view, and the Analytics menu includes several other views that can be of interest, including a particular carrier, country, user-retention, and session frequency metrics. User and application management are also carried out using links here. At the bottom of this part, users can see the current user, together with a link to log out and a change password option.

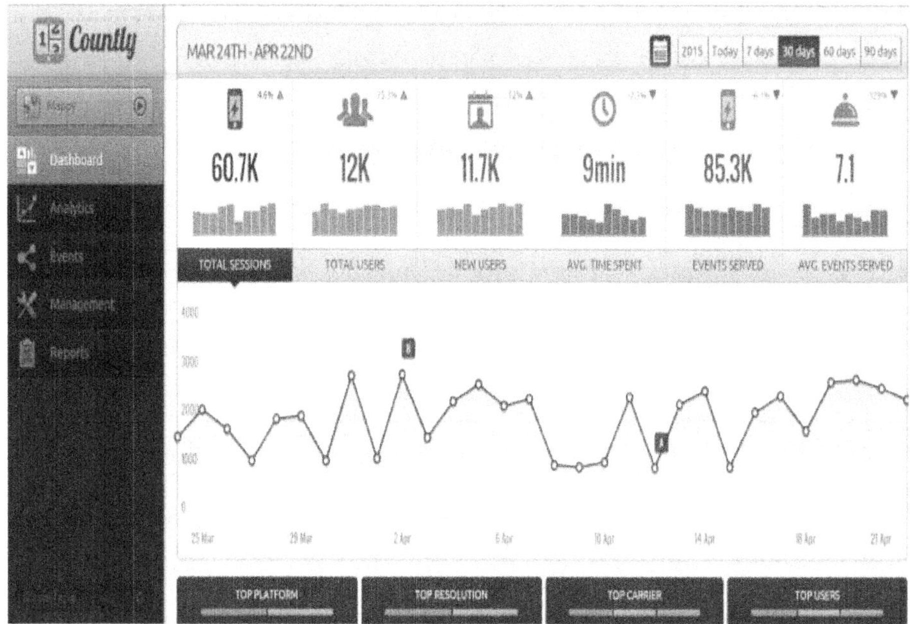

Screenshot 11.1. Countly's Dashboard

Real-Time Panel

Has the user ever wondered how many users are currently using their application at that moment? This tiny but powerful widget shows readers precisely that: online users and incoming online users. There is also a live flowchart on the right-hand side that demonstrates the status of the users—users can easily get insight into whether the numbers of online and new users are increasing and decreasing. The real-time panel is only available for business and enterprise edition users.

Quick Date Selector

On the top right of the screen, readers see a list of dates. Here, they can either use a defined period or select a date from the time selector. Note that if the reader chooses a time here, it will be automatically selected as they click on other navigation links (e.g., "Users," "Carriers," etc.). To choose a date, click on the selector, choose the start and finish dates, and click on "Apply." Graphs and corresponding boxed widgets will automatically be updated.

Analytics Panel

This panel gives a brief overview of what is happening on the dashboard. On the top, there are six widgets. When clicked, the charts under these widgets are automatically refreshed to show relevant data groups.

Each widget shows the following:

Total sessions: Number of times the application is opened. Click this item to see a time series representation of total sessions.

Total users: Number of unique devices the application is used from. Click this item to see a time series representation of total users.

New users: Number of first-time users. Click this item to see a time series representation of new users.

Time spent: Total time spent on the application. Click this item to see a time series representation of total time spent per user.

Average time spent: Total time spent using the application divided by total user count. Click this item to see a time series representation of average time spent per user.

Average requests received: Number of written API requests the Countly server received for this application divided by total user count. Click this item to see a time series representation of average events per user.

For each time series chart, there is a light gray and dark gray line. The light gray line shows the previous period for comparison purposes.

GETTING IN-DEPTH ANALYTICS

Countly's dashboard provides a quick analysis and gives a glimpse of how the application is performing. It is mostly useful for marketers who want to understand what is going on immediately. The navigation pane on the left gives more detailed information about users, sessions, countries, carriers, and more. Below we will have a look at each menu item.

Users—the "Users" tab is one of the most important parts of the analytics. Here the reader sees an overview of the total, new, and returning users based on the day. This tab will give readers the answer to the question, "How many users do I have?"

Sessions—if the user opens an application, it counts as a session until he closes it. This menu shows an overview of sessions, together with total sessions, unique sessions, and new sessions, broken down by time. This menu will provide the answer to the question, "How many times has your application been opened?"

Countries—this menu presents an overview of which countries the application is used in most. It will show the world map, total users, total sessions, and new users. This menu will provide the answer to the question, "Where do my users connect from?"

Devices—in this menu, there are three main blocks of device information. On the top, there is a list of devices, and at the bottom, these devices are shown in a table. In the middle, there are three blocks of information, showing the top platform, the top operating system version, and top resolution, respectively. Try hovering on each color line to see other top information. This menu will give the answer to the question, "Which smartphone types do my users have?"

Resolution—this menu shows two pie charts that display total users and new users and the device resolution (width x height) of their mobile device screens. The resolution menu contains reports that provide insights about which resolutions are used most so the user can focus on these screen types. Different resolution sizes within mobile devices, particularly Android-based smartphones and tablets, have presented a considerable problem for mobile application developers in the past. As a result, developers have a harder time optimizing their apps to function correctly in the massive array of Android devices. On the other hand, iOS devices are easier to manage since they have a single manufacturer (Apple) and a small set of resolution sizes.

Density—Android devices have screen densities, and this menu shows densities reported by the device. This menu is only for Android applications.

Application versions—this page shows different versions of applications; in case they are defined. A stacked chart shows total sessions and new users. The table under the chart shows total sessions, total users, and new users, respectively for each application version. This menu will give the reader the answer to the question, "How do my application versions compare?"

Carriers—the "Carriers" page shows a table of all carriers, together with total sessions, total users, and new users for a given period. On the top of the page, two pie charts are showing total users and new users of top carriers. There are only three carriers shown in this chart for compatibility, so refer to the table for a detailed carrier breakdown. This menu will give us the answer to the question, "Which operator do they use?"

Platforms—Countly provides an intuitive interface to show how different platforms (operating systems) perform. If the reader uses the same app key ("Management→Applications"), it is possible to aggregate this information and see it under this menu. This menu will give the answer to the question, "Which operating systems do my users have?"

Engagement View

This menu includes submenu items related to user engagement, such as retention, loyalty, session frequency, and session duration.

User Retention—Retention is the condition of keeping customers. This page shows the users' active days (e.g., days your customers used your application) after the first session. In the top right corner, the users can get a breakdown of daily, weekly, and monthly retention; this is one of the most critical metrics for app analytics.

User loyalty—User loyalty shows how many users started a specific number of sessions. The table indicates the number and percentage of each loyalty group compared with some sessions (e.g., one session, two sessions, and so forth). This menu will give the answer to the question, "How many users started a specific number of sessions?"

Session frequency—Session frequency shows how often mobile users open the application. It can be used to calculate the trends, or how often the application is used during a given period. The session frequency graph is very straightforward: users see a breakdown of some sessions and the corresponding number and percentage of users for each group. Most of the time, users view the number of users accumulated in the "first session" and "second session" row. This menu will give the answer to the question, "How often do you see your users open your app?"

Session duration—The "Session Duration" view shows users categorized into predefined session duration buckets. In this view, users are categorized into one of 0–0 seconds, 11–30 seconds, 31–60 seconds, 1–3 minutes, 3–10 minutes, 10–30 minutes, 30–60 minutes or >1 hour, according to this session duration. This screen will give the answer to the question, "How long do my users stay inside my application?"

Events

Countly provides a way to create custom events based on user needs. An event can be anything that managers want to measure and track, such as tracking user navigation patterns and purchase behavior. With custom events, one may be able to answer business intelligence questions such as:

- What item is purchased most?
- Which countries were top performers regarding in-app purchases?
- Which application version leads to more sales?

Business managers are able to get an understanding of how their application performs by sending data from inside the application and analyzing this information. Just like other information retrieved, custom events are true real-time. Additional information on how to create custom events is available on Count.ly's resource page: http://resources.count.ly/

Funnels

Funnels are used to track the goal completion rates of a systematic path inside the application. Funnels can, for example, be used for:

- Ranking in-app purchase conversions, understanding the paths that lead to IAPs and optimizing them
- Understanding which level or part of the application users tend to leave
- Performing A/B test analysis to see which versions perform better.

These goals (steps) are defined as custom events in Countly, and you do not need any extra/new API calls if you have already been using custom events.

Step 1: Users will be greeted by a funnel creation from where they can define the steps of their marketing funnel. A funnel needs to have at least two steps.

Step 2: After saving the funnel, users will immediately be taken to the reporting view. At the top, the reader can see how many users of the application entered this funnel by performing the first step event. Right next to it, there is the success rate and some users who have completed this funnel by performing every single event.

Step 3: Users can filter the first step event by the event's segmentation properties as well as user properties (metrics) like platform, device, country, etc.

Applications and Users

Countly provides a user interface to manage applications and system users.

Managing applications—Applications can be managed by global users (more information on users is provided later). To add an application, follow the steps below:

- Go to "Management→ Applications."
- Click on the "Add" option.
- Enter the application name, category, the time zone the user is in, and upload the application icon.
- Click "Add Application."

The user will be given an app key that is unique to that application. This key should be written in the SDK code snippet, which in turn will be embedded in the application. For more details, refer to the Countly's resources website: http://resources.count.ly/.

Alternatively, users can enter their IAP Event Key to collect IAP revenues and see it immediately on the users' dashboard.

If readers want to delete an application, just click on "Delete." There may be some cases where users want to remove all data associated with an application, but keep the application keys and other information. In this case, use "Clear data" to delete all incoming data from this application and start fresh.

Managing users—Countly provides a way to manage different types of users (e.g., global admin, admin, or user). Each user will be able to see the privileges assigned to them. For example, the user may want their marketing team to be able to see the whole dashboard, whereas the website manager, as the global admin, can quickly add/remove applications, define other users, and manage whole interfaces. Different types of users have different authorization levels:

> **Global admins** can add/remove/edit users, add/remove/edit applications and typically can do whatever is assigned them on the user interface; this is the most powerful user.
>
> **Admins** can manage applications, for example, add, edit, or delete an application from the management dashboard. If the user is the global admin and their organization controls other sub-organizations or companies, then they will probably want to add different admins to manage various applications.

Users are at the bottom of the hierarchy, and can only see the dashboard, without having the ability to manage other applications and users.

To add a user, one must be a global admin. Click "Create a new user" to get a drop-down menu where you can enter user information and credentials. Fill in the details here and click "Create user." Editing a user is straightforward: Go to the user row and click. The user will be presented with an editable form. Countly offers revenue analytics to Countly Cloud and Enterprise users for tracking in-app–purchase (IAP) data in real time. Revenue Analytics provide the following information:

- Total revenue
- Average revenue per user
- Average revenue per paying user
- Paying user count
- Paying/total users

To make revenue analytics, users need to define an in-app—purchase event. Define an event as follows.

- Go to "Management→ Applications."
- Click "Edit."
- Select an AIP event key by typing the event name.
- Click "Save Changes."

Changing Interface Language

Countly is available in several languages, including German, Spanish, Turkish, Italian, Dutch, Russian, Chinese, and more. The user can quickly switch languages from the menu on the left-hand side. Click on the name and then the language button, where the user will see the languages interface.

Source: Countly, https://count.ly/

REVIEW QUESTIONS

1. Explain the two main categories of mobile analytics.
2. What is the purpose of apps analytics?
3. Explain the different classes of mobile apps.
4. What are some key features of mobile apps?
5. Explain the different app development options.

EXERCISE 11.1: THE MOBILE APPLICATION TYPE ASSESSMENT

In this assessment, we will explore, and help the reader who is developing a mobile application, decide what type of mobile application best fits their needs.

Use the *Mobile Application Type Assessment Tool* (available from the book companion site) to help evaluate which type of mobile application will work best for the organization, whether that is a native smartphone application (Native) or a browser-based mobile application. Complete the self-assessment tab and review the results to find the mobile app that best suits the organization's needs.

With this tool, readers will be able to evaluate whether their organization should begin development on a native smartphone application (Native) or a browser-based mobile application (Web).

- In the "Questionnaire" tab, answer the questions as they relate to your organization.
- Check the "Results" tab to view your overall assessment and recommendations for your mobile.

Many of our students are working for organizations that are developing their own mobile applications. We put ourselves in the shoes of one such student and filled out the survey; the results are provided in Screenshot 11.2.

Based on the way we filled out the Mobile Application Type Assessment there is a stronger case to develop a Web Application rather than a Mobile Application. Readers can download and complete the same assessment we did, and come up with a better understanding of which type of Mobile Application to develop.

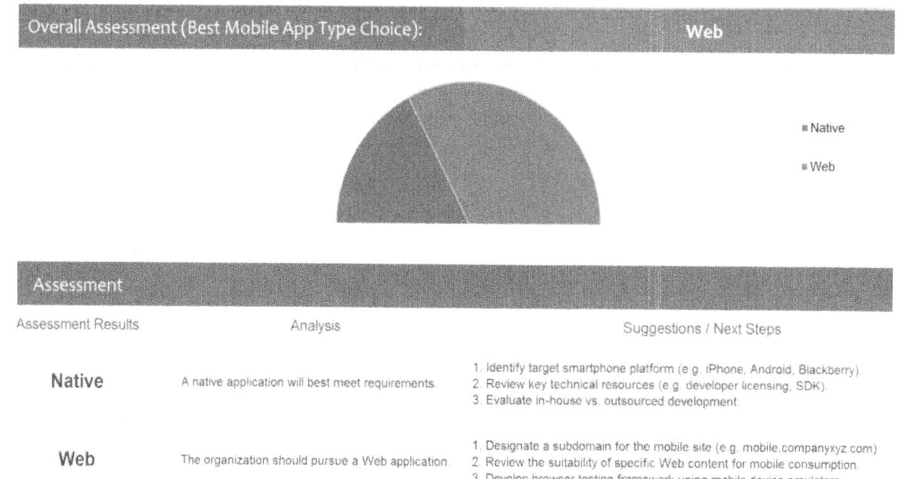

Overall Assessment (Best Mobile App Type Choice):
Web
Native
Web
Assessment
Assessment Results
Analysis
Suggestions / Next Steps
Native
A native application will best meet requirements.
1. Identify target smartphone platform (e.g. iPhone, Android, Blackberry).
2. Review key technical resources (e.g. developer licensing, SDK).
3. Evaluate in-house vs. outsourced development.
Web
The organization should pursue a Web application.
1. Designate a subdomain for the mobile site (e.g. mobile.companyxyz.com)
2. Review the suitability of specific Web content for mobile consumption.
3. Develop browser testing framework using mobile device emulators.

Screenshot 11.2. : The Mobile Application Type Assessment – Results Tab

EXERCISE 11.2: THE MOBILE MARKETING MATURITY ASSESSMENT

For readers who are employed by corporations and startups (and perhaps, non-profits), developing a successful mobile application requires mature business processes and executive buy-in. This assessment helps the reader know their readiness level to develop mobile applications. Use this assessment to audit the mobile marketing competencies of the organization to understand the current level of process maturity. In this evaluation, the reader is required to identify a way to evaluate their organization's current mobile marketing capabilities.

The *Mobile Marketing Maturity Assessment* evaluates an organization's capability across seven critical mobile marketing perspectives: Strategy, Resources, Results, Promotion, Execution, and Follow-Up and Measurement. For each of these different areas, the reader is required to select the level of process maturity they believe that they have. Once the reader has gone through the mobile marketing audit, they will be able to determine what the level of process maturity exists in their organization for each of these categories. In this resource, we also provide readers with an overall mobile marketing effectiveness score and an overall mobile marketing maturity index.

Mobile Marketing Maturity Weightings

We decided to leave the weightings of this assessment at the default in this case; readers will need to decide on how important each of these factors (shown in Screenshot 11.3) are in their organization.

Customize this tool by changing the weighting scale for each assessment category.

Weighting Scale					
Senior Management Commitment	Alignment with Business Goals & Objectives	Mobile Marketing Knowledge, Trends & Regulations	Planning	Staff, Systems, & Training	Total
20%	20%	20%	20%	20%	100%

For this assessment we left the default weightings to the default - but the reader can adjust them as needed

Screenshot 11.3. Mobile Marketing Maturity Assessment – weightings

Mobile Marketing Maturity Results

We filled out the self-assessment based on what we know about Social Listening Limited's mobile marketing capabilities (Screenshot 11.4). The results suggest that the company have a long way to go before they are able to deploy and support compelling mobile applications.

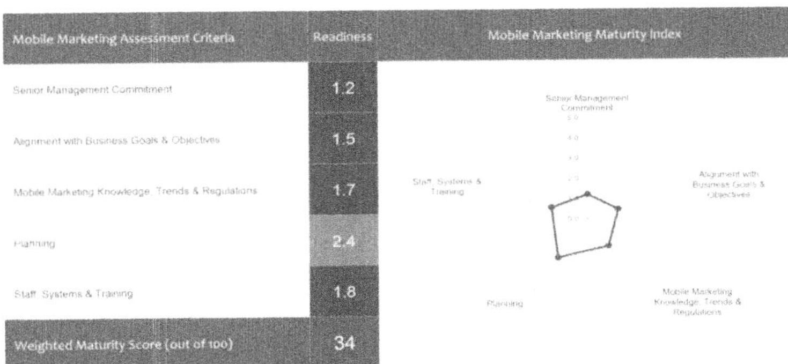

Mobile Marketing Assessment Criteria	Readiness
Senior Management Commitment	1.2
Alignment with Business Goals & Objectives	1.5
Mobile Marketing Knowledge, Trends & Regulations	1.7
Planning	2.4
Staff, Systems & Training	1.8
Weighted Maturity Score (out of 100)	34

Screenshot 11.4. Mobile Marketing Maturity results

Some of the Mobile Marketing Maturity Recommendations

This assessment provides suggestions on what the organization can do prepare for creating and deploying mobile applications. In our example, some of the following points emerged based on how the self-assessment was filled out.

- Obtain buy-in from senior management; prepare a business case and scorecard for mobile marketing, and present action plans to executives.
- Conduct research to determine if customers would benefit from the use of mobile and if it is profitable (from an ROI perspective, to do so).
- Review the competitive landscape to identify opportunities (i.e., this suggests a similar analysis to Porter's Five Forces that many marketing students study in business school).

CHAPTER 11 REFERENCES

Korf, M., & Oksman, E. (2014). Native, HTML5, or Hybrid: Understanding Your Mobile Application Development Options, available at: https://developer.salesforce.com/page/Native, HTML5, or Hybrid: Understanding Your Mobile Application Development Options.

Capturing Value with Social Media Multimedia Analytics

"A picture is worth a thousand words"—**Anonymous**

Learning Outcomes

After completing this chapter, the reader should be able to:

- Comprehend how firms create value with multimedia analytics.
- Understand image analytics concepts, tools, and applications.
- Recognize video analytics concepts, tools, and applications.
- Understand audio analytics concepts, tools, and applications.
- Comprehend Google's Cloud Vision API and its applications.
- List business uses of multimedia analytics.

INTRODUCTION

Social media *multimedia analytics* is the art and science of harnessing business value from video, images, audio, and animations, and interactive contents posted over social media outlets. A vast amount of social media content is in the form of videos, images, and animations. Every day, people post billions of pieces of multimedia content to social media platforms, such as Facebook, YouTube, Instagram, Snapchat, WhatsApp, and Flickr. The importance of multimedia content is paramount to brands. For example, research suggests that multimedia loaded content posted over social media plays a crucial role in the virility of information/posts (Bruni, Francalanci, & Giacomazzi, 2012). Similarly, multimedia content may carry useful business insights, consequently without multimedia analytics in place, brands are likely to miss out on vital visual social media conversation about their brand, products, and services. Let us discuss the three most common types of multimedia analytics.

TYPES OF MULTIMEDIA ANALYTICS

Three principal types of multimedia analytics are:

- Image Analytics
- Video Analytics
- Audio Analytics

Image Analytics

Image analytics deals with extracting business insights (e.g., faces, logos, objects, scenes, and actions) from images posted on social media. Image analytics is more formally known as image processing by the scientists working in the computer vision discipline. Computer vision is a multi-disciplinary field dealing with training computers to acquire, process, and analyze images for the purpose of extracting useful information (Szeliski, 2011). Real world application of computer vision include detection of terminal diseases, such as cancer from x-ray images, or detection of obstacles by autonomous machines, particularly self-driving vehicles, and to monitor the contents and status of retail store shelves (Marder et al., 2015).

Image analytics, when applied to social media images, may produce significant insights embedded within photos. For instance, it can be used to identify customer's sentiment, gender, age, and other unspoken conversation about brands, product, and services. Below, we explain some general and business uses of image analytics.

General Uses of Image Analytics

Google recently launched *Cloud Vision* API (application programming interface) for developers to build creative image analytics applications (Figure 12.1). Using the API developers can easily classify images into thousands of categories (e.g., "building," "tiger," "Airplane"), detect individual objects and faces within images, and likewise find and read printed words contained within images. According to Google, here are some uses of the API.

Label Detection—detects broad sets of categories within an image, ranging from manufactured and natural structures and mode of transportation to animals.

Explicit Content Detection—detects explicit content embedded within images such as adult content or violent content.

Logo Detection—pinpointing well-known brand logos and trademarks embedded within an image.

Optical Character Recognition—mining multi-lingual text that is embedded within an image. The API can also automatically recognize different languages (e.g., Chinese, French, and Arabic).

Face Detection—detects multiple faces within an image and the associated vital facial attributes such as emotional state and the accessories (such as glasses and headscarf). However, it does not include facial recognition ability.

Image Attributes—detects general attributes of the image, such as dominant colors and appropriate crop hints.

Web Detection—search the Internet for similar images.

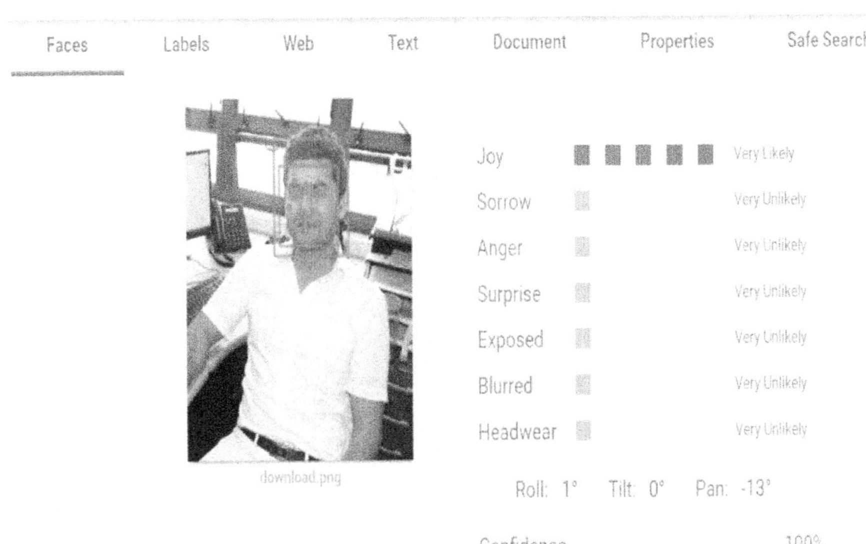

Figure 12.1. Google's Cloud Vision API demo

Business Uses of Image Analytics

Google Cloud Vision API and other similar technologies can be used for the following business-specific purposes. Huddy, a content marketing specialist at CrimsonHexagon, provided the following image analytics business uses (Huddy, 2017):

Brand Mentions

Images posted on social media can be used to identify brand *mentions*. Understanding text-based brand mentions is only half the story, as most images posted on social media do not accompany any text. For example, text analytics tools are unable to pick the Nike's visual shown in Figure 12.2.

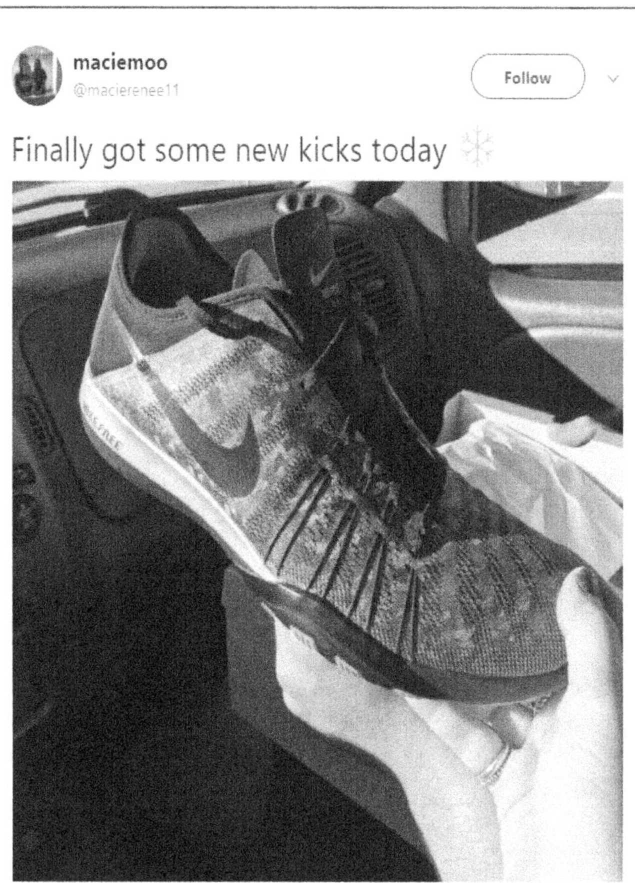

Figure 12.2. Brand visual mention example

Sentiment Analysis

Sentiment analysis is traditionally the domain of text analytics. However, when applied together with images analytic, it can reveal valuable insights. Consider the following tweet related to WhisperMint toothpaste (Figure 12.3). Only text analytics based sentiment analysis will entirely miss the visual sentiments expressed by social media users.

svt love bot @goingwithsvt ·Sep 7
Why does the brand of this toothpaste sounds like a fansite name
WhisperMint®
REFRESHING TOOTHPASTE
154
405

Figure 12.3. Visual sentiment example

Measure Sponsorship ROI

Image analytics can help brands track their *event sponsorships* by using logo tracking to see the number of photos shared that include a brand logo. Traditionally, businesses struggle to determine if placing their brand's logo in a sports stadium is worth the investment. Logo recognition technology and applications can finally start to give some answers to the "ROI of offline advertising" questions. Logo recognition technology, for example, allows users to quantify the number of impressions and exposure that a brand is getting from something like a red carpet sponsorship (Figure 12.4). In the absence of image analytics, it is tough to track visual-only mentions.

Figure 12.4. Sponsorship ROI example
Source: https://www.instagram.com/p/BPBTbYqALTB/

Find Visual Influencers

With image analytics brands can go beyond the share of voice and identify '*share of an eye*' to understand the full scope of their brand health. For example, consider the Instagram post from Skrillex displaying the Adidas logo (Figure 12.5). Regardless of the fact that it is a paid or organic investment from Adidas, they would want to monitor how influencers like Skrillex are promoting their brand.

Figure 12.5. Visual influencer example
Source: https://www.instagram.com/p/BITU0zeB8ZQ/

Identify Moments of Consumption

One of the most exciting and useful applications of image recognition technology includes identifying *moments of consumption,* i.e., the use photos to validate how, when, and where people use products and services (Figure 12.6). In other words, image analysis can identify moments of consumption without customers explicitly mentioning a brand's product in their social media posts.

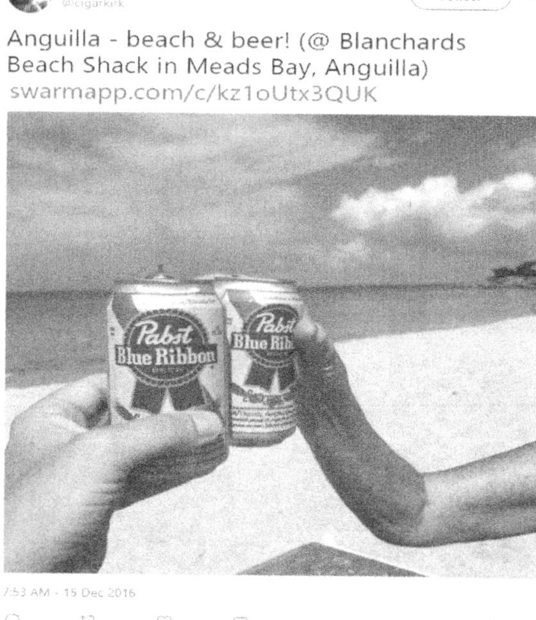
cigarkirk
@cigarkirk
Follow
Anguilla - beach & beer! (@ Blanchards Beach Shack in Meads Bay, Anguilla)
swarmapp.com/c/kz1oUtx3QUK
Pabst
Blue Ribbon
7:53 AM - 15 Dec 2016

Figure 12.6. Moments of consumption example

IMAGE ANALYTICS TOOLS

Image analytics tools are still emerging and limited in term of functionalities. Like other analytics tools, image analytics tools are available either in *on-cloud* or *on-premise* (desktop) basis. Some tools readers can try those that are (were) available at the time of writing this book.

CrimsonHexagon Image analytics

CrimsonHexagon (https://www.crimsonhexagon.com/image-analysis/) one of the leading social media analytics vendor which provides a cloud-based image analytics platform.

Simply Measured

Simply Measured (https://simplymeasured.com) a social media analytics platform provides a cloud-based image analytics tool for Instagram available for users with up to 25,000 Followers. The tool provides image related metrics including average engagement per photo, keyword analysis for comments, most active followers, and the best time to post for receiving the most engagement, top locations, and filters, etc.

Iconosquare

Iconosquare (https://pro.iconosquare.com) is a desktop image analytics tools for Instagram that provides detailed reports on total likes received, a history of your most liked photos throughout the duration of your account, the average number of likes and comments you receive per image, follower growth charts, daily lost and gain follower, and other follower demographics.

InstaFollow

InstaFollow is a mobile app for Instagram image analytics. InstaFollow provides insight specifically about your follower base including track new followers and un-followers, track followers whom you do not follow back, track users who you follow that do not follow you back, follow and unfollow users with a simple tap inside the app.

Image Memory value

At the time of this writing, there is an impressive demo that allows anyone to upload a photo, and the algorithm will determine how memorable it will be to a typical human viewer (http://memorability.csail.mit.edu/demo.html).

Pinterest Analytics

Pinterest (https://www.pinterest.com) offers its analytics platform (called Pinterest Analytics) for business users (only). Pinterest Analytics focuses on understanding a user's activity on Pinterest with the purpose of improving it. While some platforms such as Twitter offer website tracking of Twitter ads, Pinterest does not track what happens when the images or infographics pinned on a Pinterest account lead a user back to the website where they are hosted. However, Google Analytics can track visits from Pinterest (via social tracking).

Tailwind

Tailwind (https://www.tailwindapp.com/) is another analytics platform that overlaps its functionality with Pinterest analytics but also includes publishing tools for Pinterest that Pinterest analytics does not provide (probably because it is already integrated as part of Pinterest).

Curalate

Curalate (http://www.curalate.com/) is a brand monitoring and analytics platform that tracks visual imagery across platforms.

VIDEO ANALYTICS

Video analytics can be divided into two categories:

- Video Content Analysis
- Video Stats Analytics

Video Content Analytics

Video content analytics (VCA) is used to automatically analyze contents of a video to detect and determine temporal (time-bound) and spatial (space-bound) events that are captured in a video. For examples, *IBM Intelligent Video Analytics* allows an organization to use advanced search, redaction, and facial recognition analytics to find relevant and meaningful information from a digital video for public safety, security, intelligence, and investigative purposes. VCA analytics essentially detect changes that occur over consecutive frames of video, qualify these changes in each frame, correlate qualified changes over multiple frames, and finally interpret these correlated changes (Gagvani, 2008). Table 12.1 lists possible uses and applications of VCA.

Video Stats Analytics

Video stats analytics (VSA) is about monitoring and analyzing the performance of videos posted on social media channels, such as YouTube. YouTube has its own built-in analytics capability. A standard video stats analytics provide reports on the following metrics:

- Who is viewing your video content and how it is being viewed (devices, browsers, operating systems.
- How long the videos are being viewed.
- Where the viewers are located
- Advanced video stats analytics also provides detailed reports on player loads, views, viewed minutes, percent of content viewed, new viewers, unique viewers, attention span, top domains, traffic sources, search terms, and so forth.

YouTube Analytics

YouTube analytics provides very comprehensive data for the YouTube channel owner including views, likes, watch time, traffic sources, and demographics reports. For example, Figure 12.7 from the YouTube analytics shows that a majority of viewers are in the 55-64 years' range based on 660 videos.

Table 12.1. Application of video content analytics

Application	Description
Recognition	Video analytics is used for facial and object recognition (e.g., number plates) to recognize, and therefore possibly identify persons or objects. For example, the IBM video analytics tool allows users to enroll facial images of objects and people of interest in a watch list and the system compares them with faces captured by body cameras. High-quality matches are ranked for analyst review.
Detect changes in patterns	From live-streaming fixed cameras, receive automatic alerts when movement of objects (people and vehicles) is inconsistent with predefined patterns.
Flame and smoke detection	Internet-connected video surveillance cameras can be used to detect flame and smoke in 15–20 seconds or even less because of the built-in smart microchip. The microchip processes are capable of analyzing flame and smoke characteristics such as color chrominance, flickering ratio, shape, pattern, and moving direction.
Egomotion estimation	Egomotion estimation is used to determine the location of a camera by analyzing its output signal.
Motion detection	Motion detection is used to determine the presence of relevant motion in the observed scene.
Shape recognition	Shape recognition is used to recognize shapes in the input video, for example, circles or squares. This functionality is typically used in more advanced functionalities such as object detection.
Style detection	Style detection is used in settings where the video signal has been produced, for example, for television broadcast. Style detection detects the style of the production process.
Tamper detection	Tamper detection is used to determine whether the camera or output signal is tampered with.
Video tracking	Video tracking is used to determine the location of persons or objects in the video signal, possibly with regard to an external reference grid.

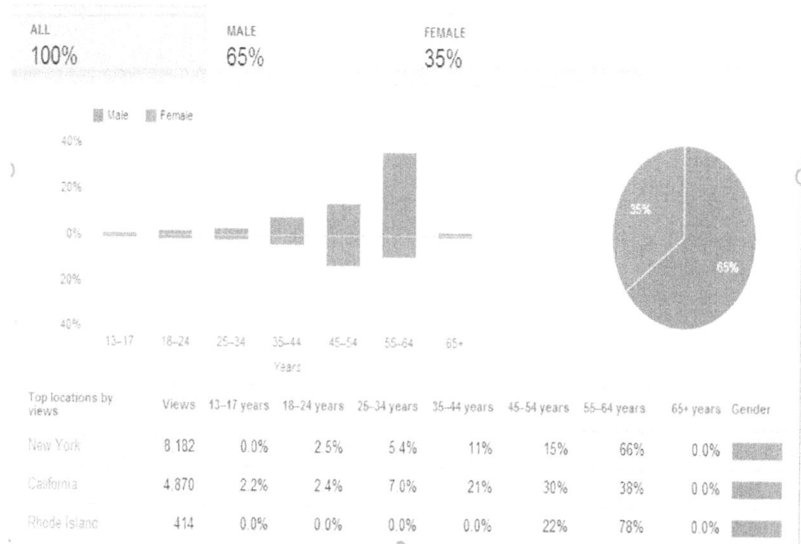

Top locations by views	Views	13–17 years	18–24 years	25–34 years	35–44 years	45–54 years	55–64 years	65+ years	Gender
New York	8 182	0.0%	2.5%	5.4%	11%	15%	66%	0.0%	
California	4,870	2.2%	2.4%	7.0%	21%	30%	38%	0.0%	
Rhode Island	414	0.0%	0.0%	0.0%	0.0%	22%	78%	0.0%	

Figure 12.7. YouTube analytics

Figure 12.7 also shows the significant locations of these viewers. Currently, it is possible to drill down to the State level, but not to exact cities or districts. Eventually, we will be able to view video consumption down to the city level - and perhaps, someday, down to the zip code. The capability exists now, but the data processing is probably too intensive for Google to want to offer this level of detail down to city or block level video views. Your Google Analytics account can also be integrated with your YouTube channel to track the traffic from external links embedded in your YouTube videos.

YouTube and Online Video Advantages

- **Low Production Costs**: Low startup costs to capture video (most digital devices can record and upload digital video to YouTube). Limitations on the length of uploaded videos (15 minutes was the limit for low traffic channels) has been relaxed; videos of almost any length can be uploaded and processed within minutes.
- **Extensible:** Sophisticated video editing tools are free or inexpensive and accessible to anyone.
- **Social Media**: Social media provides a means to gain viewers quickly through social sharing (especially if the video goes viral).
- **YouTube Advertising Network**: YouTube channel owners are given the opportunity to earn income from advertising to appear on their uploaded videos through YouTube's advertising network. Also, channel owners can run their advertising to expand the reach and audience of their videos on YouTube. When channel owners run their advertising,

they can use a variety of geo-demographic targeting options that YouTube provides.

- **Sponsorship Opportunities**: YouTube sponsors some video creators (YouTubers can be influencers and brand ambassadors) by providing an income for producing agreed-upon video content. Brands can also provide YouTube channel owners and videographers with sponsorship opportunities.
- **YouTube Production Studios**: In some cities such as New York, YouTube has studios that videographers can use or rent to produce and edit their videos.
- **YouTube Analytics**: YouTube provides sophisticated analytics to channel owners on their uploaded videos.
- **Advocacy**: Videographers and Musicians have additional training and playbook resources that encourage creators to improve their skills and build their audience.
- **Search Engine Ranking:** Online video increases the likelihood of a front-page Google search result by 96% with proper page optimization. Social media marketers suggest that the products that have videos are 95% more likely to be bought. In addition, video adds two minutes to visitors' stays on retail sites.

Issues with YouTube

- **Stiff competition:** With so much new content uploaded every moment, the videographer has a hard time gaining viewership (primarily if they have not developed an audience yet).
- **Low Attention Span**: Viewers need to engage with a video within a few seconds, or they will not watch the rest of the video. Consequently, videographers need to be good storytellers to captivate their audiences with their content.
- **Viral Sharing**: While many videographers want their videos to go "viral," few ever do. In most cases, videos need to be planned and seeded in various online locations first, which requires spending money on advertising, having a knack for appealing storylines, and great timing. Also, most of the videos that go viral are professionally produced (with rare exceptions).
- **Big Brother**: YouTube, like most social media platforms, uses the video data for a variety of purposes, including profiling of users and audiences.

The profiling goes well beyond what most videographers are aware of. While YouTube uses the data to improve its services, it also shares the information with governmental agencies, commercial brokers, and advertisers.

- **Throttling and Network Congestion**: As the Internet is getting saturated with video and audio content, it had become challenging to watch videos, especially when they stall while playing.

Issues with Video Analytics

- Third-party software such as VidStatsX, ChannelMeter provides "intermediate" metrics that are not actionable (except perhaps, advertising on a highly trafficked channel, etc.). While YouTube allows users to run advertising that targets demographics and geo-location, the actual channels that are selected are not typically shared with the advertiser.
- Most data providers including Google (Facebook and Twitter are also included) do not share the actual account (Channel) information of where your ads will appear; the rationale for that is two-fold. First, Google, Facebook, Twitter, and LinkedIn consider their 'Data' as the most valuable asset they have; they provide targeting for the advertiser, but they are not in the business ofbuilding audience lists for advertisers. The other reason is privacy. There are potential ramifications of knowing which channels and videos a video ad appears on. With enough observation, it is possible to find and build audiences, though the details of that are not covered here.

Video Analytics Tools

Several video stats analytics tools are available. Here we list some of them.

ChannelMeter—(https://channelmeter.com) is a YouTube video analytics tool, which provides reports on a variety of metrics including playlist analytics, detailed demographic reports, video drop-off analytics, and keyword monitoring, and so forth. It also allows users to track, analyze, and benchmark other channels so you know how your videos are performing as compared with others in your niche.

Vidooly—https://vidooly.com/) is a robust video analytics platform which allows users to maximize search traffic, increase their subscriber base, and see how they perform compared with others in their genre. It also allows the user to see suggested tags, suggested channels to subscribe to, and perform comment analysis.

Quintly—(https://www.quintly.com) is a YouTube analytics tool, which provides a variety of metrics on a YouTube channel and those of your competitors. Quintly's detailed subscriber statistics can play a crucial part in optimizing a YouTube channel and to keeping an eye on the competition.

RankTrackr—(http://ranktrackr.com/) is a video search engine optimization and ranking tool which helps track local rankings, search volume, track competitors, and export reports.

Socialbakers—(https://www.socialbakers.com/) is a social media analytics tool, which helps brands monitor many social media profiles, including YouTube. Using this tool, brands can track their growth, learn more about their audience, identify influencers, create scheduled reports, and more.

Ooyala—(http://www.ooyala.com) is an online video management, publishing, video analytics, and monetization tool. It also provides real-time video analytics and behavioral analysis capabilities.

Audio Analytics

Audio analytics deals with sound analysis and recognition using advanced algorithms and artificial intelligence. While the overall scope of audio analytics is broad, for example, it can be used in smart homes to prevent intrusions (Audio Analytic, 2017). In the context of social media, audio analytics deals with analyzing audio contents, such as podcast and audio messages.

Recently, Google released a cloud-based tool, which is used to convert text into speech (audio). The tool known as *Cloud Text-to-Speech* enables developers to produce natural-sounding speech in various languages and variants. *Cloud Text-to-Speech* leverages WaveNet (a neural network architecture that generates a raw audio waveform) and Google's powerful neural networks to generate more realistic-sounding human-like voices.

MINI CASE STUDIES
UNDERSTANDING AND USING IMAGE ANALYSIS

Introduction

The fact that creating and sharing images is easier than ever is not the only reason that image sharing is becoming so popular: images are more impactful than text. More memorable. More engaging. And more likely to be shared and re-shared. The power of images and the ubiquity of camera-enabled smartphones means the volume of images on the web continues to grow exponentially. There are well over three billion photos shared daily on social media. The barrier for self-expression has continued to drop as wireless network speeds, camera access, and photo quality continues to increase across the board.

Figure 12.8. Image analysis

The fastest growing social media sites are image-based. Snapchat, Instagram, and Pinterest and Tumblr put the focus on images, with text seen as secondary. Even the original social networks like Twitter and Facebook now focus much more on visual communication. Facebook is now the largest image-sharing site on the web and Twitter gives extra space to posts including images. Of course, none of this means that text-based social communication is going away anytime soon, but it is being supplemented and improved with images.

"Photos are no longer just a means of capturing a moment; they are a means of communicating."—Evan Spiegel, Snapchat Founder.

In addition to the explosion of image sharing on the web, images are proven to make your online content and social posts more engaging:

- For brands and marketers, content that contains a relevant image gets a whopping 94 percent more views (Content Marketing Institute).

- Facebook posts with images have 2.3x higher engagement than those without, and Twitter updates containing images generate 150% more retweets than text updates without images (BuzzSumo).

There is a reason behind the growth and popularity of image sharing beyond the fact that the latest technology makes creating and sharing images easier than ever. Our brains are built for visual communication. We process visuals faster, we remember them longer, and they elicit a stronger emotional response. In fact, visuals are processed 60,000x faster than text (HubSpot). It is also more efficient for the person doing the communicating. Expressing "I'm sad" is a lot faster and more efficient with an emoji (☹) than with text.

However, this influx of image-based conversation is not just changing the way we communicate with each other; it is equally changing the way brands communicate with consumers.

Why Image Analysis Matters for Business

Given that images are more impactful and memorable than text, it is evident that brands need to pay attention to photos in their social listening strategies. The increase in image sharing also provides a massive opportunity for social media analysis since images can provide new insights into your audience and industry than text.

Getting the whole story

As social and the web as a whole become visual, brands cannot rely on text alone when analyzing social media data. Of the billions of photos shared daily on social media containing brand logos, 85% do not include a text reference to the brand. Without image analysis, companies are missing a massive chunk of the social conversations about their brand, products, customers, and competitors. While image analysis technology is still new, it allows brands to gain more powerful insights on who is using their product, how they are using it, and how they feel about it—all without the need for text.

There are some significant advantages to looking at both text and images when analyzing social media data:

- Images do not require translation, making image analysis extremely useful in a global strategy.
- Looking at a more complete data set enables businesses to

incorporate social insights into decision-making more effectively.

- Images can tell an entirely different story than text mentions (Example: Text-based analysis of conversation around Disney's Frozen, shows the audience as adults in their 30s. Image analysis of the same conversation shows the movie's actual audience, children.)

Images can also tell a very different story than text mentions. The technology behind image analysis is advancing quickly—making image analysis at a scale much more accessible. Images show contextual, environmental, and emotional factors that you cannot get with just text. However, how does image analysis actually work?

How Image Analysis Works

When looking at how to apply image analysis to social data, it is helpful to think in the same terms as traditional text-based social analysis. Nevertheless, what are the differences in the technology? Can image analysis do everything text analysis can do? Here's a chart explaining the progression of analytics technology in terms of business value and degree of difficulty:

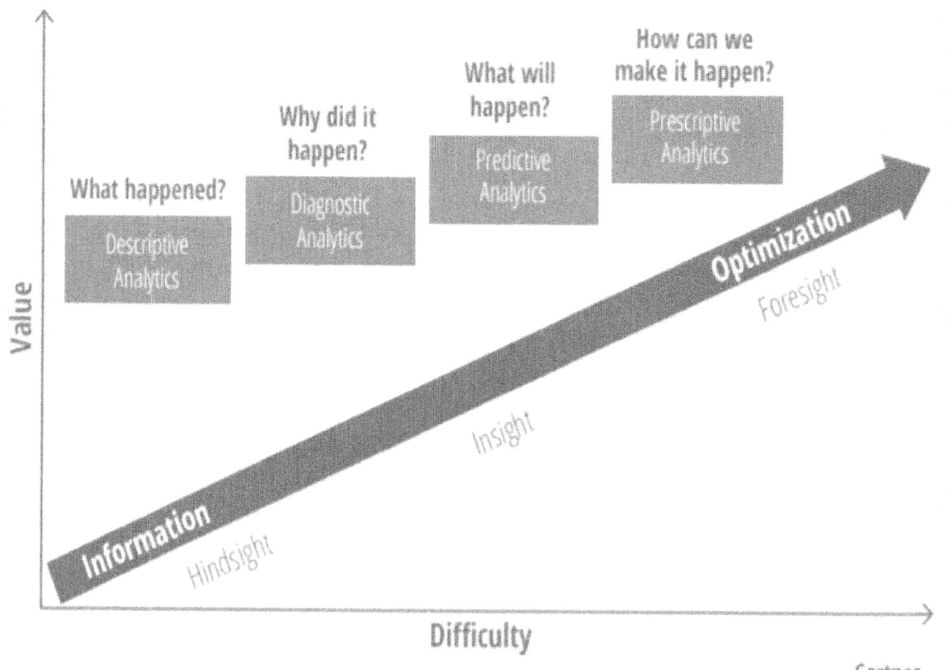

Figure 12.9. Types of analytics and business value

Let us look specifically at how image analysis fits in this framework.

What happened?

Descriptive Analysis can recognize multiple elements within a photo like logos, faces, activities, objects, and scenes (Figure 12.10). The technology can also automatically caption images, i.e., "Boy riding a bicycle outside with dog wearing Nike T-shirt."

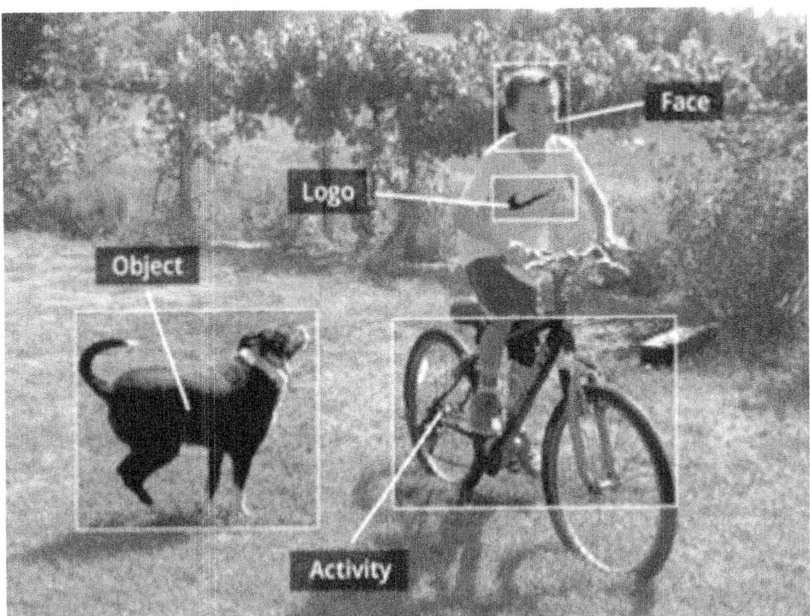

Figure 12.10. Descriptive image analytics example

Why did it happen?

Diagnostic analysis is one area where image analysis is just not quite there yet. The reason it is not here yet is that it requires the technology to have a common-sense understanding of the world, which is much more difficult for a machine to learn. For example, current image analysis technology would not be able to know "why" people are laughing at something in a photo or why a particular photo is funny.

What will happen?

Predictive Analysis can look at an image and determine what is likely to happen next. While this technology is still very new, MIT recently demonstrated that their image analysis technology could predict things like a kiss or a handshake based on the setting and body language in photos.

Figure 12.11. Predictive image analytics example

How can we make it happen?

Prescriptive Analysis gives recommendations based on image data. A recent example comes from OpenAI research scientist, Andrej Karpathy, who analyzed selfie photo data and determined what types of photos got the most likes (Figure 12.12). He developed a program that did not just give recommendations on how to improve your selfies, but actually edited selfies to optimize them for more likes based on the data.

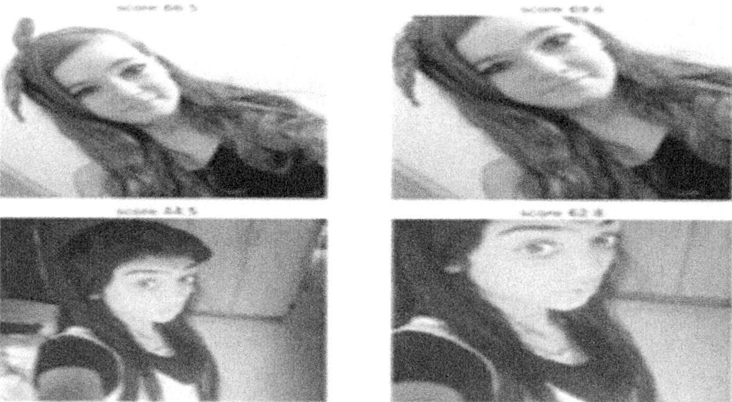

Figure 12.12. Prescriptive image analytics example

Practical Business Use Cases for Image Analytics

Image analysis technology may sound great, but it is not helpful to your strategy if it is all theoretical. It is important to look specifically at how companies can use social image analytics to uncover new insights about their audiences and industries.

Measure ROI with Logo Recognition

Beyond just looking at a brand's share of the visual or text-based conversation, there are many more specific uses for brand-related image analysis. One of the most accessible and most helpful is logo detection. While the concept of crawling the web to find images that contain your logo is straightforward, logo detection technology can be applied in multiple ways. How can you determine if your brand's logo in a sports stadium is worth the investment (Figure 12.13)? Was it worth it to sponsor that big event? These types of questions have been raised in marketing discussions for years, but logo recognition technology can finally start to give some answers to the "ROI of offline advertising" question

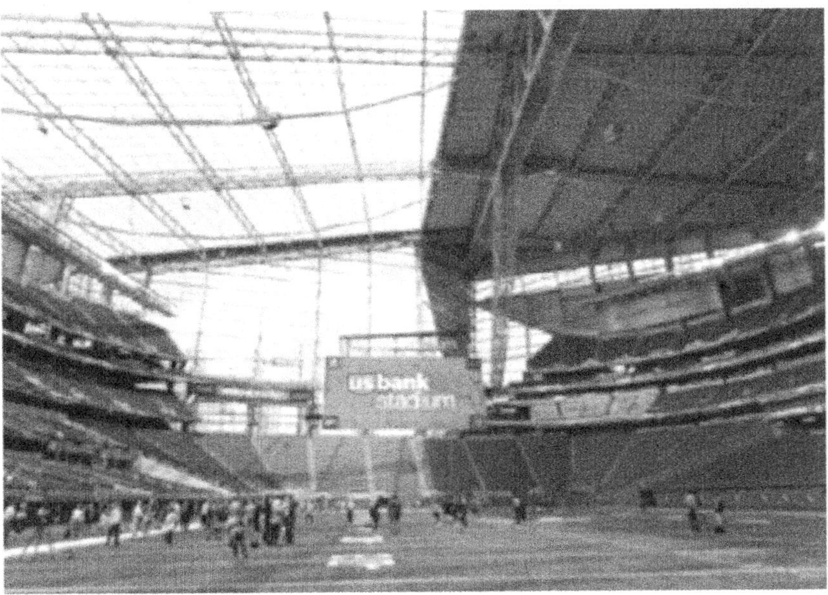

Figure 12.13. Measure ROI with Logo recognition example

Source: http://www.twincities.com/2016/07/19/vikings-us-bank-stadium-ugly-on-the-outside-better-interior/

Finally, understand the full value of your sponsorships

Typically, people measure something like a sports sponsorship by looking at how many people were at the game and how many people watched on TV, but there is not a right way to analyze the sponsorship ROI on social. People posting about the game on social media are not going to be directly mentioning the sponsoring brands, but they are posting photos of the stadium and the players that are heavily branded. Logo recognition technology allows you to quantify the number of impressions and exposure that your brand is getting from something like a stadium sponsorship (Figure 12.14). Otherwise, you have no way to track those visual-only mentions. Anyone who has been to Boston knows there is no shortage of Dunkin' Donuts in the city. In addition to having hundreds of locations in the greater Boston area, it makes sense that Dunkin' would be a big sponsor of Boston-area sports teams. Venues like TD Garden, Fenway Park, and Gillette Stadium always seem to have the Dunkin' logo in multiple prominent locations, season after season. Nevertheless, how can a brand identify which of these sponsorships are helping them achieve their brand goals? With text-based social analysis, they could track brand mentions associated with games and events with one of the sponsored stadiums, but like earlier examples, it is unlikely that sports fans will be explicitly mentioning Dunkin' in their posts. With prominent brand placement somewhere like the scoreboard at Fenway Park, many fans are exposed to their sponsorship, but few are explicitly mentioning it.

Figure 12.14. understanding the full value of your sponsorships example

Enter logo recognition, which allows a company like Dunkin' to analyze how many photos posted on social media contain their sponsorship branding. This technology opens up many possibilities for optimizing these stadium sponsorships based on data that previously would have been impossible to collect. Logo recognition allows you to measure which sponsorships, in which locations within each stadium, are being photographed the most. The most shared branding is also likely the most valuable as the reach goes far beyond just those in attendance at a game or watching on TV. The results of such an analysis could allow Dunkin' to double down on the most photographed locations for their logo and remove or reduce sponsorship from places that are not photographed as often. These insights on the visual reach of sponsorship could allow a brand like Dunkin' Donuts to make better sponsorship decisions to boost brand Image from Dunkin Donuts awareness.

Track Visual Mentions

When a big brand like Nike wants to measure the impact of a new ad campaign, one of their first steps may be to analyze their share of voice on social. How much of the social conversation do they own compared to major competitors like Adidas or Under Armour? How many people are using their branded hashtags? Who is specifically mentioning new products? However, as we have discussed, looking at these direct mentions is only one piece of the puzzle. What about the sportswear conversation that does not involve text? This is where the "share of an eye" is essential.

Share of Eye

When measuring your brand's reach, it is crucial to not only look at posts involving words alone but also images, especially logos. Given that recall increases by 55% with image-based content when compared to text, you want to make sure your brand is getting enough visual mentions. Here is an example to illustrate the power of visual communication: What's the first insurance company that comes to mind off the top of your head? If your answer is Geico, you are not alone. Geico's share of an eye is much larger than any of their competitors. Just think of all of the different, memorable Geico ads you have seen over the years. Some could argue their lack of consistency in their mascots and ad themes could be a misstep, but it is clear that their constant visual representation of the brand is enough to keep them ahead of the pack when it comes to consumer awareness.

Asking the right questions

Just as a brand wants to understand their "share of voice" on social media and across the web, they also want to look at their "share of an eye" in terms of visual mentions. Tracking your share of an eye efficiently requires asking the right questions. Otherwise, you are just looking at all of your visual mentions with a lack of context or goals. Here are some questions you should be asking when tracking your share of an eye:

- How do your visual mentions across the web compare to your competitors?
- What impact did your recent campaign or sponsorship have on your share of an eye?
- How has your (or your competitors' share of an eye changed month over month?
- What are the overarching themes and sentiments behind your visual mentions?
- What is the primary source of your visual mentions? (e.g., sponsorships, product use photos, promotional photos, etc.).
- Who is sharing these images?
- What are their other interests?

Without incorporating images into your social analysis, all of these critical questions go unanswered.

Identify Moments of Consumption

One of the most exciting and useful applications of image recognition technology is identifying moments of consumption. Every company wants to know as much as possible about how, when, and where people are using their products, but the limits of text analysis cannot provide a complete picture of actual product use. No mention? No problem. Unlike text, images provide real-life validation that someone is using your product. Without image analysis, your fans and customers have to explicitly mention your product, which is less likely to happen. For example, think of the amount of brand logos that appear on clothing and beverages in social media photos. The person posting the photo is unlikely to tag or even mention the brands in the photo. Rarely would someone say, "Here's me wearing a Lacoste shirt drinking Coca-Cola." Nevertheless, image analysis would allow Lacoste and Coke to track those specific uses of their products and the context around their use. Tracking visual evidence of product usage in the wild provides a much more powerful metric for brands. Taking it a step further, you can start to correlate sales data with the number of times your product appears in social photos. Crimson Hexagon's research has shown a strong correlation between sales numbers and the volume of social photos showing the use of your product.

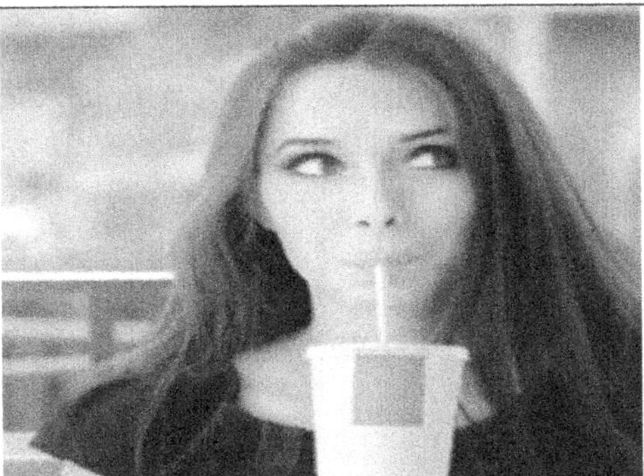

Figure 12.15. Identify moments of consumption example

Going beyond sales data

Big beer brands spend a lot on advertising, but how can they make sure the themes in their ad campaigns appeal to their target audience? How can they ensure that they are making the right advertising and branding decisions? Sales data can tell them how much beer they are selling and where, but it is particularly challenging to get specific context around how people are actually enjoying their products.

Beyond the general point of sale data for where people are buying cases of Miller Lite, how do people drink it? At home? At parties? In the backyard? Weeknights or weekdays? Like the other examples, there will undoubtedly be a small segment of people drinking Miller Lite who will explicitly mention the brand in posts, but the vast majority of photos containing cans or bottles will not have any text reference to the brand. Combining image recognition and text analysis in your social listening allows you to find all of the mentions of your brand, with or without a specific tag or mention. Beyond providing a far more accurate view of the social conversation around your brand, an analysis of the image results gives you the ability to identify scenes and get context and volume data around the use of your product.

Making data-driven decisions

For example, say that sales data shows a spike in Miller Lite sales in Chicago in October. That data does not give any context as to "why." With combined image and text analysis, perhaps you will find that social photos show a trend toward drinking Miller Lite while watching the Chicago Cubs in the playoffs (Figure 12.16). That data could be compared to the number of photos of Chicagoans drinking Miller Lite while watching the Bears or the Blackhawks.

The results could then be used to make decisions about which team's games are best to run ads during. If it turns out that Cubs fans are also the biggest Miller Lite fans, ads during televised Cubs games and Wrigley Field sponsorships for next season might be the best bet. As image recognition technology advances, other factors like facial recognition can give brands a better idea of the demographics of their customers. It is already possible to get an accurate estimate of someone's age with facial recognition. Miller would be interested in knowing the average age of people appearing in social photos with their beer. Are the majority in their 20s or over 40? How does the average age of the Miller Lite drinker compare with the average age of the Coors Light drinker? How can MillerCoors use that data to identify how to market each of these similar light beer products better?

Figure 12.16. Making data-driven decisions using an image

Conclusion: What is next?

The use cases we have discussed are only scratching the surface of the possible business applications of image analysis technology. As features like scene and emotion recognition evolve, it will be possible to measure and categorize consumer behavior and sentiment in brand new ways. While every use case for text analytics can be further augmented by image analytics, there are many insights that can only be gleaned from the images themselves. Ultimately, the combination of text and image-based social analysis is the only way to get the full picture of what is happening on social and ensure that your insights are accurate and actionable.

END CHAPTER QUESTIONS

1. What is Google's Cloud Vision API and what are its business applications.
2. Explain what multimedia analytics is and how it can be used for business intelligence purposes?
3. Briefly explain image analytics concepts, tools, and applications.
4. Briefly explain video analytics concepts, tools, and applications.
5. Briefly explain the advantages and disadvantage of YouTube Analytics.
6. List some real world application of video content analysis.

CHAPTER 12 REFERENCES

Audio Analytic, L. (2017). https://www.audioanalytic.com/about-us/.

Bruni, L., Francalanci, C., & Giacomazzi, P. (2012). The Role of Multimedia Content in Determining the Virality of Social Media Information. *Information & Management, 3*, 278-289.

Gagvani, N. (2008). Introduction to video analytics, avialable at: https://www.eetimes.com/document.asp?doc_id=1273834.

Huddy, G. (2017). What is image analysis: how brands can use image analysis for brand insights, https://www.crimsonhexagon.com/blog/what-is-image-analysis/.

Marder, M., Harary, S., Ribak, A., Tzur, Y., Alpert, S., & Tzadok, A. (2015). Using image analytics to monitor retail store shelves. *IBM Journal of Research and Development, 59*(2/3), 3:1-3:11. doi:10.1147/JRD.2015.2394513

Szeliski, R. (2011). *Computer Vision: Algorithms and Applications*. New York: Springer.

Part 4: Sustaining the Value

Chapter 13

Social Media Analytics Capabilities

"A business capability is the firm's ability to integrate, build, and reconfigure internal and external competencies to address rapidly changing environments." **—Pearl Zhu**

Learning Outcomes

After completing this chapter, the reader should be able to:

- Comprehend social media analytic capabilities.
- Recognize the role of SMA capabilities in competitive advantage.
- Understand operational and dynamics capabilities.
- Explain different technological, organizational, people, environmental, and cultural capabilities and routines that organization need to define, align, capture, consume, and sustain SMA value creation.
- Comprehend social media analytics capability frameworks.

INTRODUCTION

If harvested and appropriately consumed, social media data can potentially lead to a *competitive advantage*. Competitive advantage is a property, condition, or circumstance that a company can have over its rivals. For example, having sound social media analytics (SMA) capabilities can place a firm in a superior business position, which can generate greater value for a firm and its shareholders. To do so, however, organizations need to possess sophisticated *social media analytics capabilities and routines.*

SOCIAL MEDIA ANALYTICS CAPABILITIES

Social media analytics capabilities and routines are the interlocking systems of *competencies* and *practices* that enable organizations to create value through social media data (Shank & Bekmamedova, 2011). In order to harness value from big data and analytics, firms need both 1) operational and 2) dynamic capabilities (Shank & Bekmamedova, 2011).

Operational Capabilities

Operational capabilities that are valuable, rare, inimitable, and non-substitutable lead to organizational value and competitive advantage. These include technological, organizational, people, environmental, and cultural capabilities and routines that organization need to define, align, capture, consume, and sustain SMA value creation and support effective organizational decision-making (Karim et al., 2016). For instance, to capture value from unstructured social media data (such as tweets), a brand needs to allocate appropriate technological assets and people with relevant analytics competencies. To interpret and consume the insights gained from decision-making, organizations need to embed it into daily business practices.

Dynamic Capabilities

Dynamic capabilities are needed to operate in constantly changing business environments. Dynamic capabilities are "the capacity of an organization to purposefully create, extend, or modify its resource base" (Helfat et al. 2007, p. 4). Dynamic capabilities consist of two organizational routines, 1) search and select and 2) asset orchestration (Shank & Bekmamedova, 2011).

Search and Select

Search is the process of understanding and identifying new business opportunities and the need for change (Vogel, Evanschitzky, & Ramaseshan, 2008). The *selection process* is concerned with formulating actions and allocating resources to respond to the opportunity by:

- Designing new business models
- Selecting configurations of co-specialized assets
- Selecting investments and courses of action to invest in, and
- Selecting organizational, governance and incentive structures (Helfat et al., 2007).

Asset Orchestration

Asset orchestration is the ability to put search and select decisions into action by executing new blends and co-alignment of assets (Teece, 2009; Teece, Pisano, & Shuen, 1999). The core element of asset orchestration capabilities is the regularly sanctioned managerial processes to commence change. The changes may be in the form of new products, new processes, new technology, new decision-making routines, new reporting relationships, etc. Asset orchestration often requires a high degree of coordination across business unit boundaries to undertake changes (Shank & Bekmamedova, 2011).

SOCIAL MEDIA ANALYTICS CAPABILITY FRAMEWORK

In the management literature, several *business analytics* (BA) capability frameworks are available (e.g., see Cosic, Shanks, & Maynard, 2015; Watson, Ariyachandra, & Matyska, 2001; Yeoh & Koronios, 2010). However, a sound *social media analytics capability framework* is lacking, mainly because SMA is a relatively new, but emerging, field of research. The capabilities needed to leverage social media data are significantly different from the conventional BA capabilities. The core notions of both BA and SMA are to produce actionable business insights. However, the scope, nature, and type of data mined is significantly varied (Khan, 2015) (refer to chapter 3 for a discussion on the difference between BA and SMA). BA leverages the internally generated and business owned structural data; whereas, SMA deals with semi-structural and unstructured public data generated on social media.

In light of these differences, Karim et al., (2016) have developed a *social media analytics capability framework* that organizations can utilize to efficiently harvest and consume social media data (Figure 13.1). Overall, the authors suggested five higher-level social media analytics capabilities, which are further grouped into twenty-four sub-capabilities (as detailed in the Table 13.1 and explained below in detail).

Social Media Technical Capabilities

These are the overall *technical capabilities* and *infrastructure* needed to extract, mind, and interpret social media, such as data mining, sentiment analysis, and including capabilities needed to mine the eight layers of social media data model discussed earlier in the book.

Data mining

Data mining is concerned with discovering insights from large-scale data. Data mining comprises the core algorithms that enable one to gain fundamental insights and knowledge from massive data. It is an interdisciplinary field merging concepts from various areas like database systems, statistics, and pattern recognition. Actually, it is part of a more extensive knowledge discovery process (Zaki & Jr., 2014).

Text Mining

As an emerging area, *text mining* or analytics aims to extract meaningful information from unstructured textual social media data. As users continue to post textual information (e.g., tweets and comments) on various social media sites, there is a growing interest in using text mining, sentiment analysis, and social network analysis approaches to process large amounts of user-generated data and extract meaningful knowledge and insights (He, Wu, Yan, Akula, &Shen, 2015).

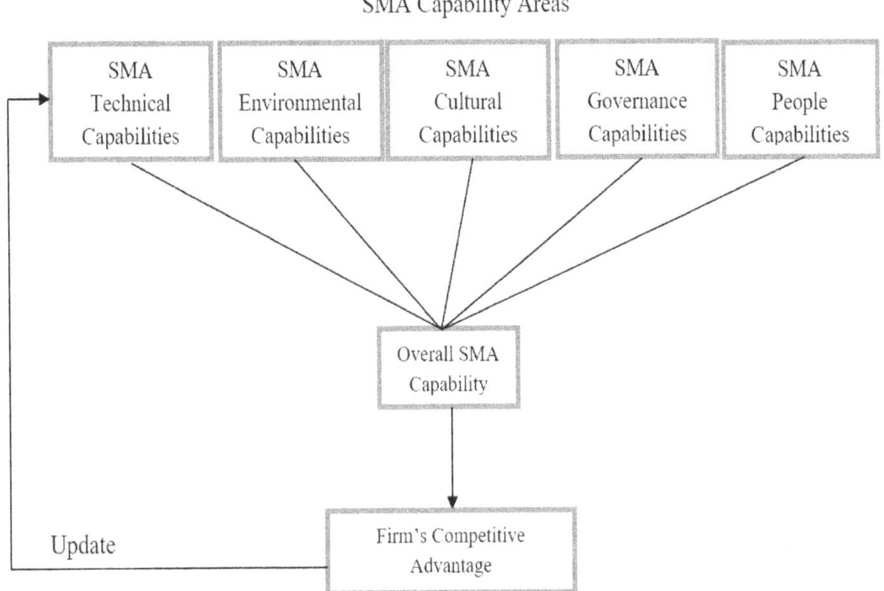

Figure 13.1. Social media analytics capability framework
(Source: Karim et al., 2016)

Today, numerous customers and users share their experiences using various social media sites such as Twitter, Facebook, and blogs. It has become a big challenge for organizations to monitor and understand what people post on the social media sites.

Traditional content analysis methods are no longer able to meet organizations' needs to analyze a significant amount of new content on a daily basis. To glean useful information from a large number of social media texts quickly, it has become imperative to use automated computer techniques. Different from the traditional content analysis, the primary purpose of text mining is to automatically extract knowledge, insights, useful patterns, or trends from a given set of textual documents. Some significant applications of text mining include cluster analysis, categorization, information extraction (text summarization), and link analysis (Abrahams, Fan, Wang, Zhang, & Jiao, 2015).

Sentiment Analysis

Sentiment analysis is the computational detection and study of opinions, sentiments, emotions, and subjectivities in social media texts. As a particular application of text mining, sentiment analysis is concerned with the automatic extraction of positive or negative opinions from texts. Given that texts often contain a mix of positive and negative sentiments, it is often useful to identify the polarity of sentiment in texts (positive, negative, or neutral) and even the strength of the sentiments expressed (Pang & Lee, 2014). There is a growing interest in using sentiment analysis methods to mine user-generated social media data. Sentiment analysis has been used to determine the attitude of customers and online users on some specific topics, such as consumer product (e.g., books, movies, electronics) reviews, hotel service reviews, public relations statements, and financial blogs (He et al., 2015).

Networks Analytics

Social media *network analytics* extract, analyze, and interpret personal and professional social media networks, for example, Facebook, Friendship Network, and Twitter. The principal business objective of network analytics is to identify influential nodes (e.g., people and organizations) and their position in the network.

Hyperlinks Analytics

Hyperlink analytics is used to extract, analyze, and interpret social media hyperlinks (e.g., in-links and out-links). Hyperlink analysis is helpful in understanding Internet traffic patterns and sources of incoming or outgoing traffic to and from a corporate website.

Search Engine Analytics

Search engines analytics focuses on analyzing historical search data for gaining valuable insights into a range of areas, including trends analysis, keyword monitoring, search results, advertisement history, and advertisement spending statistics (Khan, 2015).

Apps Analytics

Apps analytics deals with measuring and optimizing user engagement with mobile applications (or apps for short), such as analyzing and understanding in-app purchases, customer engagement, and mobile user demographics (Khan, 2015).

Location Analytics

Location analytics, also known as geospatial analytics, is concerned with mining and mapping the locations of social media users, contents, and data.

Data Visualization

As the amount of data is gaining magnitude, the importance of *data visualization* is also increasing exponentially. The goal of data visualization is to clearly communicate the information that has been extracted in schematic form.

Multimedia analytics

Multimedia analytics deals with analyzing social media multimedia contents, such as audio, video, and photos.

Data Cleansing

This refers to the cleaning of *unstructured textual data* (e.g., normalizing text). The high-frequency streamed real-time data is challenging to handle and could still present numerous problems and research challenges, which is why it is necessary to normalize it.

Website Analytics

Website analytics is mostly focused on characteristics, actions, and behaviors of corporate website visitors. One of the analytics that is increasingly gaining popularity is Google Analytics. By monitoring the job-searching portals like seeks.com.au, we observed that companies now want their potential employees to have skills in Google analytics.

News Analytics

News analytics deals with the measurement of the various qualitative and quantitative attributes of textual (unstructured data) news stories. Some of these attributes are sentiment, relevance, and novelty.

Social Media Environmental Capabilities

These are the overall organizational understanding and awareness related to regulations, security, ethical, and privacy issues surrounding social media use and data.

Laws and Regulations

Companies should be aware of the local government *laws* regarding the accessibility of public information while practicing social media analytics. In some countries, the government controls the political environment, and therefore the access to information on social media is restricted, which makes it challenging to gather social media data. In other countries, obtaining users' social media data is illegal and can have serious implications for the organization. Thus, understanding and adhering to laws and regulations related to social media data mining is crucial. It is vital for the ethical implications of the big data industry that the firms supplying the data should be assessed on how it respects privacy in the collection of information. Each country has a different set of rules and regulations about the collection of social media data/big data. For example, the use of big data in Europe faces a distinct set of regulatory constraints governed by the EU's Data Protection Directive (95/46/EC) and, for example, the United Kingdom's Data Protection Act 1998 (Martin, 2015).

Privacy Issues

As social media is proliferating, a critical concern for users is their *privacy*. Marketers need access to personal information on social media in order to make effective decisions, but users have a right to restrict the access of personal information to third the parties. The social media privacy issue got much momentum due to the large-scale "*Facebook Experiment*" carried out in 2012. Facebook deliberately manipulated the news feeds feature of thousands of people to see if emotion contagion occurs without face-to-face interaction (and absence of nonverbal cues) between people in social networks (Kramer, Guillory, & Hancock, 2014). Such experiments and social media data extraction practices for analytic purposes raise severe concerns regarding obtaining informed consent from participants and allowing them to opt out.

Social Media Cultural Capabilities

These capabilities include the overall *tacit* and *explicit* organizational norms, values, and behavioral readiness for social media data-based decision making (Leidner & Kayworth, 2006). The four core cultural capabilities are.

Executive Support and Leadership

The support of *top management* is vital for a social media data decision making culture. Leadership is needed to motivate and empower an organization to responsibly identify, collect, analyze, and interpret insights from social media data.

Solidarity

Solidarity refers to the degree to which an organization's members pursue shared objectives quickly and efficiently regardless of personal ties (Goffee & Jones, 1996). In an organization's cultural context, it is critical that the members of that organization have a sense of solidarity for social media data-based decision making. Having solidarity and a shared sense of responsibility could speed up the gathering, analyzing, and, efficient consumption of social media data.

Innovativeness

Innovativeness refers to the organization's values that emphasize challenge and risk-taking (Wallach, 1983). Organization innovativeness is the art of social media analytics. It consistently requires finding new ways to analyze and consume social media data efficiently. The organization should have the ability to take risks and explore new opportunities by employing social media data.

Organizational Supportiveness

It is the degree to which an organization has concerns for its employees (Wallach, 1983). Organizational support enables employees to work as a team, which in turn lead to higher performance in the collection, analyzing, and use of SMA data.

Social Media Governance Capabilities

These organizational capabilities include the overall organizational *adaptability*, *innovativeness*, and *alignment* of social media with business objectives.

Decision Making

Effective decisions making regarding the management of social media data is crucial for any organization. This includes the overall management of the appropriateness, availability, usability, integrity, ethics, and security of the social media data. To leverage it effectively organizations should have a sound *social media data governance program*, which includes a governing body, a defined set of procedures, and a plan to execute those procedures.

Strategic Alignment

This refers to the ability to *align* social media analytics goals and objectives with business objectives (Khan, 2015). To leverage it to its full potential, a social media analytics initiative should be strategically aligned with business goals and objectives.

Adaptability and Flexibility

Adaptability of an organization is defined as its capacity for internal change in response to external conditions (Denison & Mishra, 1995). Social media tools and technologies are in a constant state of flux. Social media data-driven decision-making requires flexibility and adaptability in all aspect of management. Be it willingness to consider social media data seriously or experimenting with new tools and platforms.

Change Management

This refers to the process of transitioning organizations to a social media *data-driven decision-making* culture. This may require management of resistance and provision of training to all sharcholders affected by business analytics initiatives.

Social Media People Related Capabilities

The social media people related capabilities are the capability area that is relevant to the human capital of the organization, such as, sociability and communication, and the availability of trained personnel in the field of SMA.

Sociability and Communication skills

These include both external and internal *sociability* and *communications* abilities of an origination. Social media data primarily comes from the organizational social media platforms where they interact and communicate with their customers. Consequently, organizational sociability and external communication abilities will determine the quality of data they can glean from their social media data. The rule is simple, the more significant and effective the engagement over social media, the better will be the data available for analytics purposes. Internal communication abilities are also crucial. Furthermore, the ability to effectively communicate analytics initiatives and results are necessary abilities for organizations embarking on social media data-driven decision-making.

Training and Empowerment

Social media data is highly unstructured and to make it work requires skilled data analysts, sophisticated tools, and technologies. To leverage social media data, *skilled data scientists* should be available and empowered to glean business insights from social media data.

Business Skills and Knowledge

One of the prime responsibilities of a social media analytics team is to translate and to communicate insights from data to the executives. However, doing so will be virtually impossible without having proper knowledge of business concepts, needs, and objectives. On the other hand, business executives should be aware of the social media potential and limitations.

Updating the Capabilities

And finally, due to the turbulent nature of social media technical and social environment, the SMA capabilities need to be consistently updated and adjusted as the usage of social media patterns, and the requirements of the organizations change over time.

Table 13.1. Social media analytics capabilities

Capabilities	Sub-capabilities	Definition
Social Media Technical Capabilities: The overall technical capabilities and infrastructure needed to extract, mind, and interpret social media data.	*Text Mining*	Text mining aims to extract meaningful information from unstructured textual, social media data, such as tweets, posts.
	Data Mining	Data mining is used to discover business insights from large-scale data.
	Networks Analytics	Social media network analytics extract, analyze, and interpret personal and professional social media networks.
	Sentiment Analysis	Sentiment analysis is the computational detection and study of opinions, sentiments, emotions, and subjectivities in a text.
	Website Analytics	Website analytics deals with analyzing website visitors' data and behavior.
	Multimedia Analytics	Multimedia analytics deals with analyzing social media multimedia contents.
	Data Cleansing	It refers to the cleaning of unstructured textual data, for example, normalizing text.
	Apps Analytics	Apps analytics deals with analyzing mobile applications data and behavior.
	Location Analytics	Location analytics deals with mining locations of social media users, contents, and data.
	Data Visualization	Refers to the visual representation of data with the goal of communicating it clearly.
	Search Engine Analytics	Search engines analytics focuses on analyzing historical search data.
	Hyperlink Analytics	Hyperlink analytics is used to extract, analyze, and interpret social media hyperlinks.
	News Analytics	It is the measurement of the various

Capabilities	Sub-capabilities	Definition
		qualitative and quantitative attributes of textual (unstructured data) news stories.
Social Media Environmental Capabilities: The overall organizational understanding and awareness related to social media data mining laws, regulations, security, and privacy issues.	*Laws and Regulations*	Organizations have to follow region specific and global laws in order to access data on social media.
	Privacy Issues	The questionable use of social media data is accessed by organizations without the users' consent
Social Media Cultural Capabilities: The cultural capability is the overall tacit and explicit organizational norms, values, and behavioral readiness for social media data-based decision making.	*Executive Support and Leadership*	Support from the top management and effective leadership.
	Solidarity	The degree to which an organization's members pursue shared objectives quickly and efficiently regardless of personal ties.
	Organizational Supportiveness	The degree to which the organization has concerns for its employees.
Social Media Governance Capabilities: The overall organizational adaptability, innovativeness, and alignment of social media with business objectives.	*Adaptability and Flexibility*	The capacity for internal change in response to external conditions.
	Innovativeness	Innovativeness refers to the organization's values that emphasize challenge and risk-taking.
	Strategic Alignment	The ability to align social media analytics goals and objectives with business objectives.
Social Media People related capabilities: The capability area that is relevant to the human capital of the organization.	*Sociability and Communication*	The tendency toward sincere friendliness among members of a community is sociability.
	Training and Empowerment	Personnel should be trained in the field of SMA and empowered to make decisions.

Capabilities	Sub-capabilities	Definition
	Business Skills and Knowledge	People in business analytics management areas execute the role of translating and communicating insights from data to the top management. That is why they need to understand (through business skills and knowledge) the value and utilization of such data.

REVIEW QUESTIONS

- What is the role of SMA capabilities in competitive advantage?
- Explain different technological and organizational skills and capabilities needed to define, align, capture, consume, and sustain SMA value creation.
- Explain different people, environmental, and cultural capabilities that analytics-driven organization must have.
- Briefly explain Karim et al., 2016's Social Media Analytics Capability Frameworks.

CHAPTER 13 REFERENCES

Abrahams, A. S., Fan, W., Wang, G. A., Zhang, Z., & Jiao, J. (2015). An Integrated Text Analytic Framework for Product Defect Discovery. *Production and Operations Management, 24*(6), 975-990. doi:10.1111/poms.12303

Cosic, R., Shanks, G., & Maynard, S. B. (2015). A business analytics capability framework. *2015, 19*. doi:10.3127/ajis.v19i0.1150

Denison, D. R., & Mishra, A. K. (1995). Toward a Theory of Organizational Culture and Effectiveness. *Organization Science, 6*(2), 204-223.

Goffee, R., & Jones, G. (1996). What Holds the Modern Company Together? . *Harvard Business Review, 74*(6), 133-148.

He, W., Wu, H., Yan, G., Akula, V., & Shen, J. (2015). A novel social media competitive analytics framework with sentiment benchmarks. *Information & Management, 52*(7), 801-812. doi:https://doi.org/10.1016/j.im.2015.04.006

Helfat, C. E., Finkelstein, S., Mitchell, W., Peteraf, M. A., Singh, H., Teece, D. J., & Winter, S. G. (2007). *Dynamic Capabilities: Understanding Strategic Change in Organisations*. Blackwell, Carlton.

Karim, A., Khan, N., & Khan, G. F. (2016). *A SOCIAL MEDIA ANALYTICS CAPABILITY FRAMEWORK FOR FIRM'S COMPETITIVE ADVANTAGE*. Paper presented at the PACIS 2016 Proceedings, Taiwan.

Khan, G. F. (2015). *Seven layers of social media analytics: Mining business insights from social media text, actions, networks, hyperlinks, apps, search engine, and location data.* CreateSpace.

Kramer, A. D. I., Guillory, J. E., & Hancock, J. T. (2014). Experimental evidence of massive-scale emotional contagion through social networks. *Proceedings of the National Academy of Sciences, 111*(24), 8788-8790. doi:10.1073/pnas.1320040111

Leidner, D. E., & Kayworth, T. (2006). A Review of Culture in Information Systems Research: Toward a Theory of Information Technology Culture Conflict. *MIS Quarterly, 30*(2).

Martin, K. E. (2015). Ethical issues in the big data industry. *MIS Quaterly Executive, 14*(2), 67-85.

Pang, B., & Lee, L. (2014). *A sentimental education: Sentiment analysis using subjectivity*. Paper presented at the Proceedings of ACL.

Shank, G., & Bekmamedova, N. (2011, 29th November to 2nd December 2011). *Creating Value from Business Analytics Systems: A Process-oriented Theoretical Framework and Case Study* Paper presented at the 22nd Australasian Conference on Information Systems, 29th November to 2nd December 2011, Sydney.

Teece, D. J. (2009). *Strategic Management and Dynamic Capabilities*. New York.: Oxford University Press.

Teece, D. J., Pisano, G., & Shuen, A. (1999). Dynamic capabilities and strategic management. *Strategic Management Journal, 18*, 509-533.

Vogel, V., Evanschitzky, H., & Ramaseshan, B. (2008). Customer Equity Drivers and Future Sales. *Journal of Marketing, 72*(6), 98-108. doi:10.1509/jmkg.72.6.98

Wallach, E. J. (1983). "Individuals and Organizations: The Cultural Match. *Training and Development Journal 37*(2), 28-35.

Watson, H., Ariyachandra, T., & Matyska, R. J. (2001). Data Warehousing Stages of Growth. *Information Systems Management, 18*(3), 42-50. doi:10.1201/1078/43196.18.3.20010601/31289.6

Yeoh, W., & Koronios, A. (2010). Critical Success Factors for Business Intelligence Systems. *Journal of Computer Information Systems, 50*(3), 23-32. doi:10.1080/08874417.2010.11645404

Zaki, M. J., & Jr., W. M. (2014). *Data mining and analysis*: Cambridge University Press.

Chapter 14

Social Media Legal, Privacy, and Security Issues

"Getting information off the Internet is like taking a drink from a firehose."—**Mitchell Kapor**

Learning Outcomes

After completing this chapter, the reader should be able to:

- Understand common social media risks and privacy issues.
- Comprehend social media risks management framework.
- Understand social media risks mitigation strategies.
- Know the different types of social media data and the privacy issues surrounding them.
- Be familiar with techniques and strategies to secure social media accounts.

INTRODUCTION

Engaging through social media introduces new challenges related to privacy, security, data management, accessibility, social inclusion, governance, and other information security issues such as hacking and cyber-warfare.

Risk is the possibility of losing something of value such as intellectual or physical capital. A comprehensive definition of risk is provided by the *National Institute of Standards and Technology* (NIST), which states, "Risk is a function of the likelihood of a given threat sources exercising a particular potential vulnerability, and the resulting impact of that adverse event on the organization." Here, we will focus on the risk arising from social media use and define it as the potential of losing something of value (such as information, reputation, or goodwill) due to the use of social media. In this chapter, we will discuss three aspects of social media risks:

- Legal Risks
- Privacy Risks
- Security Risks

LEGAL RISKS

Legal risk is the potential of losing something of value (such as information, reputation, or goodwill) due to the lack of knowledge of the way laws and regulations apply to a business. When it comes to legal issues surrounding social media, it essentially answers the question: *what your customer and competitors can sue or be sued for*. We will try to answer this question in light of the following significant social media legal risks:

- Defamation: Libel and Slander.
- Copyright: Sharing something that is not yours.
- Trademark: confusing customers about trademarks.
- Spam: sending unwanted messages/posts.
- Negligence: assuming a duty and not fulfilling it.
- Discrimination in hiring practices, and
- Sexual harassment and unwanted social media posting.

Next, we briefly explain some of these in the context of social media.

Defamation

Defamation is a false statement (written or spoken) about someone, which damages that person's reputation. It has two forms:

Libel

Libel is a defamatory statement in written form (e.g., social media comments or post).

Slander

Slander is when a defamatory statement is in spoken form (e.g., audio or video posted on social media).

Defamation and Social Media

Posting defamatory content on social media can have serious consequences. For example, a former Orange High School student was ordered to pay $10,500 in damage for defaming a school teacher on Facebook and Twitter (Figure 14.1).

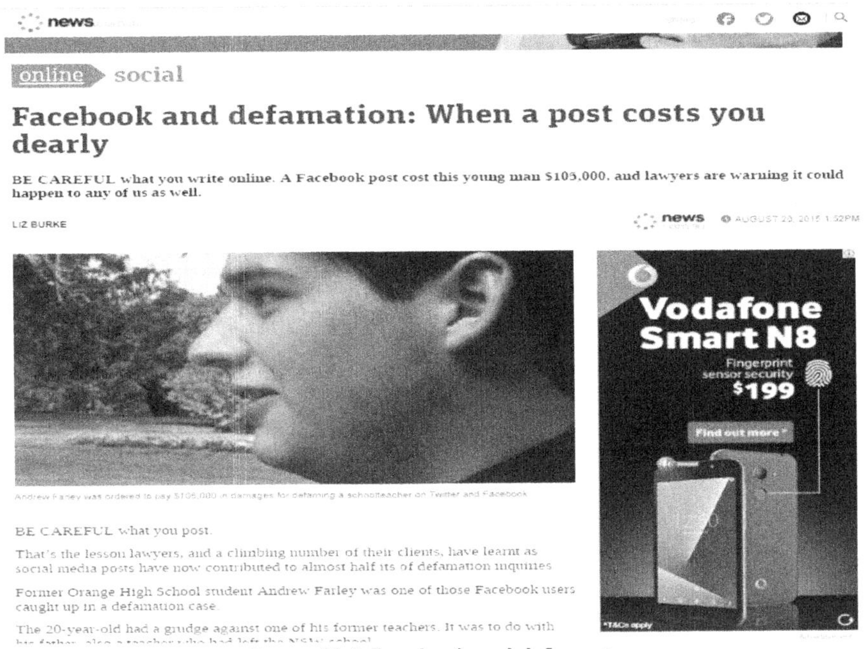

news

online social

Facebook and defamation: When a post costs you dearly

BE CAREFUL what you write online. A Facebook post cost this young man $105,000, and lawyers are warning it could happen to any of us as well.

LIZ BURKE

news AUGUST 20, 2015 1:52PM

Andrew Farley was ordered to pay $105,000 in damages for defaming a schoolteacher on Twitter and Facebook

BE CAREFUL what you post.

That's the lesson lawyers, and a climbing number of their clients, have learnt as social media posts have now contributed to almost half its of defamation inquiries

Former Orange High School student Andrew Farley was one of those Facebook users caught up in a defamation case.

The 20-year-old had a grudge against one of his former teachers. It was to do with

Figure 14.1. Facebook and defamation

Defamation in the context of social media is, however, a complicated issue. To understand its complexity, consider the case of KitchenAid: an American home appliance brand owned by Whirlpool Corporation. KitchenAid came under scrutiny when one of its employees posted defamatory remarks about President Obama from the KitchenAid official account (see Figure 14.2). Essential questions that are raised here are (note that answering these questions will largely depend on the country where you live):

Q1. Does Libel law even apply to a tweet?
Yes. In most countries "Libel laws apply to the Internet the same way they do to newspapers, magazines, books, films, and other similar publications" (Luara, 2014, p.53). Thus, in most countries, the medium for communication is irrelevant in defamation laws. It could be a letter, an email, a social media post, a video, an audio, and other communication methods.

Obamas gma even knew it was going 2 b bad! 'She died 3 days b4 he became president'. #nbcpolitics

Figure 14.2. Defamatory tweet by KitchenAid employee

Q2. Can Twitter be held liable for defamatory comments posted by its users?
No. Under the United States Law, Twitter is protected under the Communications Decency Act (CDA) 1996, which provides immunity from liability for service providers and users who publish information provided by others (user-generated content). However, to qualify for protection, a service provider must follow a proper notice and takedown procedure, inform its customers of its policies, and meet several other requirements set by law.

Q3. Who is responsible for the Kitchen Aid tweet? The employee who tweeted and/or the company who owns the Twitter account.
KitchenAid may also be protected under the CDA act, given that they have clear policies, guidelines, and training about using cooperate social media. However, the actual outcome will depend on the nature of the case. So, one can assume that the employee who tweeted is responsible.

Q4. Does the responsibility extend to those around the world who retweeted the tweet?
It depends. The actual legal implication of retweeting (retransmitting) a defamatory statement may vary based on a country, a Twitter user's location, and the location of the Twitter account, among other things. For example, based on the CDA, "*no provider or user of an interactive computer service shall be treated as the publisher or speaker of any information provided by another information content provider.*" In other words, this means a person cannot be sued for something they retweet, even if the original tweet is defamatory, as long as the libelous content was created by a third-party. However, according to Judith Delaney (an attorney who specializes in online privacy issues):

> "*If you or an entity tweets or retweets something defamatory, and even if you or an entity quickly deletes it and follows it up with a correction or an apology, no matter where you or that entity may be in most parts of the world, such actions most likely will not affect the potential viability of a libel claim against you and/or an entity whether as the "Tweeter" or the "Retweeter"*." (Delaney, 2013).

Similarly, based on New Zealand's Harmful Digital Communications Act 2015 (HDCA), a person may be held liable for spreading information that was already in the public domain (e.g., re-tweeting a defamatory tweet or sharing someone's data which was deliberately made available by a hacker), given that it harms the individual whom the information is about, and it is unfair and unreasonable for a person to share that data.

The HDCA (which became law on 3 July 2015) is intended to discourage, prevent, and reduce harmful digital communications posted online through emails, text, websites, applications, or social media. Examples of harmful digital communications include:

- sending or publishing threatening or offensive material.
- spreading harmful stories.
- sending or publishing sensitive personal information such as humiliating photos and videos.

Here are the 10 principles of the HDCA:

Principle 1—a digital communication should not disclose sensitive personal facts about an individual.

Principle 2—a digital communication should not be threatening, intimidating, or menacing.

Principle 3—a digital communication should not be grossly offensive to a reasonable person in the position of the affected individual.

Principle 4—a digital communication should not be indecent or obscene.

Principle 5—a digital communication should not be used to harass an individual.

Principle 6—a digital communication should not make a false allegation.

Principle 7—a digital communication should not contain a matter that is published in breach of confidence.

Principle 8—a digital communication should not incite or encourage anyone to send a message to an individual for the purpose of causing harm to the individual.

Principle 9—a digital communication should not incite or encourage an individual to commit suicide.

Principle 10—a digital communication should not denigrate an individual by reason of his or her color, race, ethnic or national origins, religion, gender, sexual orientation, or disability.

Intellectual Property

Intellectual property (IP) is the creations of the mind, which includes computer programs, music, and literature, discoveries, inventions, words, phrases, symbols, and designs, etc. Intellectual Property Rights (IPRs) are the rights granted to the creators of IP, which includes:

Copyright

The purpose of *copyright* is to protect works of authorship (books, work of art, photos, and computer code). The legal question that surfaces here is *who owns the IP rights of content (ideas, documents, pictures, and songs) posted on social media?* The answer is obvious, the original creator. However, most social media posting (e.g., tweets and comments) may not meet the minimum IP creativity criteria and may not have copyright protection.

Trademarks

The purpose of a *trademark* is to protect words, phrases, and logos used in commerce. You may, for example, be held liable for creating a brand handler/account similar to competitors that may confuse social media users. There may also be a liability for the use of a competitor's trademarks in Google AdWords, AdSense, and website meta-tags.

Trade Secrets

Trade secrets are any business information not generally known to the public. Trade secrets may include, for example, a formula, algorithm, design, recipes, process, and a method. Trade secrets can easily be leaked on social media, often mistakenly. An employee leaking trade secrets through social media (or any other medium) breaches:

- The duty of loyalty.
- Breach of contractual confidentially.
- Non-disclosure agreement.
- Misappropriation of trade secrets.

Breaching the above agreements can lead to job termination and legal consequences. Here are some strategies to stop it from happening:

- Have an updated social media use policies (e.g., the policy should clearly state that employees should not discuss the company's plans over social media).

- Always have an updated non-disclosure agreement in place; being a legal document, it prohibits material, knowledge, or information exchange with third parties.
- Always conduct exit interviews.
- Have a comprehensive training and awareness program related to social media use and trade secrets.

Spam

A commercial, irrelevant, or unsolicited message sent over the Internet is considered *spam*. An electronic message is considered commercial if it promotes products, services, land, an interest in land, or an investment opportunity. Most countries have laws regulating spam. For example, in New Zealand, the Unsolicited Electronic Messages Act 2007 regulates spam or junk or unwanted messages. To comply with the law, the following actions are recommended.

Obtain Consent

Prior to sending any commercial message, *obtain consent* (written or verbal). In the social media context, send messages only to people who follow you. People who follow over Twitter, for example, have already opted (through Twitter's service agreement) to receiving your direct messages. For any other commercial electronic messages, always use *opt-in* and *opt-out* options.

Provide opt-in and opt-out options

Opt-in require a customer to actively tick a box to receive further messages (Figure 14.3).

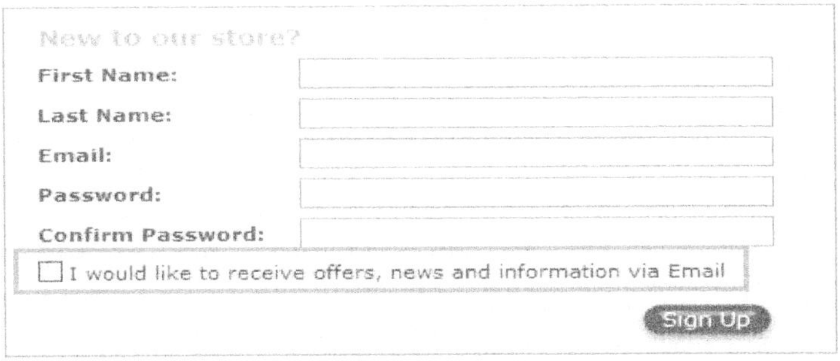

New to our store?
First Name:
Last Name:
Email:
Password:
Confirm Password:
I would like to receive offers, news and information via Email
Sign Up

Figure 14.3. Opt-in example

Opt-out requires customers to un-tick a pre-ticked box to not receive further correspondence (Figure 14.4). Furthermore, a commercial message should clearly and correctly identify the sender and the message should include precise information about how the recipient can readily contact the sender.

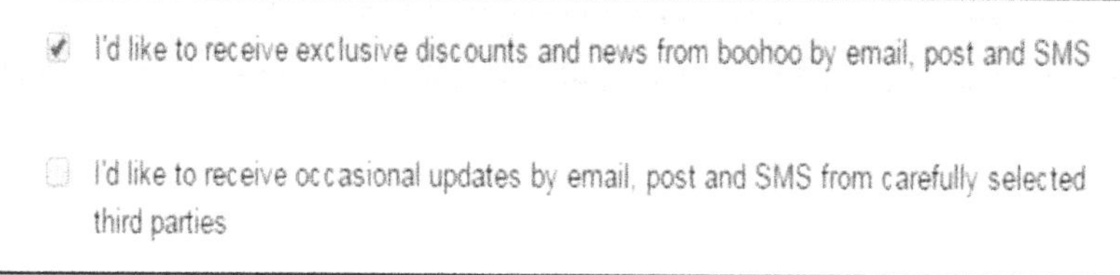

I'd like to receive exclusive discounts and news from boohoo by email, post and SMS
I'd like to receive occasional updates by email, post and SMS from carefully selected third parties

Figure 14.4. Opt-out example

SOCIAL MEDIA PRIVACY ISSUES

Privacy is "the right to be let alone" (Warren & Brandeis, 1980) (p.195). In other words, it is the right of a person to isolate themselves, or information about themselves, and thereby express themselves selectively. Engaging through social media has essential privacy implication for brands. Privacy in the context of social media is the ability to decide what *information* one discloses or withholds about oneself on social media, who has access to such information, and for what purposes one's information may or may not be used. On social media, the issue of privacy may surface if a person's information is accessed, used, and shared when the individual had a reasonable expectation of privacy. It is interesting to note that social media users voluntarily sacrifice their privacy in exchange for using the social media platforms and services. Research into privacy issues suggests that people are more likely to voluntarily sacrifice privacy if the data collector is perceived to be transparent about the nature of the information being collected and how it is used (Oulasvirta, 2014). The following is summary of the fundamental concepts related to privacy (Solove, 2008):

1. **The right to be let alone**—the fundamental right of an individual to isolate themselves, or information about themselves, and thereby express themselves selectively.
2. **Limiting access to one's personal information**—it refers to a person's ability to participate in society without having other individuals and organizations collect information about them.
3. **Secrecy**—the option or ability to conceal any information from others.
4. **Control over information**—it is the control over others' use of information about oneself. Control over one's personal information is the concept that "privacy is the claim of individuals, groups, or institutions to determine for themselves when, how, and to what extent information about them is communicated to others." (Solove, 2008) (p. 24).

5. **States of privacy**—there are four states of privacy: 1) solitude, 2) intimacy, 3) anonymity, and 4) reserve (Westin, 1967). *Solitude* is state of a physical separation from other individuals in a society/community. *Intimacy* is a "close, relaxed, and frank relationship between two or more individuals" that normally results from the isolation of a pair or small group of individuals. *Anonymity* is the "desire of individuals for times of 'public privacy." Finally, *reserve* is the "creation of a psychological barrier against unwanted intrusion;" this creation of a psychological barrier requires others to respect an individual's need or desire to restrict communication of information concerning himself or herself.

PRIVACY AND SOCIAL MEDIA DATA

A wide array of *data types* are generated, stored, and distributed over social media platforms. Understanding social media data types is crucial not only for analytical purposes but also for *social media privacy issues*. Later in this chapter, we discuss various social media data types and the privacy concerns associated with them. However, speaking from a user's perspective, social media data can be divided into, a) public data and b) private data. *Public data* is something that is seen by anyone connected to the Internet. Examples of public data on Facebook include profile photos, social media ID (handler), country, the public groups a user is a member of, and anything that a user has made available to the public. Similarly, any data that a user has not made available to the public is *private data*, for example, address, gender, work address, email, and phone numbers. In essence, deciding if some data is public or private hinges on the privacy settings of the social media applications in use. Normally, social media applications allow users to control what information they want to make public or private. Facebook users, for example, can use the "View As" tool (available from the profile page) to check how their profile looks to the outside world. This will let a user know which portion of their information is publically available. However, one thing to note is that regardless of a user's privacy settings, both private and public information is always available to the social media platforms. For example, Facebook privacy policy describes what information they collect, how it is used and shared.

> *"We collect the content and other information you provide when you use our Services, including when you sign up for an account, create or share, and message or communicate with others. This can include information in or about the content you provide, such as the location of a photo or the date a file was created. We also collect information about how you use our Services, such as the types of content you view or engage with or the frequency and duration of*

your activities." (Facebook Privacy Policy, 2018).

Social Media Data and Third Party Apps

Most social media *third-party apps* and games request personal information before it can be used. Consequently, when a social media user installs an app, they give it permission to access their information (e.g., name, profile pictures, username, user ID, networks, friends' info, gender, age range and locale, and any info the users choose to make publicly available). The information collected from social media platforms (e.g., Facebook) by third-party apps (e.g., Facebook games) is subject to their own terms and policies. In other words, they can do whatever their terms and policies allow them to do. For example, Cambridge Analytica harvested and used the data of 87 million Facebook users to psychologically profile voters during the 2016 US election. Technically, the third-party app developers should use the information to (but it is not always the case):

- Help the users find friends that also use the app.
- Provide a personalized experience to the user.
- Make it easier to share information with friends on social media (e.g., Facebook).

However, due to the recent *Cambridge Analytica* data breach, social media data access and use policies will significantly change. At the time of writing this book, *Mark Zuckerberg* (while giving testimony to Senate committees) promised to significantly alter the way Facebook data is accessed and shared with third-party application developers.

Disable or Revoke Third-Party Apps

Third-party apps are developed by other companies but have access to social media platforms (e.g., Facebook) via its *application programming interface* (API). While third-party apps improve your social media experience (e.g., if you allow access to the WordPress app, your Facebook updates will automatically appear on your wordpress.com blog), some of them may be vulnerable to attacks or may handle users information insecurely. Here is how to disable the vulnerable apps on Facebook.

Steps: Login to your account → "Account Settings" → "Apps and Websites" → "Logged in with Facebook" → Select and → "Remove."

However, by disabling access to third-party apps, a Facebook user will not able to:

- Log into apps or websites using Facebook.

- Apps and websites you have logged into with Facebook may delete your accounts and activity.
- Play some games on Facebook, and your gaming activity may be deleted
- Your posts, photos, and videos on Facebook that apps and websites have published may be deleted.
- To interact with or share content from other apps and websites on Facebook using social plugins such as the Share and Like buttons.

Collecting Personal Data

Most privacy laws require that businesses should not collect personal information on individuals unless 1) the information is collected for a legal purpose necessary to carry out certain functions or activity of the company and 2) the functions or activities cannot be performed without the collection of the information. In addition, where the information collection is paramount and it is not publically available, it should be collected directly from the individual concerned. Based on New Zealand's Privacy Act 1993 (and the subsequent amendments), when information is directly collected from an individual, the agency must make sure that the individual is aware of:

a) the fact that the information is being collected; and
b) the purpose for which the information is being collected; and
c) the intended recipients of the information; and
d) the name and address of the agency that is collecting the information; and
e) the agency that will hold the information; and
f) if the collection of the information is authorized or required by or under the law; the particular law by or under which the collection of the information is so authorized or required; and
g) whether or not the supply of the information by that individual is voluntary or mandatory; and
h) the consequences (if any) for that individual if all or any part of the requested information is not provided; and
i) the rights of access to, and correction of, personal information provided by these principles.

An important question to ask is *under what circumstances can businesses access social media data*? In reference to New Zealand's Privacy Act 1993, an individual's information may be collected from other sources (e.g., social media) and not directly from the individual if the entity collecting the information believes (on reasonable grounds) that:

a) the information is publically available, or
b) consent is obtained from the individual concerned, or
c) the information will be used for statistical or research purposes, or
d) the information will not be published in a form that could reasonably be expected to identify the individual concerned, or
e) compliance is not reasonably practicable in the circumstances of the particular case (for detailed discussion on the other exceptions, read New Zealand's Privacy Act 1993).

To fully comprehend social media privacy and legal issues, let us discuss different social media data types.

SOCIAL MEDIA DATA TYPES

While there is no universally accepted social media data framework, Richthammer et al., (2014) have developed a *taxonomy* for classifying social media data types. The framework also provides the privacy implications stemming from different data types. Figure 14.5 provides an overview of the taxonomy which comprises 13 data types that are integrated into a hierarchical structure (Richthammer, et al., 2014). From the perspective of parties involved, we can classify social media data into two classes.

- **Service providers related data**: service providers (such as Facebook) provide social media platforms and related services whereas the users' personal data commonly provides the basis of their business model.
- **Social media users' related data**: Social media users use personal data to get access and use a social media platform.

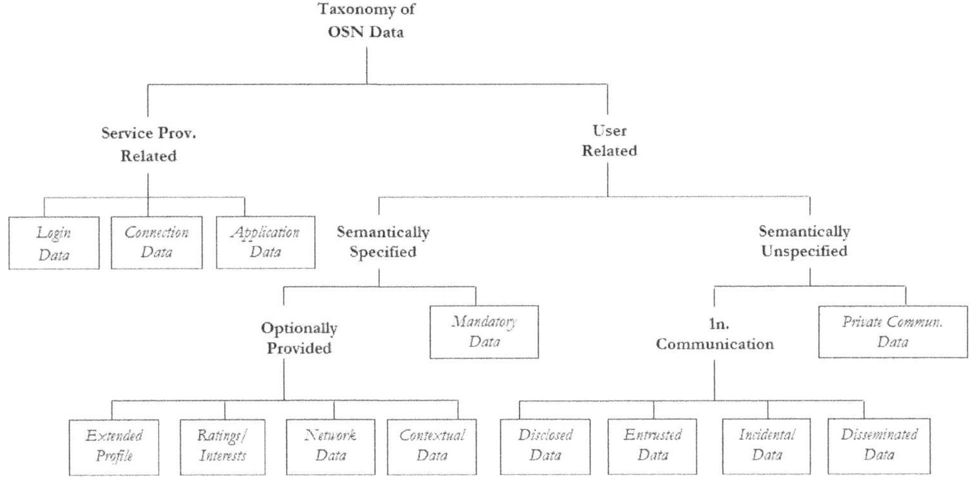

Figure 14.5. Social media data type taxonomy

Service Provider Related Data Types

Mainly, there are three types of service provided related social media data types: login data, connection data, and application data. Below, we discuss each of it with accompanying privacy concerns.

Login data

Login data is required for verification purposes to identify social media users and prevent identity theft. Common types of such data are a username, password, and an email address.

> *Privacy Implications*—uniquely identifiable information used to access social media platforms, such as, an email address and username may allow other users to access a user's personal information that was not intended for them. Thus, access to login data may lead to privacy violation of the social media users.

Connection Data

Connection data—which is not social media specific and used to connect to and use Internet—includes user's IP (Internet Protocol) address, the type of communication devices (smartphone or personal computers), information related to the browser and the operating system, and location (derived from the IP address or using GPS).

Privacy Implications—connection data leave a variety of digital traces that are considered private information. Particularly the Internet browsing habits and user's location data are considered sensitive information. It may violate user's privacy when made available (without a user's consent) to social media service providers through internet cookies and browsing history. Research suggests that cyber-attacks, such as browser fingerprinting attacks, can be employed to identify Internet users solely based on their HTTP headers (an HTTP header is used to communicate between a client computer and a web server) (Eckersley, 2010). The header data may not be sensitive from the privacy perspective per se, but rather the potential to use this data to invade privacy through de-anonymizing users and linking previously unrelated personal information.

Application data

Application data includes data originating from the use of third-party services that have access to the social media platforms, for example, through APIs (application users interface). Well-known examples of application data include social media application usage statistics, social media games, or in-app purchase data such as credit card information.

Privacy Implications—application data has both privacy and security risks. Application data security mostly hinge on the honesty and protection mechanisms of the service provider (e.g., Facebook) and third-party service providers (e.g., Facebook games) who have access to a social media user's account. If application data is not handled carefully, it may lead to grave consequences such as credit card fraud and identify theft. Privacy may be threatened if third-party usage statistics become available publically. For instance, an employer may notice that one of her employees is spending time on social media games during working hours.

User-Related Data Types

While users engage with social media platforms in many ways and generate a variety of data types; user-related social media data can be essentially classified into two: *semantically specified* and *semantically unspecified* data (Richthammer et al., 2014).

- **Semantically Specified**: this data type has a clearly defined meaning and can be easily understood, such as profile name, birthdate, and hometown.
- **Semantically Unspecified**: unlike semantically specified data, this data is not clearly defined and let users freely express aspects of their personality. Examples include discretion, posts, and status updates.

However, considering the diverse nature of social media, it is not always possible to classify data types into one or other type, as some parts of a data type are semantically specified while others remain unspecified.

Semantically Specified

Semantically specific data is used for self-description and expression of one's personality. It can be further subdivided into mandatory and optional data types.

Mandatory data

Mandatory data is the minimum amount of personal data required (mainly at registration stage) by a social media platform for user discovery, profile creations, and verification purposes. This data is primarily required to get things started. Examples of such data include a user's age and name.

> *Privacy Implications*—Privacy implications for mandatory data depend on the actual privacy setting of the social media platforms. It needs to be examined whether mandatory data becomes part of a user's profile and if the privacy settings are available to restrict its visibility.

Optionally Provided Data

In addition to the mandatory data, several *optional data* types are stored on social media platforms. Here we discuss some essential types.

Extended Profile Data*:* This data includes several other types of predefined profile attributes that can be used to describe particular aspects of one's personality, such as postal address, education, hobbies, favorite actors, favorite films, and interests.

> *Privacy Implications*—since this data type is optionally required, the privacy risks associated with this data are manageable as it is up to the user to decide whether to disclose a particular personal attribute. However, the available privacy settings are to be considered as these define the granularity of the potential audience that may access an attribute.

Ratings/Interests*:* this type of data covers expressed interests and symbolic reactions to social media contents through liking, sharing, commenting, and viewing.

> *Privacy Implications*—ratings, interested, and reactions to social media contents are typically widely distributed across social media and the

Internet. Therefore, from the privacy point of view, a user's expressed ratings and interests are crucial, as it may allow others to draw inferences from all instances of this data type about a user's personality. Major social media platforms use this data to offer personalized suggestions and commercial ads.

Network Data: By its very nature, social media is a *network media*, i.e., users forge friendship ties and relationship with other users. Thus, *network data* includes all the data related to the network the user has built around themselves on social media. The network data which is the collection of all connections of a particular user is also known as the social graph (Beye et al., 2012). As discussed in an earlier chapter, social media networks include friendship networks, following-follower network, and fan networks, and so forth.

Privacy Implications—access to social media network data can have significant privacy and security implications. For example, knowledge of a user's social graph can be used to draw inferences about the identity and behavior of a user. Furthermore, knowledge of a social graph can also be used to launch 'Sybil attacks' where attackers use false/forged identities to gain unlawful access to a secure system (Carminati, Ferrari, & Viviani, 2013). Research also suggests that partial knowledge of a social graph (such as knowledge of groups a person is a member of) is enough to reveal the identity of a social media user (Wondracek, Holz, Kirda, & Kruegel, 2010).

Contextual data: contextual data is usually a *byproduct* of its primary data type, which normally is not clearly visible to the user. For example, a shared picture (primary data) may contain a variety of information including the camera model, camera owner, and location (contextual data). Contextual data is often machine-processable.

Privacy Implications— the machine-readable and by-product nature of the contextual data, for example, allows social media service providers to gather information without the knowledge of the social media users. Hence, subject to privacy concerns.

Semantically Unspecified

Semantically unspecified data refers to data types whose format is *predefined* (by the social media service providers), but the data content per se is left to the user to manipulate. For example, a photo album feature predefines the format (digital photos) but leaves the picture content to the user to fill in. Currently, machines cannot interpret this data. Nevertheless, technology developments (such as face image recognition) are increasingly making it possible to make these datatypes machine-readable.

Privacy Implications—due to its nature, on the one hand, it is problematic to draw a conclusion based on privacy risks associated with semantically unspecified data types, where risks mainly hinge on nature of the content. On the other hand, the absence of semantic specification obstructs social media service providers from mechanically processing this data.

Private Communication Data

This class includes data originating from *private communication* between two social media users. Although private communication may encompass text messages including other media formats, their content is not semantically specified. Examples include private messages with or without attachments, private video chats, as well as smaller interactions such as poking other users.

Privacy implications—private communication data is usually not visible to third parties outside the conversation. Hence it does not bear any privacy risks as long as the communication partner can be trusted. The social media security mechanisms prevent third parties from getting access, and the social media service provider does not inspect the messages to an extent higher than automatically scanning them for illegal content.

n Communication

In addition to private communication between two social media users, data with semantically unspecified content can be shared with an 'n' number of other social media users. This mode of information sharing or communication is concerned with semantically unstructured data (such as photos, status messages, and comments) and leads to three possible data types:

- Disclosed Data
- Entrusted Data
- Incidental Data
- Disseminated Data

Note that from the Table 14.1, though the data elements are of similar nature, a differentiation is made between the creator (the original author of the content), publisher (of the content), and the domain (logical boundary of user's social media sphere) log in which the data element is published.

Disclosed Data: it is the data/content/information created and published by a social media user in their *own domain* or within the logical boundary of their social media sphere. Examples of disclosed data include posting comments, photos, and videos on one's own social media profile or wall.

Privacy Implication—privacy of disclosed data mainly depends on the privacy settings of the social media applications (e.g., the data can be visible to the world or only to one's friends). Apart from this, privacy rights may not be breached, as the user is both the creator and publisher of the item (i.e., the person intentionally wants the data to be visible to others), and it is shared within the domain of the user (no other users are affected with the shared item).

Entrusted Data: *Entrusted data*, however, refers to information that is both user-generated and user-published but in the domain of another social media user (a friend for example). Posting or commenting on the other user's social media profile, wall/news feed, or blog.

Privacy Implication—once the data is posted in the domain of another social media user, control passes over to the domain owner who controls its visibility. Privacy implications mainly arise from the loss of control once the data element is published.

Table 14.1. Differences between disclosed, entrusted, incidental, and shared data

	Creator	Publisher	Domain
Disclosed data	User	User	User
Entrusted data	User	User	Contact
Incidental data	Contact	Contact	User
Disseminated data	User	Contact	Contact

(Source: Richthammer et al., 2014)

Incidental Data: *Incidental data* is the inverse of entrusted data. It originates from a social media friend (contact) sharing a data element on the user's wall. In this case, the friend is both the creator and publisher; however, the information is shared in the user's domain.

Privacy Implication—in this scenario, the user gains control over the data, whereas the extent depends on the social media platform privacy sharing settings.

Disseminated Data: This type includes the user-generated data elements that are further distributed by a *contact* (friend) within their own domain or within the logical boundary of their social media sphere. This may include data elements that the user has initially shared with a contact or provided to him/her using other communication channels (such as face-to-face and private communication).

Privacy Implication—in this scenario serious privacy issues may arise because the contact remains the only person to control the visibility of the data. However, the social media platform may prevent the contact from publishing the item with a larger than the user's intended audience and grant additional permissions to the user.

OTHER SOCIAL MEDIA PRIVACY AND ETHICAL ISSUES

Some other crucial social media privacy and ethical issues to be aware of include the following.

Correlation of Low Sensitivity Data

Crunching, analyzing, and correlating *individual instances* of social media data (such as gender, age, and postal code) can potentially reveal sensitive information. According to Buytendijk and Heiser (Financial Times, 2013), "the triple identifier" (birthday, gender and postcode) are all that is required to identify at least 87% of American citizens in publically available databases.

Lack of Consent

Users of social media platforms often *ignore privacy warnings* and terms of use. As a result, users may be unaware that multiple parties are using their data without their consent and that it likely has identifiable information attached.

Vulnerable Participants

Social media makes it difficult to identify *vulnerable participants* such as children, the elderly, or those with special needs. People often shield their identity on social media platforms making it hard to identify who is providing the information.

Managerial Actions

When it comes to social media data privacy and ethics, businesses should take the following actions to ensure that they are not violating these issues.

Accessing Public and Protected Data

Just because data is publically available, it does not mean it is legal and ethical to access it. As mentioned early, you may be liable for accessing publically available information, if it harms the individual whom the information is about and it is unfair and unreasonable for you to share that data. Similarly, accessing *protected data* (e.g., one that requires membership approval) or if the group is password protected is illegal and unethical. Thus, always seek informed consent from participants before using the data that you suspect may have ethical and privacy consequences.

Anonymity

If data is used outside the organization that obtained it, ensure *anonymity* of data sources unless informed consent is requested from users. Maintaining anonymity can be difficult, particularly with social media where individual data such as tweets are reproduced or retweeted on a regular basis.

Comply with social media terms

Ensure you are complying with the *terms and conditions* of social media platforms. Some social media platforms enforce terms and conditions regarding data such as the use of data by third-parties. These terms and conditions can continuously change, thus keep yourself updated.

Be aware of vulnerable participants

Attaining data through social media makes it difficult to *identify vulnerable participants*. While an individual may display himself or herself as particular age or gender, there is no guarantee that this information is accurate. If you suspect that the data has originated from a vulnerable participant, exclude this information immediately.

Dealing with sensitive data

Personal data such as date of birth, phone, email, criminal activity, financial data, health data, and sexuality have the potential to harm a user. If you feel the data you are accessing is *sensitive*, obtain consent and anonymize it, to make sure it cannot be tracked back to a user's personal profile. If neither is possible, consider disregarding the information entirely (Townsend & Wallace, 2016).

Ensure you have a good privacy policy

Ensure that you have a sound *privacy policy* based on the relevant data privacy laws in your country. In your privacy policy, include clauses relating to what information you are collecting, how the data will be used, how the data will be stored and shared, and who will have access to the data.

MANAGING SOCIAL RISKS

Social media related risks need to be adequately managed, both from the strategic and technological points of view. Organizations need *proactive*, rather than reactive, *social media risk-management strategy*. A simple but effective way to proactively manage social media risks is through the social media crisis management loop (Figure 14.6), which includes four iterative steps:

- **Identify** - In the identification stage, potential risks are identified.
- **Assess** - In the assessment stage, risks are assessed and prioritized regarding the probability of occurrence and impact on the organization.
- **Mitigate** - In the mitigation stage, risk reduction strategies are formulated and implemented.
- **Evaluate** - Periodic assessment and reviews are carried out in the evaluation stage of the risk-management loop.

Below, we discuss each step in detail.

Risk Identification

Risk identification is the process of identifying social media threats regarding vulnerabilities and exploits that could potentially inhibit the organization from achieving its objectives. At this stage, the goal is to determine potential accidental or malicious risks that can come from within or outside the company. Examples of social media related security breaches are hacking, information leaks, phishing, and impersonation. Phishing and hacking are examples of malicious outsider attacks.

While not exactly a social media platform, 500 million Yahoo! Accounts were breached in 2014, but the public did not get to find out about until the news was announced in February 2016. The theft included names, email addresses, telephone numbers, dates of birth, and in some cases, encrypted or unencrypted security questions, and answers. Yahoo believed the theft (the most significant security breach ever to have taken place in the history of the United States) was state-sponsored (i.e., Russia, China, and Iran). Well-known social media platforms (such as Facebook, Twitter, and YouTube) are more prone to security breaches (Webber, 2012).

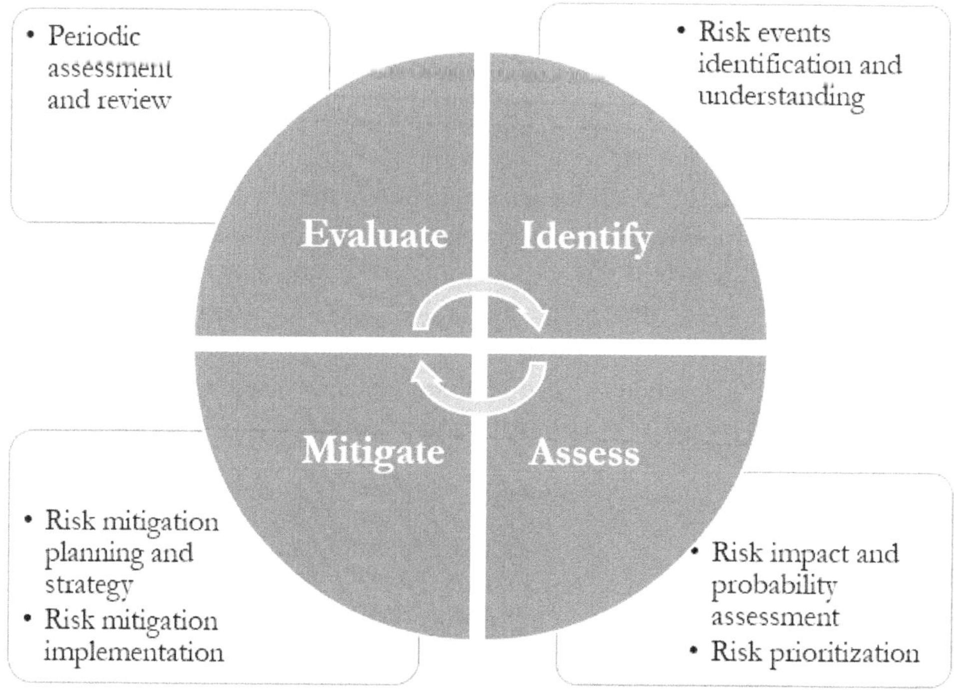

Figure 14.6. Social media risk management framework

According to a study based on surveys and interviews with ninety-nine professionals and thirty-six companies (Webber, 2012), the main social media risks identified are the following.

- Damage to reputation
- The release of confidential information
- Legal, regulatory, and compliance violations
- Identity theft and hijacking
- Loss of intellectual property

Other potential social media risks include malware, loss of privacy, and social engineering attacks.

Risk Assessment

Risk assessment is "the process of assessing the probabilities and consequences of risk events if they are realized" (MITRE, 2014). The risk evaluation process determines the likelihood of a social media risk event that could influence the organization economically, technically, politically, and socially. The potential risks identified in the earlier step are prioritised and ranked based on the probability of occurrence and impact on an organization (Garvey, 2008).

Probability (P) is the likelihood of occurrence of a risk event and can take a value from 0 to 1. Probability can, for example, be assigned to risks events as follows.

- *Certain to occur (P=1)*—the risks with a P value equal to 1 are the risks that will undoubtedly happen. In other words, they have a 100 percent chance of occurring.

- *Extremely sure to occur (P=> 95 <1)*—the risks, for example, with a probability value greater than 0.95 and less than 1.0 can be considered as "extremely sure to happen" risks. In other words, they have a 95–100 percent chance of occurring.

- *Almost sure to occur (P= > 0.85 <= 0.95)*—the risks with a probability value greater than 0.85 and less than or equal to 0.95 can be considered as "very likely to occur" risks. The can be said to have an 85–95 percent chance of occurring.

- *Very likely to occur (P=> 0.75 <=0.85)*—these are the risks with a 75–85 percent chance of occurring.

- *Likely to occur (P=> 0.65 <=0.75)*—these are the risks with a 65 to 75 percent chance of occurring.

- *Slightly likely to occur (P=> 0.55 <=0.65)*—these are the risks with a 65 to 75 percent chance of occurring.

- *Evenly likely to occur* (P=> 0.45 <=0.55)—these are the risks with a 45 to 55 percent chance of occurring.

The impact of a risk event can be characterized as:

- Severe
- Significant
- Moderate
- Minor
- Minimal

A risk event is considered severe if it has devastating economic, technological, political, or social impact on the organization. Moreover, a risk is deemed minimal if its impact is minimal or negligible. Based on the incidence and probability, social media risks can be prioritized as:

- High
- Medium
- Low

High priority hazards—the risks that, if they happen, will have severe economic, technological, political, or social impact on the organization. These are the risks that need immediate attention and should be managed carefully.

Medium priority risks—the medium-probability risks that, if they happen, will have considerable economic, technological, political, or social impact on the organization.

Low priority risks—the low probability risks that, if they happen, will have low economic, technological, political, or social impact on the organization.

As shown in Figure 14.7, stakeholders can assign other probabilities similarly.

Probability (P)	Chance of occurrence	Priority
P=1	Certain to occur	High Priority Risks
P=> 0.95 <1	Extremely sure to occur	High Priority Risks
P=> 0.85 <= 0.95	Almost sure to occur	High Priority Risks
P=> 0.75 <=0.85	Very likely to occur	High Priority Risks
P=> 0.65 <=0.75	Likely to occur	High Priority Risks
P=> 0.55 <=0.65	Slightly likely to occur	Medium Priority Risks
P=> 0.45 <=0.55	Evenly likely to occur	Medium Priority Risks
P=> 0.35 <=0.45	Less than an even chance	Medium Priority Risks
P=> 0.25 <=0.35	Less likely to occur	Low Priority Risks
P=> 0.15 <=0.25	Not likely to occur	Low Priority Risks
P=> 0.00 <=0.15	Certainly sure not to occur	Low Priority Risks

Figure 14.7. Risk probability and prioritization assessment

Risk Mitigation

The risks prioritized and ranked in the earlier stage should be physically, technically, and procedurally managed, eliminated, or reduced to an acceptable level. Depending on the nature of the risks, different strategies should be used. The uncalculated risks posed by employees (e.g., posting copyright material online or tweeting some confidential information) can be eliminated by a training, and awareness program. It also helps to have a sound social media policy in place to minimize risks. Hacking attacks are another type of security risk that is mitigated using updated antivirus systems and by creating an extra layer of security. Typical risks mitigation strategies are:

Risks Management Governance

New governance structures, roles, and policies should be created within the business for adequately managing social media risks. These activities may involve identifying and empowering a social media risk management manager, developing a business-wide risk-management strategy, the identification of actions and steps needed to implement the strategy, and determining the resources required to mitigate the risks (Garvey, 2008). This risk assessment should include IT, finance, public relations, human resources, legal, and communications. All of these components play a significant role in identifying and mitigating social media risks.

Training and Awareness

Provide education and spread awareness on legal issues such as copyright, intellectual property, defamation, slander, and antitrust issues.

Social Media Policy

Create a sound and easily accessible *social media policy* that outlines the relative rights and responsibilities of employers and employees. A study by business consulting firm Protiviti in 2013 reported that seventy-three percent of US companies did not have a social media security policy for employees.

Secure Social Media Platforms

Secure social media platforms to minimize the impact or likelihood of the security risk from occurring. *Security measures* are set up at the platform level (i.e., Facebook sets up its own security protocols), but there are some programs that can scan social media accounts, such as Facebook pages, for malicious words in visitor posts. When malicious words are detected, the posts are automatically flagged and hidden from view until the page owner examines them.

Managing Social Media Security

Use the following techniques to use to secure various social media platforms:

- Use strong passwords—to protect the social media accounts (Twitter, Facebook, YouTube, blogs, etc.), always use strong passwords.
- The password should be at least ten characters long.

- The password should be a combination of uppercase and lowercase letters, numbers, and symbols.
- The password should not include personal information such as phone numbers, birthdays, name, etc.
- The password should not use standard "dictionary words" words.
- Does not use alphabetical sequences (such as "abcd1234") or keyboard sequences (such as "qwerty").
- Is not reused across websites; for example, the Twitter account password should be unique to Twitter.
- Is memorized or kept in a safe place if written.

Securing Facebook Accounts

The following are some techniques to secure your Facebook account.

Two-Mode Authentication

Many organizations are following this model. Facebook's *two-mode authentication* (or login approval, as Facebook calls it) is an excellent way to secure your account. It provides an extra layer of security that uses a phone to protect user accounts. For example, if an account is compromised or someone figures out a user password, the hacker will still not be able to access the account unless the hacker has physical access to a security token such as a 4-digit pin. Each time user's login in from an unknown browser or computer, they will need to provide a security code to access their account (unless the device is listed as secure). The security code is only provided to the user through their phone via a text message or through a third-party code application installed on a smartphone, such as the Google Authenticator application.

> **Steps**: Login to your Facebook account → Go to "Account Settings" → "Security & Login" → "Use two-factor authentication" → "Get Started."

Clicking on the "Getting Started" button will take you through a systematic process to enable the two-mode authentication. Note that the codes cannot be texted to a landline or Google Voice, so you will need a mobile phone to configure the authentication correctly.

Trusted Contacts

The *trusted contact* is an account recovery feature provided by Facebook to help you access your account securely through your friends if you have trouble accessing your account. You can select three to five friends to be your trusted contacts who can be reached through means other than Facebook (e.g., phone or e-mail). In the case of emergency, you can contact your trusted contacts and Facebook will provide each of them a security code for you with instructions on how to help you. You can then use the codes to recover your Facebook account.

Steps: Login to your account → "Account Settings" → "Security & Login" → "Trusted Contacts" → "Choose Trusted Contacts."

Review Your Login History

It is a good practice regularly to review your account login history and location.

Steps: Login to your account → "Account Settings" → "Security & Login" → "Where you're Logged In."

Your location is estimated with your public IP (Internet protocol) or address. Bringing your cursor over the location will display the IP used to access the account. Make sure the IP address is associated with the organization. The page will also provide information about other devices used to access the account (e.g., Chrome on Windows 7 or Android-based device). If you notice any strange devices or locations, you can end the session by clicking on the "End Activity" button.

Login Notification

Enable your Facebook *login notification* so that you can be notified by e-mail or text message when your account is accessed.

Steps: Login to your account → "Account Settings" → → "Security & Login"→ "Login Notification" → "Get alerts about unrecognized logins."

The notification e-mail provides detailed information about the login, including the IP address used, location, time, and type of device used to access the account.

Securing Your Twitter Account

The following are some techniques to secure your Twitter account.

Use Login Verification

Like Facebook, Twitter also provides two-mode authentication known as *login verification.* After enabling the login verification feature, you will need both your password and your phone to log in to your Twitter account. When you log in to Twitter.com, you will receive a text message with a login code or a push notification.

Steps: "Settings" → "Security and Privacy Settings" → "Send login verification requests to my phone" → when prompted, click "Okay, send me a message"→ if you receive the verification message, click "Yes."

Before using this feature, make sure that you verify your e-mails, add a phone number, and check that your service provider is Twitter-supported. Instructions on how to confirm your e-mail address are provided here: https://support.twitter.com/articles/97942

Revoke Third-Party Apps

Like Facebook, Twitter also provides access to *third-party apps*. While these apps make your Twitter experience more convenient, as mentioned earlier, some of them may be *vulnerable* to attacks or may handle your account information insecurely. Here is how to disable them.

Steps: Log in to your account→ "Settings" → "Apps" → you will be provided with a list of apps that have access to your account → "Revoke Access."

Securing Your Blog

The following are some techniques to secure your blog.

Two-Mode Authentication

Steps: Go to your blog and click on your avatar (or profile picture if you have uploaded one) available in the upper right-hand corner of the -window → "Account Settings" → "Security" → "Two-Step Authentication."

Disconnect Third-Party Applications

Steps: "Account Settings" → "Security" → "Connection Applications" → click on any unwanted applications that you want to remove → "Remove App Connection."

Back Up Your Blog

You can back up your blog's content (including posts, pages, comments, custom fields, terms, navigation menus, and custom posts), which then can be restored in case of emergency. Here is how to do it.

Step 1: Go to your blog by typing its address into your Internet browser.

Step 2: Click on the "WP Admin" option, this will bring you to the blog's "Dashboard."

Step 3: Once in the Dashboard click on the "Tools" available at the lower left corner of the dashboard, and then on "Export." There are two export options: "Export" and "Guided Transfer." Select the "Export" option.

Step 4: You will be offered a "Choose What to Export" option. Click on the default "Select All Content" and click "Download export file." Save the file in a secure location. It can be restored when needed.

To restore the blog content, you have exported earlier use the following steps.

Steps: "WP Admin" → "Tools" → "Import" → from the available systems select "WordPress" → "Choose the file" you have saved to your computer → "Upload File and Import."

Risk Evaluation

Social media risk management is a rigorous process that requires professional as well as informed stakeholders. In the face of rapid technological, political, and social change, social media risks should be *periodically reviewed.* The continuous evaluation and monitoring effort will make sure that the initial assumption made about the external and internal risks are still relevant.

CASE STUDY 14.1
SOCIAL MEDIA RISK ASSESSMENT FOR ABC APPLIANCES

Introduction

ABC Appliances (not its real name) has been operating in the Waikato for over 70 years well before social media became part of everyday life. ABC started using social media, particularly in March 2013. Since then ABC Appliances has attracted 7,487 page-likes and 7,243 followers on Facebook. Facebook is the primary platform for social media used by ABC Appliances. An Instagram page was formed in August 2016 and has attracted 161 followers. Using social media is rewarding, but not risk free. For example, negative feedback posted by respondents, inappropriate content posted by employees, and negative feedback posted by market competitors has the potential to jeopardize the highly-regarded brand and reputation created over those 70 years. In this case study, working with ABC's social media team, an in-depth risk mitigation plan was proposed which provides ABC Appliances with a step by step, practical guideline for social media risk mitigation. Based on extensive review of the literature, several key approaches are recommended including the creation of a customer-centric environment, creation of alternative social media channels, investment of fit-for-purpose technologies, and social media specific policies and training.

Company Background

ABC Appliances is a family owned and operated appliance retailer and service center operating in the Waikato for over 70 years. ABC Appliances hold a variety of products including whiteware appliances, small appliances, televisions, audio, IT, beds, cameras, etc. ABC Appliances is a medium-sized enterprise employing approximately 100 staff across all aspects of the business. ABC Appliances has four retail stores in Morrinsville, Te Awamutu, Hamilton City, and The Base Hamilton (as well as an online store that ships nationally). The service center and air conditioning center are based in the Hamilton City store. ABC Appliances has achieved several awards in the past 5 years including a large retail store of the year in 2013, 2014, and 2016 as well as best in service in 2013 and 2014. The appliance retail industry ABC Appliances operates in is mature and extremely competitive. ABC Appliances competes against several large companies including Harvey Norman, Noel Leeming, and JB Hifi. Many of the products sold are the same between all these retailers resulting in consumers having high purchasing power, and point of difference limited to price, service, and brand recognition.

Risk Mitigation Plan

We used the MITRE risk management framework (see Figure 2) to create a risk mitigation plan for ABC Appliances. The MITRE risk management tool has the following steps.

Step 1: Risk Identification: The first step involved identifying the potential risks faced by ABC. Through a risk assessment interview, overall we noted 26 risks (explained in detail in the proceeding section; also available in Table 14.2).

Step 2: Risk impact assessment: this step entails assessing the impact and consequences of each identified risk. Based on the interview and subsequent risk assessment, a risk impact assessment model was done by converting the High, Medium, and Low ratings into High = 3, Medium = 2, and Low = 1.

Step 3: Risk prioritization—next step involve prioritizing risks with the highest impact. The risk impact was then calculated as *Impact X Priority= Risk Rating*. The risk impact was then graphed in Figure 3.

Step 4: Risk mitigation planning, implementation, and progress monitoring—finally based on the risk rating, a risk mitigation, and implementation plan was created.

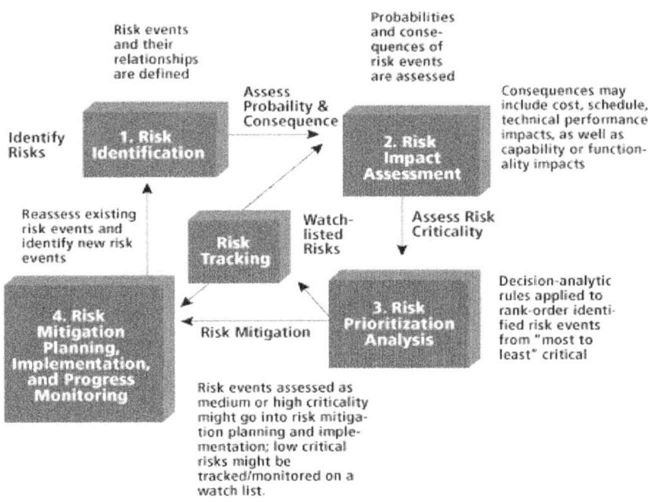

Figure 14.8. METRE Risk Management Framework

Step 1 to 3: Risk Identification, Impact Assessment, and Prioritization

During the interview, it was identified that risks could be segregated to either internal or external to ABC Appliances, which is used to assess the risks.

Internal Risks

Looking internally, there are several risk events that were identified as having a high impact on ABC Appliances (see Table 14.2 for details). These include:

- having an incomplete social media strategy
- lack of buy-in from senior executives
- selecting the incorrect media channels
- lack of control over corporate content
- inappropriate content posted by employees, and
- access granted to the incorrect person

High impact risks such as *incomplete social media strategy* and *lack of buy-in from senior management* will adversely affect two essential goals: 1) increasing sales and 2) improve brand recognition. The management is actively pushing the social media team to develop and grow their social media presence and in doing so ensures a social media plan is completed and communicated to the marketing team at the beginning of each week. Selecting the *incorrect social media channels* is a moderate risk as it limits ABC Appliances from interacting with a range of customers and connecting with new customers. During the interview, ABC Appliances social media team explained that Facebook was their primary focus followed by Instagram as they were the most significant channels in New Zealand.

Similarly, the risks: 1) *having a lack of control of corporate content*, 2) *inappropriate content posted by employees*, and 3) *having access granted to the incorrect person* are also substantial risks to consider. The likely outcome of these risk events is that incorrect information may be presented to their customers, consequently misrepresenting ABC Appliances and decreasing its brand equity. The probability, however, is moderate as there is a vast amount of information available on a lot of products stocked by ABC Appliances, some of which are highly technical and have very slight differences between each other. Even when social media content is provided by suppliers, it can be incorrect or change from being available to being out of stock. It was identified that the employees posting content are likely to require in-depth knowledge of products and their features and selling points as well as how the industry and supplier operates.

External Risks

The external risks appear significantly more worrisome. The notable risks include: *Negative and inappropriate feedback or content posted by unhappy customers, disgruntled past employees, and market competitors.* These risks influence sales and the bottom line as well as decreasing brand equity and reputation. It was identified that these risks occur more often than any other identified risk. The social media team described further issues in which it is often hard to identify if negative interactions are false or true. It was identified that these risks are unpreventable to a degree; however, treating staff fairly could reduce the likelihood of past employees group posting negative feedback or contents.

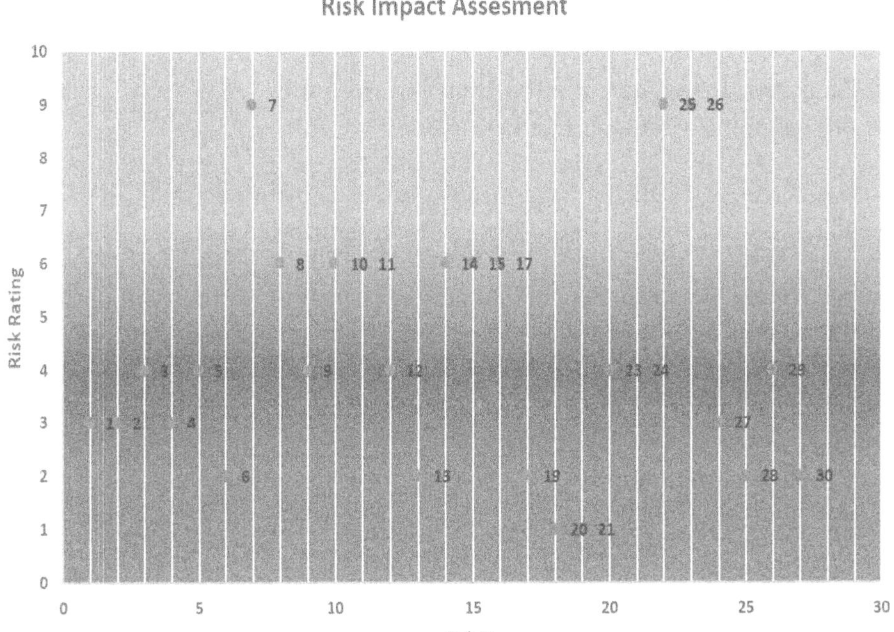

Figure 14.9. Risks Impact Rating

Further external risks include *data theft and identity theft*, which were expected to have a harmful outcome to ABC Appliances' brand and reflect poorly on the security of customer information held by ABC Appliances. The probability of this occurring is medium as access is limited to only four staff members' personal accounts. However, given the highly competitive industry, others may wish to harm the ABC Appliances' brand.

Additionally, bandwidth issues, technical difficulties, and virus and malware contraction were also identified as risks to ABC Appliances. The outcome is predicted to be moderate and includes downtime, which causes end user frustration and dissatisfaction. With the risk of viruses and malware, the outcome could result in stolen data, which presents a higher impact.

Step 4: Risk Mitigation Planning

Step 4 entails risk mitigation planning, implementation, and progress monitoring based on the results of step 3. The high priority risk will be mitigated individually while the medium and low risks will be tracked and re-assessed. Suggested mitigation plans for each of the three high risks are outlined below.

Risk 1: Negative Feedback Posted by Respondents

Here is the risk mitigation plan for these risks.

Step 1. Create a customer focus environment and staff training to reduce the likelihood of the risk event occurring in the first place.

Step 2. In the event, negative feedback is posted by respondent, address customer concerns immediately and take the conversation out of public view (within minutes of feedback being posted whenever possible). In the event that the respondent is incorrect, do not want to humiliate them.

A suggested comment on Facebook back to respondent is:

> *"Hi (customer name), sorry to hear about your poor experience. We are hoping to make it up to you and fix (issue/experience name). Please check your private messages we require a few more details on your experience."*

The suggested plan will aim to show the public the event has been addressed quickly and professionally.

Step 3. Depending on feedback, the post may also be hidden; however, transparency is preferred.

Risk 2: Inappropriate Content Posted by Employees

Step 1. Limit access authority to social media pages to selected employees.

Step 2. Create a social media policy, which all employees must read, and sign.

Step 3. Provide training to those with access to social media pages.

Step 4. Develop a review system where all content is reviewed before being published by the relevant category manager. If the category manager is unavailable, the content can be reviewed by another category manager or by a member of the marketing team.

Risk 3: Negative Feedback Posted by Market Competitors

This risk appears somewhat unpreventable to a degree. To mitigate this risk, it is suggested ABC Appliances try minimizing threats to competitors.

Step 1. Stick to the Waikato region with marketing efforts. Dropping mailers and activity and pursuing other regions may cause pushback from competitors. It is suggested that customers will still find ABC Appliances online through price comparison websites and Google PageRank and advertising. Their superior service can still provide slow growth outside of Waikato.

Step 2. In the event of negative feedback, ABC Appliances are to treat all as severe and work to identify if the feedback is legitimate or false through contacting the respondent offline.

Step 3. If the negative feedback posted by respondents, is identified as false, hide feedback where possible and block/report respondent to the social media provider. However, if the feedback is legitimate, blocking it will further escalate the issues. In such a case, it should be handled professionally.

Recommendations

The following recommendations are aimed at risk mitigation for both ABC Appliances social media strategies and ABC Appliances as an organization to strengthen its market position by using social media as a business tool.

- As several high risks stemmed from customer and employee interactions, including risks 7, 8, 9 (see Table 14.2), a customer-centric social media strategy is recommended. A customer-centric approach seeks to fulfill the individual needs and wants of customers(Chaffey, 2015). It is a personal approach, connecting with customers as people instead of a faceless corporation. It is suggested this approach will fit the in-store customer service culture which as stated in the background has won awards. Furthermore, this approach is likely to result in customer loyalty and provides a point of difference from competitors that sell exactly the same products(Laroche, Habibi, & Richard, 2013).

- Based on the analysis of risks 3 and 4, it is recommended ABC Appliances vary their social media channels to not just interact with the same customer base. Suggested channels include Twitter, YouTube, and Snapchat. It is suggested ABC Appliances start with YouTube and Twitter as they already have accounts although they are not very active. These two social media forms fit well with the products available at ABC Appliances. It is understood that ABC Appliances has limited human resource to manage social media and it is expected that many of the videos shared through Facebook and Instagram as well as the messages will easily be transferable to Twitter and YouTube.
- It is recommended ABC Appliances invest in fit for purpose technologies to support the social media strategy or contract out to a third party. This will aid in mitigation of risks 1, 5, 15, 17, 18, and 19. These technologies include;
- The use of corporate social media accounts allows the organization to monitor accounts.
- The use of tools to do capacity management to ensure that bandwidth of the internet links is not over utilized.
- As several of the risks are likely to be caused by staff usage of social media, including risks; 11, 12, 13, 23, 24, 27, 28, 29, 30 (as shown in the Table 14.2), it is recommended ABC Appliances establishes a social media policy and training program. John and James (2014) suggest two policies be established, one for personal social media use and the second for social media use on behalf of the organization. The authors also suggest the training program should be specific to the organization and include the following areas (John & James, 2014):
    - Online brand promotion and protection
    - Style guidelines
    - Privacy and confidentiality
    - Guidelines for conducting conversations and responding to comments

Conclusion

ABC Appliances has gained a modest social media presence in the 5 years they have been present with over 7000 likes on Facebook as well as

Instagram, YouTube, and Twitter accounts. ABC Appliances industry is fast moving and highly competitive and has created some common social media risks and events including; negative feedback from respondents, inappropriate content posted by employees, and negative feedback from competitors. Key to mitigating these risks include establishing superior customer service and a customer-centric approach to business which is reflected both in-store and online. At the core of this is ABC Appliances employees who require training and guidelines to implement this approach, as well as the awareness of the risks and impacts their actions have on social media. A challenge to ABC Appliances is mitigating the risks caused by false feedback from competitors. Not only is it somewhat unpreventable but also challenging to identify. However, it is a reflection that ABC Appliances are on the right path and competitors are becoming threatened by this small but capable business.

Source: this case study was conducted by Keri O'Connell, Mark Swanepoel, and Chandra Singh graduate students at Waikato Management School under the supervision of Dr. Gohar Khan.

Table 14.2. Risk assessment results

Risk	Event Description	Expected Outcomes	I[5]	P[6]	Risk Mitigation Plan
1	Incomplete Social Media Strategy	Social media project will be ineffective or fail	**High**	**Low**	Plan 3 months in advance and communicate weekly to the marketing team. The impact is high as with a strategy and plans to achieve the strategy it would be absent or inconsistent. Probability is low as social media strategy is developed and changed within marketing team to align with marketing goals.
2	Lack of Buy-In from Senior Executives	Insufficient funding and social media project will be ineffective	**High**	**Low**	Emphasis the value/ROI created from social media in comparison to traditional forms of marketing used such as newspaper advertisements, mailers, and radio. The impact is high as to generate any momentum in social media funding is required. Probability is low as owner understands this and is actively pushing for better social media growth.
3	Insufficient Resources	Employee backlash due to workload	**Med**	**Med**	Collaboratively work with procurement and marketing team and readily accept content and feedback from them. The impact is medium as fewer posts/slow responses are not likely to have a significant impact. Probability is medium as ABC Appliances is a small-medium business where Liam is also coordinating website sales amongst other ad-hoc responsibilities.
4	Selecting the Wrong Social Media Channels	Lack of online engagement	**High**	**Med**	Focus on Facebook as it is the most significant social media channel in New Zealand. The impact is high as would be at a disadvantage from competitors without one (due to the industry). Furthermore, if the focus/resources were not directed significantly to Facebook, it would likely be directed towards traditional

[5] I = Impact
[6] P = probability

Risk	Event Description	Expected Outcomes	I[5]	P[6]	Risk Mitigation Plan
					forms of advertising. The probability is low, and the social media strategy revolves around Facebook.
5	Incorrectly Measuring Social Media Metrics	Difficulty in demonstrating ROI	**Med**	**Med**	Allocate time weekly to measure/assess social media performance and to pay consultants to provide performance, competitor's performance, and feedback on social media every two weeks. The impact is medium as without recognition of performance cannot look to alter and improve performance and drive ROI. However, low impact to business overall. The probability is medium, as Liam has limited experience in reporting and not his primary role at ABC Appliances. In addition, there is only a moderate incentive for consultants to provide accurate feedback and reporting as they are paid regardless of thoroughness.
6	Potential Leak of Corporate Strategy	Direction & goals exposed	**Med**	**Low**	Limited knowledge of social media strategy and plan to the marketing team. Ensure consultants sign non-disclosure agreements. Low impact as there are always many rumors of competitors strategies. Low probability as limited people know the corporate strategy.
7	Negative Feedback Posted by Responden ts	Impact on sales and bottom line	**High**	**High**	Ensure customer service is a priority for all staff to give customer no reason to provide negative feedback. Act immediately to fix the customers issues as soon as they become evident. Contact customer/user privately on the issue so not to draw further attention to shortcomings. Post public message to feedback advising

Risk	Event Description	Expected Outcomes	I[5]	P[6]	Risk Mitigation Plan
					customer they have been contacted privately to show the public that the issue has been addressed immediately. High impact as ABC Appliances sells products that are the same to those sold in competitors' stores. The defining factor is often price and reputation. A lot of negative feedback from customers/users brings reputation to disrepute. The probability is high as several factors are out of control including the lifespan of products purchased, delivery, and shipping delays. This is the most common event for ABC Appliances and the retail industry.
8	Inappropriate Content Posted by Respondents	Decrease brand equity	**High**	**Med**	Set Facebook profanity filter to medium to block content posted by respondents that have words that are commonly reported as offensive. Have several members of marketing team regularly review content posted by respondents, hide, and block anything offensive. The impact is high as it reflects negatively on the mid-premium brand and product offering associated to ABC Appliances. The probability is medium as dissatisfaction with products and service are common in the retail industry.
9	Lack of Participation by Consumers	Goals will not be reached	**Med**	**Med**	Ensure content allows for participation by consumers including the open-ended question, giveaway incentives. The impact is medium as although high participation is desirable to grow social media presence it is only one of several media including in-store and radio. The probability is medium as although staff and staff family members participate many consumers require an incentive such as a giveaway or chance to win.

Risk	Event Description	Expected Outcomes	I[5]	P[6]	Risk Mitigation Plan
10	Lack of Control Over Corporate Content	Employees posting incorrect Info online	**High**	**Med**	Have an approval process in place, where posts need to be approved before going online. It is recommended each category manager needs to approve posts relating to their category and the marketing a marketing team member for the other posts. The impact is high as incorrect/inaccurate/inappropriate content impacts brand perception and the bottom line. The probability is medium as products and availability are always changing. Information provided by the supplier is not always 100% accurate.
11	Inappropriate Content Posted by Employees	Decrease brand equity	**High**	**High**	Have a social media use policy signed by all staff member outlining use.
12	Excessive use of Social Media by Employees	Loss of productivity	**Med**	**Med**	Have a social media use policy signed by all staff member outlining use. Limiting Wi-Fi access to specific staff members. The impact is medium as although there may be some loss it is unlikely to be significant. The probability is medium due to the high visibility of staff by managers and the high access to computers and mobile devices.
13	Using Personal Accounts for Work Purposes	Misrepresentation of the company	**Med**	**Low**	Have a social media use policy signed by all staff member outlining use and retributions. The impact is medium as it also humanizes employees and identifies them with customers.
14	Data Theft	UN/PW could be hacked to enter the system	**High**	**Med**	Uncontrollable to some degree. High impact as could harm the reputation of entire business security. Medium probability as 4 staff members have access although as they are linked to private accounts will want to keep secure for personal reasons.

Risk	Event Description	Expected Outcomes	I[5]	P[6]	Risk Mitigation Plan
15	Identity Theft	Misrepresentation/Brand Hijacking	**High**	**Med**	Uncontrollable. High impact as could negatively influence brand and reputation. Medium probability as it is a highly competitive and large industry. Some competitors may wish to harm the brand.
16	Loss of Business Reputation	Inconsistent brand messaging	**High**	**Med**	Ensure customer service remains a priority and content and message match mid-premium brand associated with ABC Appliances and products offered. High impact as customer service and mid to premium is something that has taken years to develop. Medium probability as easy to be caught up in competition and compete on price or lack of service.
17	Risk of Contracting Viruses and/or Malware	System Crash/Risk of Stolen Data. End User Frustration & Dissatisfaction.	**High**	**Low**	Continue to contract security to 3rd party specialists. The impact is medium, as many social media channels remain isolated from PC. Low probability as security is contracted to 3rd party specialists and has not been an issue in the past.
18	Technical Difficulties	Downtime End-User Frustration & Dissatisfaction	**Med**	**Low**	Have adequate training and problem-solving/ troubleshooting procedures. The impact is medium as this is easily solved with the right personnel. Probability is low, as the staff member should have a sufficient level of knowledge before entering the position.
19	Bandwidth Issues	Downtime due to excessive usage. End User Frustration & Dissatisfaction.	**Med**	**Low**	Encourage management to have a reliable and sufficient internet provider. Would have a medium impact, would affect efficiency and time taken to complete tasks. Probability is low as the majority of companies invest in a quality internet, but a small possibility.
20	Negative Feedback Posted by Disgruntled Past	Impact on sales and bottom line	**Med**	**Med**	Uncontrollable to some degree. Attempt to treat staff fairly and give them no reason to act negatively. The impact is medium as reach can be limited/deleted.

Risk	Event Description	Expected Outcomes	I[5]	P[6]	Risk Mitigation Plan
	Employees				Probability is medium as it has happened in the past but are isolated cases.
21	Inappropriate Content Posted by Disgruntled Past Employees	Decrease brand equity	**Med**	**Med**	Uncontrollable to some degree. Attempt to treat staff fairly and give them no reason to act negatively. The impact is medium as reach can be limited/deleted. Probability is medium as it has happened in the past but are isolated cases.
22	Negative Feedback Posted by Market Competitors	Impact on sales and bottom line	**High**	**High**	Uncontrollable. High impact as often difficult to distinguish between legitimate customer issues. Impacts on reputation and brand. High probability as a competitive industry with competitors doing anything for an advantage.
23	Access granted to the wrong person	Impact on sales and bottom line and misrepresentation of the company	**High**	**Low**	Changing of passwords regularly and adequate security, and protection of information. The impact would be high if financial or customer information became available to the wrong person.
24	Poorly run competitions and giveaways	Decrease brand equity	**Med**	**Low**	Have an approval process in place, where competitions require approval before going online. Also, have a fair 3rd method for selecting winners and ensuring that if the staff member in charge of the giveaway is away someone else can complete/pick winners. Medium impact as will impact on reputation if not completed fairly, however, it may not be noticed if the winner was announced a day or two late or did not use a 3rd party app. Probability is low as competitions are usually planned thoroughly and reminders set on the calendar for at least two staff members.
25	Violation of	Potential legal problems	**Med**	**Med**	Source content directly from the supplier for product content.

Risk	Event Description	Expected Outcomes	I[5]	P[6]	Risk Mitigation Plan
	copyright laws				Most product content is readily available from suppliers with permission to use for marketing purposes.
26	Content misalignment with other marketing	Inconsistent information and brand messaging	**Med**	**Low**	Base social media strategy on a business marketing plan and collaboratively work with procurement and marketing team. Medium impact as can provide the customer with incorrect information or brand message. However, due to a significant amount of advertising in the industry also becomes lost. The probability is low for this risk, as social media content is based on business marketing calendar and strategy.

REVIEW QUESTIONS

1. What are some common social media risks?
2. Explain the four steps in social media risk management.
3. Explain common social media risk mitigation strategies.
4. Explain different techniques to secure social media accounts.
5. Understand the different types of social media data and the privacy issues surrounding them.
6. Harnessing social media data (for analytics purposes) to solve business problems introduces new challenges related to privacy and ethics. Explain various privacy and ethical issues surrounding social media data analytics that they need to consider.

EXERCISE 14.1: SOCIAL MEDIA RISK ASSESSMENT

Engaging through social media introduces new challenges related to privacy and security risks. Risk is the possibility of losing something of value such as intellectual or physical capital. Social media related risks need to be adequately managed, both from the strategic and technological points of view. Organizations need a proactive, rather than reactive, social media risk-management strategy.

Your task

This assignment requires you to find and interview a business manager to help them identify and mitigate risks associated with their business use of social media. Ideally, you should approach a business that has a social media presence (e.g., have a Facebook fan page or Twitter).

To complete the task, use the *Social Media Risk Assessment* template available from the course companion site (see Figure 14.10). Working with the business manager, you should:

- In the *Risk Assessment tab* at the bottom of the spreadsheet, conduct your risk assessment.
- Enter a description for an event that could put the company at risk (example events are provided; however, you are encouraged to come up with risk events that are more relevant to the business in question).
- Consider the expected outcome resulting from this risk entered into the appropriate column (example risks and impacts are provided in the template; you are encouraged to come up with risks and impacts that are more relevant to the business in question).

- Assess the level of impact resulting from this risk being realized (select from the drop-down list: High, Medium, and Low).
- Determine the probability of this risk occurring (select from the drop-down list: High, Medium, and Low).
- Develop a risk mitigation plan for each risk and prioritize efforts based on the level of impact and probability of occurrence.

Your Goal

Your goal is to write a report on the risk assessment exercise you have completed. The report should talk about the potential risks the company face, why, and how it will affect the business. Then sketch out a detailed risk mitigation plan for the company. In the process, you may use MITRE's risk management tool introduced earlier. Your final report should also include information about the company you selected, the person you interviewed, and the rationale behind your choice. If possible, record the interview and/or include photos as proof.

Formatting Guidelines

- The report should be no more than five pages single-spaced, 12-point font, and one-inch margins.
- Include page numbers to facilitate review.
- The first page should provide a title, the writer's name, and email address.
- An abstract, of not more than 250 words, should precede the body of the paper.
- Literature cited should follow APA style references.

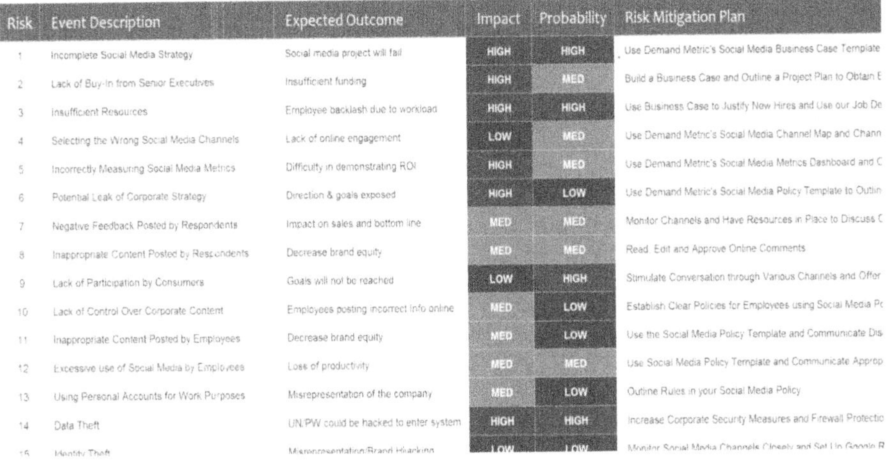

Risk	Event Description	Expected Outcome	Impact	Probability	Risk Mitigation Plan
1	Incomplete Social Media Strategy	Social media project will fail	HIGH	HIGH	Use Demand Metric's Social Media Business Case Template
2	Lack of Buy-In from Senior Executives	Insufficient funding	HIGH	MED	Build a Business Case and Outline a Project Plan to Obtain E
3	Insufficient Resources	Employee backlash due to workload	HIGH	HIGH	Use Business Case to Justify New Hires and Use our Job De
4	Selecting the Wrong Social Media Channels	Lack of online engagement	LOW	MED	Use Demand Metric's Social Media Channel Map and Chann
5	Incorrectly Measuring Social Media Metrics	Difficulty in demonstrating ROI	HIGH	MED	Use Demand Metric's Social Media Metrics Dashboard and C
6	Potential Leak of Corporate Strategy	Direction & goals exposed	HIGH	LOW	Use Demand Metric's Social Media Policy Template to Outlin
7	Negative Feedback Posted by Respondents	Impact on sales and bottom line	MED	MED	Monitor Channels and Have Resources in Place to Discuss C
8	Inappropriate Content Posted by Respondents	Decrease brand equity	MED	MED	Read, Edit and Approve Online Comments
9	Lack of Participation by Consumers	Goals will not be reached	LOW	HIGH	Stimulate Conversation through Various Channels and Offer
10	Lack of Control Over Corporate Content	Employees posting incorrect info online	MED	LOW	Establish Clear Policies for Employees using Social Media Pc
11	Inappropriate Content Posted by Employees	Decrease brand equity	MED	LOW	Use the Social Media Policy Template and Communicate Dis
12	Excessive use of Social Media by Employees	Loss of productivity	MED	MED	Use Social Media Policy Template and Communicate Approp
13	Using Personal Accounts for Work Purposes	Misrepresentation of the company	MED	LOW	Outline Rules in your Social Media Policy
14	Data Theft	UN/PW could be hacked to enter system	HIGH	HIGH	Increase Corporate Security Measures and Firewall Protectio
15	Identity Theft	Misrepresentation/Brand Hijacking	LOW	LOW	Monitor Social Media Channels Closely and Set Up Google R

Figure 14.10. Social media risk assessment template

CHAPTER 14 REFERENCES

Beye, M., Jeckmans, A., Erkin, Z., Hartel, P., Lagendijk, R., & Tang, Q. (2012). Privacy in online social networks. computational Social Networks: Security and Privacy. London: Springer.

Carminati, B., Ferrari, E., & Viviani, M. (2013). Security and Trust in Online Social Networks. Synthesis Lectures on Information Security. Synthesis Lectures on Information Security, Privacy, and Trust, 4(3), 1-120.

Chaffey, D. (2015). Digital business and e-commerce management Harlow, United Kingdom: Pearson Education Limited.

Delaney, Judith, 2013, Are You Liable for Tweeting and/or Retweeting an Offensive Tweet? Available at: https://melissaagnes.com/are-you-liable-for-tweeting-andor-retweeting-an-offensive-tweet/

Eckersley, P. (2010). How unique is your web browser? Paper presented at the 10th International Conference on Privacy Enhancing Technologies PETS'10, Berlin, Heidelberg.

Garvey, P. R. (2008). Analytical Methods for Risk Management: A Systems Engineering Perspective. United States: Taylor & Francis Group.

John, C., & James, F. (2014). Managing the risks of social media: Ways to ensure that online behavior is always appropriate. Human Resource Management International Digest, 22(5), 39-41. doi:10.1108/HRMID-07-2014-0103

Laroche, M., Habibi, M. R., & Richard, M.-O. (2013). To be or not to be in social media: How brand loyalty is affected by social media? International Journal of Information Management, 33(1), 76-82.

Laura Scaife, 2014, Handbook of Social Media and the Law, Informa Law from Routledge, New York.

doi:https://doi.org/10.1016/j.ijinfomgt.2012.07.003

MITRE. (2014). Risk Impact Assessment and Prioritization, available at: https://www.mitre.org/publications/systems-engineering-guide/acquisition-systems-engineering/risk-management/risk-impact-assessment-and-prioritization.

Oulasvirta, Antti; Suomalainen, Tiia; Hamari, Juho; Lampinen, Airi; Karvonen, Kristiina (2014). "Transparency of Intentions Decreases Privacy Concerns in Ubiquitous Surveillance". Cyberpsychology, Behavior, and Social Networking. 17 (10): 633–38. doi:10.1089/cyber.2013.0585.

Richthammer, C., Netter, M., Riesner, M., Sänger, J., & Pernul, G. (2014). Taxonomy of social network data types. *EURASIP Journal on Information Security, 2014*(1), 11. doi:10.1186/s13635-014-0011-7

Solove, Daniel J. *(2008).* Understanding Privacy. *Cambridge, Mass.: Harvard University Press.* ISBN 9780674027725.

Warren, S. D., & Brandeis, L. D. (1980). The Right to Privacy. *Harvard Law Rev, IV*(5), 193-220.

Webber, A. (2012). Guarding the Social Gates: The Imperative for Social Media Risk Management, available at:http://www.slideshare.net/Altimeter/guarding-the-social-gates-the-imperative-for-social-media-risk-management.

Westin, Alan (1967). Privacy and Freedom. New York: Atheneum.

Wondracek, G., Holz, T., Kirda, E., & Kruegel, C. (2010, 16-19 May 2010). *A Practical Attack to De-anonymize Social Network Users.* Paper presented at the 2010 IEEE Symposium on Security and Privacy.

INDEX

A

B

C

D

E

F

G

H

I

J

K

L

M

N

O

P

Q

R

S

T

U

V

W

Y

Made in the USA
Columbia, SC
07 September 2019